XII XI X IX VIII VII VI V IIII III II I

Dawn of the Arcana

12

Story & Art by
Rei Toma

characters

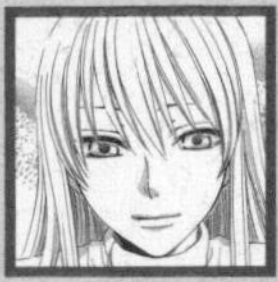

Sara
King Guran's concubine. Deceased.

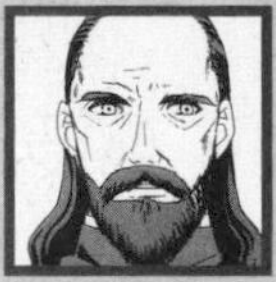

Guran
King of Belquat.

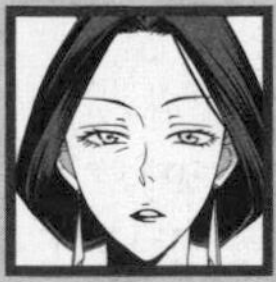

Rosenta
Queen of Belquat.

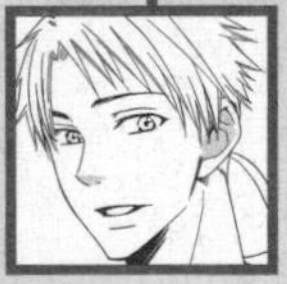

Cain
First-born prince of Belquat. Caesar's brother. He was killed by Loki.

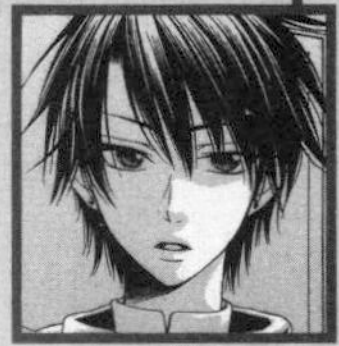

Caesar
The second-born prince of Belquat. He breaks up with Nakaba and marries Louise.

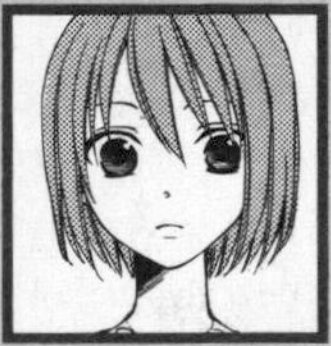

Nakaba
The princess royal of Senan. Strong of will and noble of spirit, she possesses a strange power.

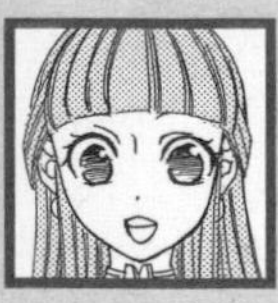

Lemiria
Bellinus's younger sister. Fond of her big brother.

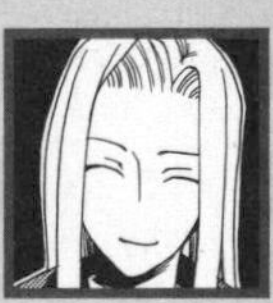

Bellinus
Caesar's attendant. Always cool and collected.

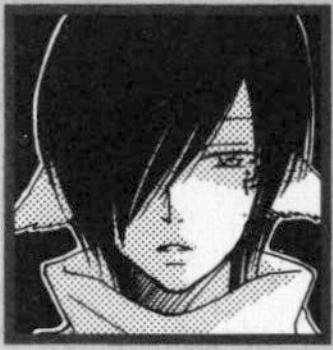

Loki
Nakaba's attendant. His senses of perception are unmatched.

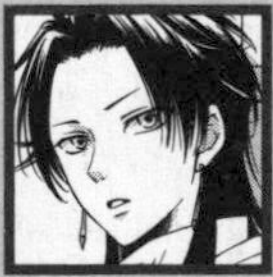

Adel
Successor to the throne of Senan. Married to Nakaba.

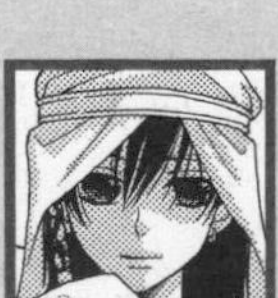

Akhil
Fifth-born prince of Lithuanel.

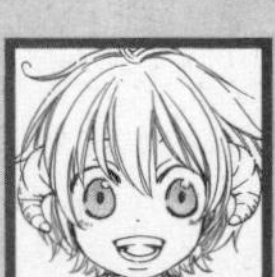

Rito
Nakaba's attendant.

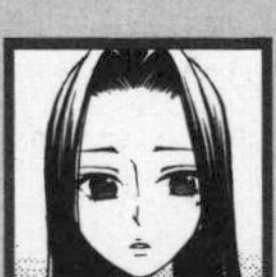

Louise
The daughter of a Belquat general.

story

• Wed to Prince Caesar as a symbol of the peace between their two countries, Nakaba is actually little more than a hostage. Unbeknownst to King Guran, she is a survivor of the race he tried to destroy for fear of their power. Nakaba herself possesses the Arcana of Time, so she can see the past and the future. The political marriage between Nakaba and Caesar gets off to a rocky start, but as they grow to know each other, they fall in love.

• Unfortunately, Caesar and Nakaba are unsuccessful with their mission in Lithuanel to establish diplomatic ties. In order to change a world full of absurd wars and battles for the throne, Caesar heads to Belquat while Nakaba heads to Senan. They hope to become rulers of their respective countries and merge the two one day. They still think of each other often.

• When Caesar returns to Belquat, he does as his mother bids and marries Louise, who was formerly engaged to his late brother, Cain. Meanwhile, Nakaba returns to Senan and uses her Arcana power as a bargaining tool to marry Adel, who is next in line for the Senan throne.

• When the king of Senan falls ill and collapses, Nakaba has a chance to gain real power. As things stand, the king's death would make Adel king and Nakaba herself queen. Nakaba knows she can never truly rule Senan unless she deals with Adel, but she's become fond of him and is reluctant to take extreme measures.

• Things change when the Arcana shows Nakaba a future in which Loki kills Adel. To keep Loki from taking that step, she goes to the king of Senan and threatens to kill Adel if the king doesn't name her his successor. The king does as she says and draws up a will. When he passes away soon afterward, Nakaba takes the throne in his place!

Neighboring Kingdoms

Senan
A poor kingdom in the cold north of the island. Militarily weak.

Belquat
A powerful country that thrives thanks to its temperate climate.

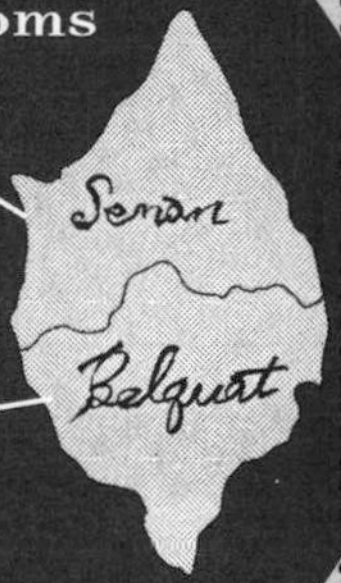
Senan
Belquat

Dawn of the Arcana

Volume 12

XII

XI

X

CONTENTS

IX

VIII

VII

VI

Chapter 46

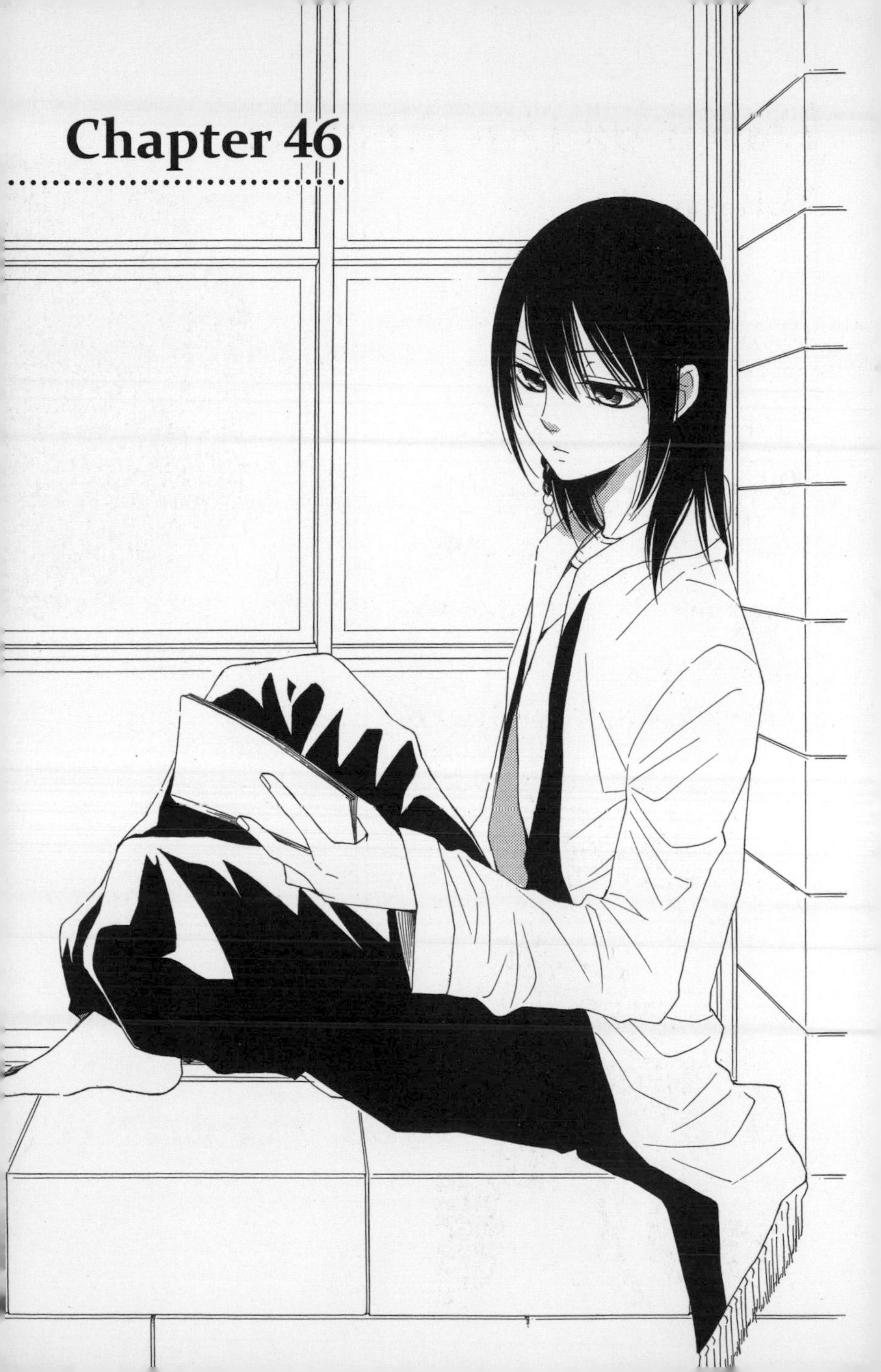

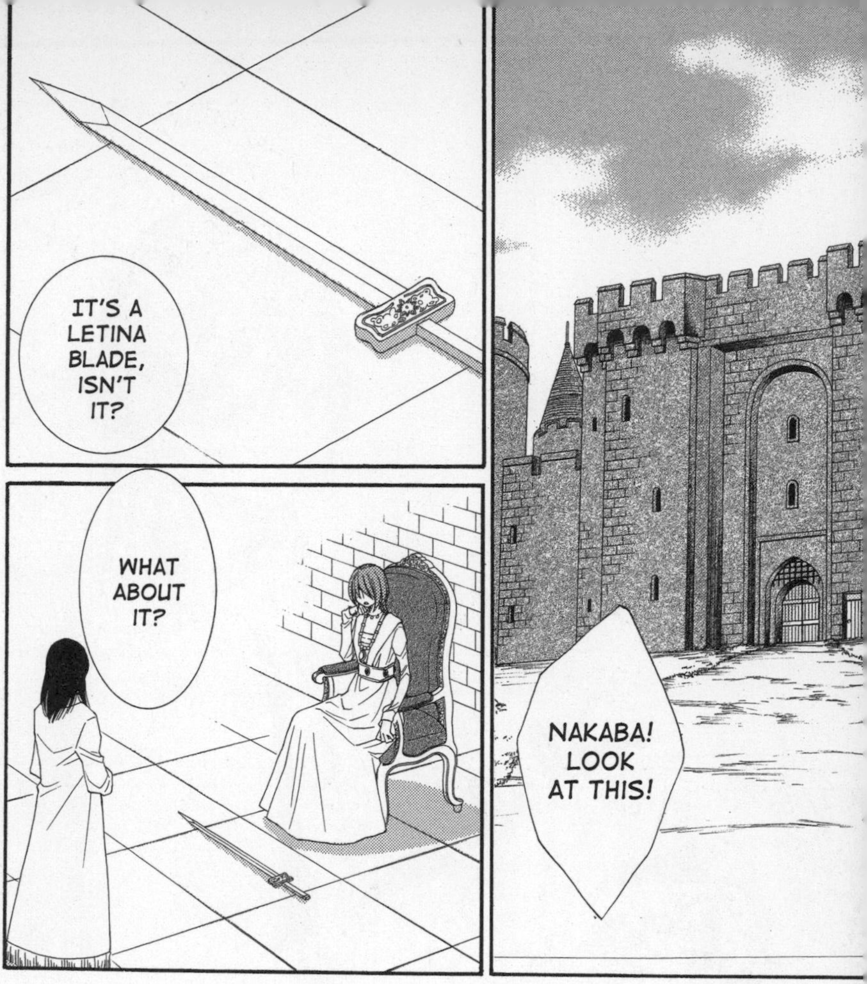
NAKABA! LOOK AT THIS!
IT'S A LETINA BLADE, ISN'T IT?
WHAT ABOUT IT?

Dawn of the Arcana

WATCH
CLOSELY.

KACHIK

SIZZLE

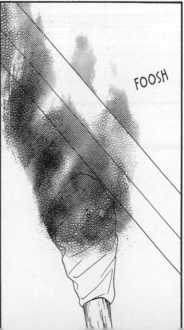

FOOSH

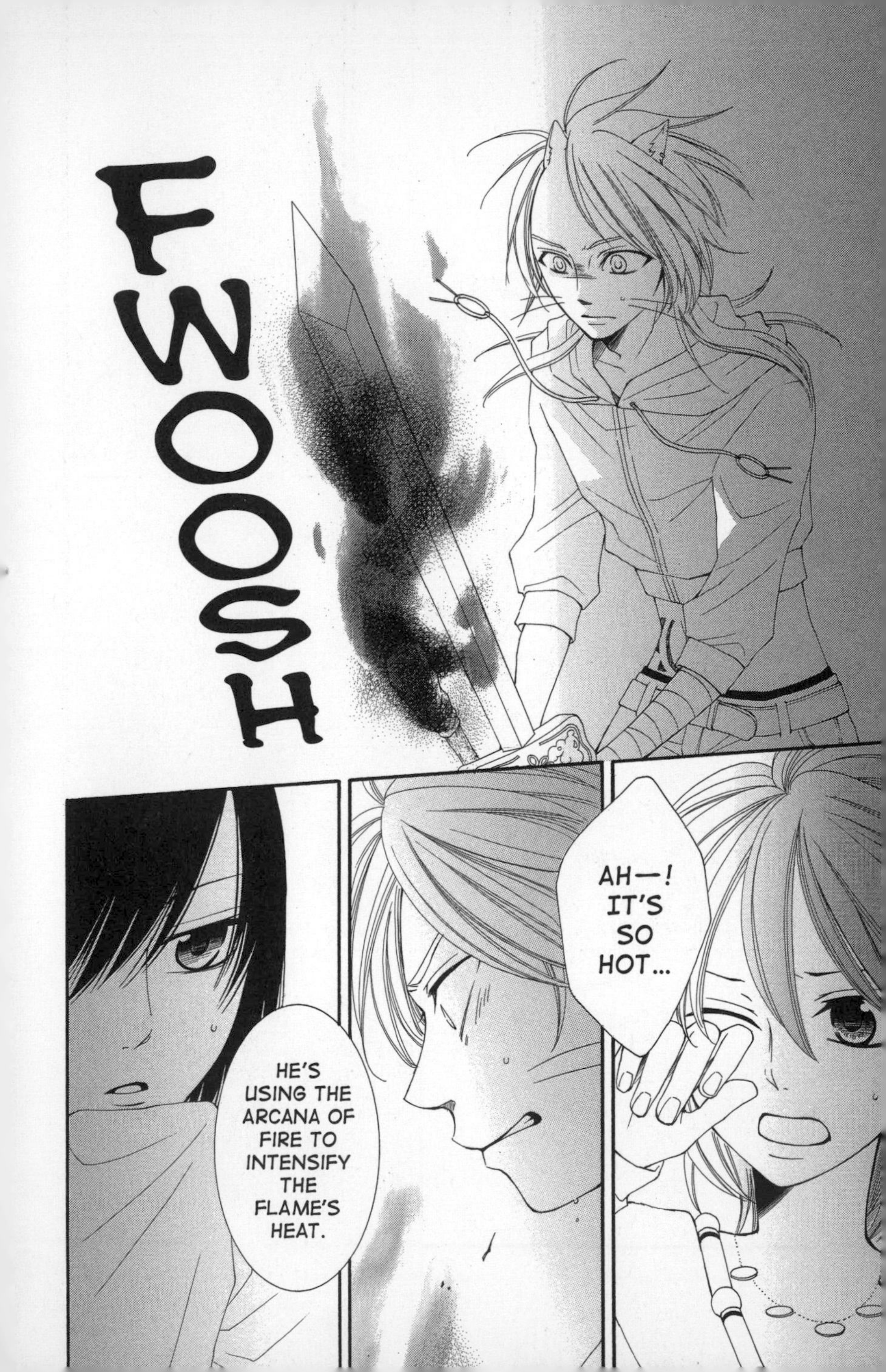
FWOOSH
AH—! IT'S SO HOT...
HE'S USING THE ARCANA OF FIRE TO INTENSIFY THE FLAME'S HEAT.

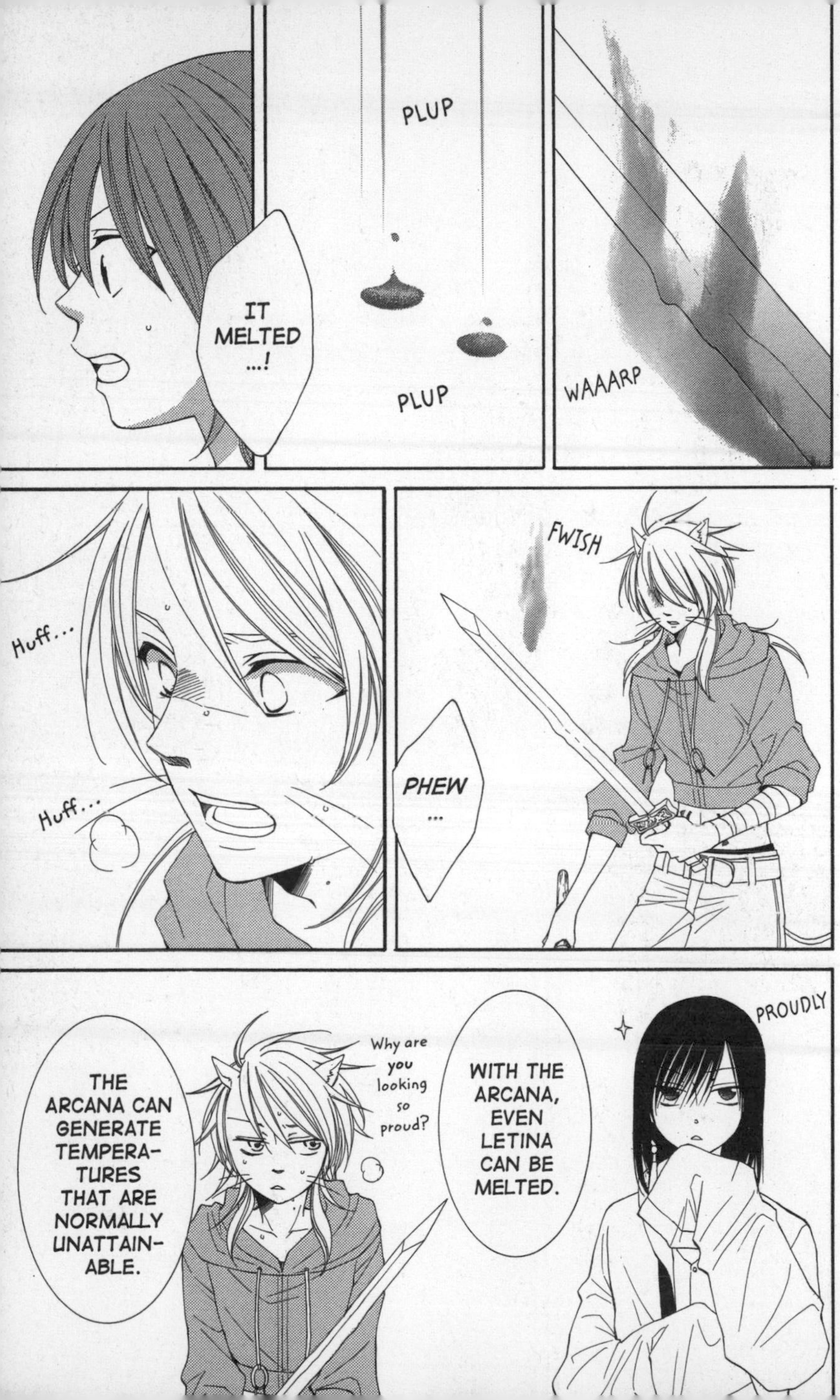
WAAARP
PLUP
PLUP
IT MELTED ...!
FWISH
PHEW ...
Huff...
Huff...
PROUDLY
WITH THE ARCANA, EVEN LETINA CAN BE MELTED.
Why are you looking so proud?
THE ARCANA CAN GENERATE TEMPERA-TURES THAT ARE NORMALLY UNATTAIN-ABLE.

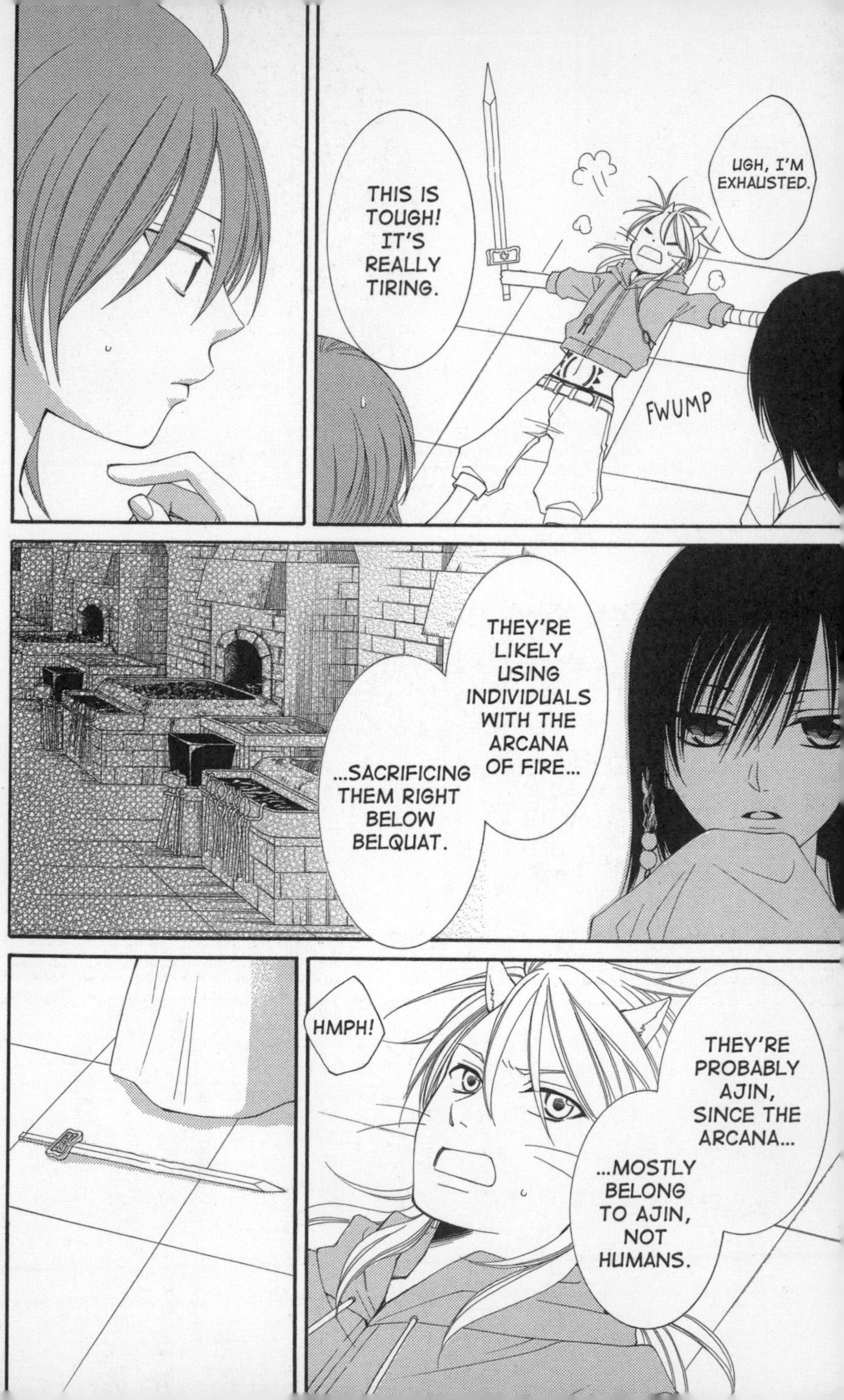
UGH, I'M EXHAUSTED.
THIS IS TOUGH! IT'S REALLY TIRING.
FWUMP
THEY'RE LIKELY USING INDIVIDUALS WITH THE ARCANA OF FIRE...
...SACRIFICING THEM RIGHT BELOW BELQUAT.
THEY'RE PROBABLY AJIN, SINCE THE ARCANA...
...MOSTLY BELONG TO AJIN, NOT HUMANS.
HMPH!

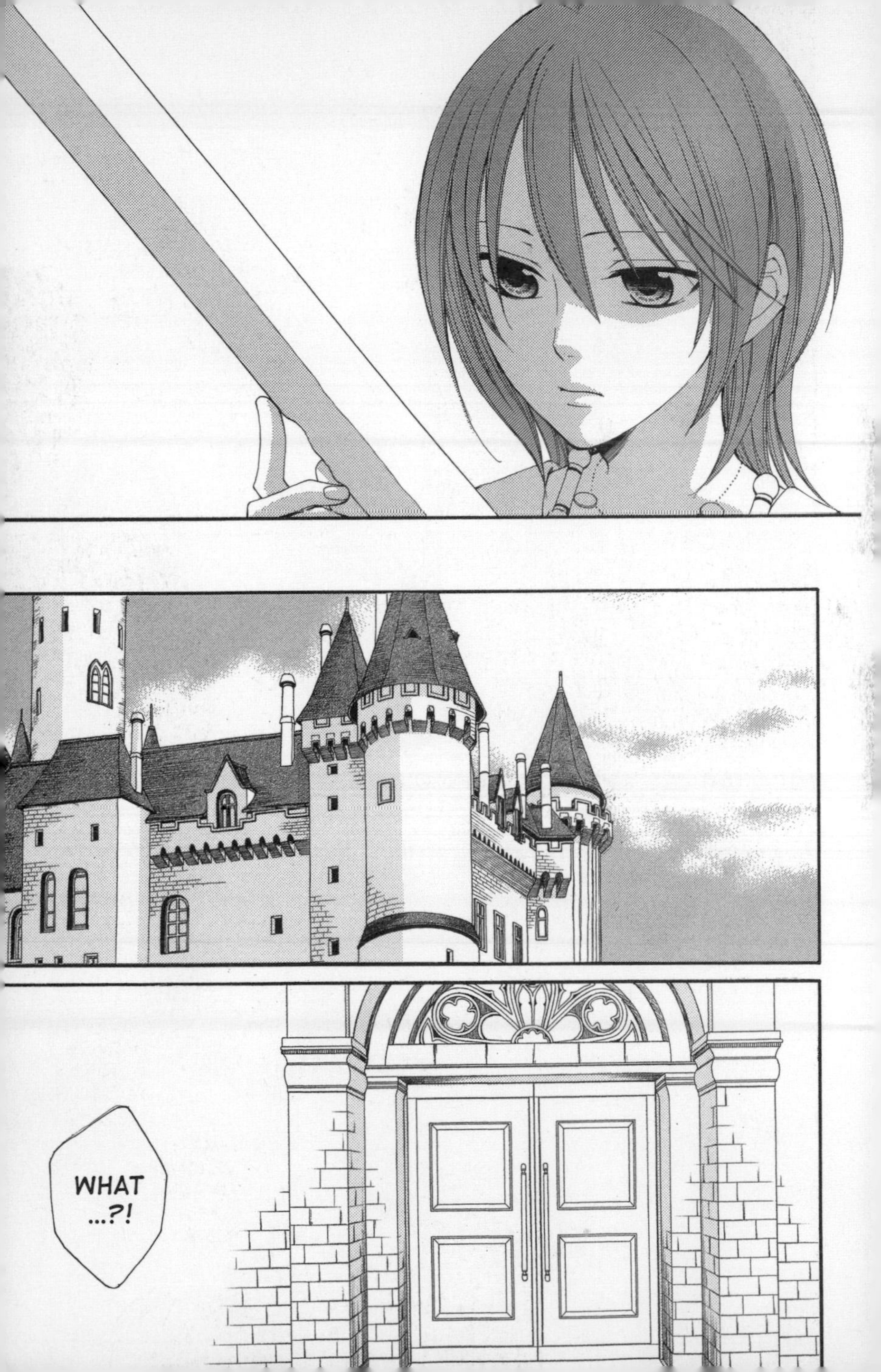
WHAT ...?!

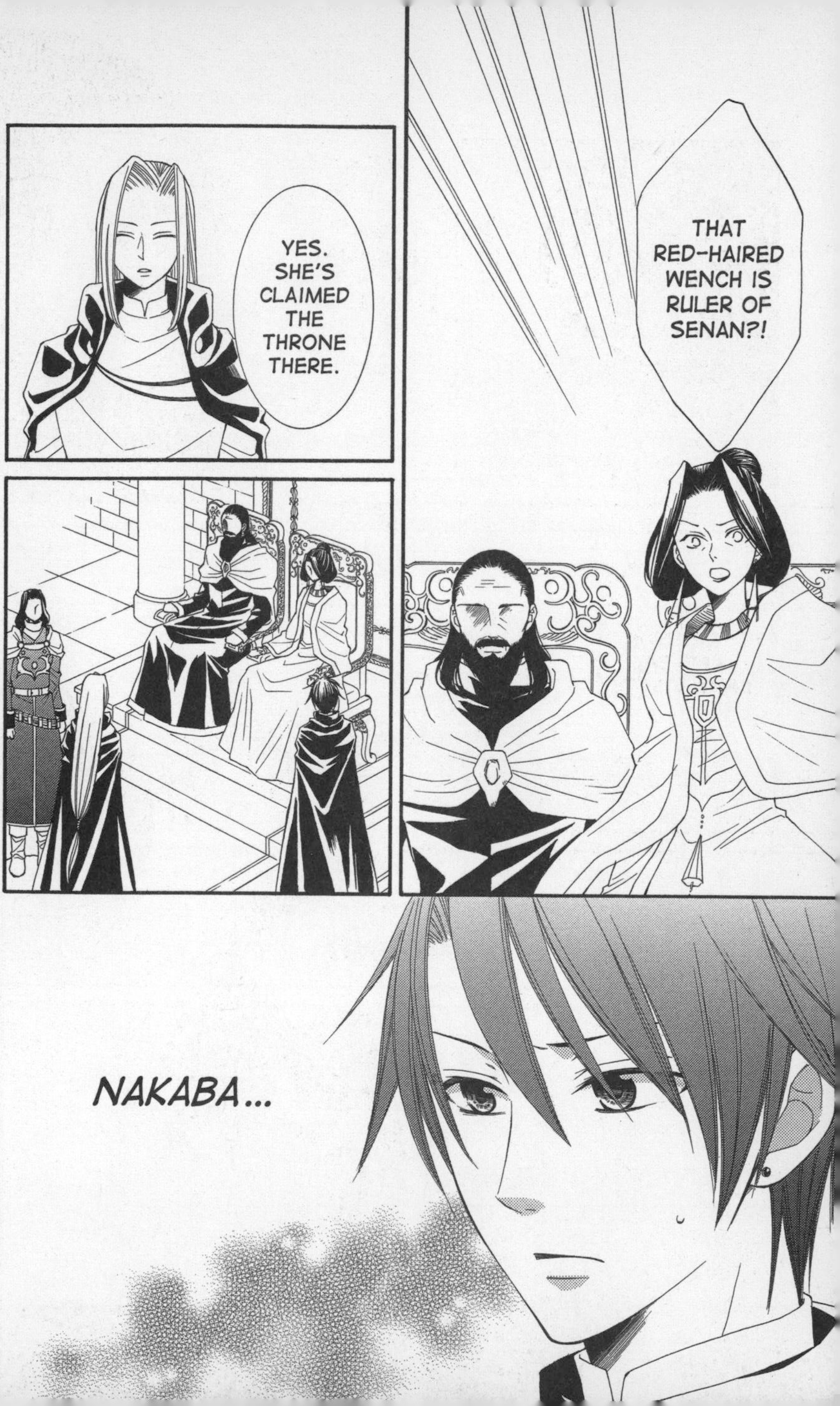
THAT RED-HAIRED WENCH IS RULER OF SENAN?!
YES. SHE'S CLAIMED THE THRONE THERE.
NAKABA...

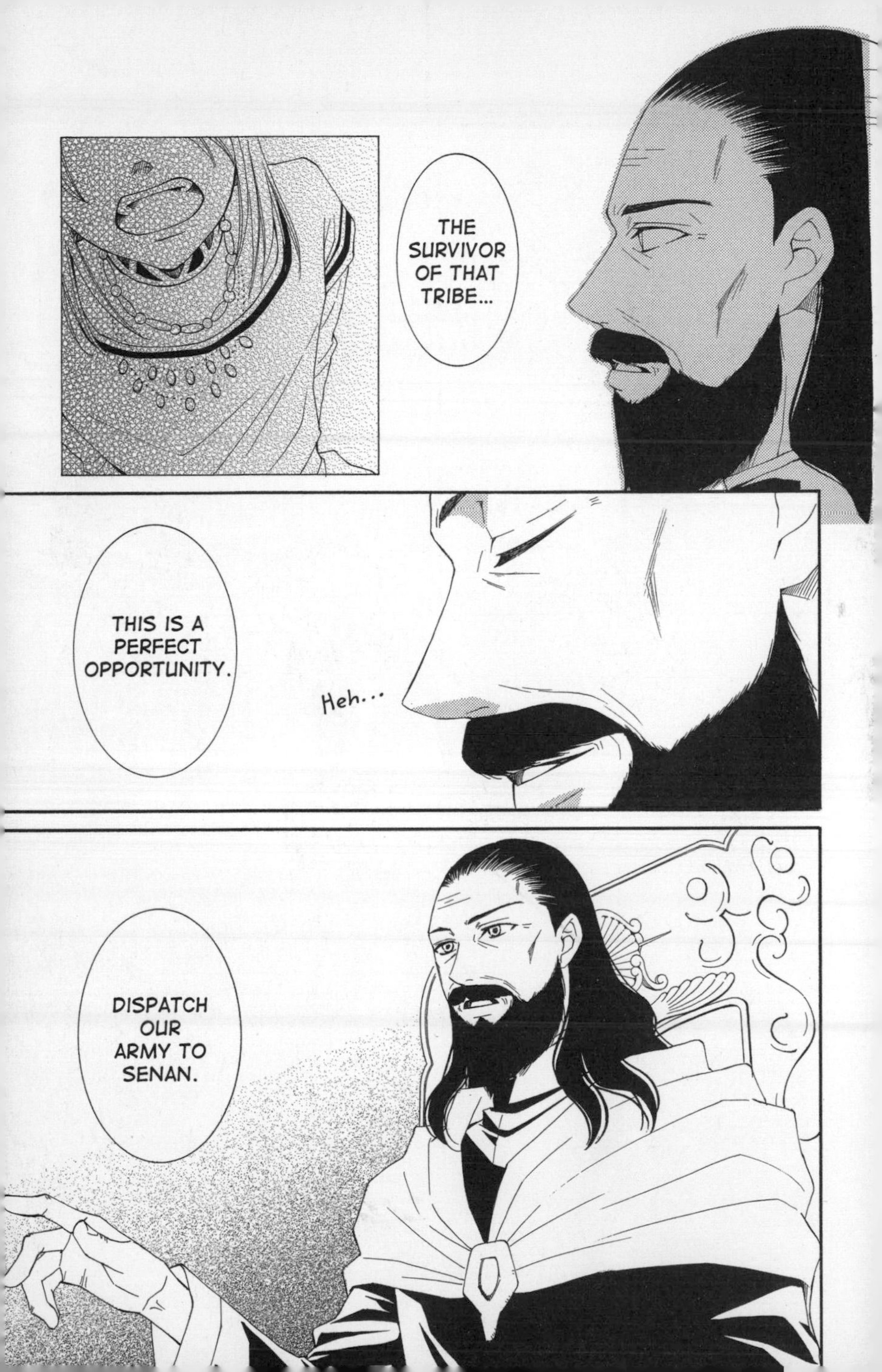
THE SURVIVOR OF THAT TRIBE...
THIS IS A PERFECT OPPORTUNITY.
Heh...
DISPATCH OUR ARMY TO SENAN.

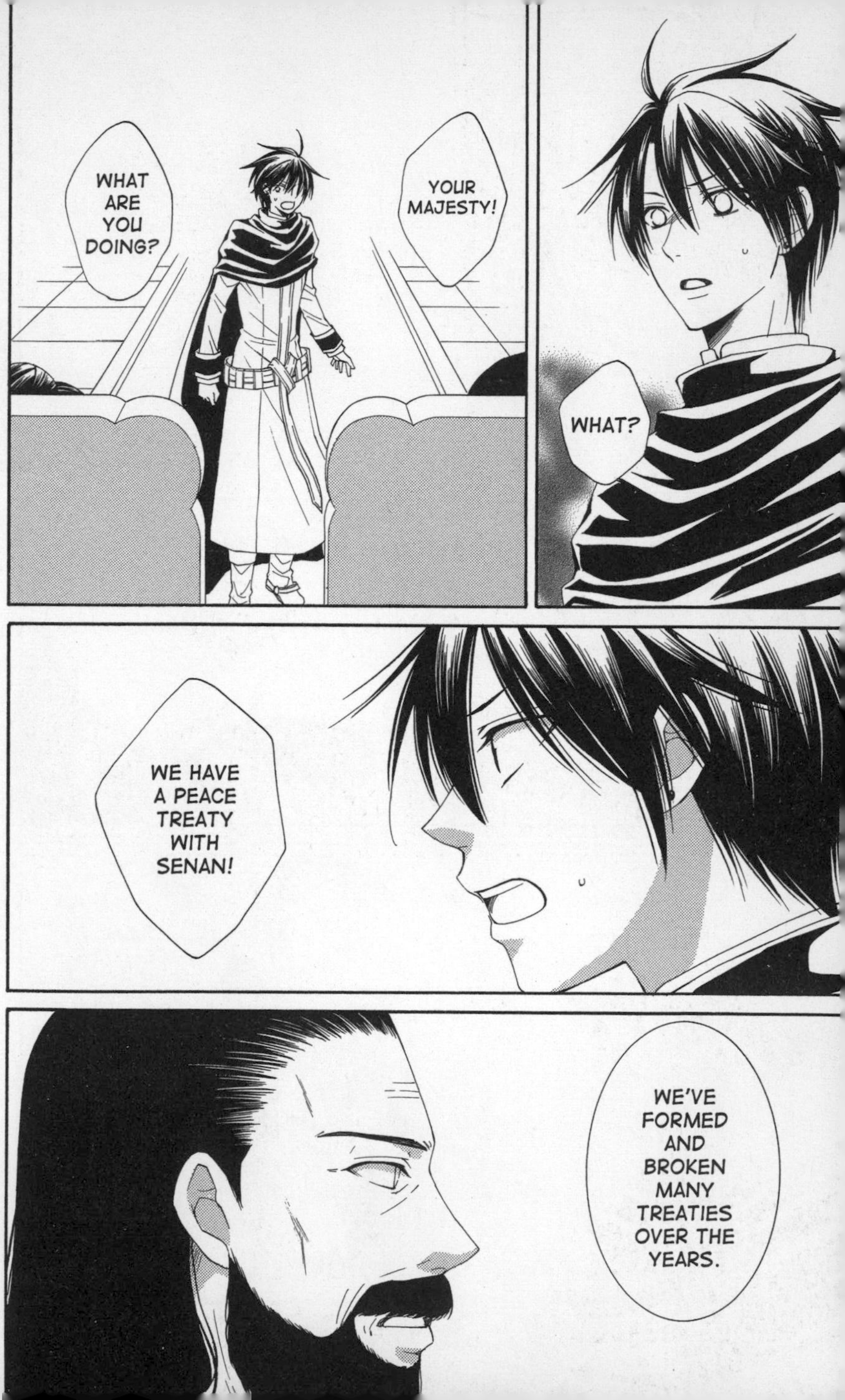
WHAT?
YOUR MAJESTY!
WHAT ARE YOU DOING?
WE HAVE A PEACE TREATY WITH SENAN!
WE'VE FORMED AND BROKEN MANY TREATIES OVER THE YEARS.

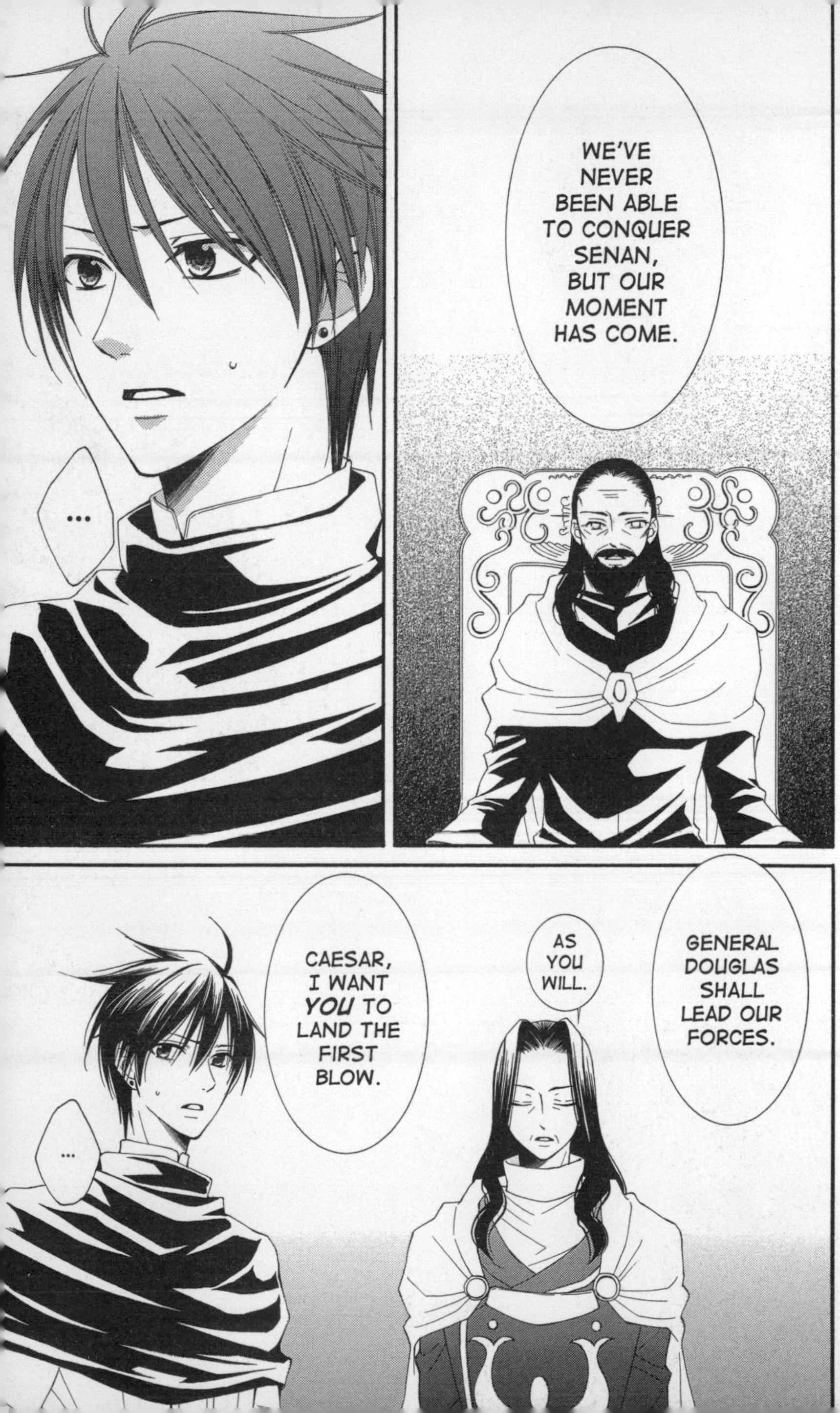
WE'VE NEVER BEEN ABLE TO CONQUER SENAN, BUT OUR MOMENT HAS COME.
...
GENERAL DOUGLAS SHALL LEAD OUR FORCES.
AS YOU WILL.
CAESAR, I WANT *YOU* TO LAND THE FIRST BLOW.
...

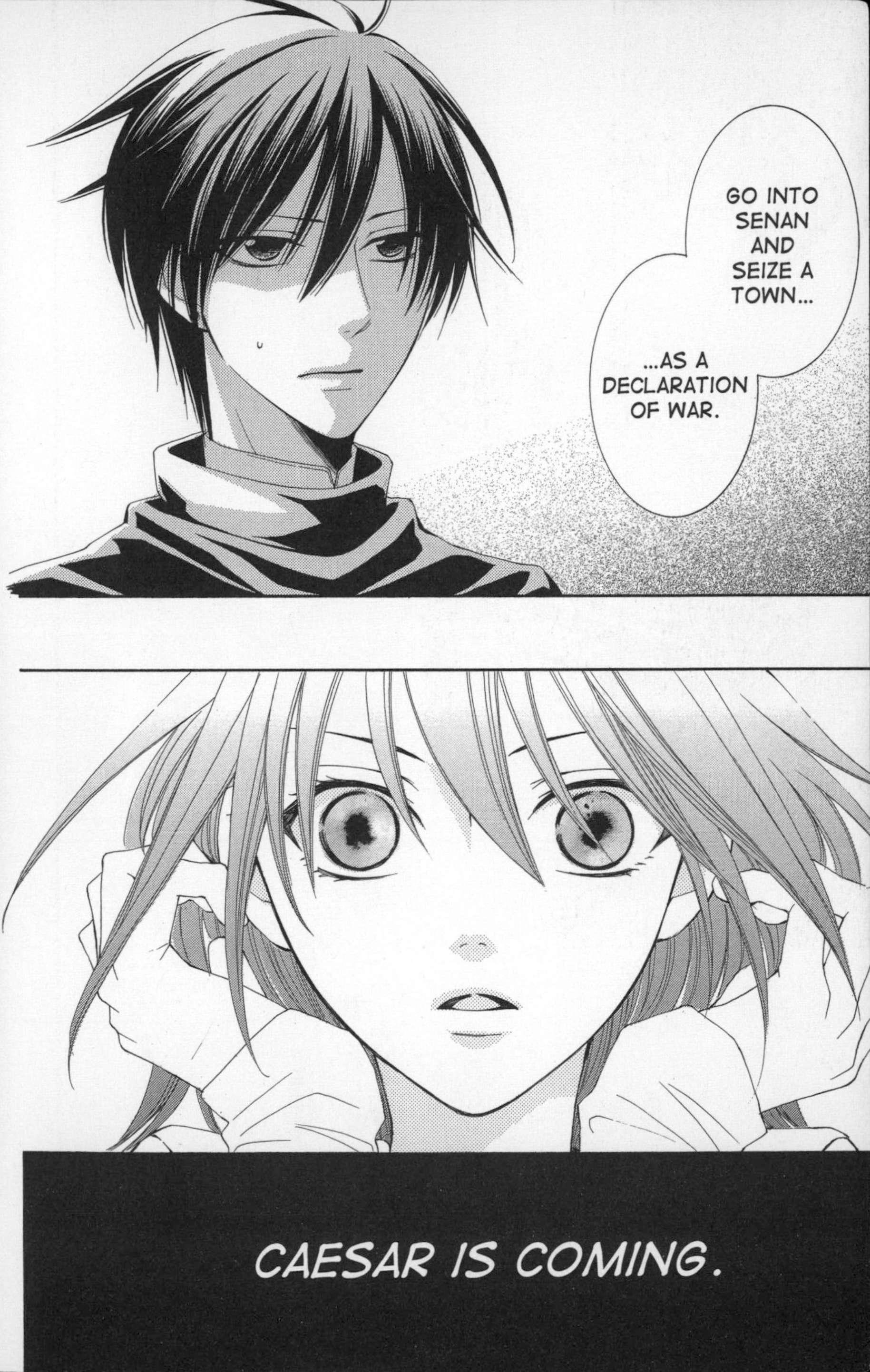
GO INTO SENAN AND SEIZE A TOWN...
...AS A DECLARATION OF WAR.
CAESAR IS COMING.

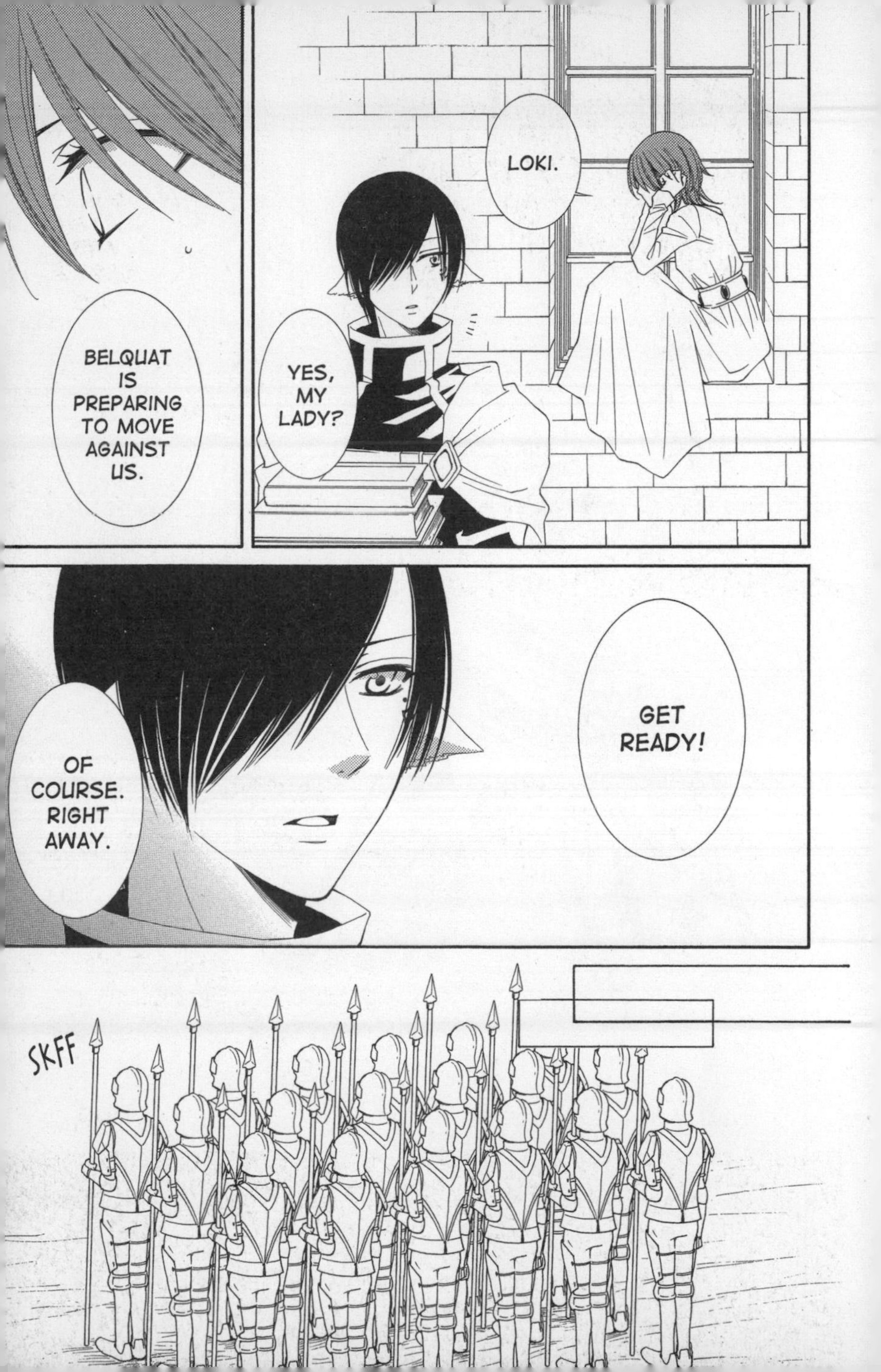
LOKI.
YES, MY LADY?
BELQUAT IS PREPARING TO MOVE AGAINST US.
GET READY!
OF COURSE. RIGHT AWAY.
SKFF

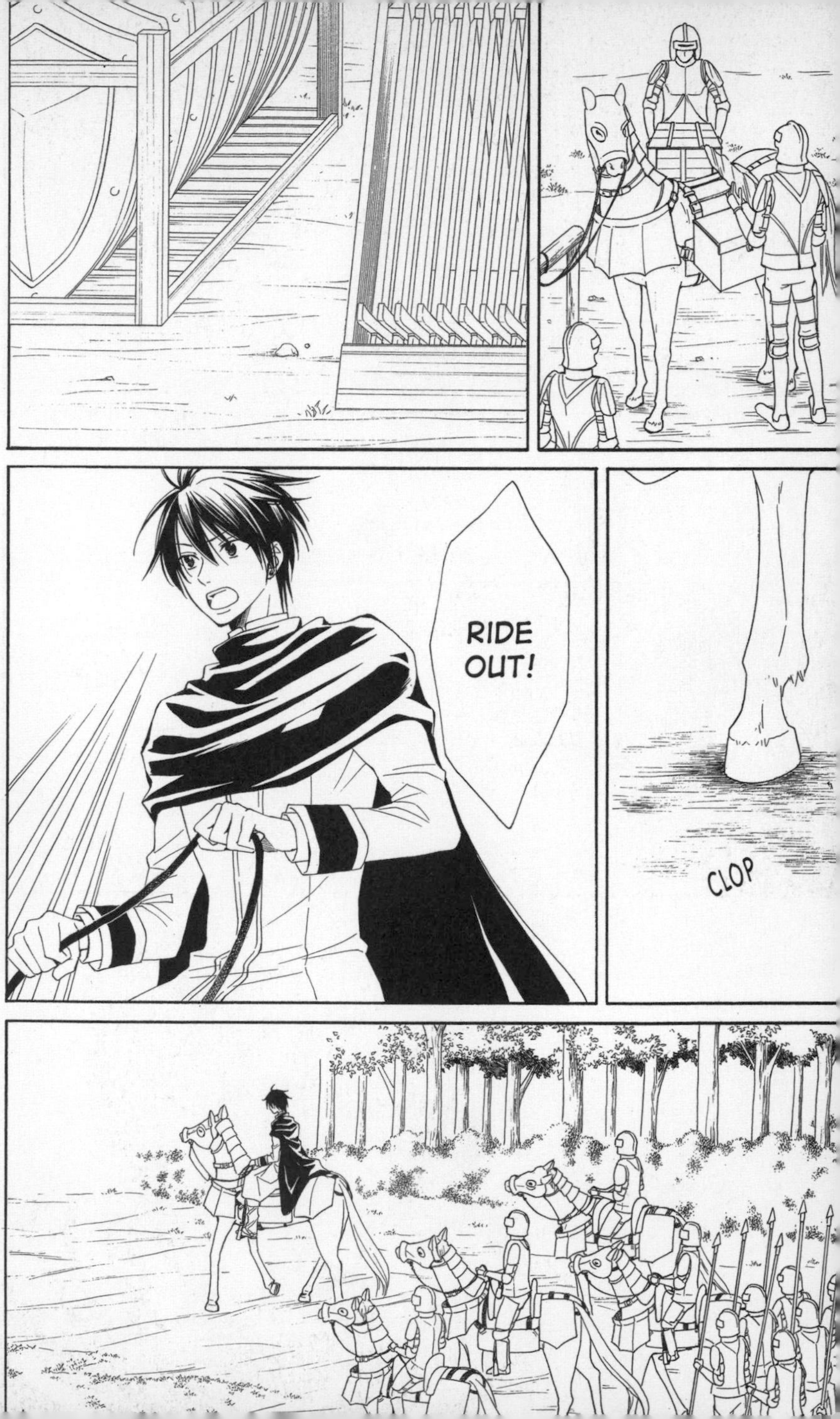
CLOP
RIDE OUT!

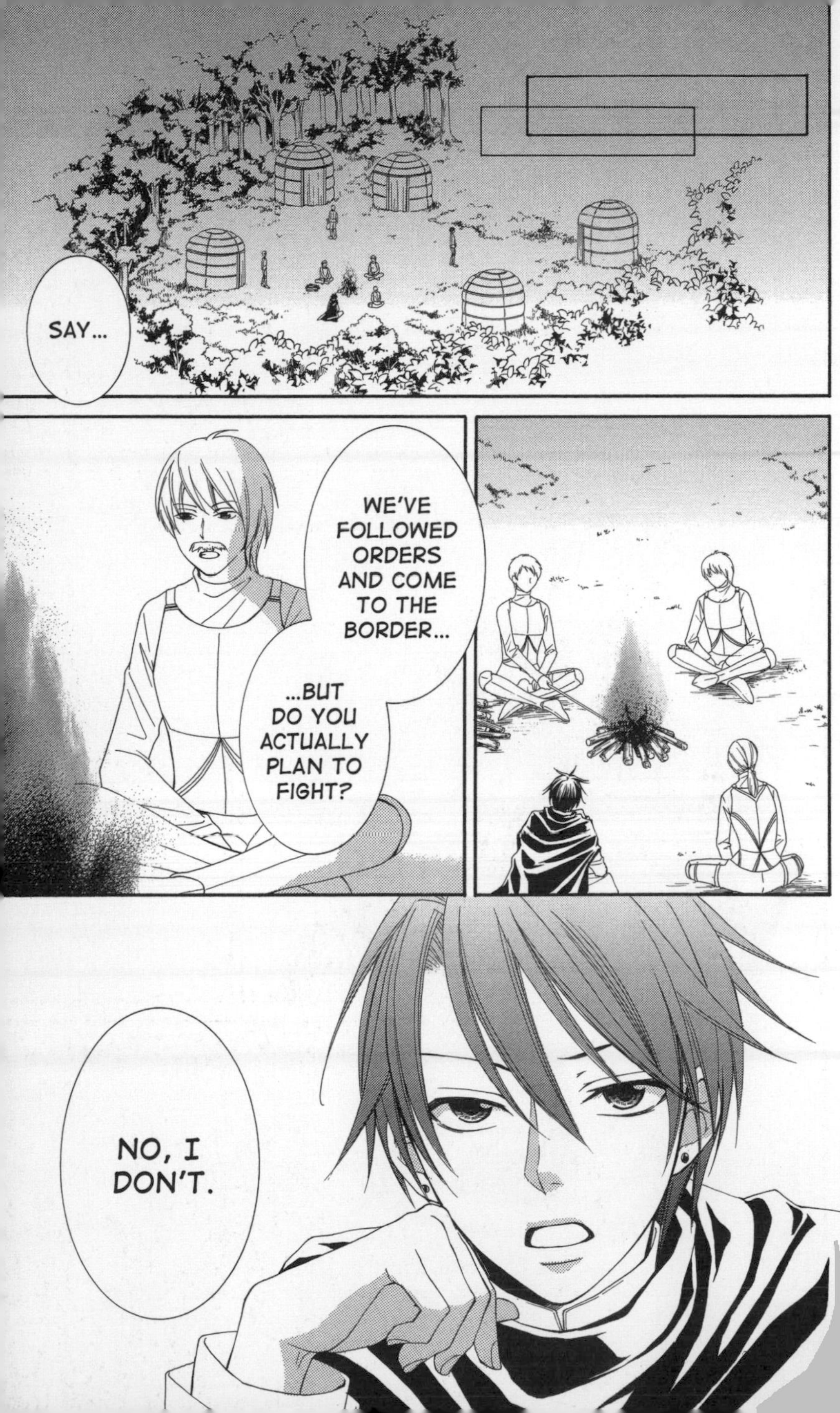
SAY...
WE'VE FOLLOWED ORDERS AND COME TO THE BORDER...
...BUT DO YOU ACTUALLY PLAN TO FIGHT?
NO, I DON'T.

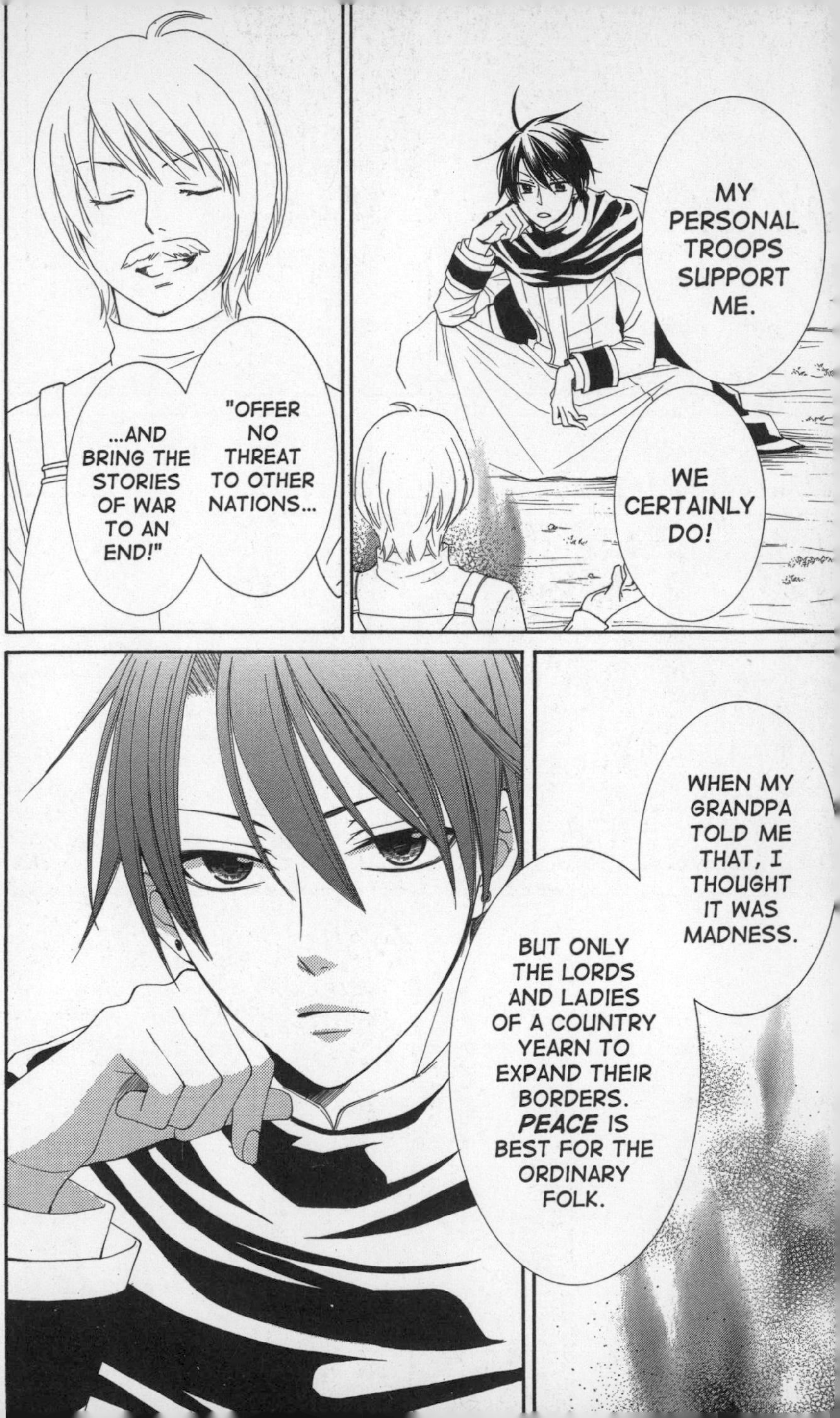
MY PERSONAL TROOPS SUPPORT ME.
WE CERTAINLY DO!
"OFFER NO THREAT TO OTHER NATIONS...
...AND BRING THE STORIES OF WAR TO AN END!"
WHEN MY GRANDPA TOLD ME THAT, I THOUGHT IT WAS MADNESS.
BUT ONLY THE LORDS AND LADIES OF A COUNTRY YEARN TO EXPAND THEIR BORDERS. *PEACE* IS BEST FOR THE ORDINARY FOLK.

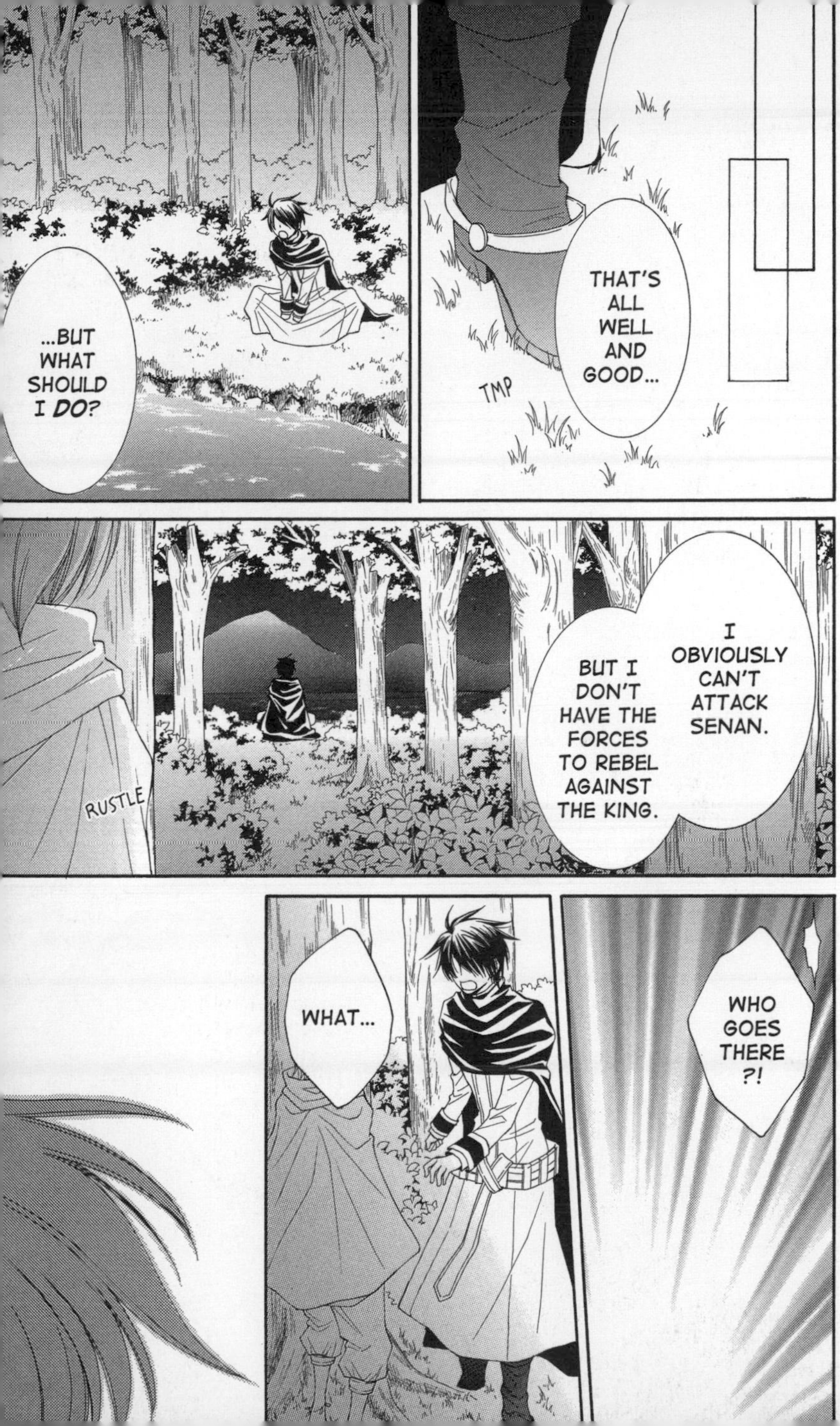
THAT'S ALL WELL AND GOOD...
TMP
...BUT WHAT SHOULD I *DO*?
I OBVIOUSLY CAN'T ATTACK SENAN.
BUT I DON'T HAVE THE FORCES TO REBEL AGAINST THE KING.
RUSTLE
WHO GOES THERE?!
WHAT...

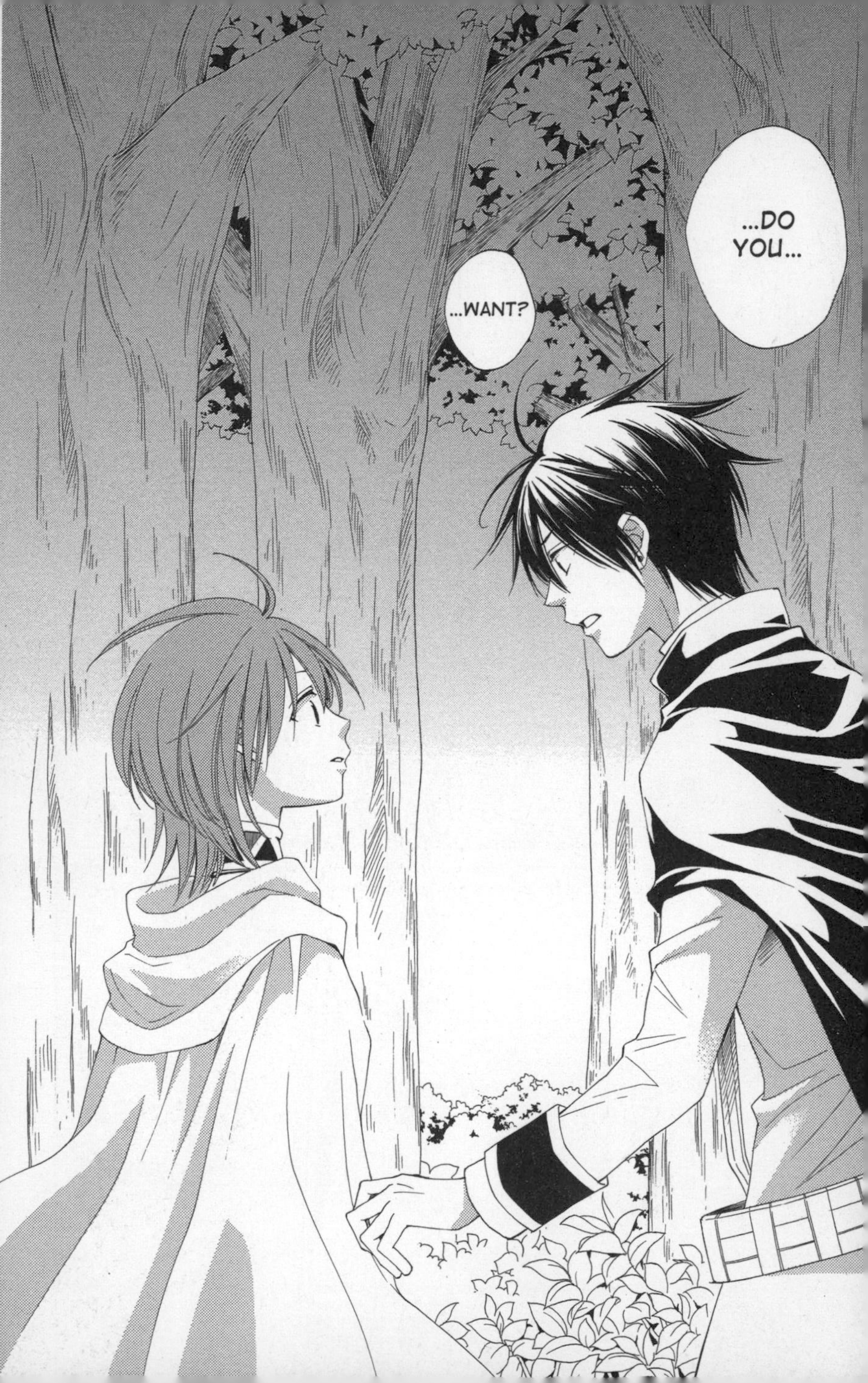
...DO YOU...
...WANT?

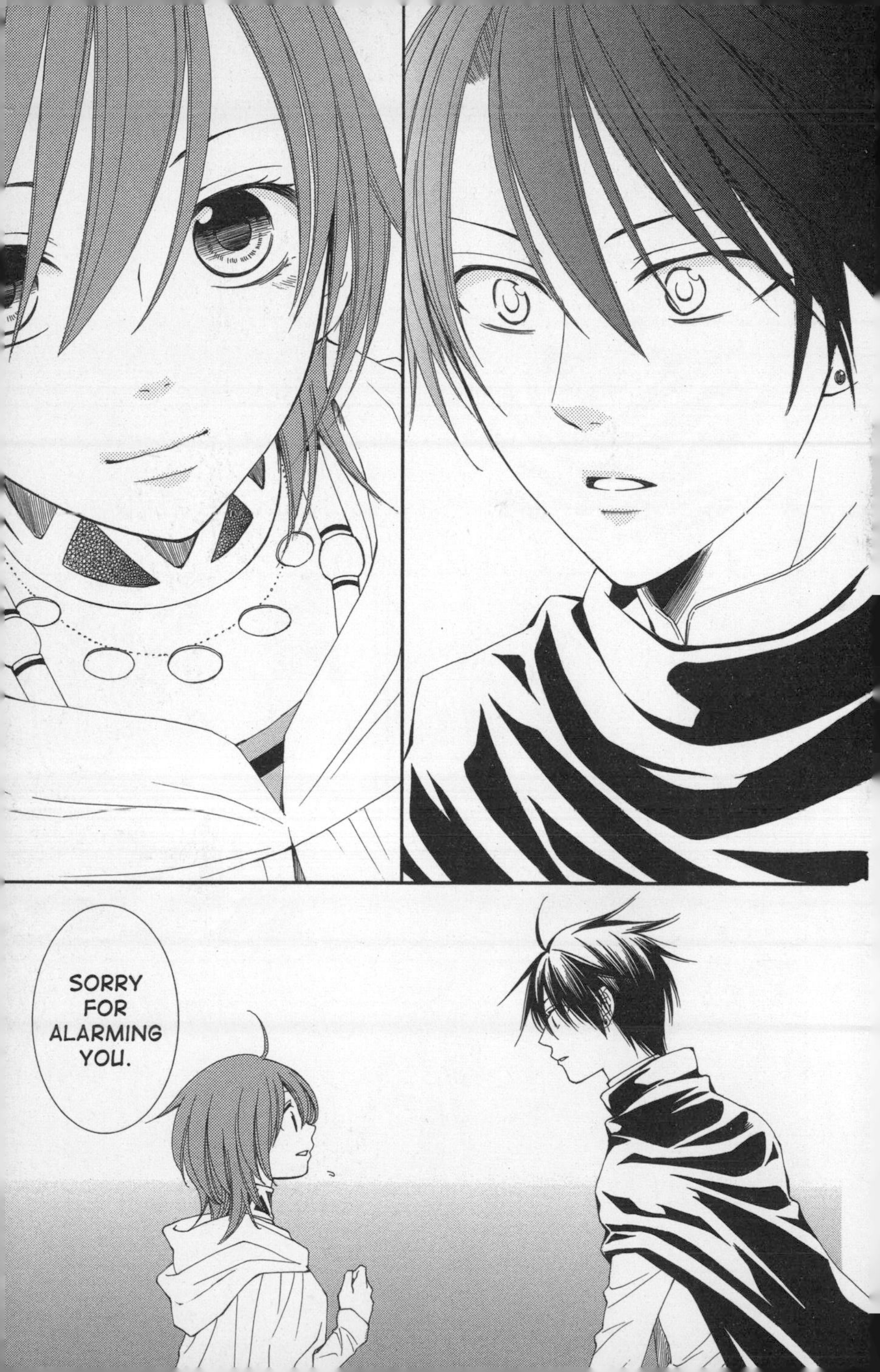
SORRY FOR ALARMING YOU.

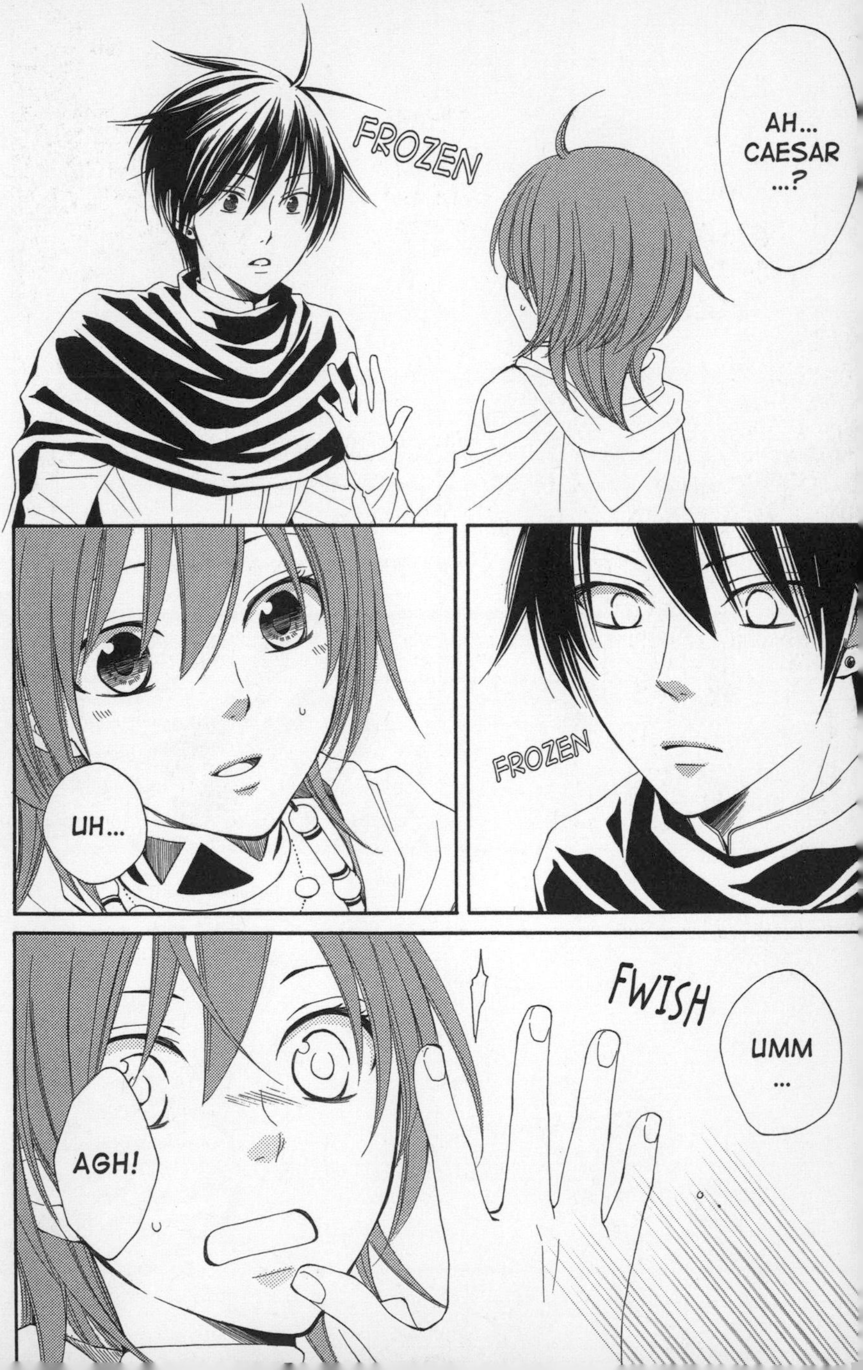
AH... CAESAR ...?
FROZEN
FROZEN
UH...
UMM ...
FWISH
AGH!

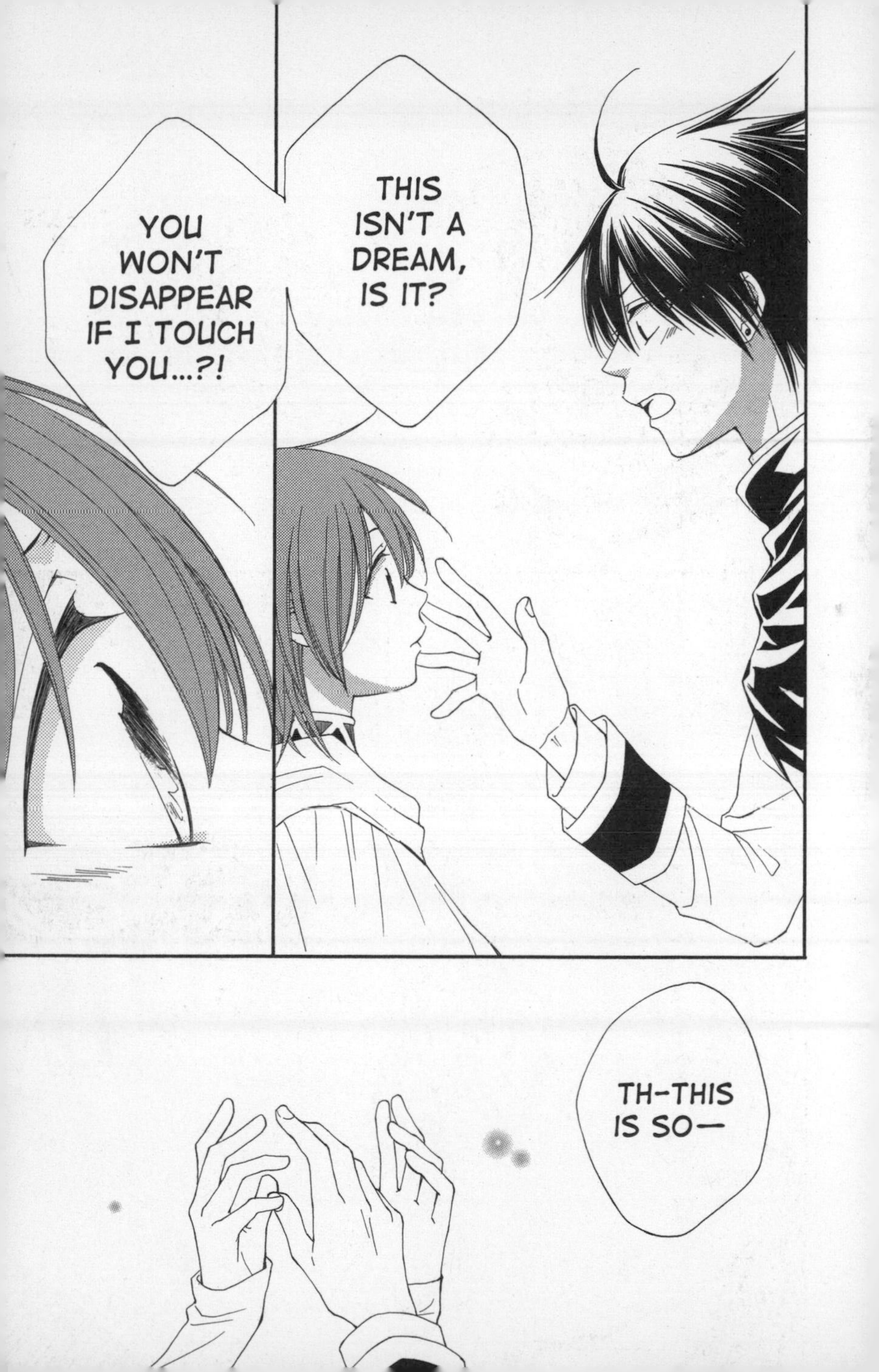
THIS ISN'T A DREAM, IS IT?
YOU WON'T DISAPPEAR IF I TOUCH YOU...?!
TH-THIS IS SO—

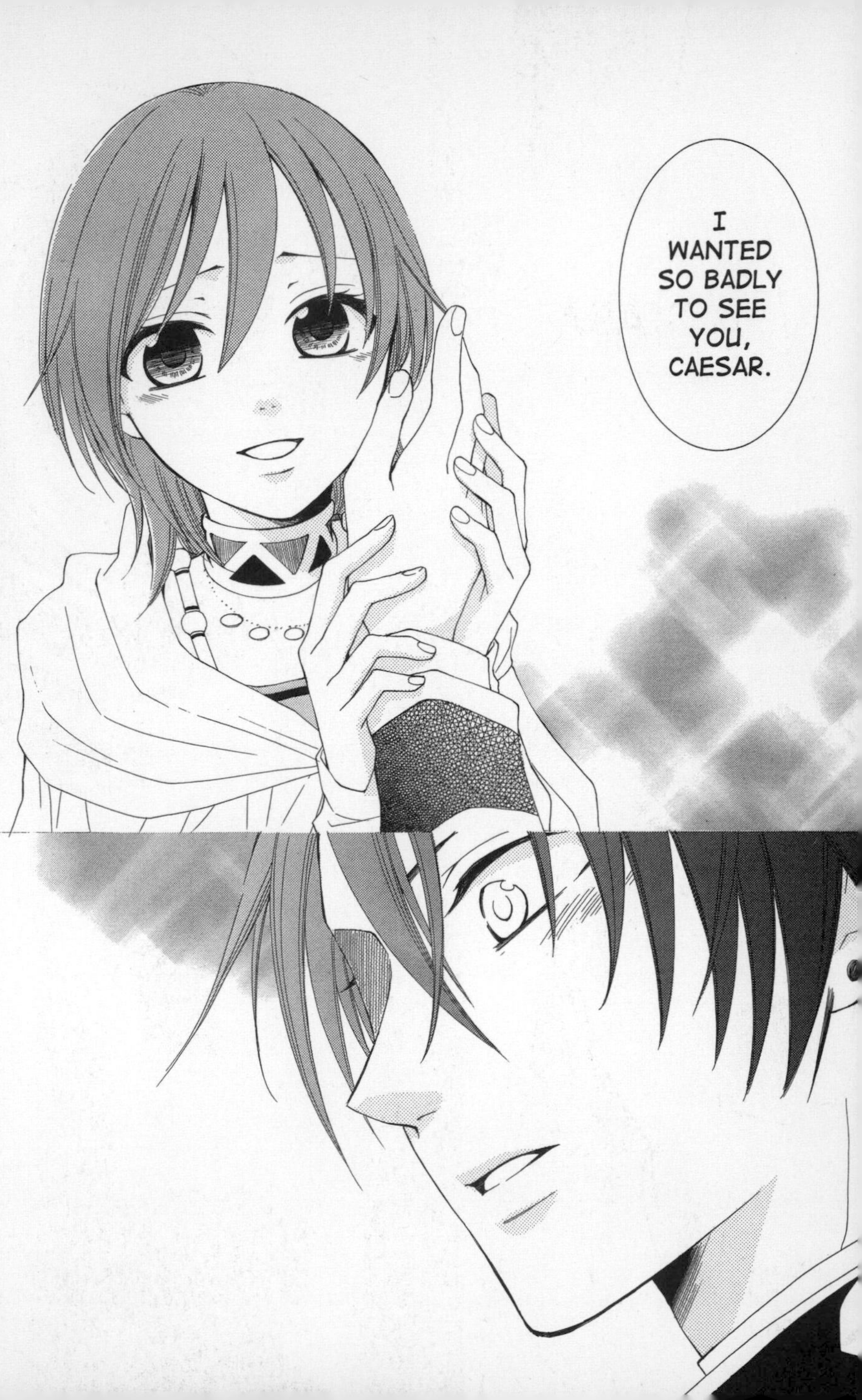
I WANTED SO BADLY TO SEE YOU, CAESAR.

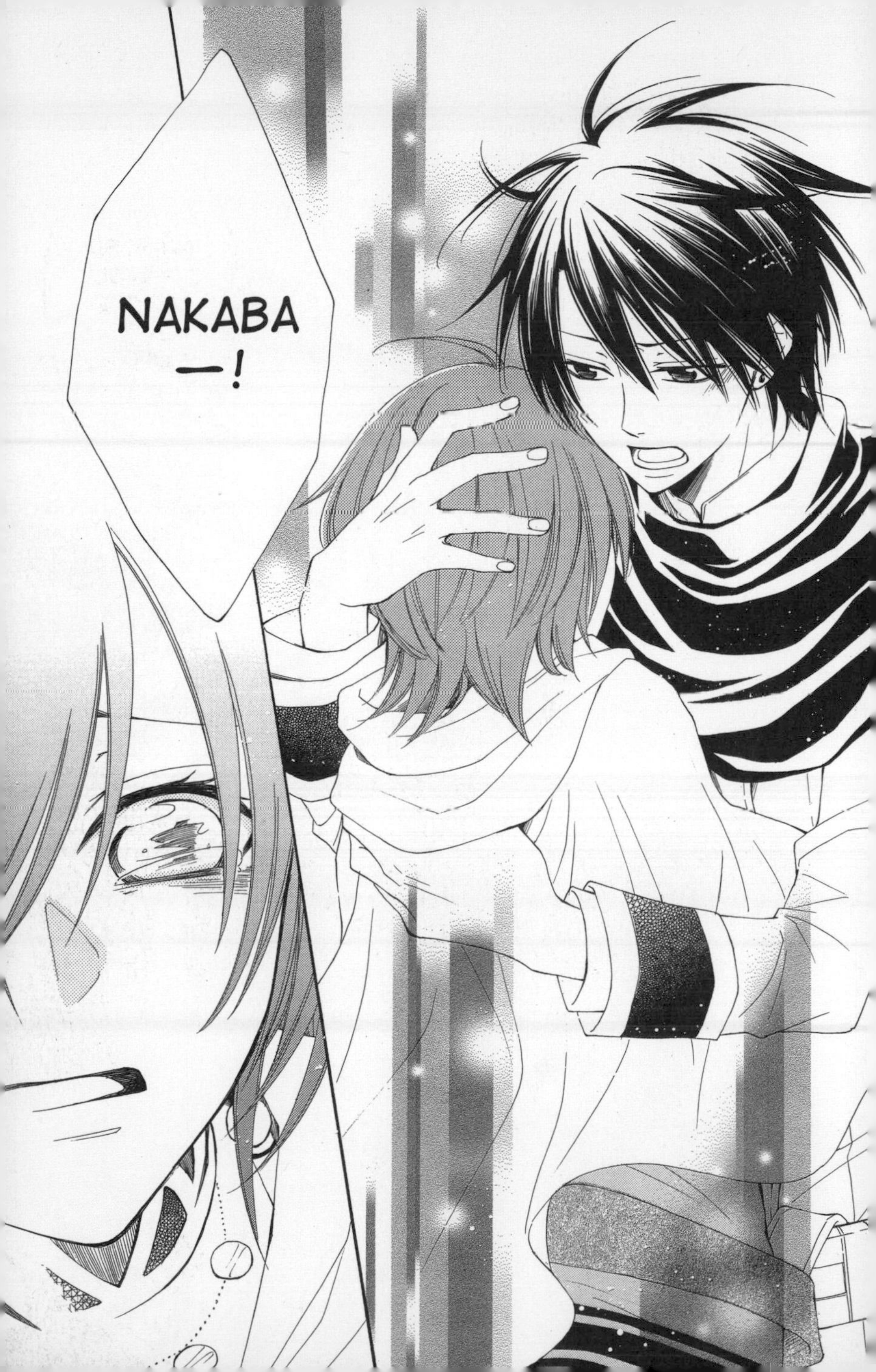
NAKABA
—!

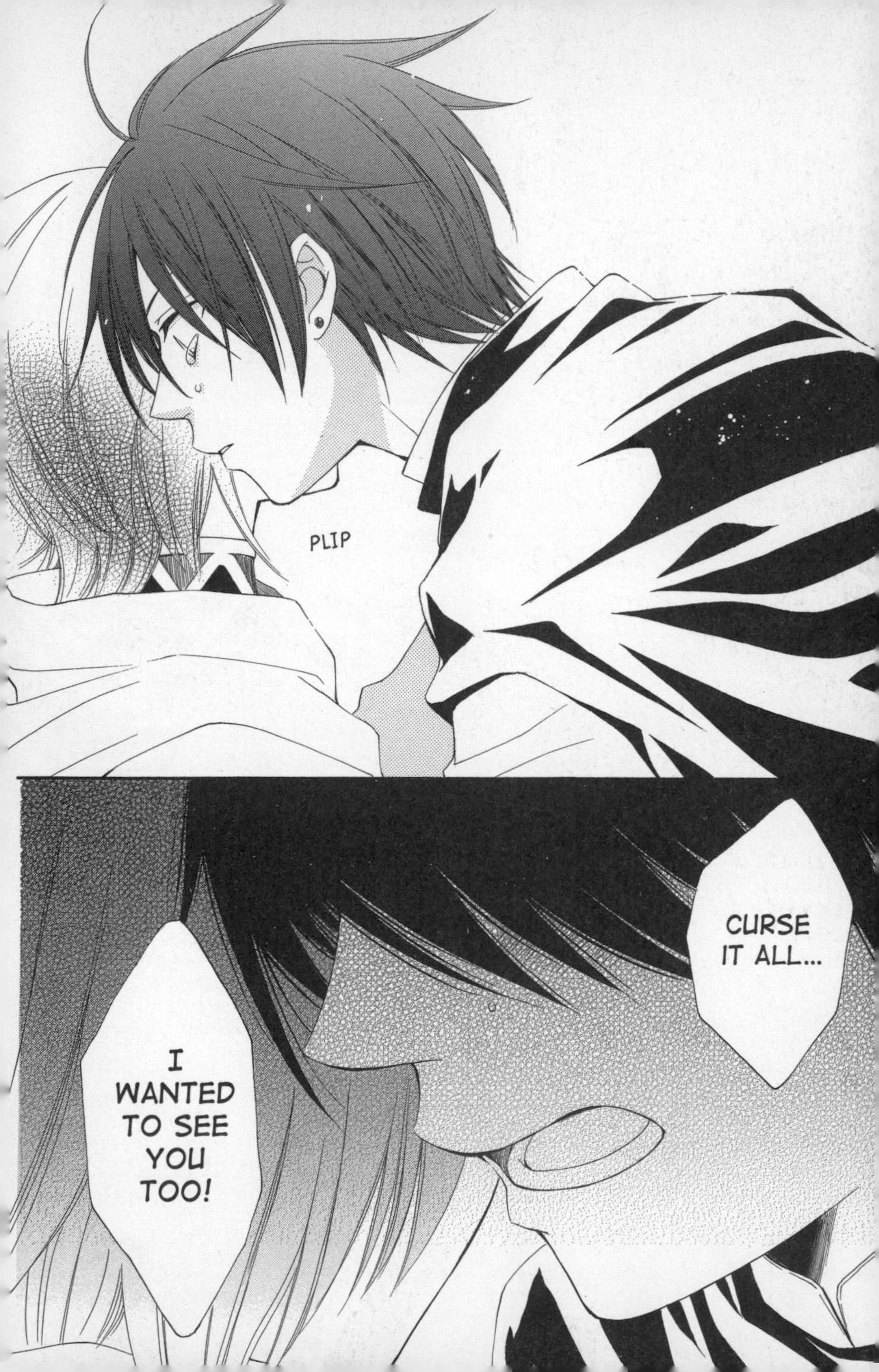
PLIP
CURSE IT ALL...
I WANTED TO SEE YOU TOO!

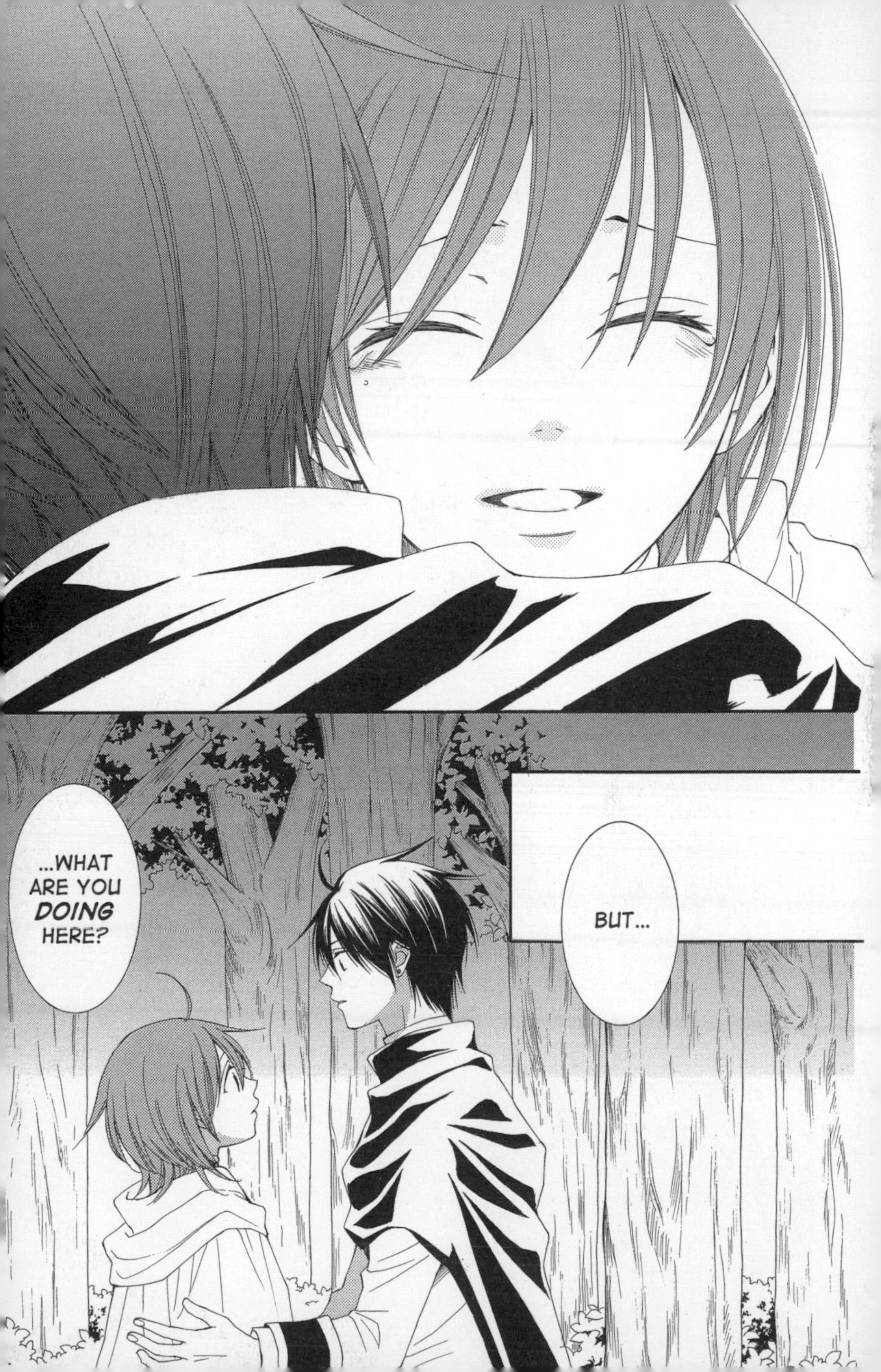
BUT...
...WHAT ARE YOU *DOING* HERE?

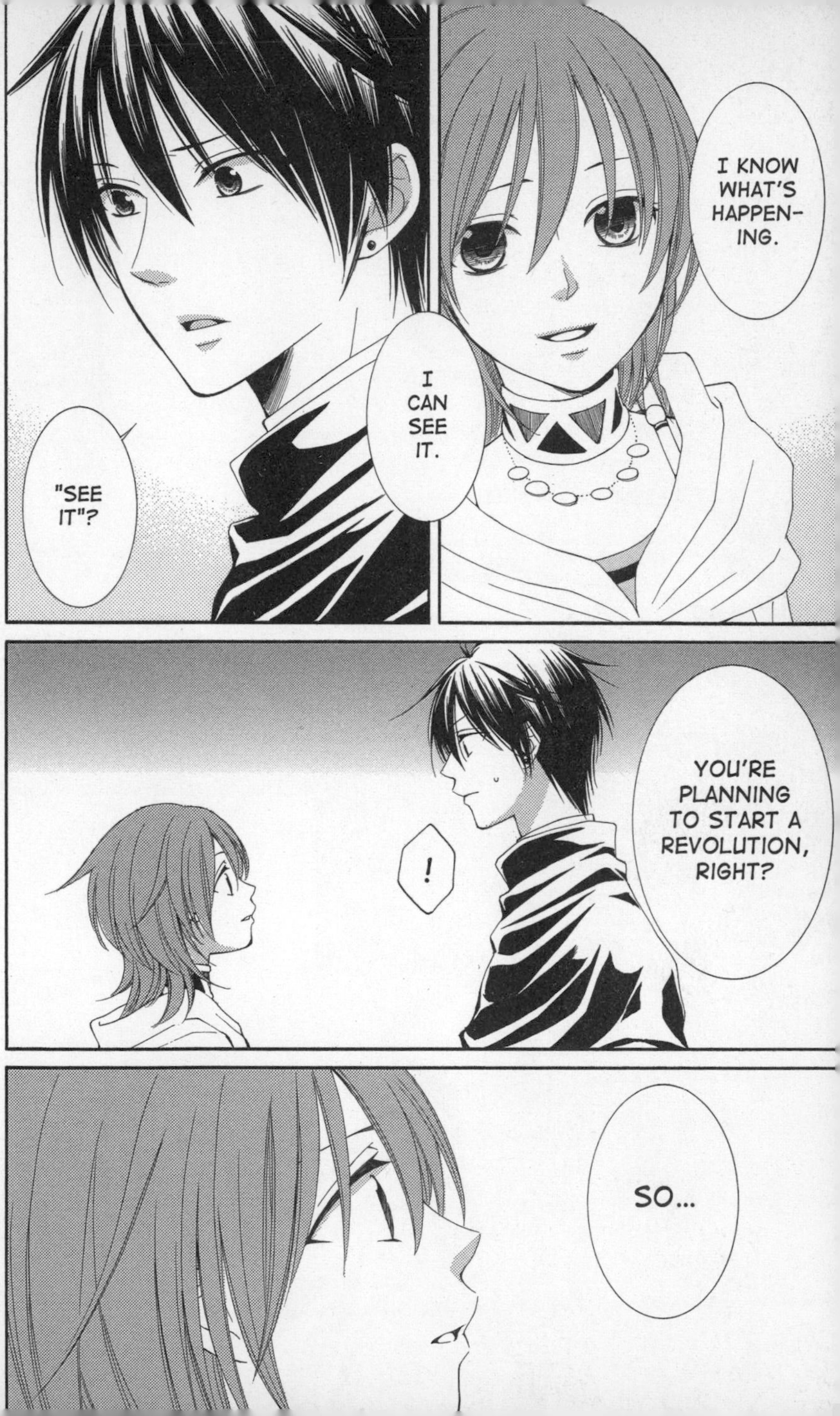
I KNOW WHAT'S HAPPENING.
I CAN SEE IT.
"SEE IT"?
YOU'RE PLANNING TO START A REVOLUTION, RIGHT?
!
SO...

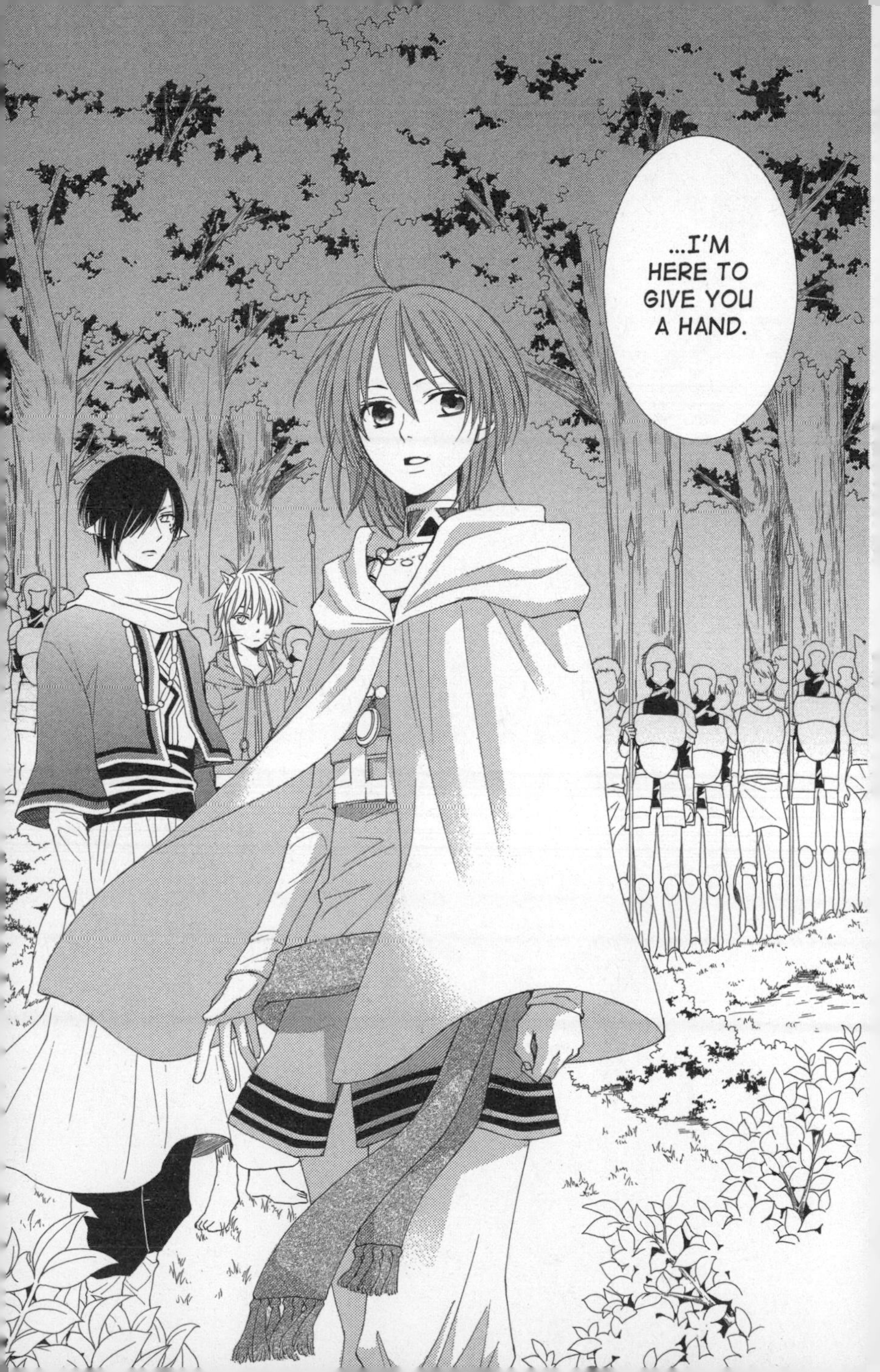
...I'M HERE TO GIVE YOU A HAND.

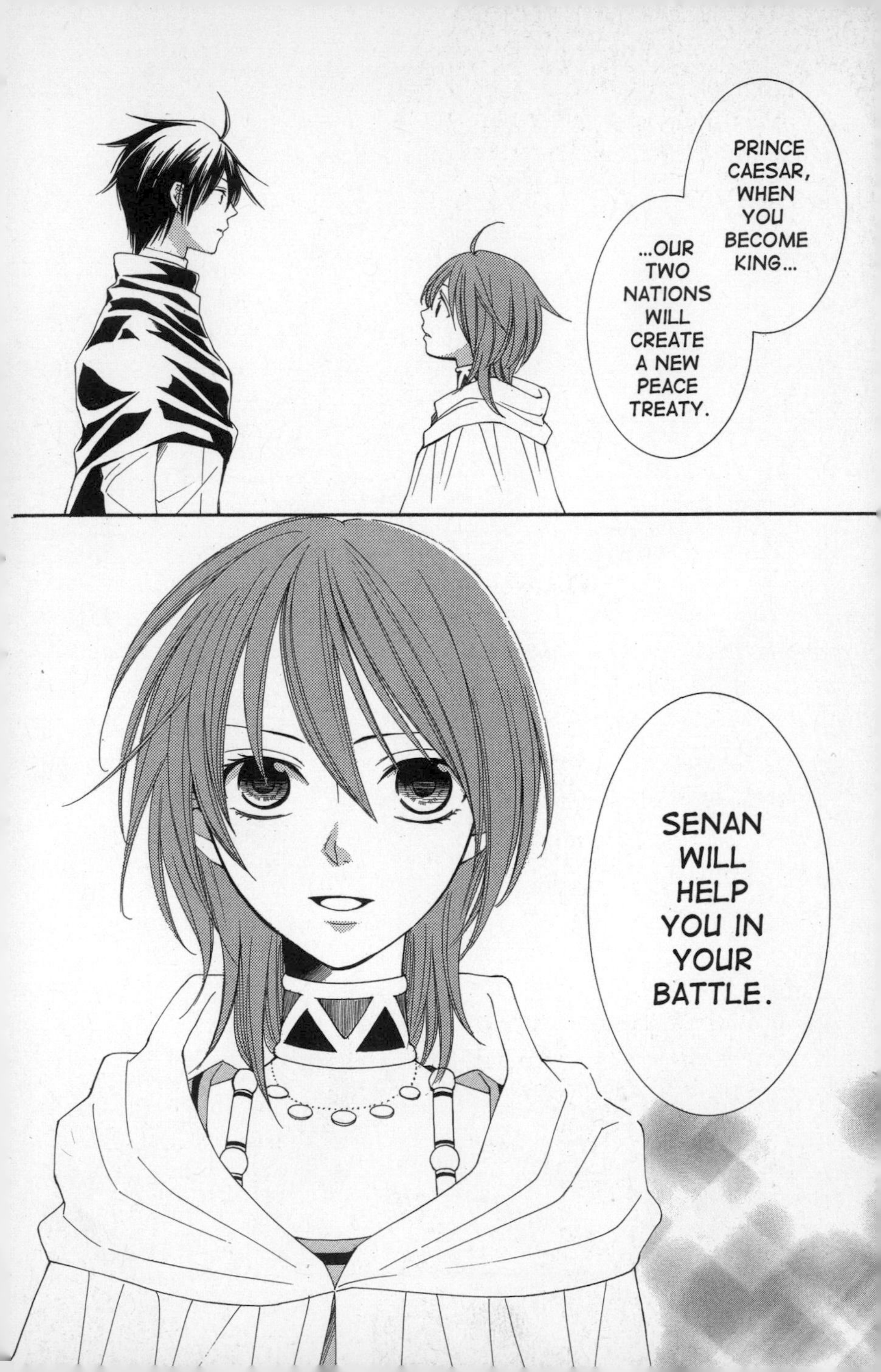
PRINCE CAESAR, WHEN YOU BECOME KING...
...OUR TWO NATIONS WILL CREATE A NEW PEACE TREATY.
SENAN WILL HELP YOU IN YOUR BATTLE.

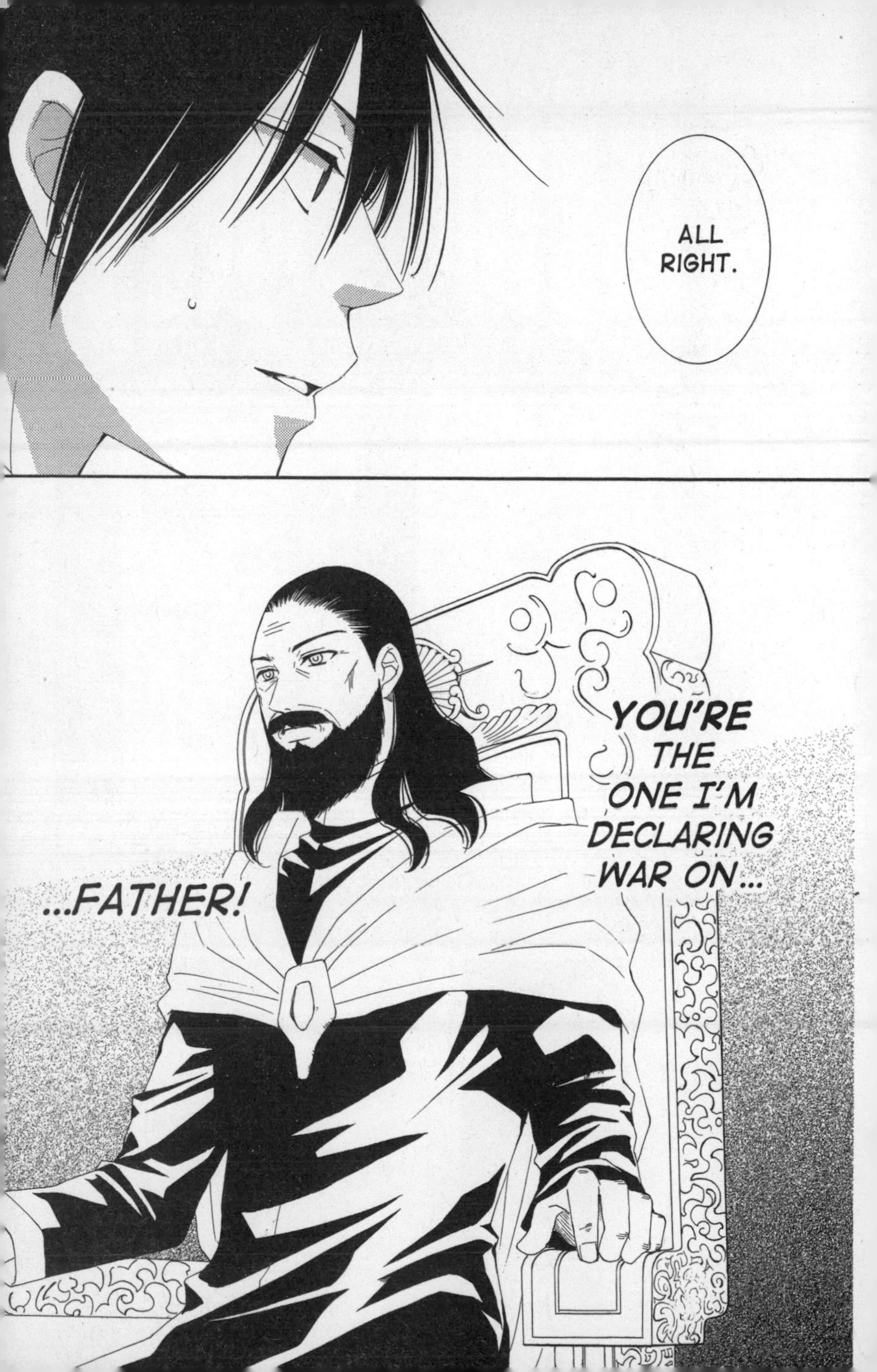
ALL RIGHT.
YOU'RE THE ONE I'M DECLARING WAR ON...
...FATHER!

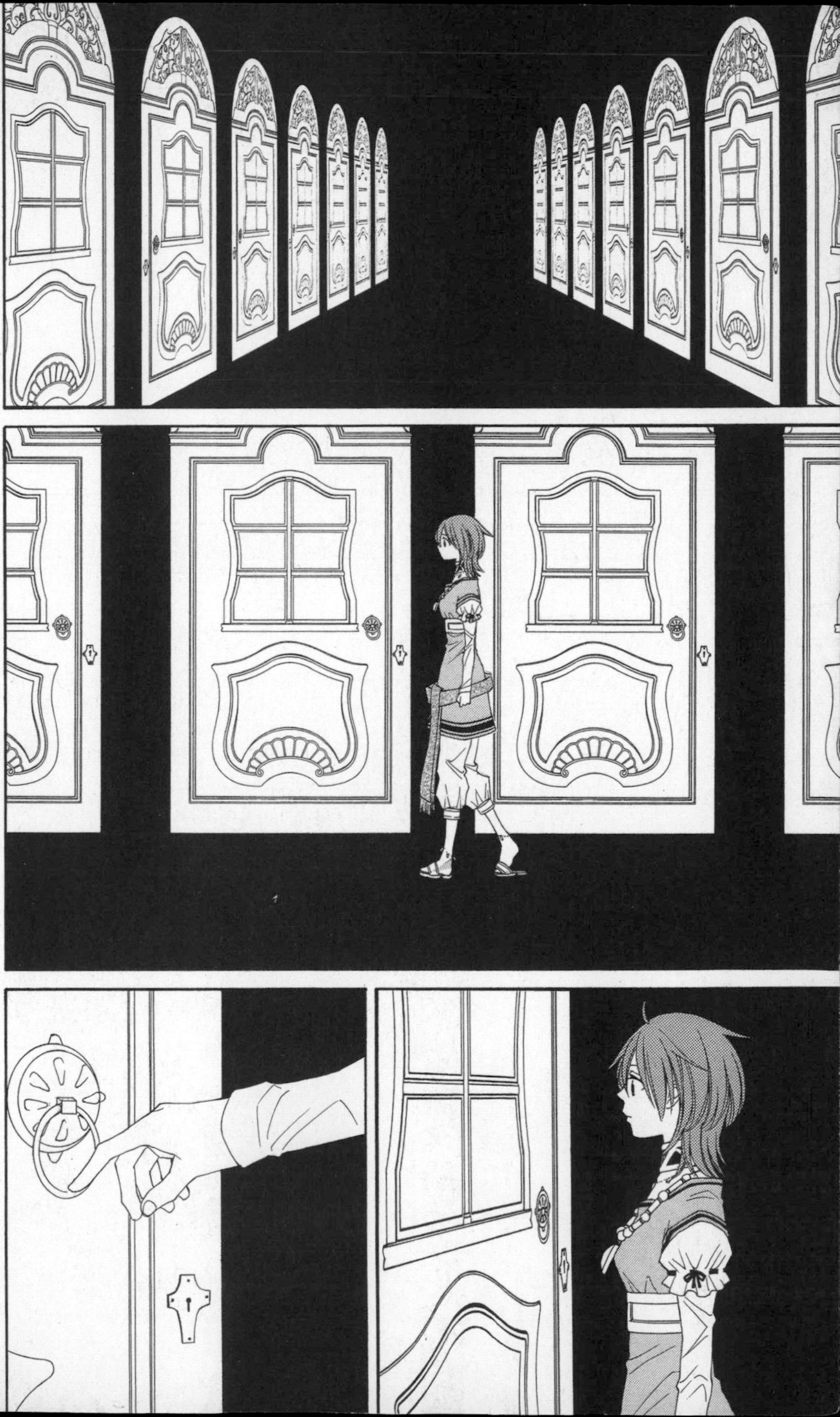

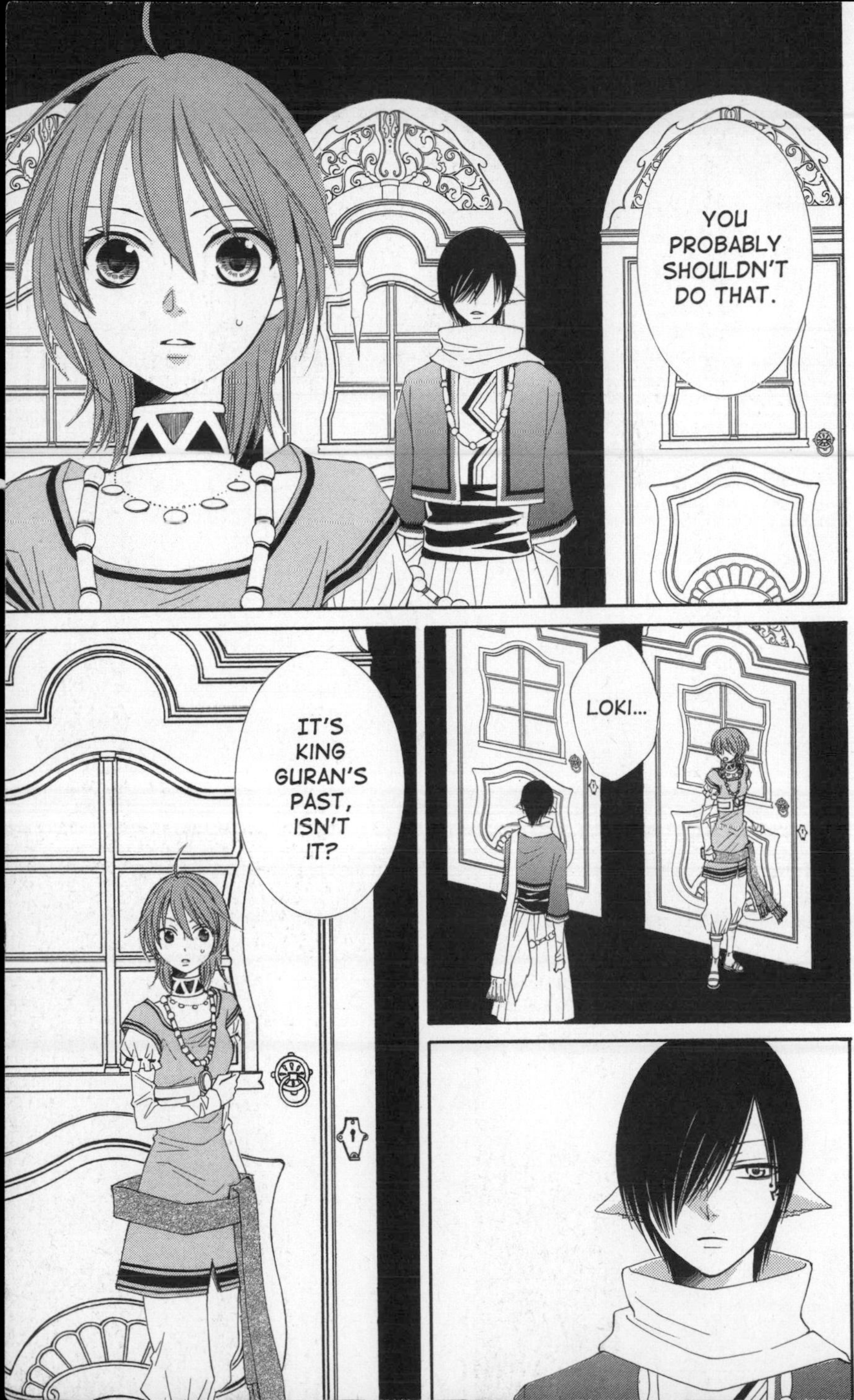
YOU PROBABLY SHOULDN'T DO THAT.
LOKI...
IT'S KING GURAN'S PAST, ISN'T IT?

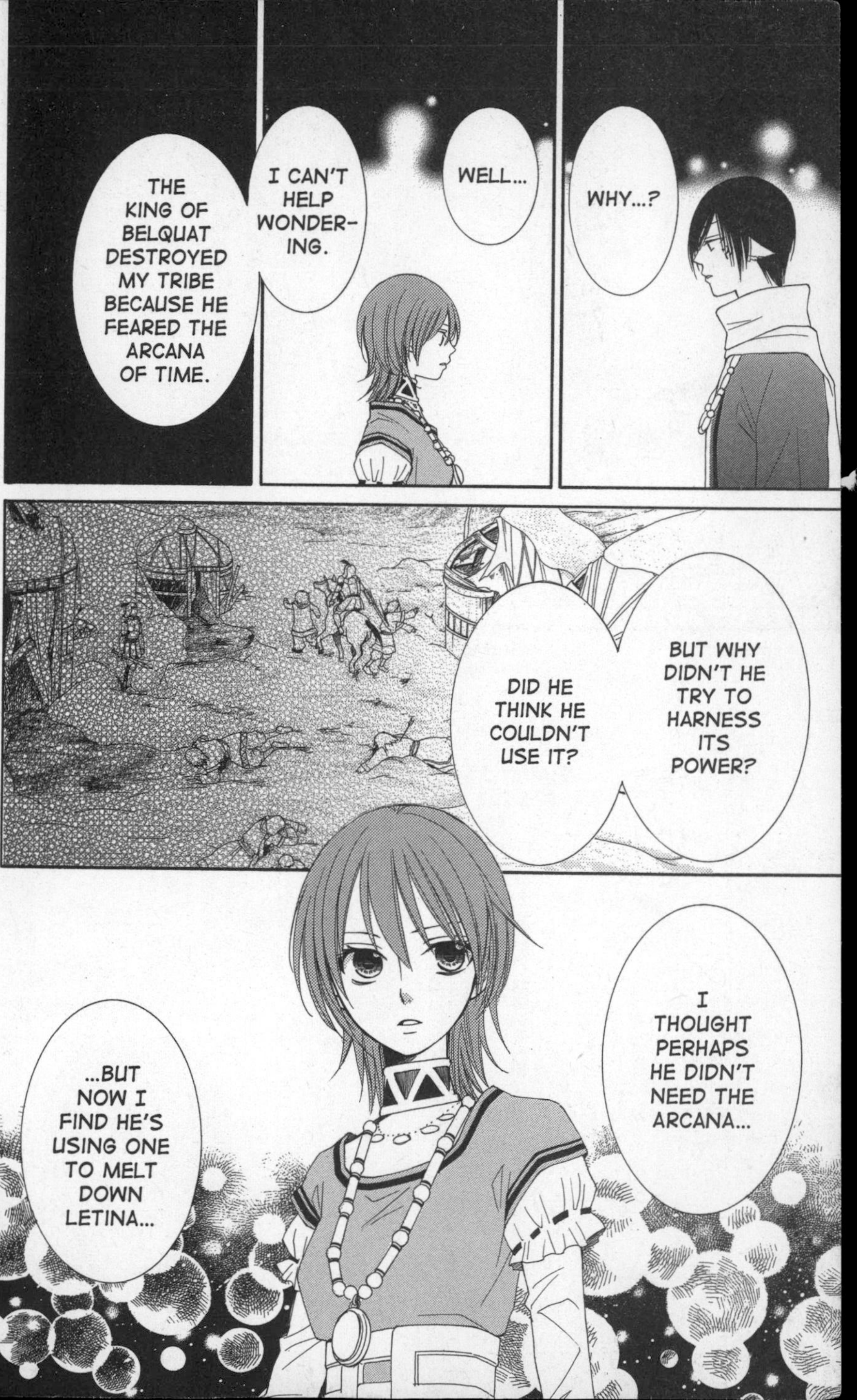
WHY...?
WELL...
I CAN'T HELP WONDER-ING.
THE KING OF BELQUAT DESTROYED MY TRIBE BECAUSE HE FEARED THE ARCANA OF TIME.
BUT WHY DIDN'T HE TRY TO HARNESS ITS POWER?
DID HE THINK HE COULDN'T USE IT?
I THOUGHT PERHAPS HE DIDN'T NEED THE ARCANA...
...BUT NOW I FIND HE'S USING ONE TO MELT DOWN LETINA...

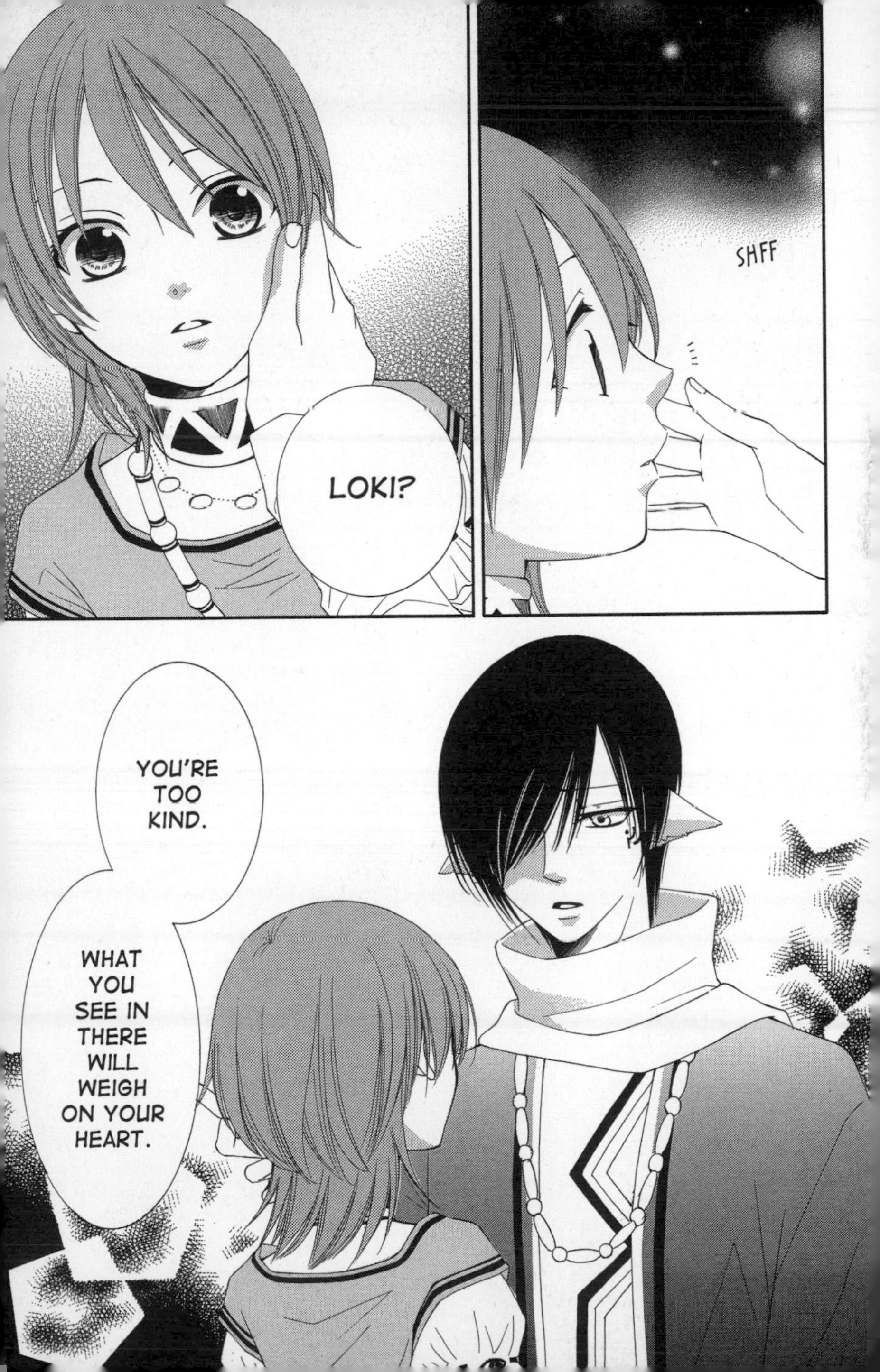
SHFF
LOKI?
YOU'RE TOO KIND.
WHAT YOU SEE IN THERE WILL WEIGH ON YOUR HEART.

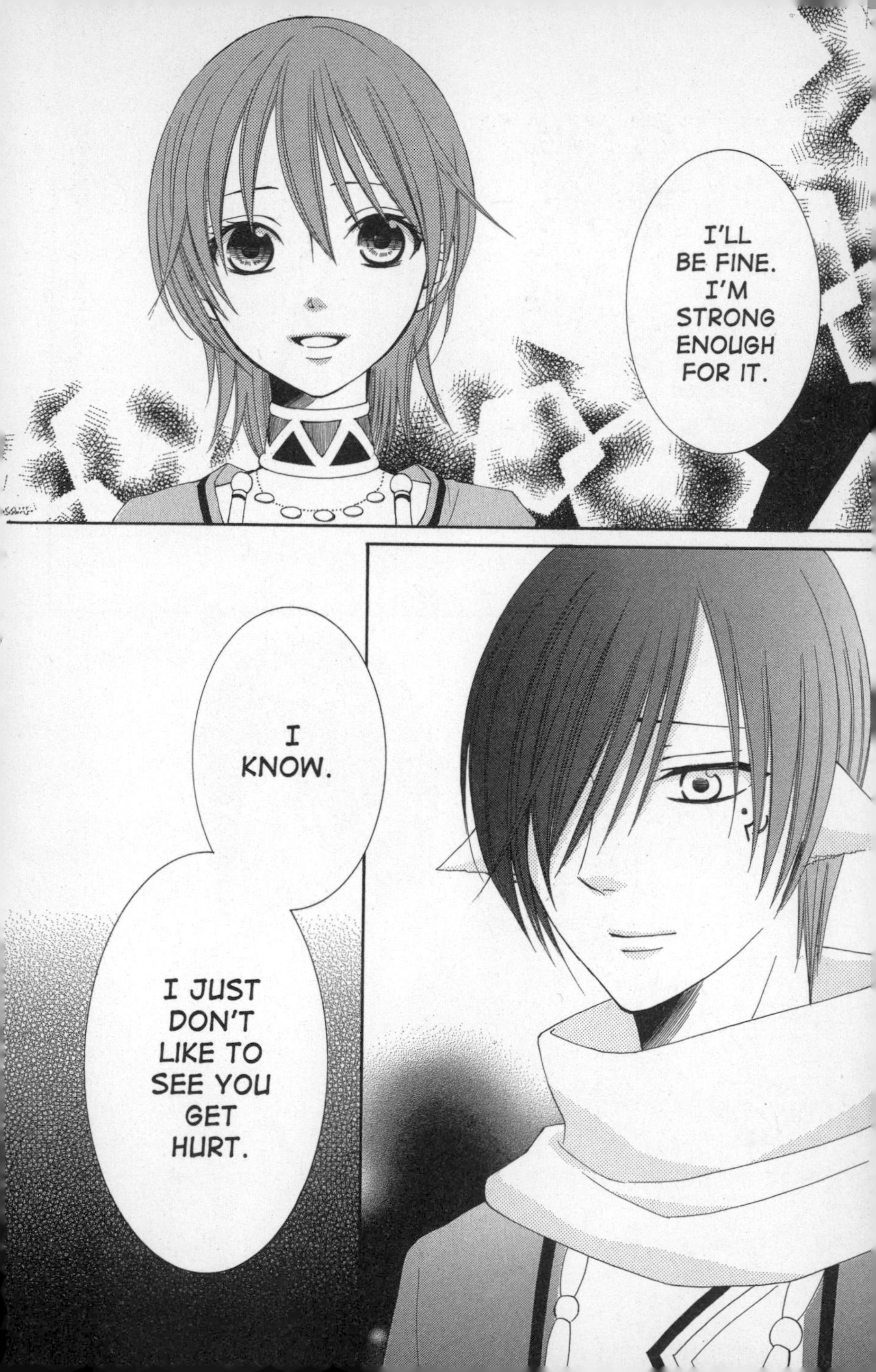
I'LL BE FINE. I'M STRONG ENOUGH FOR IT.
I KNOW.
I JUST DON'T LIKE TO SEE YOU GET HURT.

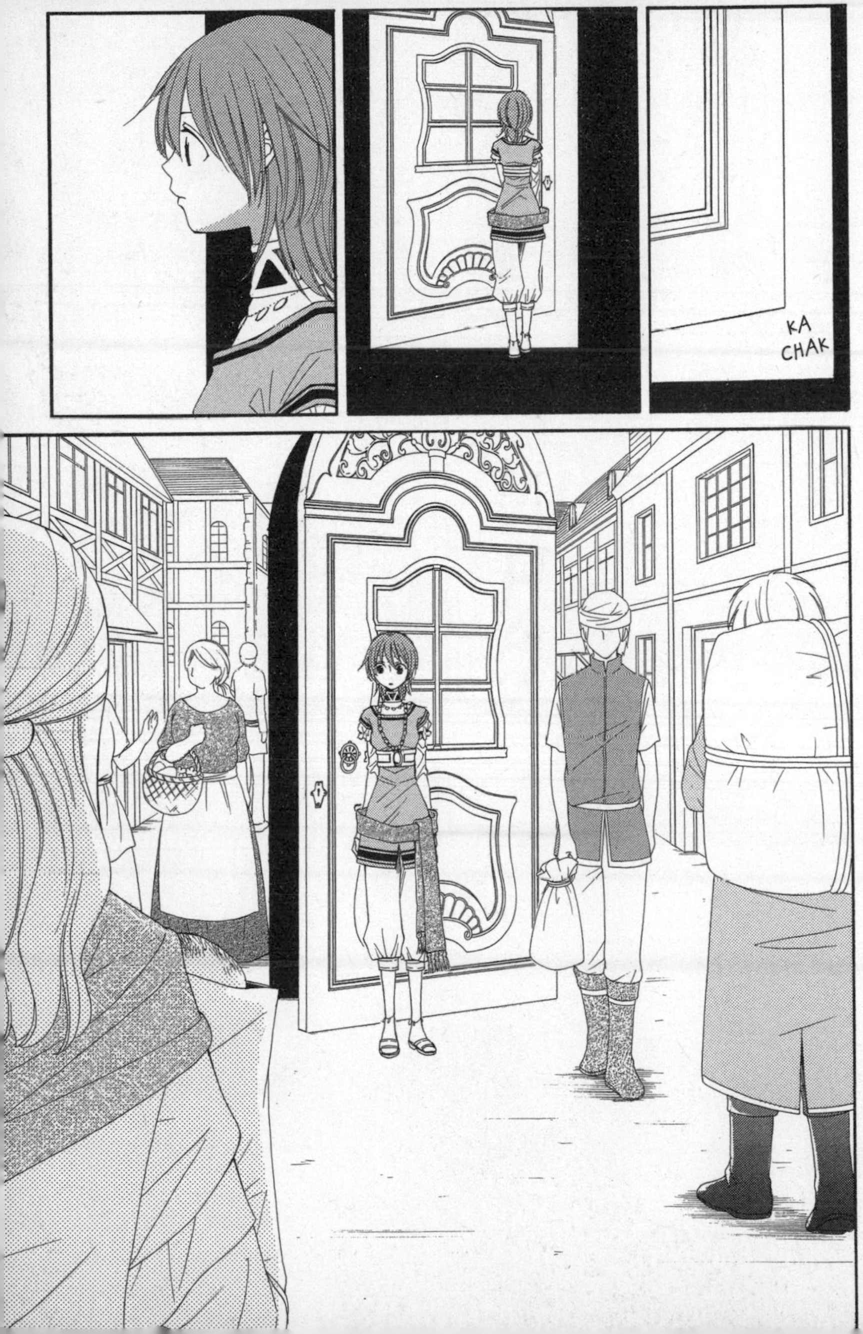
KA
CHAK

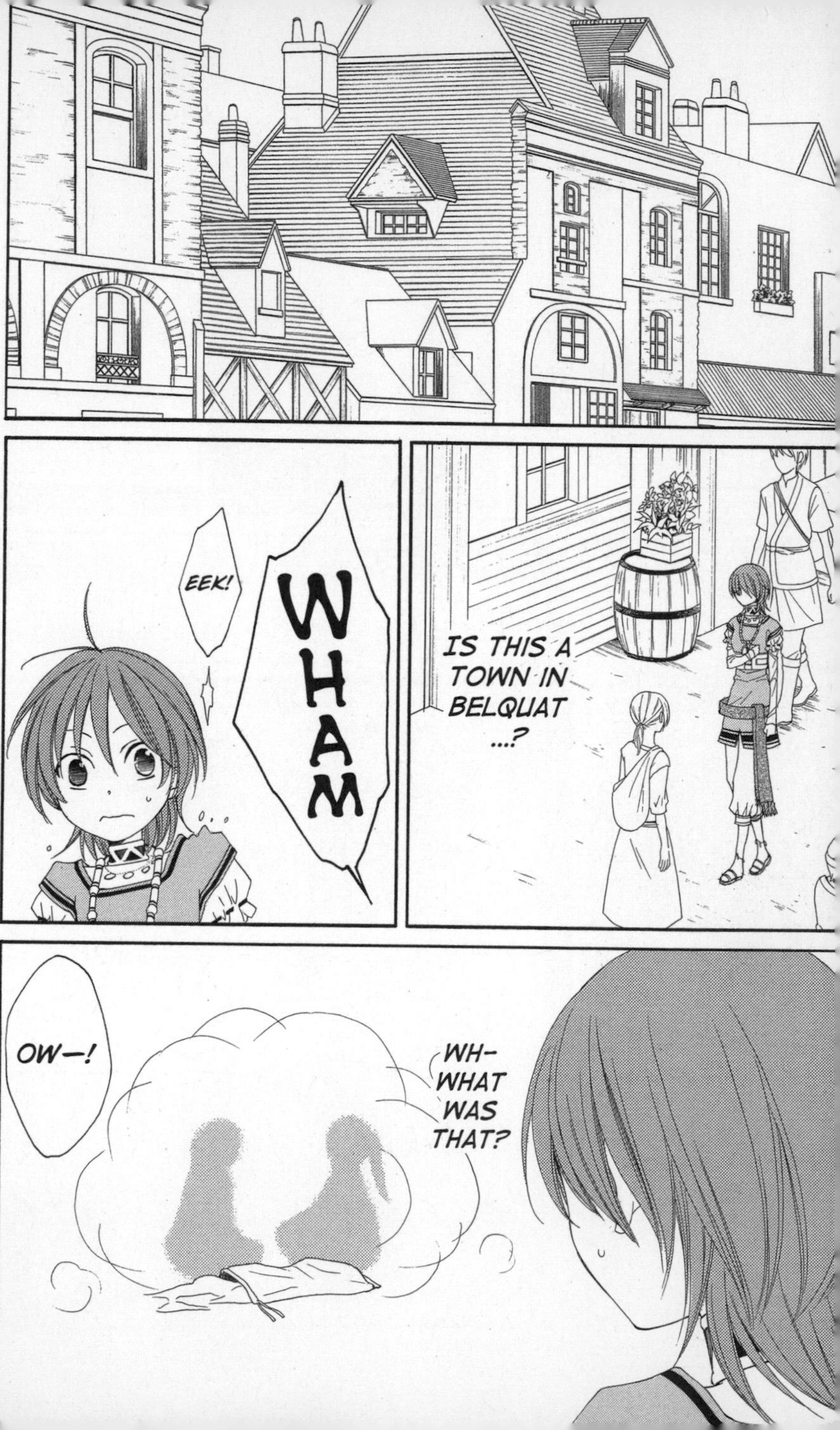
IS THIS A TOWN IN BELQUAT ...?
WHAM
EEK!
WH- WHAT WAS THAT?
OW—!

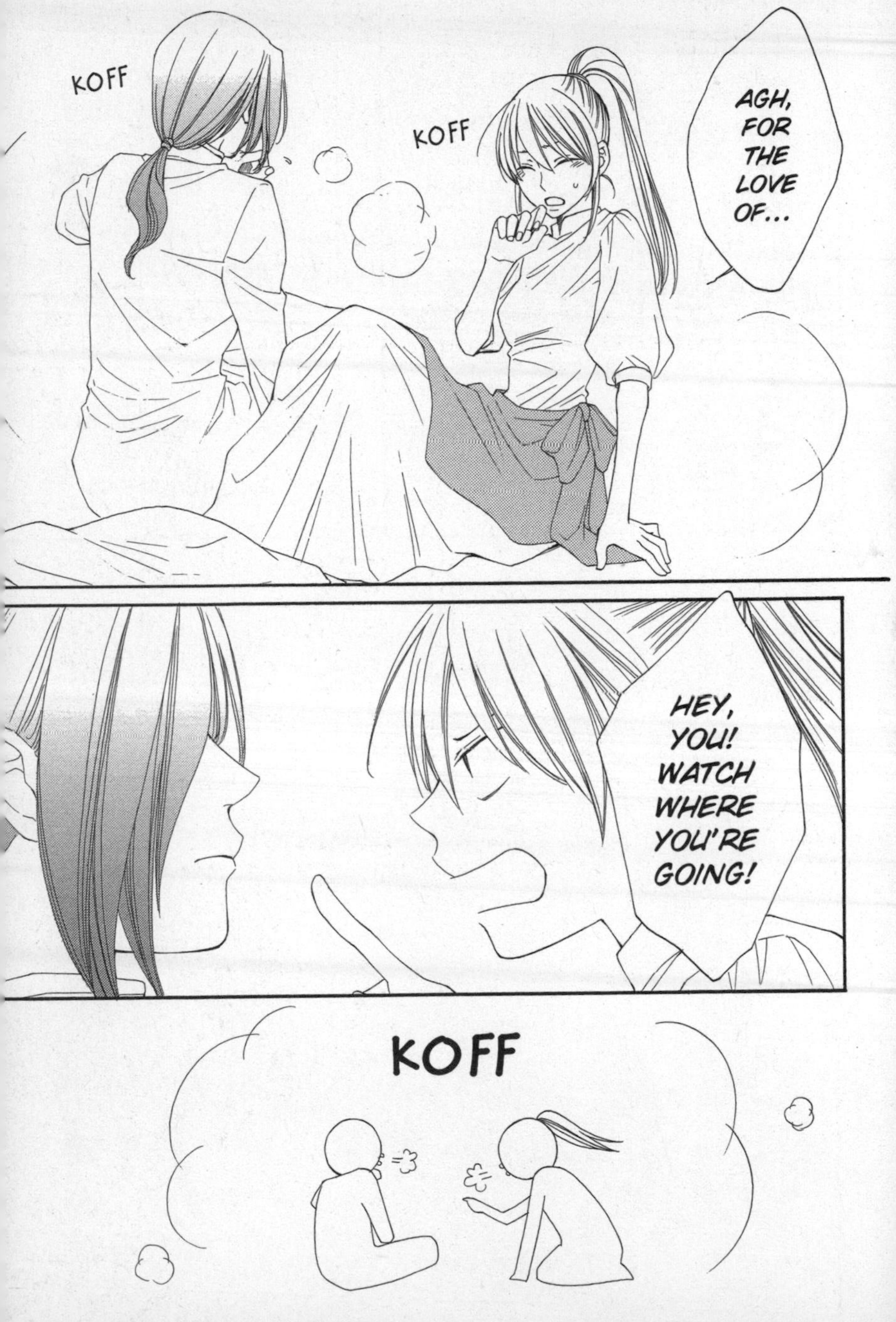
AGH, FOR THE LOVE OF...
KOFF
KOFF
HEY, YOU! WATCH WHERE YOU'RE GOING!
KOFF

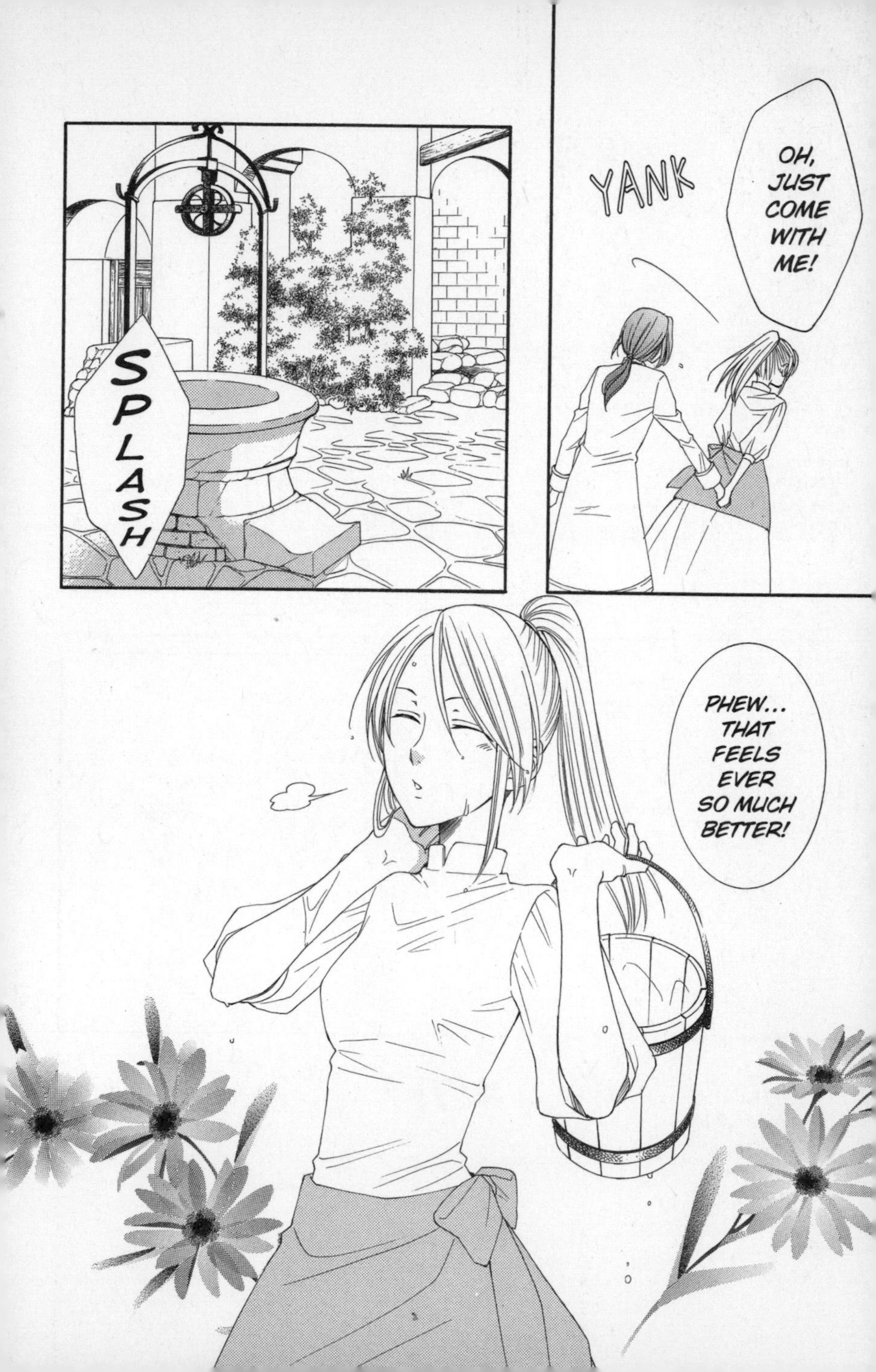
YANK
OH, JUST COME WITH ME!
SPLASH
PHEW... THAT FEELS EVER SO MUCH BETTER!

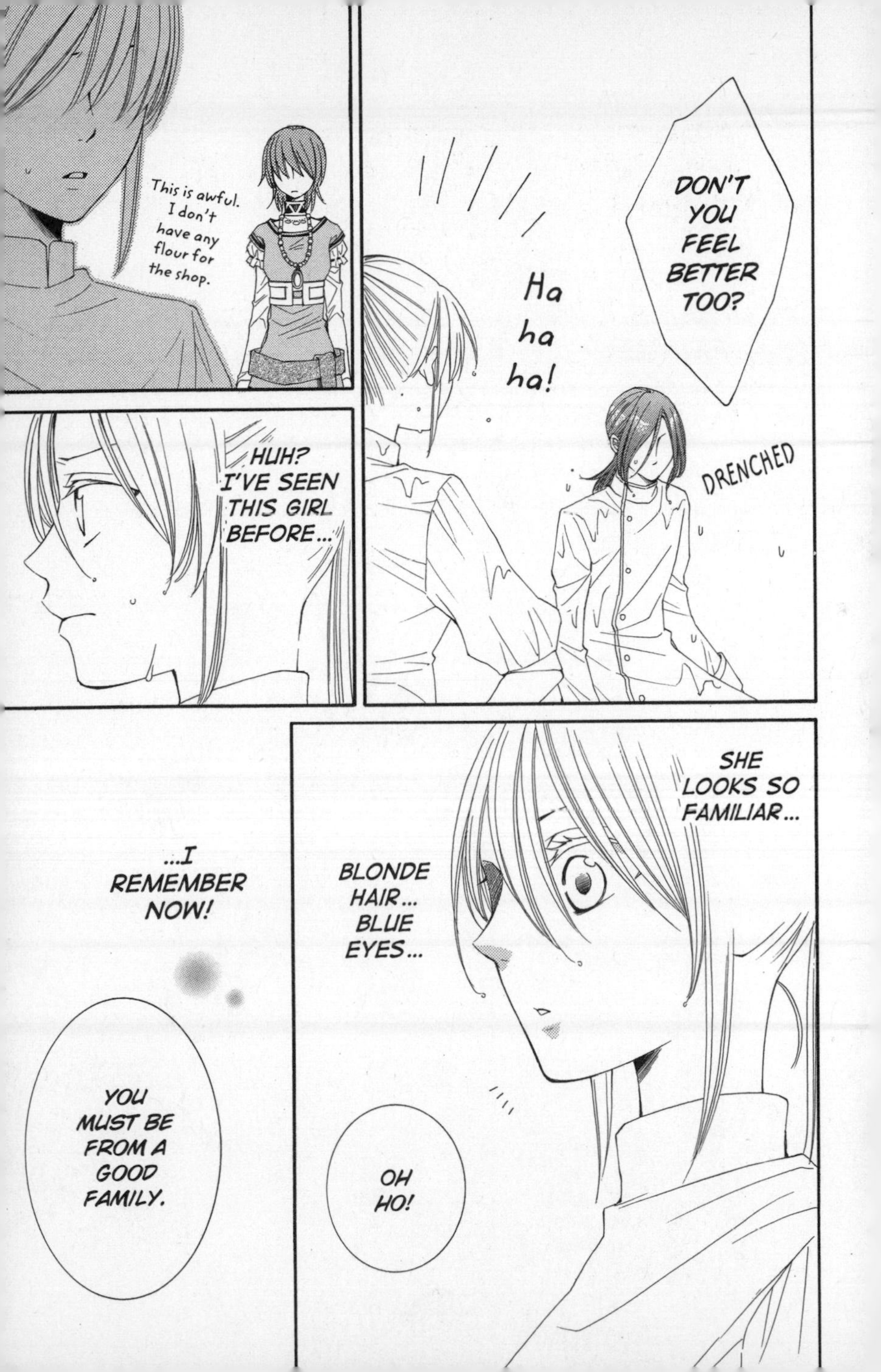
DON'T YOU FEEL BETTER TOO?
Ha ha ha!
DRENCHED
This is awful. I don't have any flour for the shop.
HUH? I'VE SEEN THIS GIRL BEFORE...
SHE LOOKS SO FAMILIAR...
BLONDE HAIR... BLUE EYES...
OH HO!
...I REMEMBER NOW!
YOU MUST BE FROM A GOOD FAMILY.

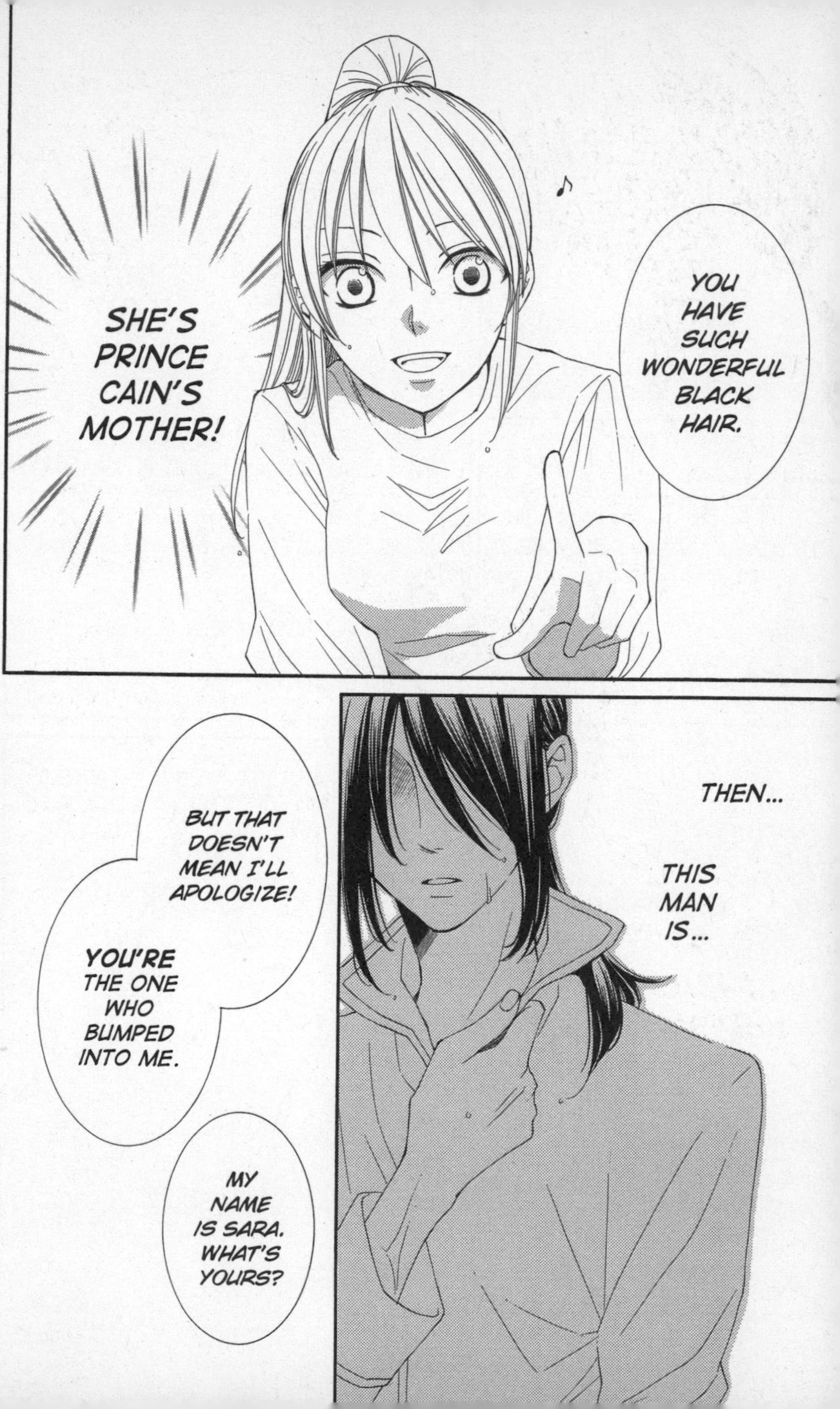
YOU HAVE SUCH WONDERFUL BLACK HAIR.
SHE'S PRINCE CAIN'S MOTHER!
THEN...
THIS MAN IS...
BUT THAT DOESN'T MEAN I'LL APOLOGIZE!
YOU'RE THE ONE WHO BUMPED INTO ME.
MY NAME IS SARA. WHAT'S YOURS?

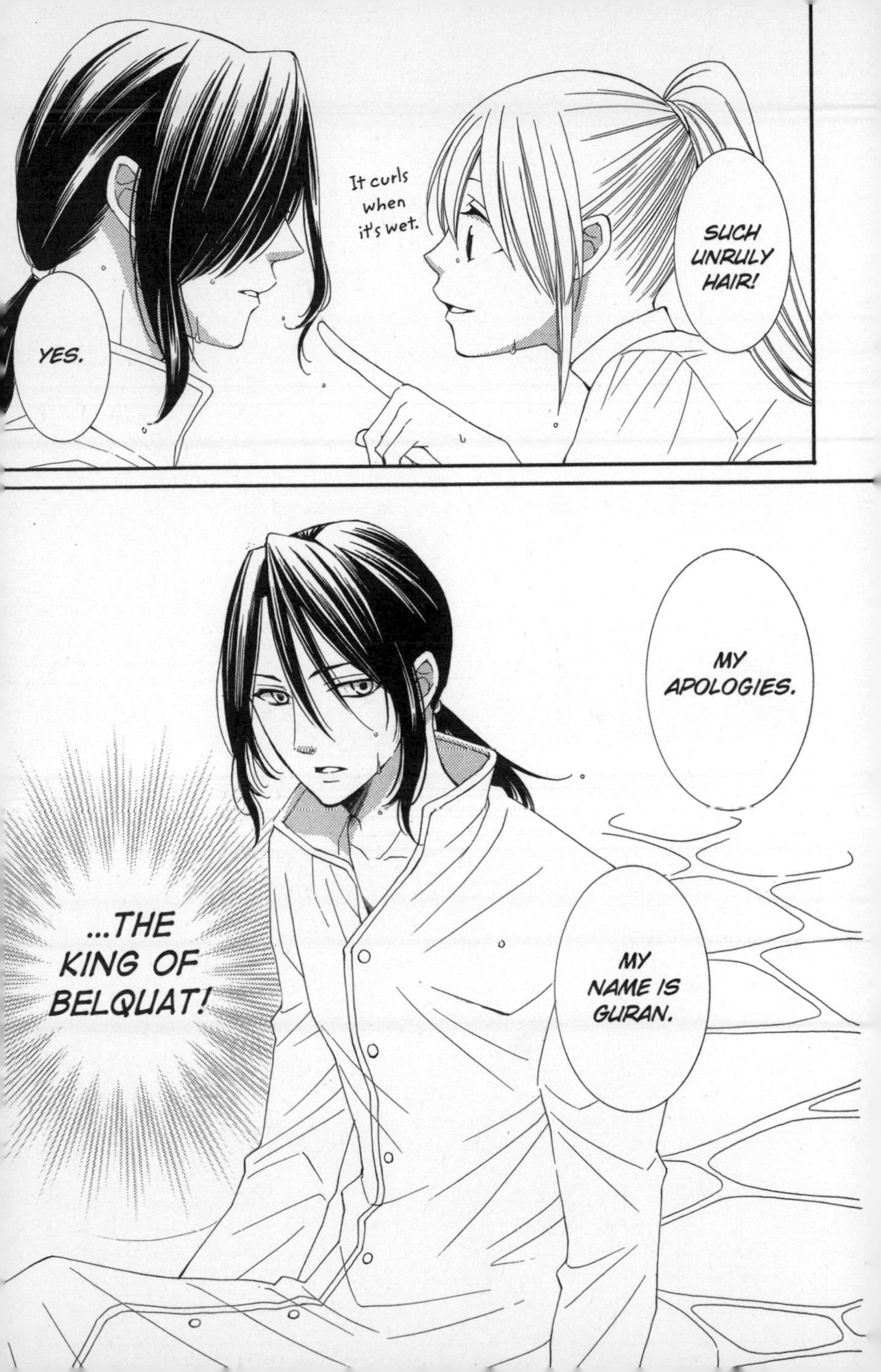
SUCH UNRULY HAIR!
It curls when it's wet.
YES.
MY APOLOGIES.
MY NAME IS GURAN.
...THE KING OF BELQUAT!

KOFF

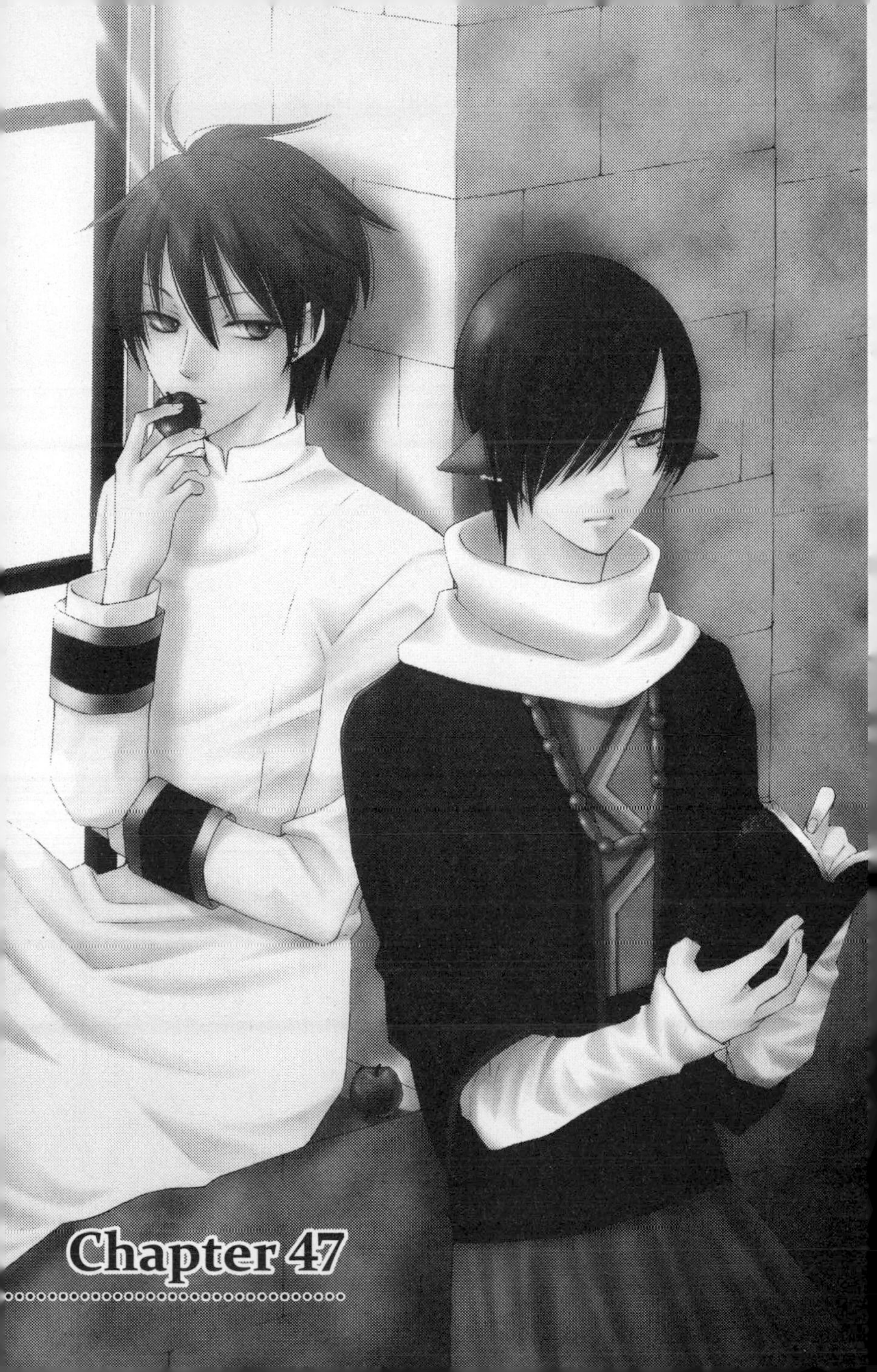
Chapter 47

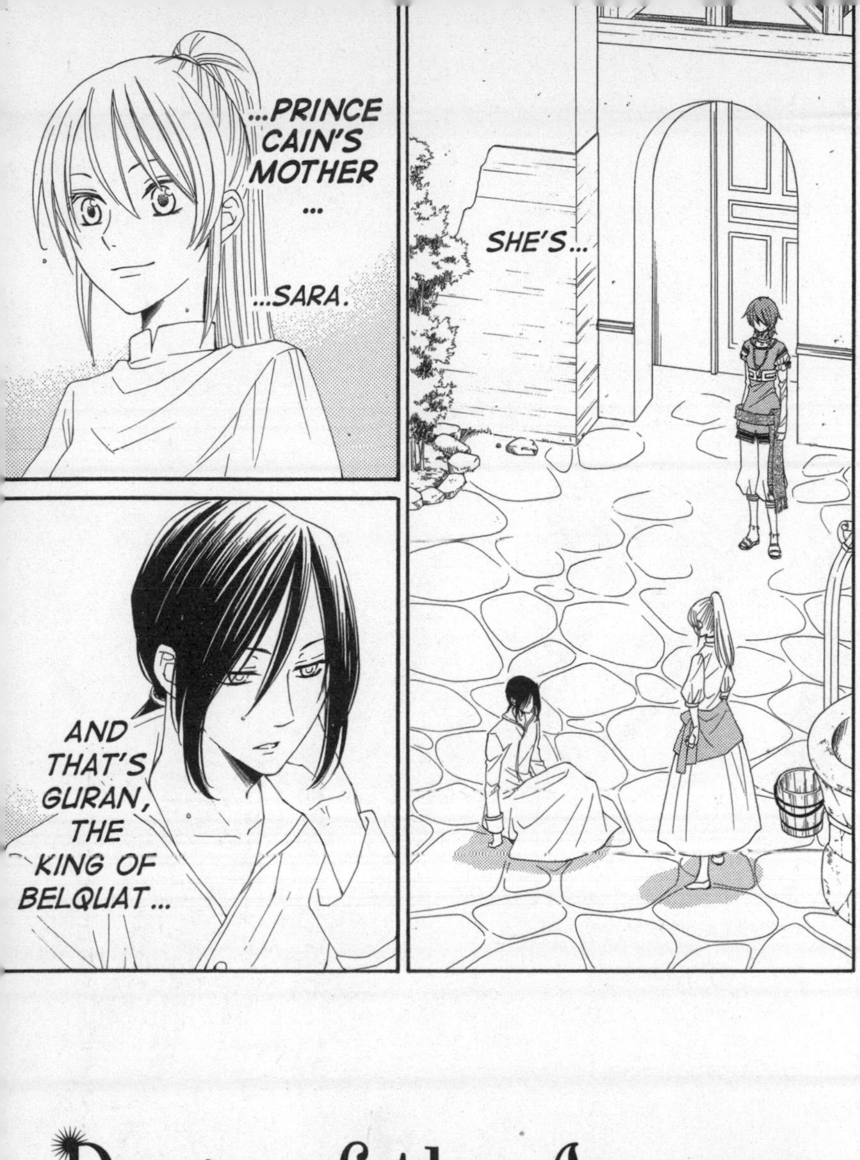
SHE'S...
...PRINCE CAIN'S MOTHER ...
...SARA.
AND THAT'S GURAN, THE KING OF BELQUAT...

Dawn of the Arcana

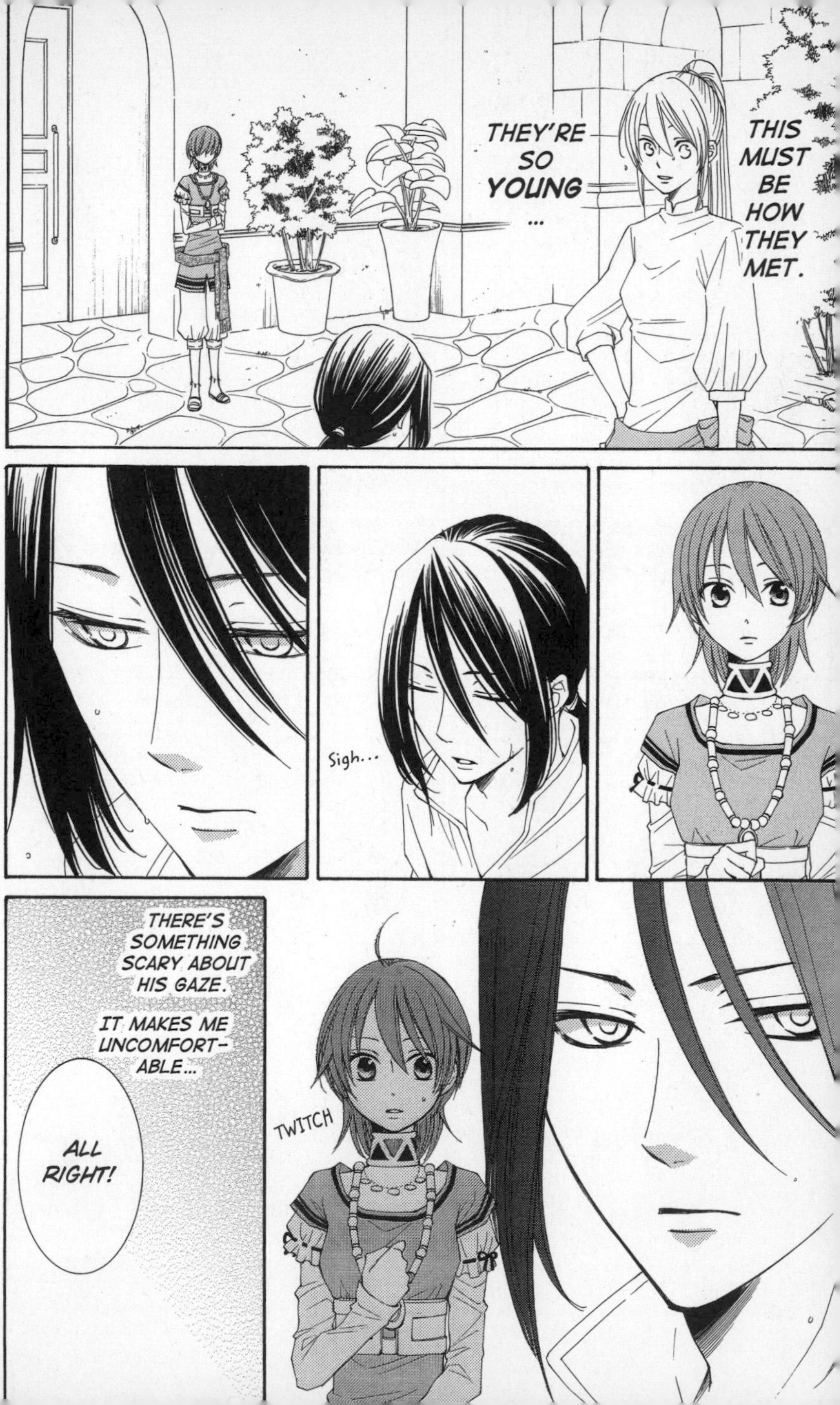
THIS MUST BE HOW THEY MET.
THEY'RE SO YOUNG...
Sigh...
THERE'S SOMETHING SCARY ABOUT HIS GAZE.
IT MAKES ME UNCOMFORTABLE...
TWITCH
ALL RIGHT!

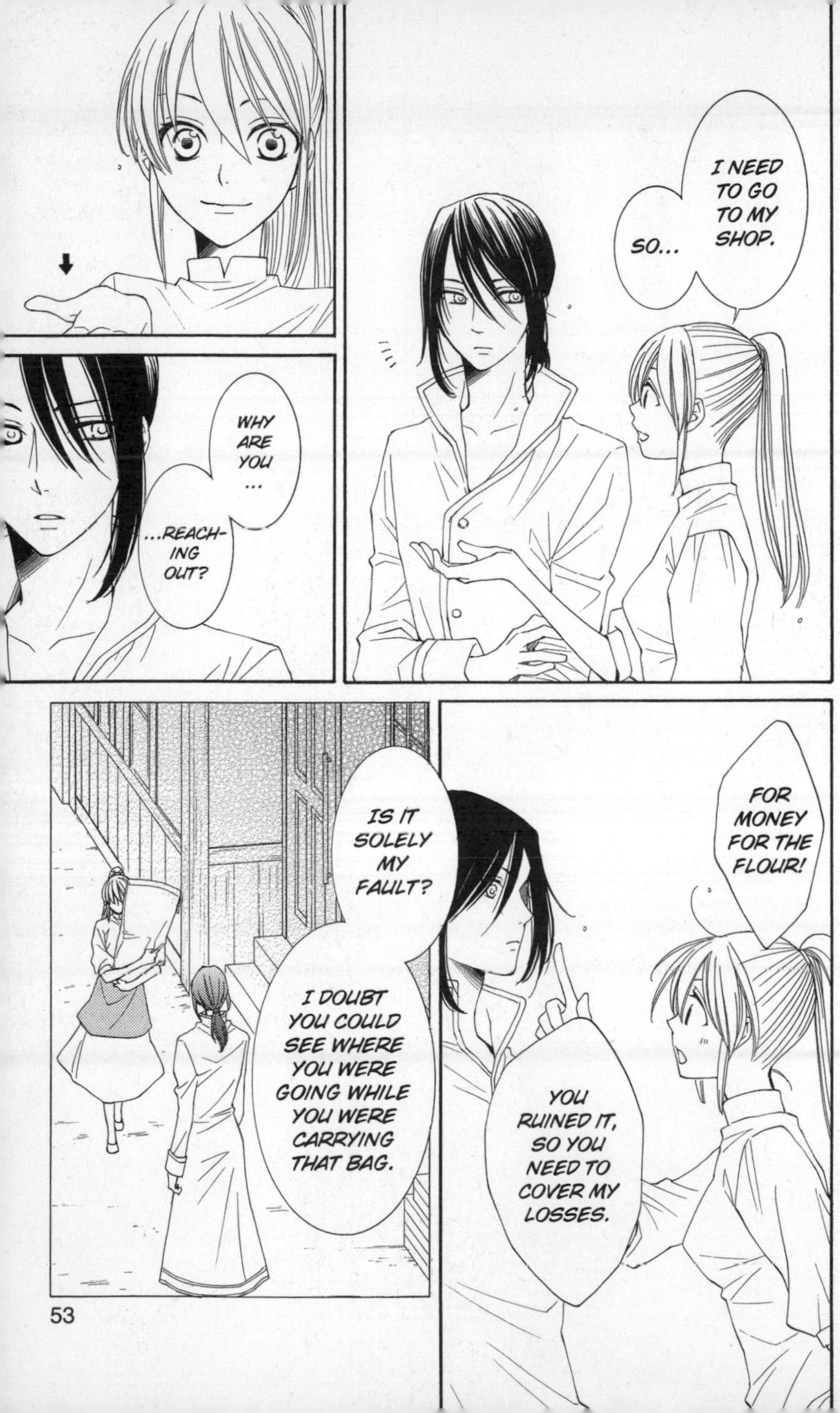
SO...
I NEED TO GO TO MY SHOP.
WHY ARE YOU...
...REACHING OUT?
FOR MONEY FOR THE FLOUR!
YOU RUINED IT, SO YOU NEED TO COVER MY LOSSES.
IS IT SOLELY MY FAULT?
I DOUBT YOU COULD SEE WHERE YOU WERE GOING WHILE YOU WERE CARRYING THAT BAG.

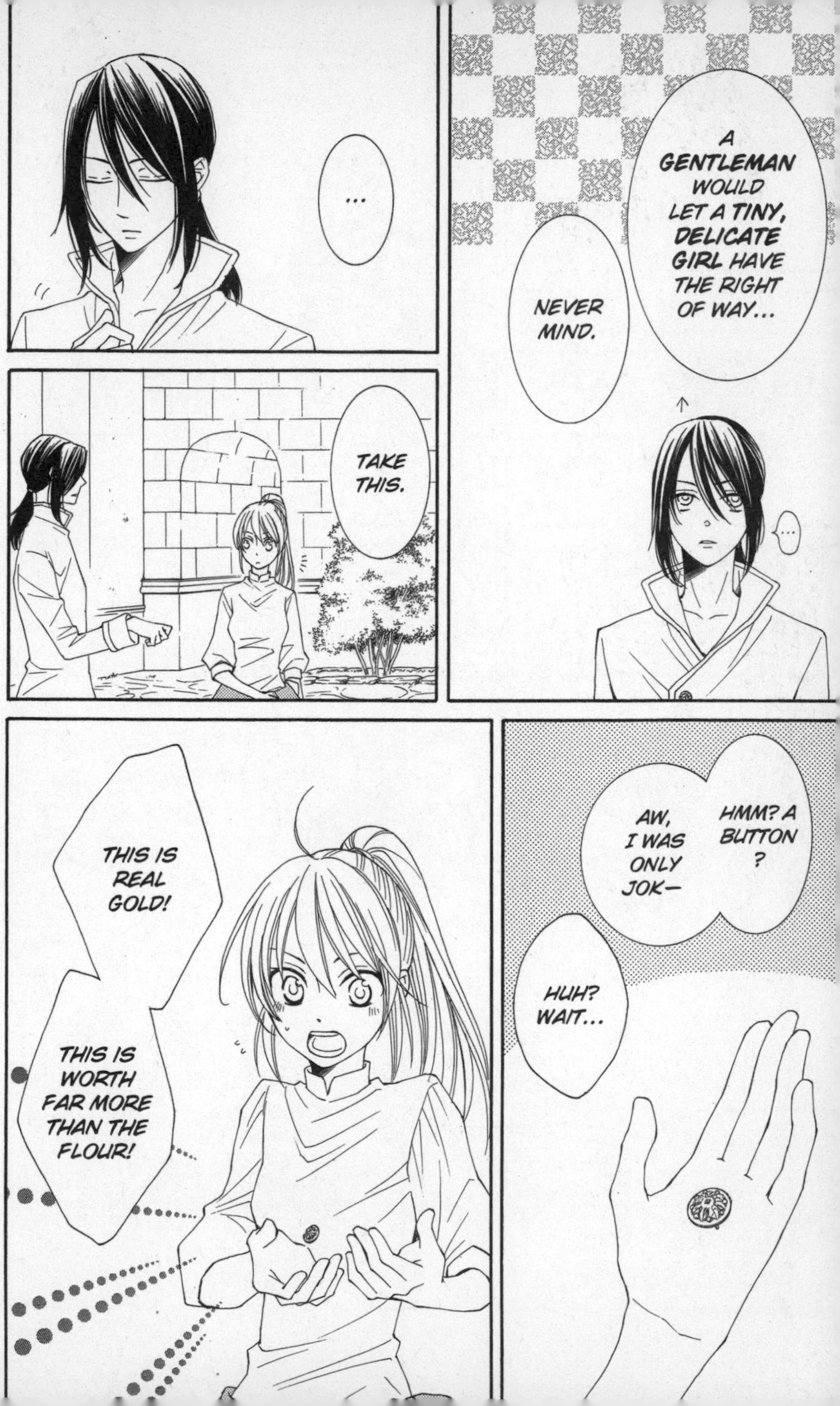
A GENTLEMAN WOULD LET A TINY, DELICATE GIRL HAVE THE RIGHT OF WAY...
NEVER MIND.
...
...
TAKE THIS.
HMM? A BUTTON?
AW, I WAS ONLY JOK—
HUH? WAIT...
THIS IS REAL GOLD!
THIS IS WORTH FAR MORE THAN THE FLOUR!

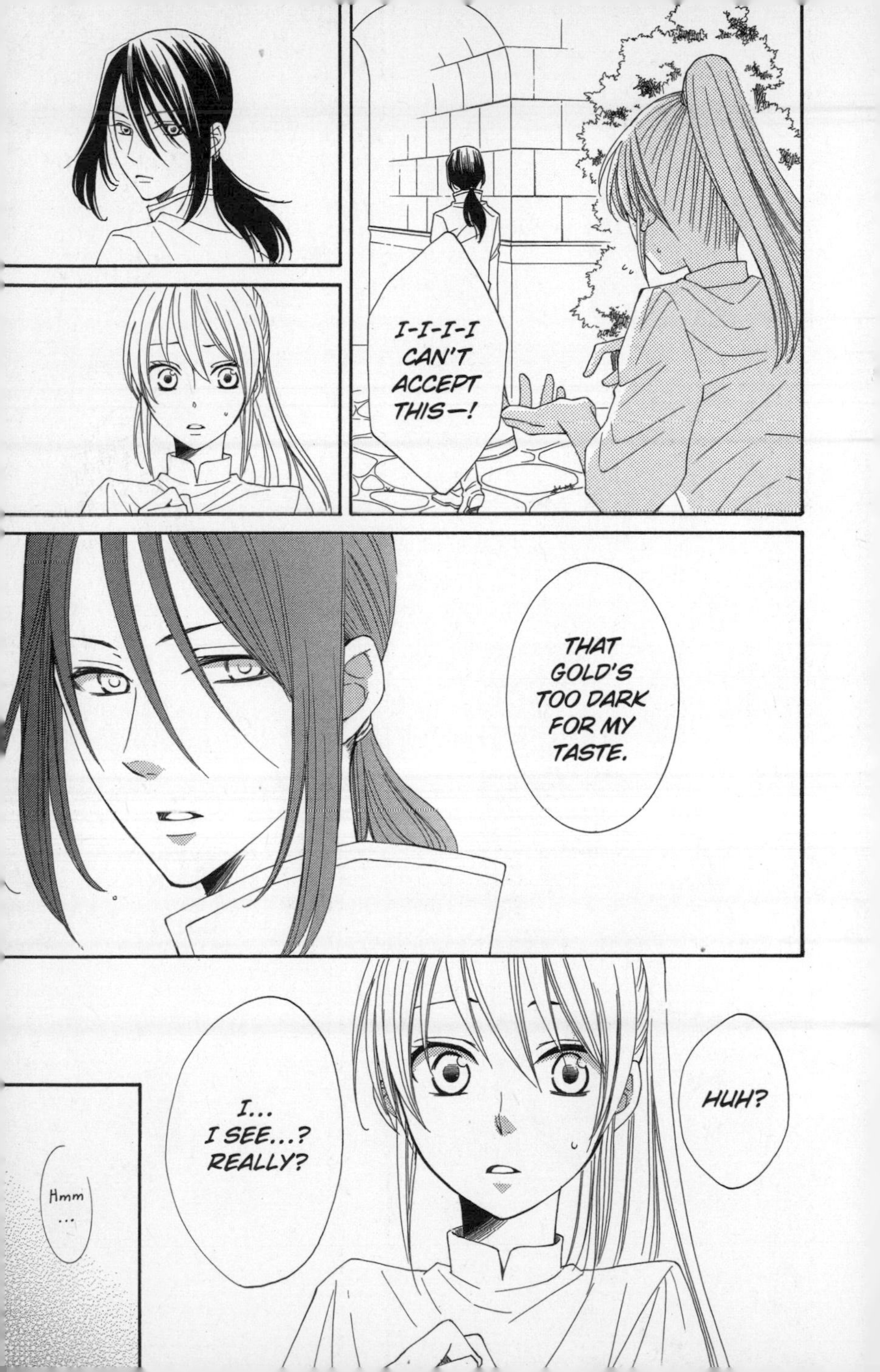
I-I-I-I CAN'T ACCEPT THIS—!
THAT GOLD'S TOO DARK FOR MY TASTE.
HUH?
I... I SEE...? REALLY?
Hmm...

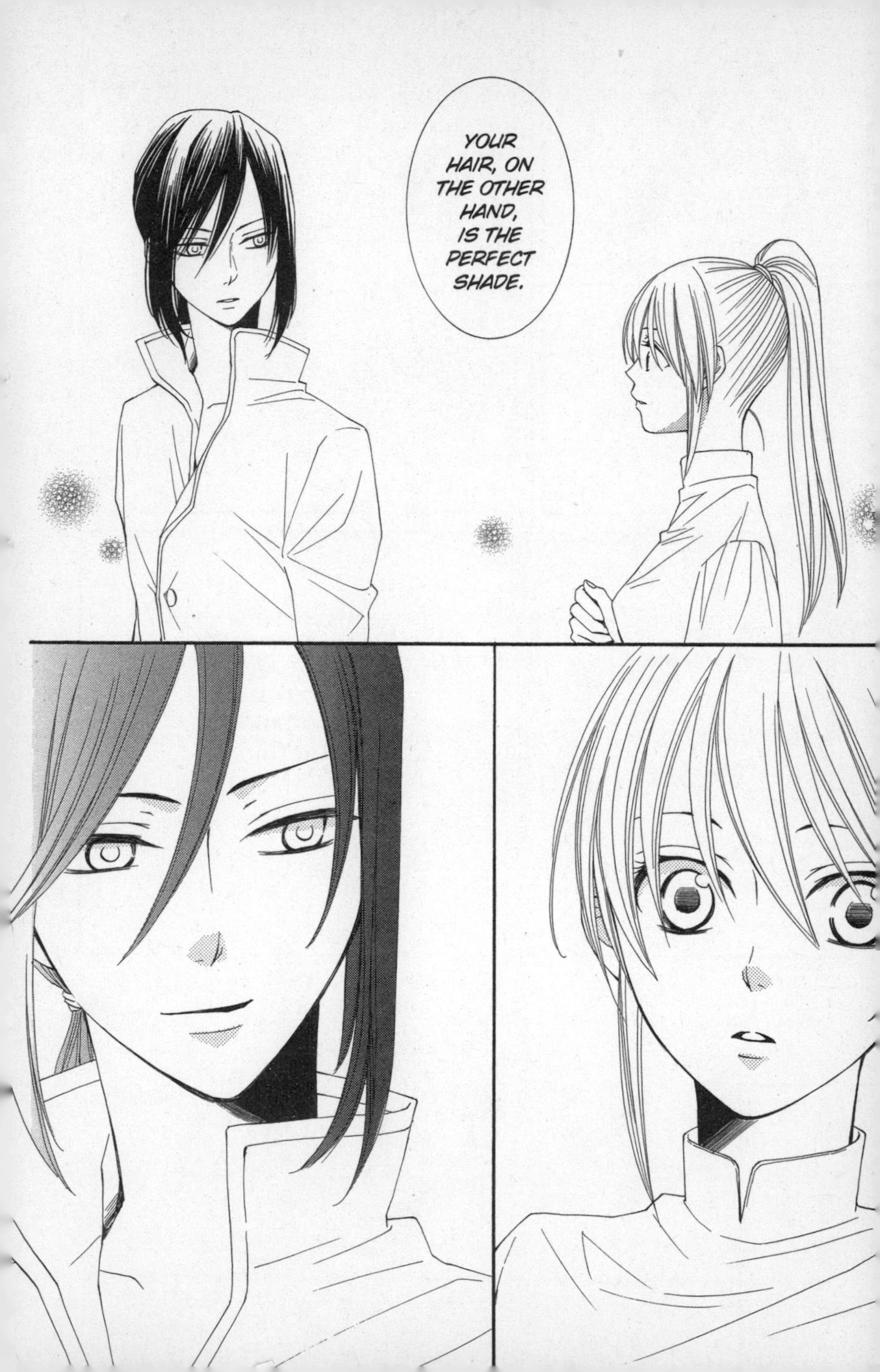
YOUR HAIR, ON THE OTHER HAND, IS THE PERFECT SHADE.

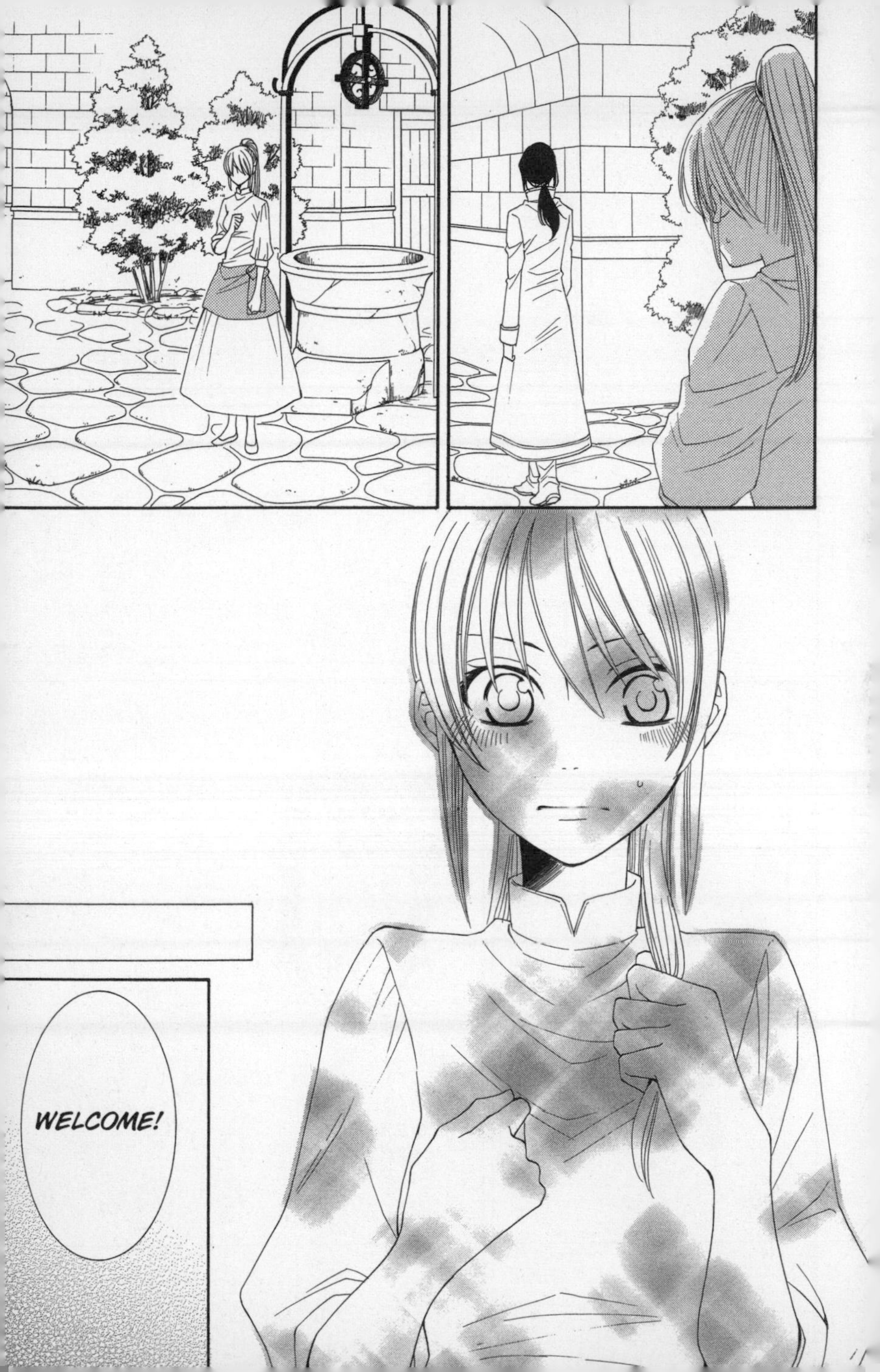
WELCOME!

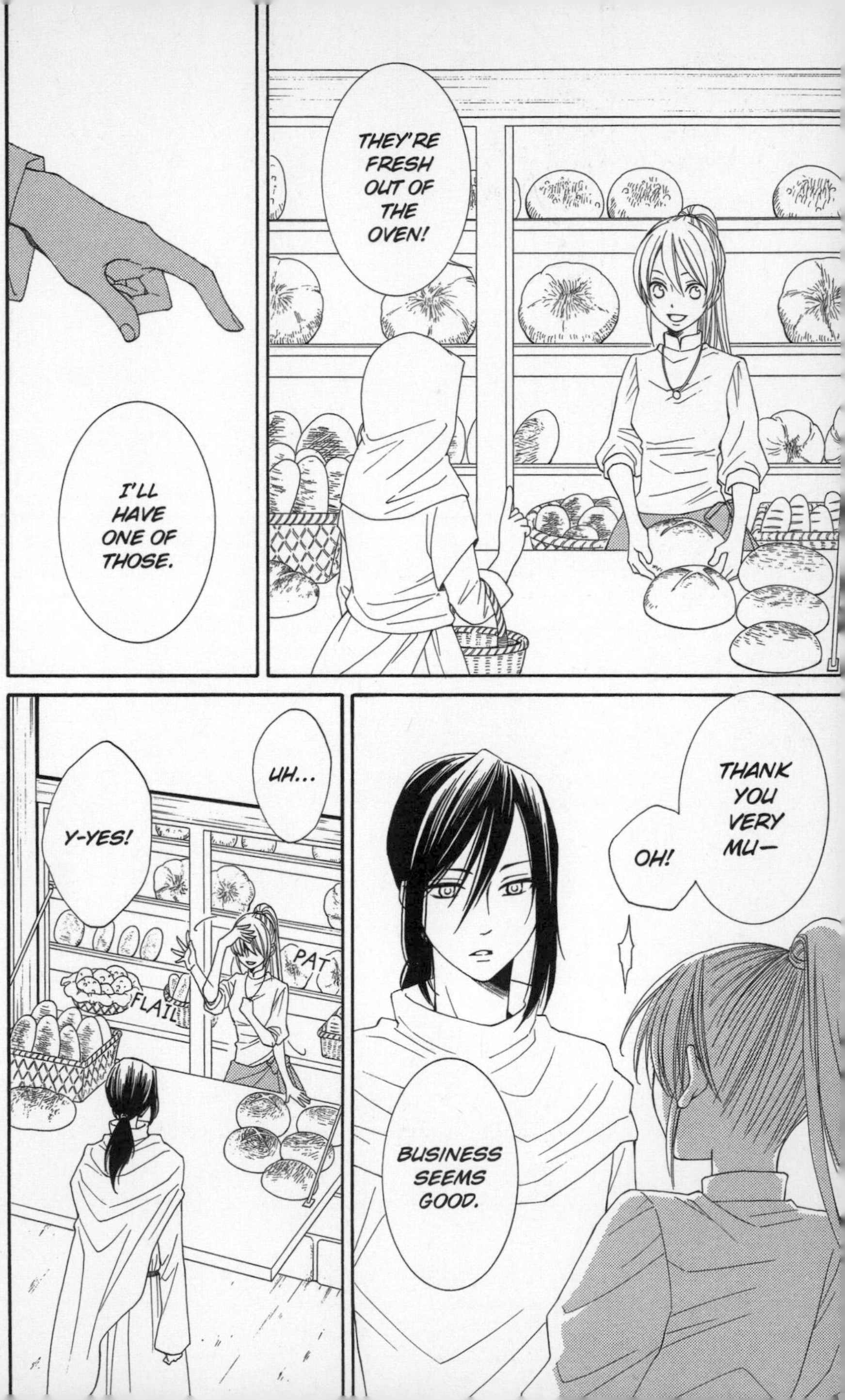
THEY'RE FRESH OUT OF THE OVEN!
I'LL HAVE ONE OF THOSE.
THANK YOU VERY MU—
OH!
BUSINESS SEEMS GOOD.
UH...
Y-YES!
PAT
FLAIL

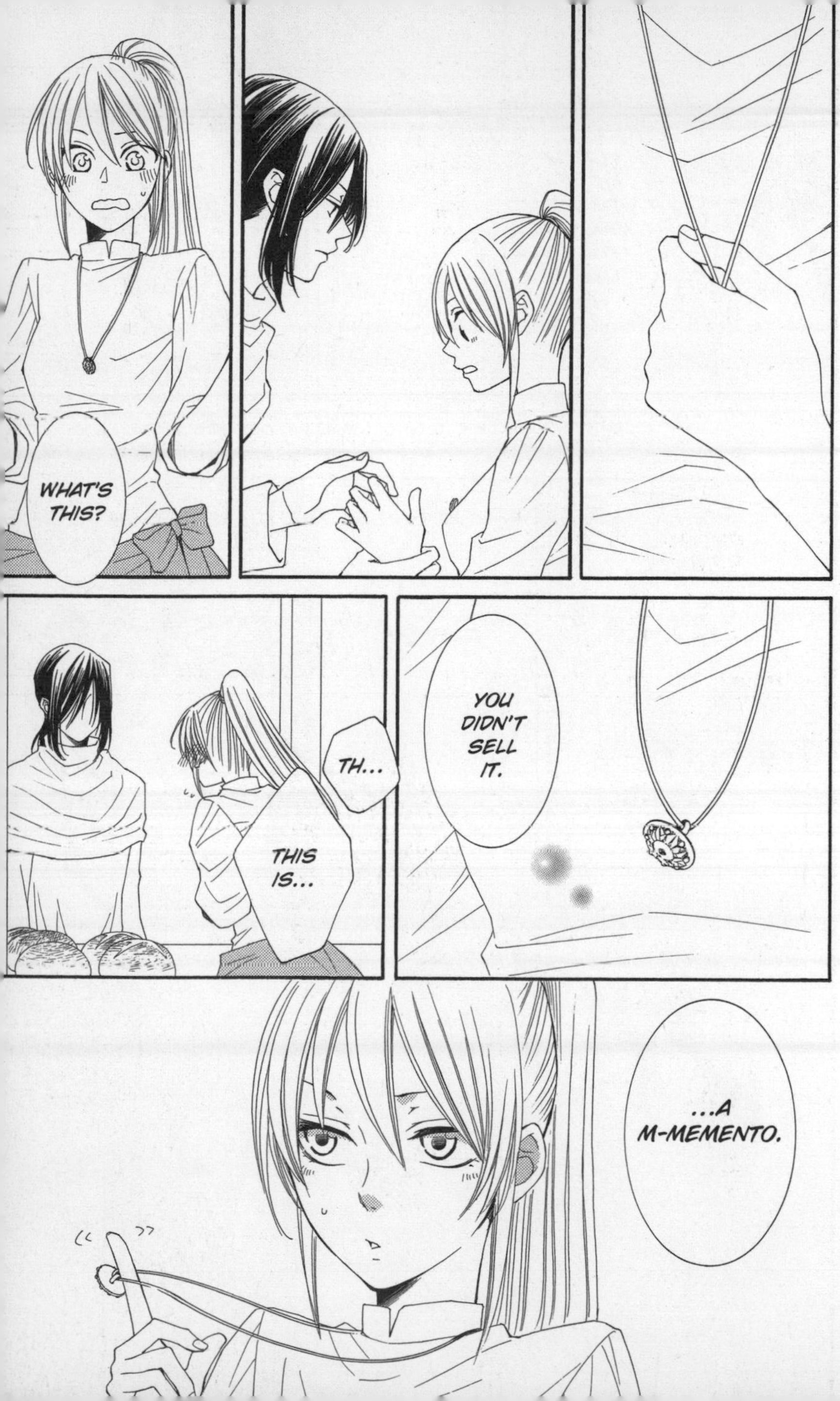
WHAT'S THIS?
YOU DIDN'T SELL IT.
TH...
THIS IS...
...A M-MEMENTO.

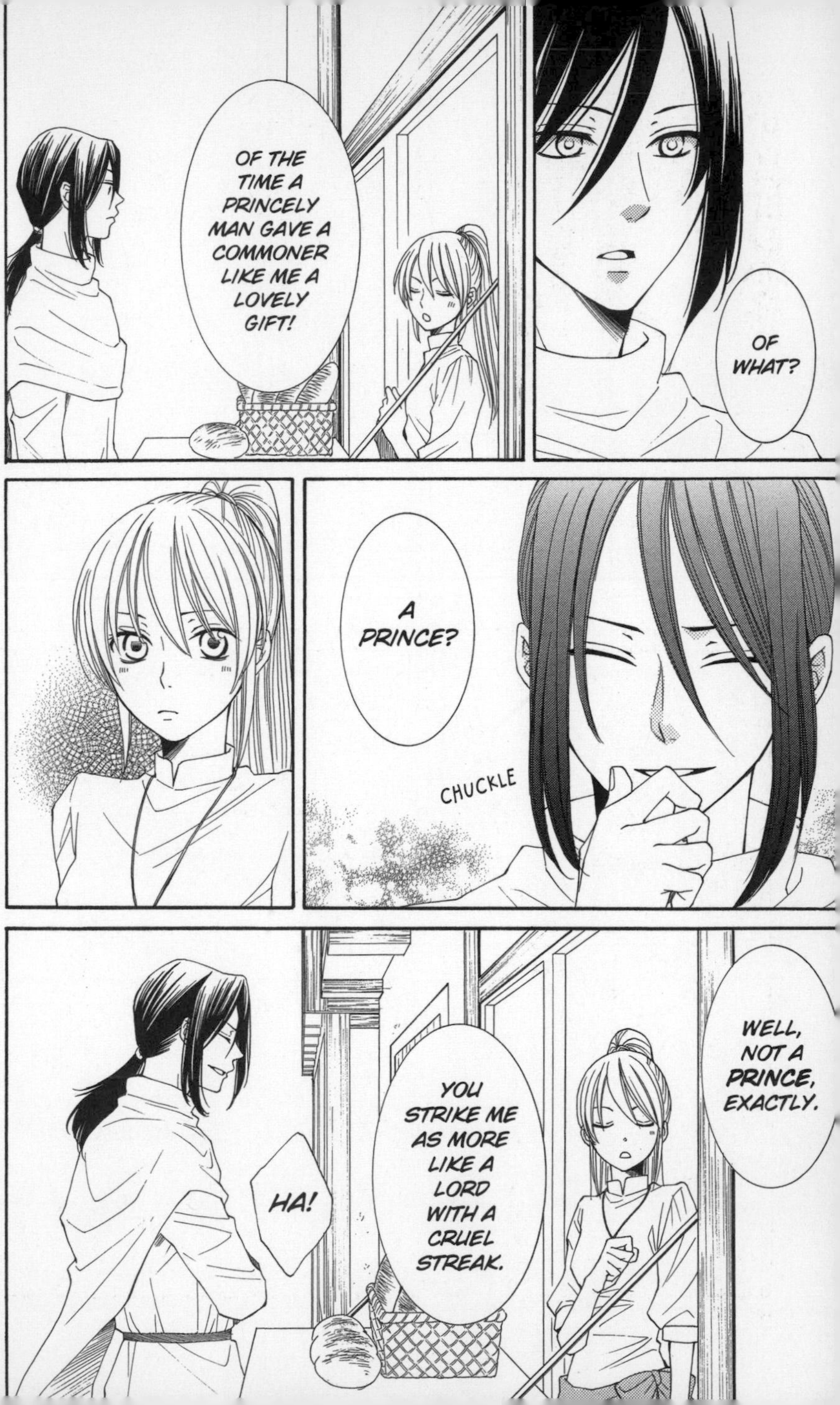
OF WHAT?
OF THE TIME A PRINCELY MAN GAVE A COMMONER LIKE ME A LOVELY GIFT!
A PRINCE?
CHUCKLE
WELL, NOT A PRINCE, EXACTLY.
YOU STRIKE ME AS MORE LIKE A LORD WITH A CRUEL STREAK.
HA!

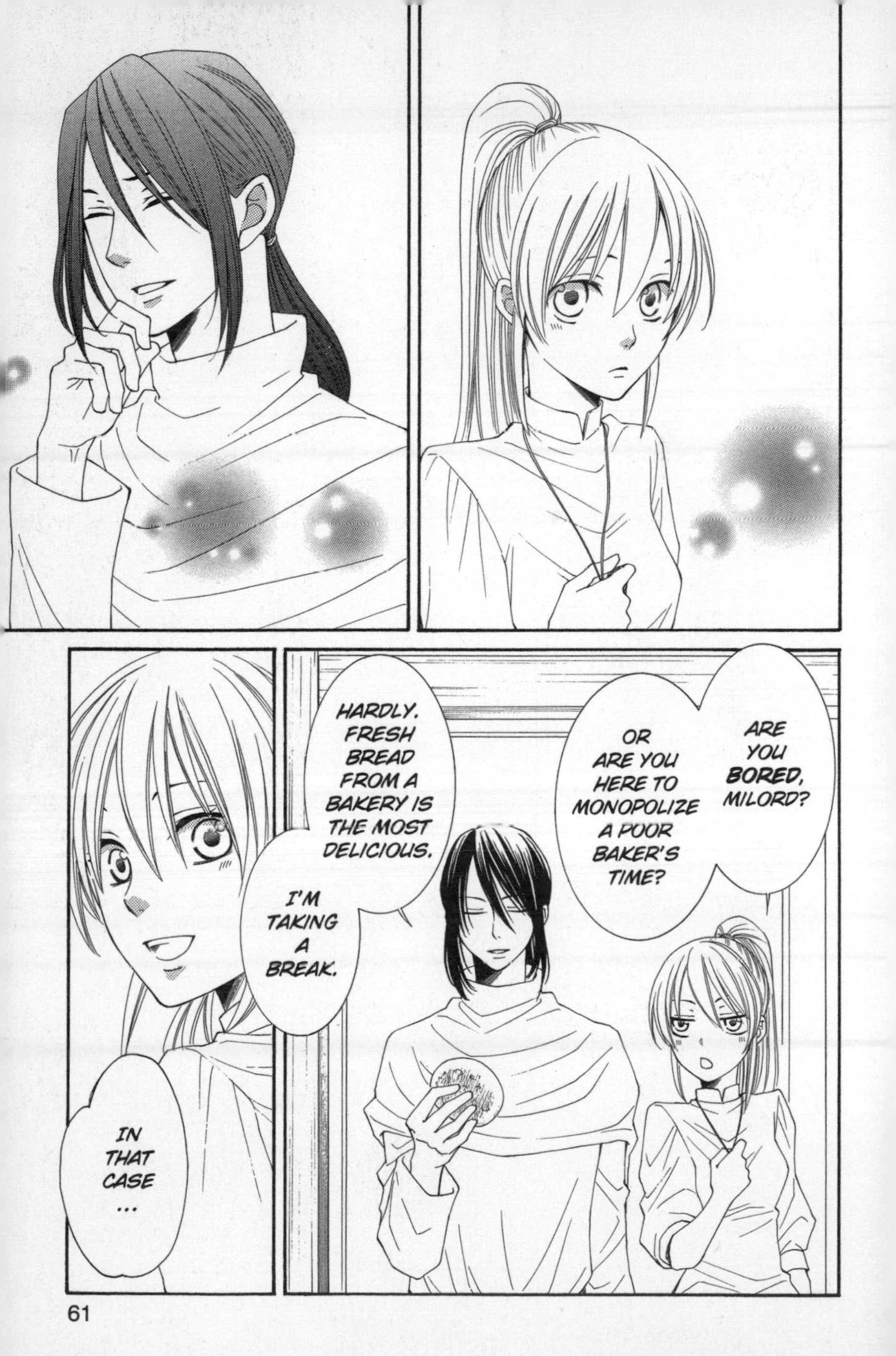
ARE YOU BORED, MILORD?
OR ARE YOU HERE TO MONOPOLIZE A POOR BAKER'S TIME?
HARDLY. FRESH BREAD FROM A BAKERY IS THE MOST DELICIOUS.
I'M TAKING A BREAK.
IN THAT CASE...

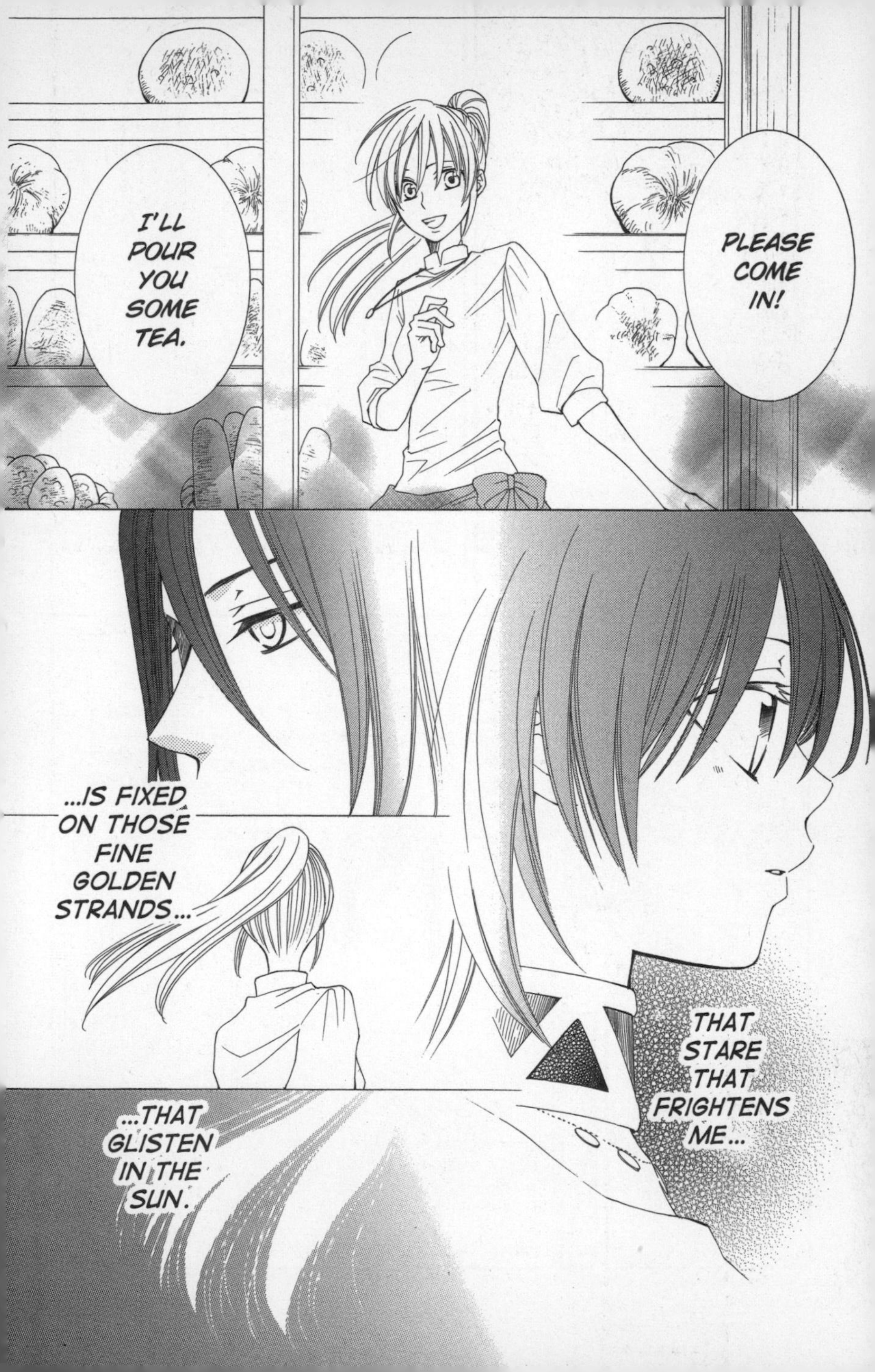
PLEASE COME IN!
I'LL POUR YOU SOME TEA.
THAT STARE THAT FRIGHTENS ME...
...IS FIXED ON THOSE FINE GOLDEN STRANDS...
...THAT GLISTEN IN THE SUN.

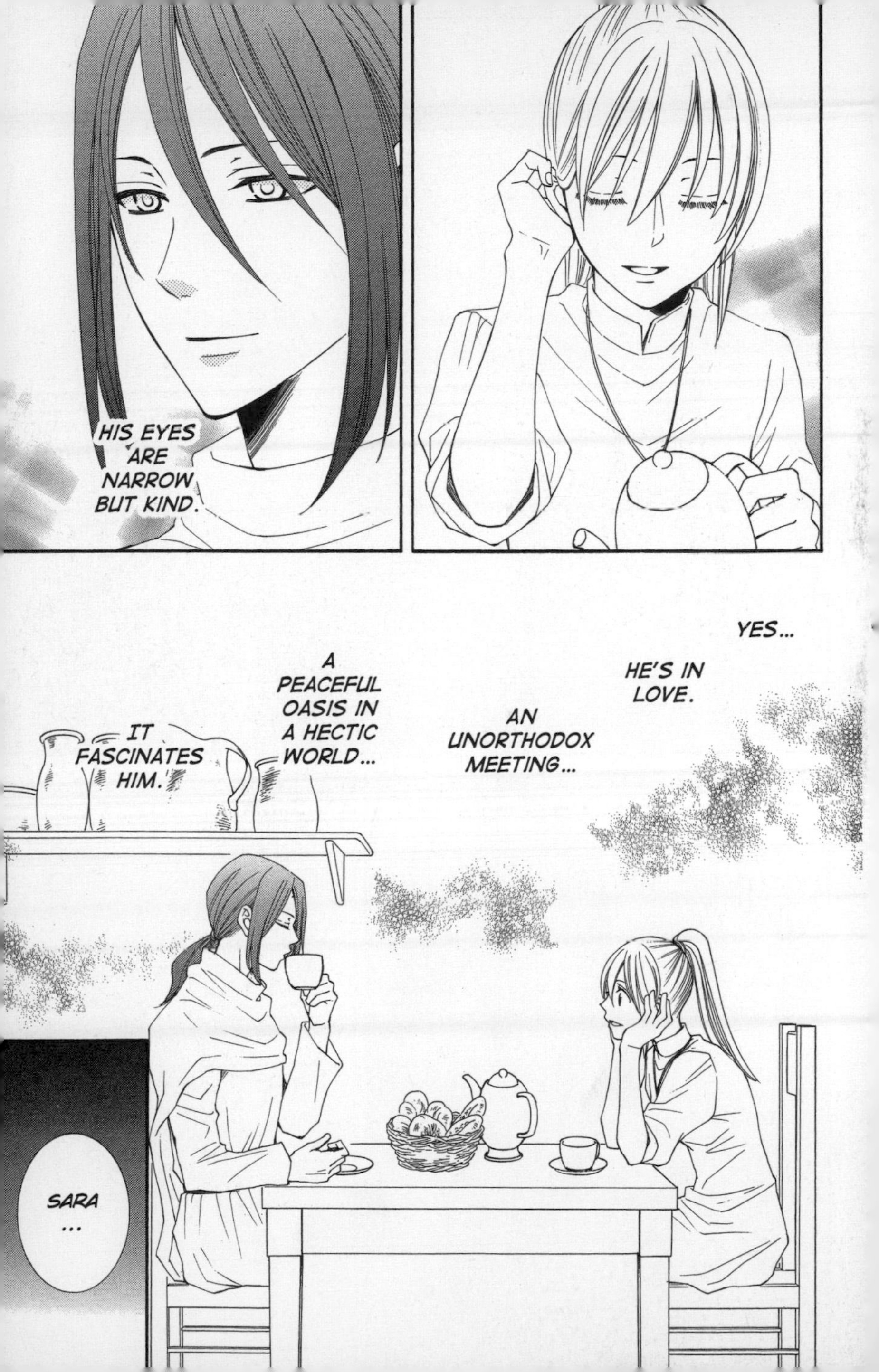
HIS EYES ARE NARROW BUT KIND.
YES...
HE'S IN LOVE.
AN UNORTHODOX MEETING...
A PEACEFUL OASIS IN A HECTIC WORLD...
IT FASCINATES HIM.
SARA ...

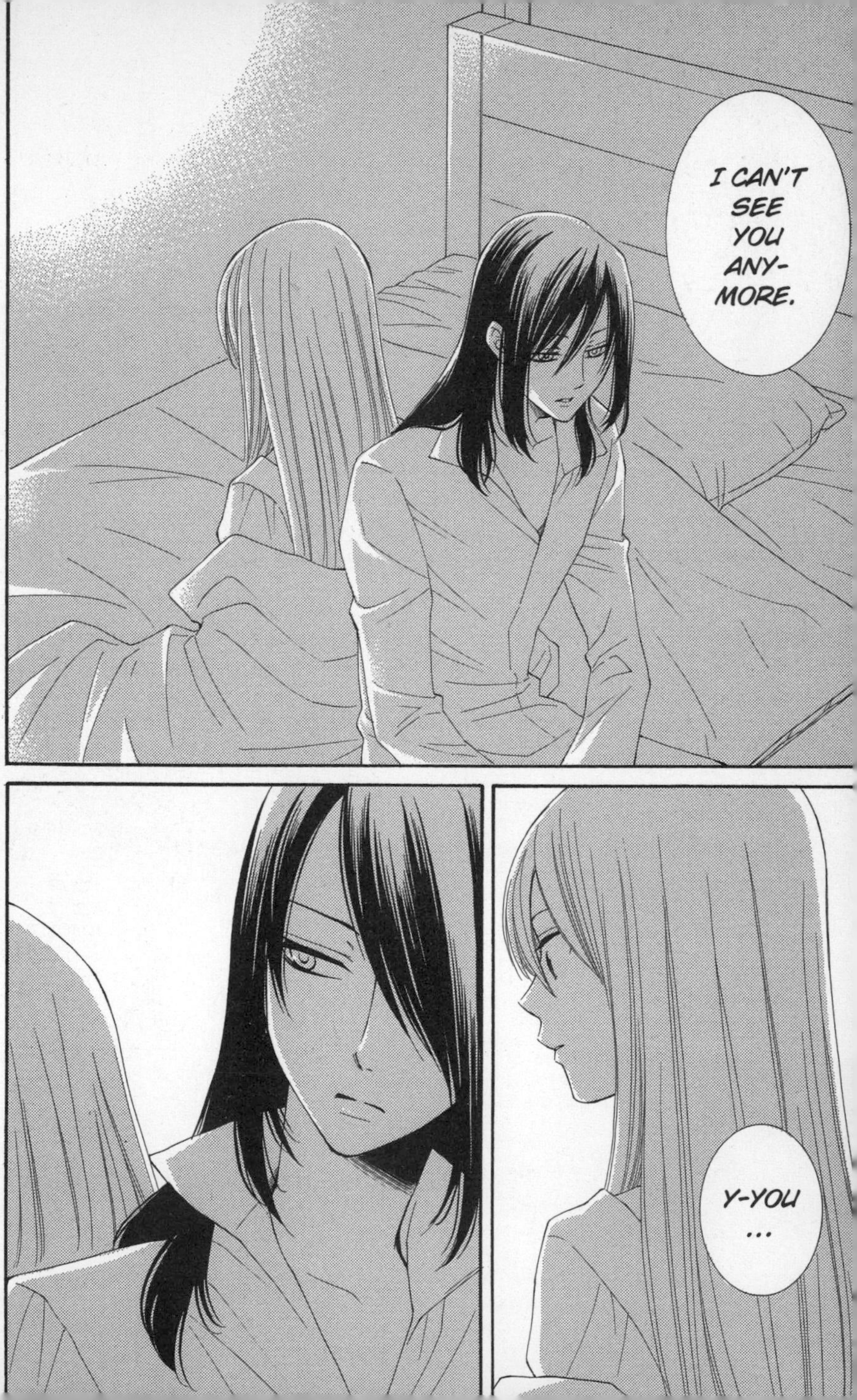
I CAN'T SEE YOU ANY-MORE.
Y-YOU ...

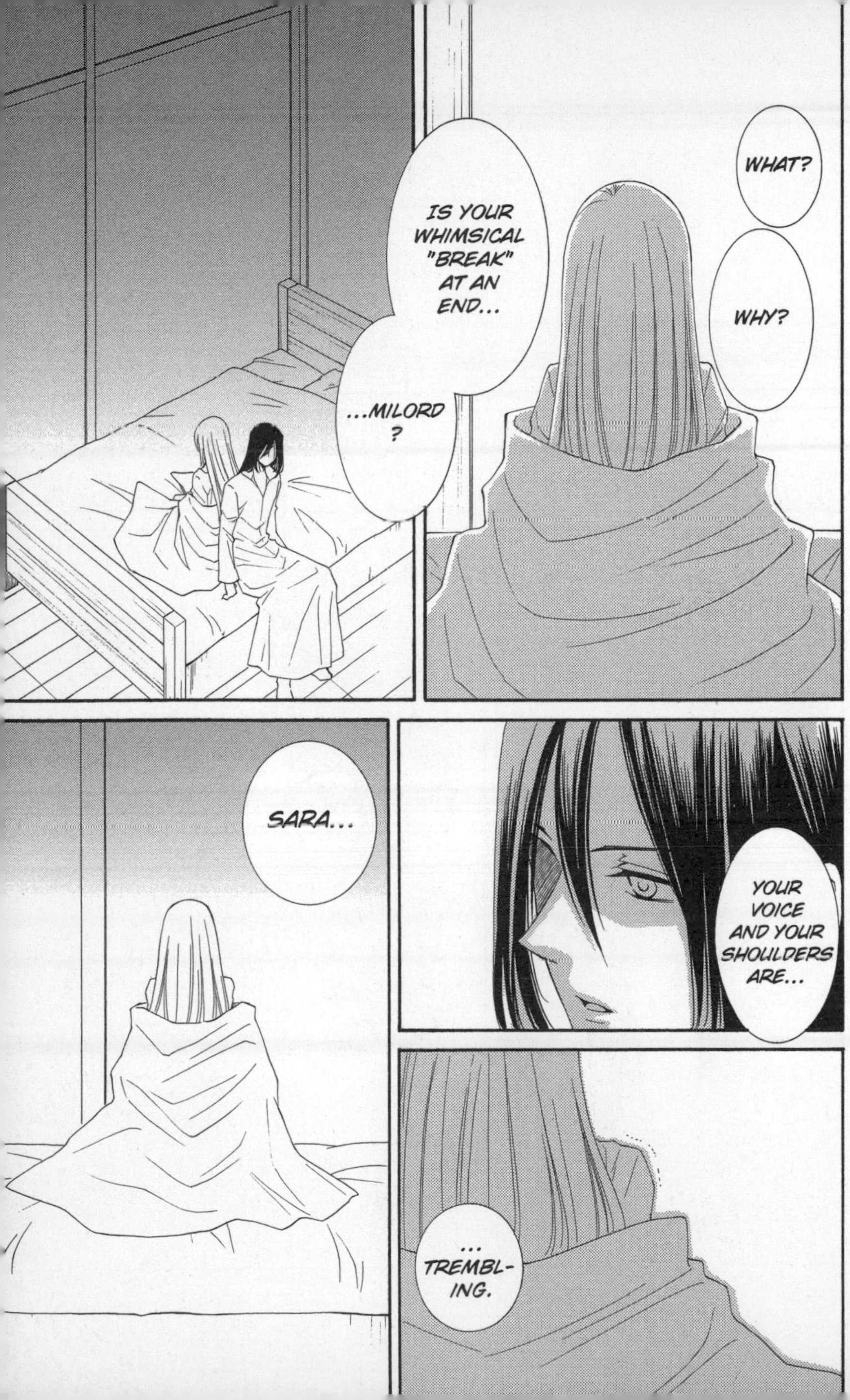
WHAT?
WHY?
IS YOUR WHIMSICAL "BREAK" AT AN END...
...MILORD?
YOUR VOICE AND YOUR SHOULDERS ARE...
...TREMBLING.
SARA...

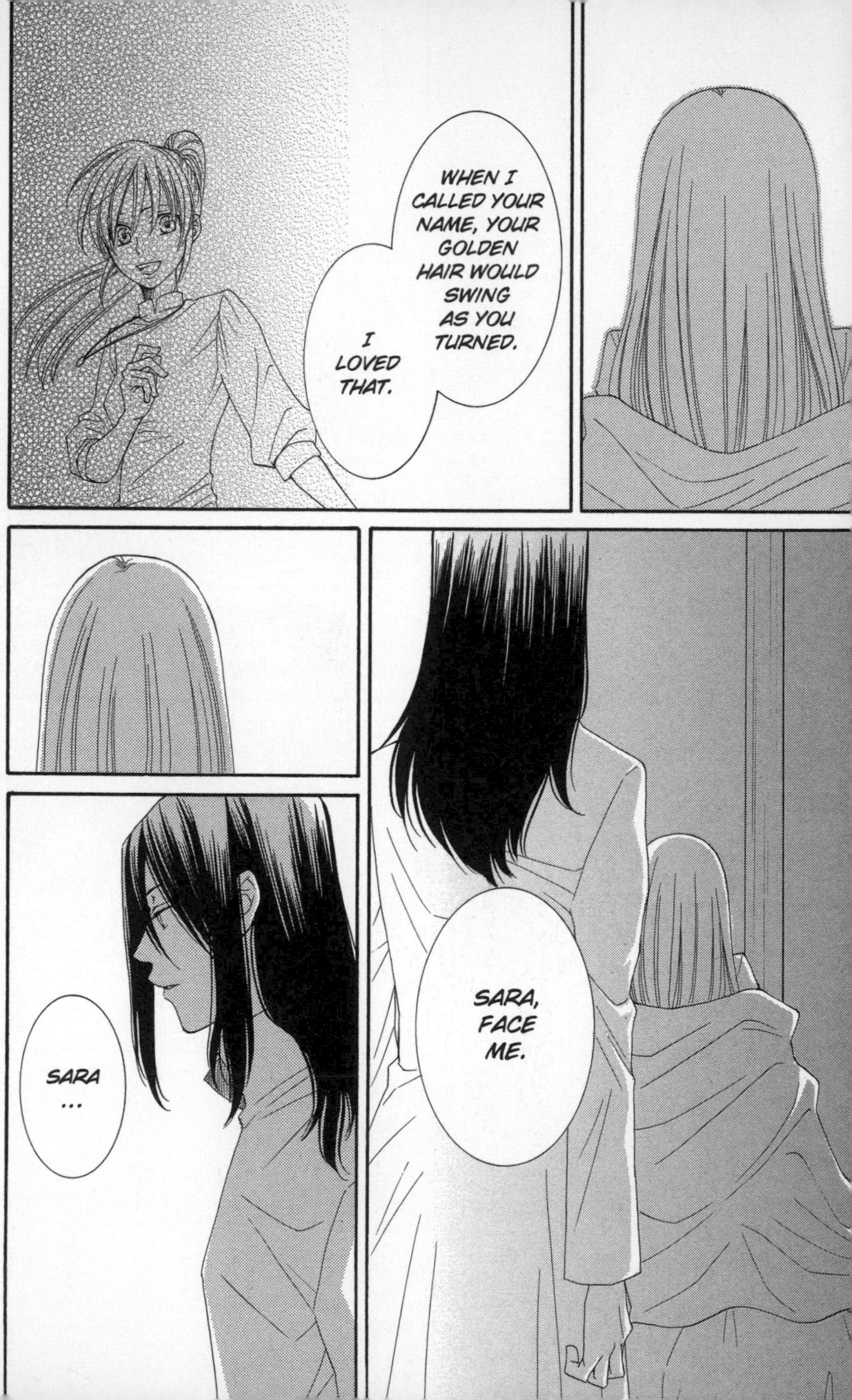
WHEN I CALLED YOUR NAME, YOUR GOLDEN HAIR WOULD SWING AS YOU TURNED.
I LOVED THAT.
SARA, FACE ME.
SARA ...

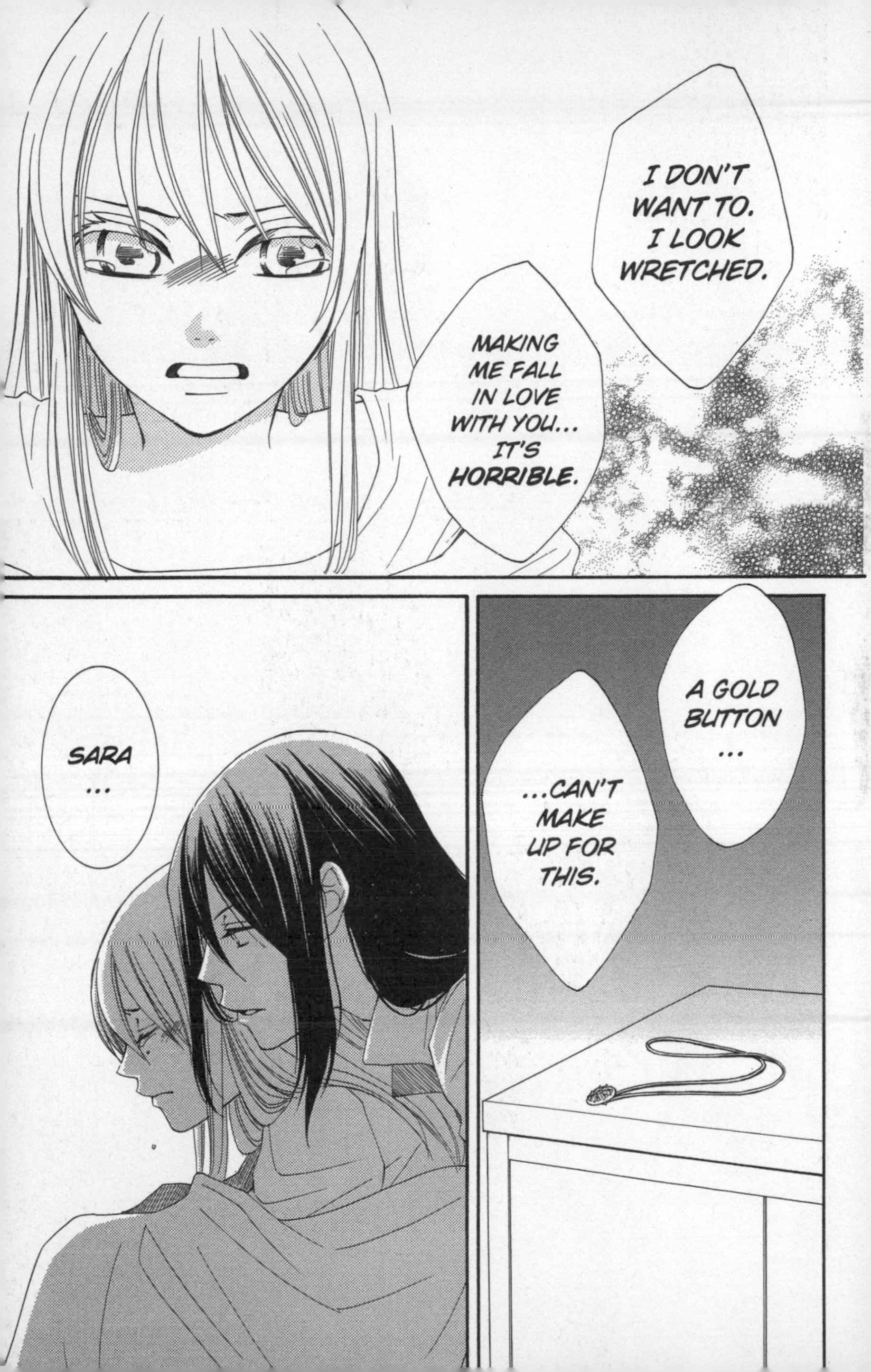
I DON'T WANT TO. I LOOK WRETCHED.
MAKING ME FALL IN LOVE WITH YOU... IT'S HORRIBLE.
A GOLD BUTTON ...
...CAN'T MAKE UP FOR THIS.
SARA ...

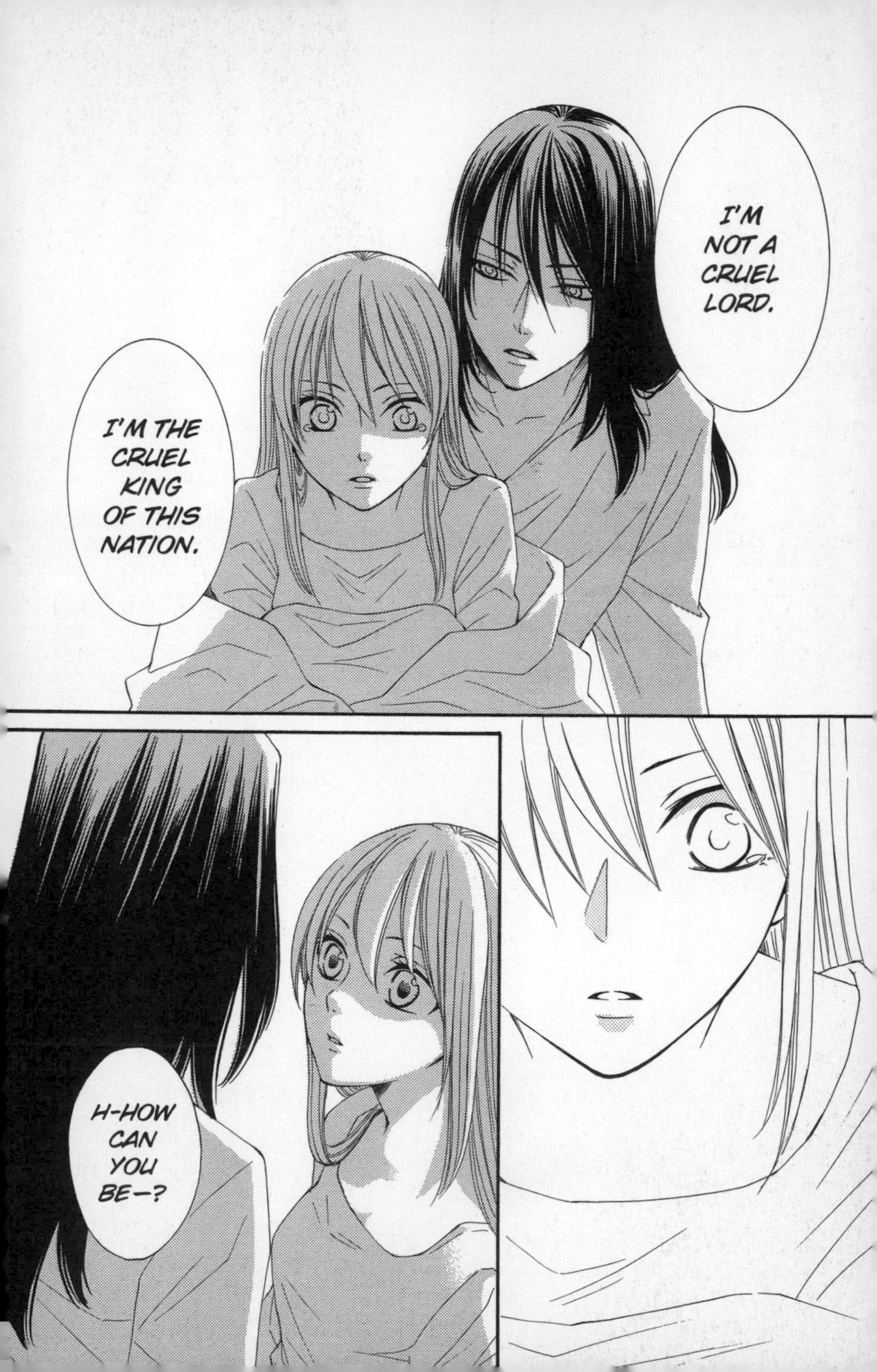
I'M NOT A CRUEL LORD.
I'M THE CRUEL KING OF THIS NATION.
H-HOW CAN YOU BE—?

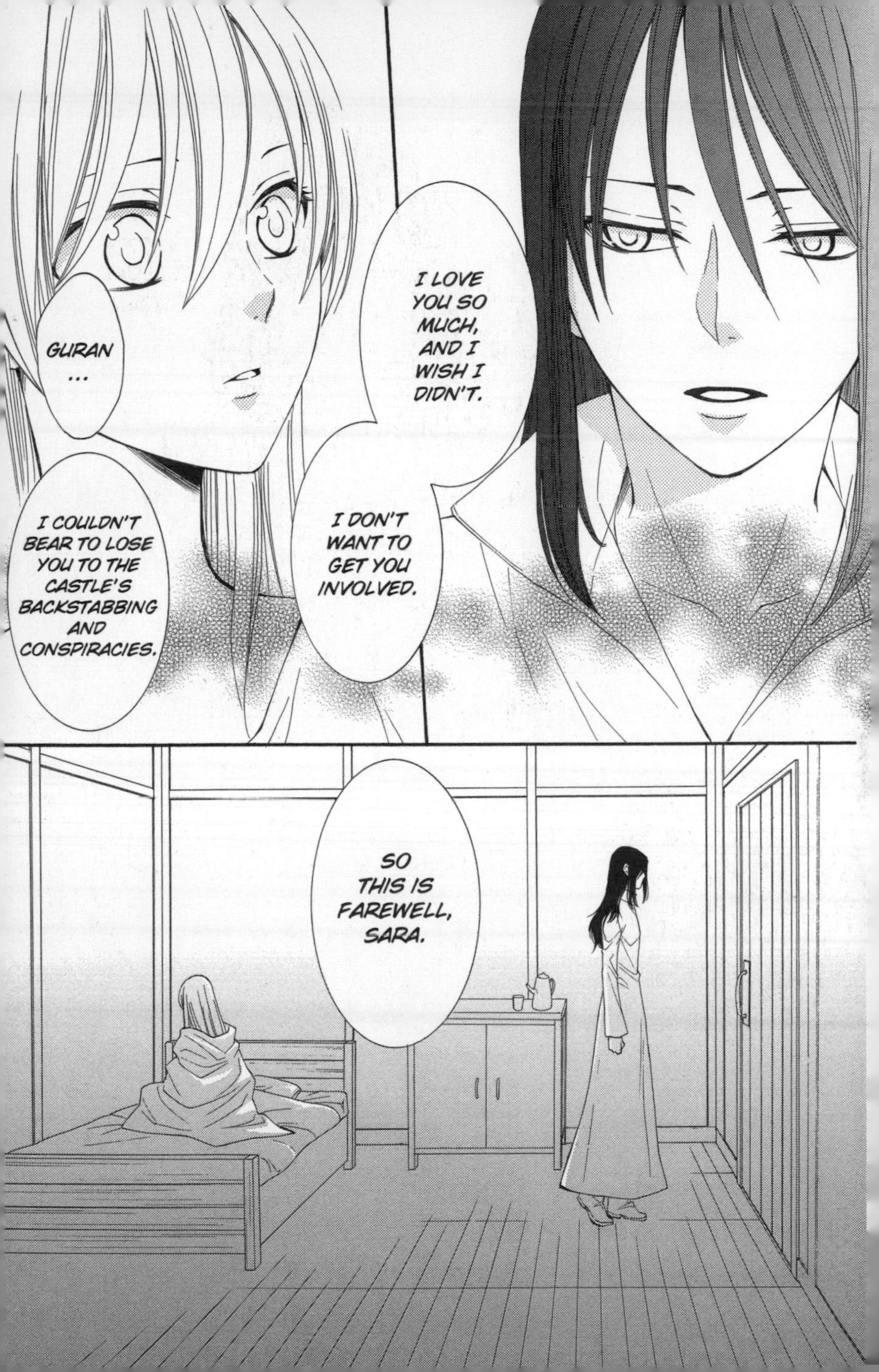
I LOVE YOU SO MUCH, AND I WISH I DIDN'T.
GURAN ...
I DON'T WANT TO GET YOU INVOLVED.
I COULDN'T BEAR TO LOSE YOU TO THE CASTLE'S BACKSTABBING AND CONSPIRACIES.
SO THIS IS FAREWELL, SARA.

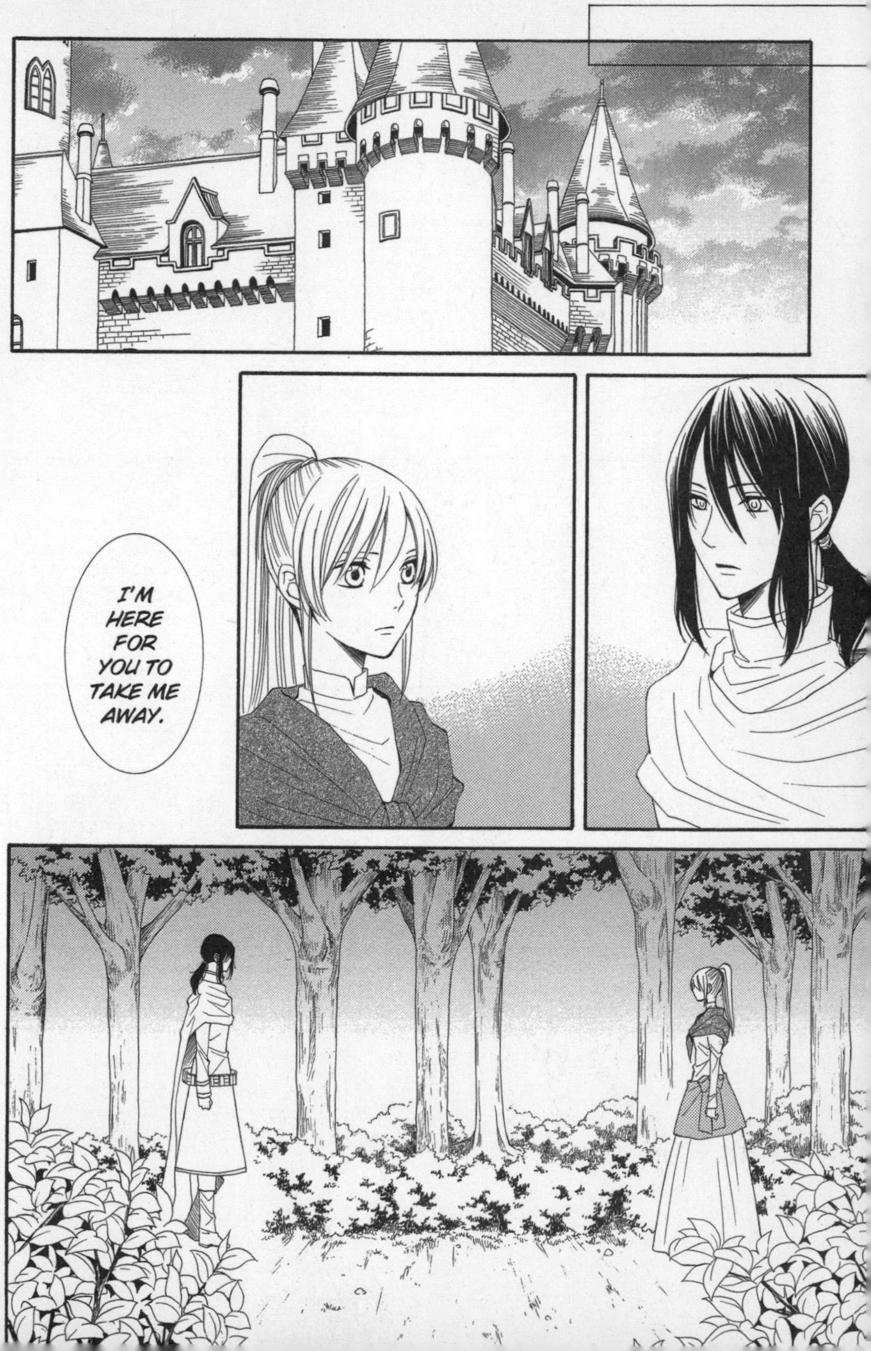
I'M HERE FOR YOU TO TAKE ME AWAY.

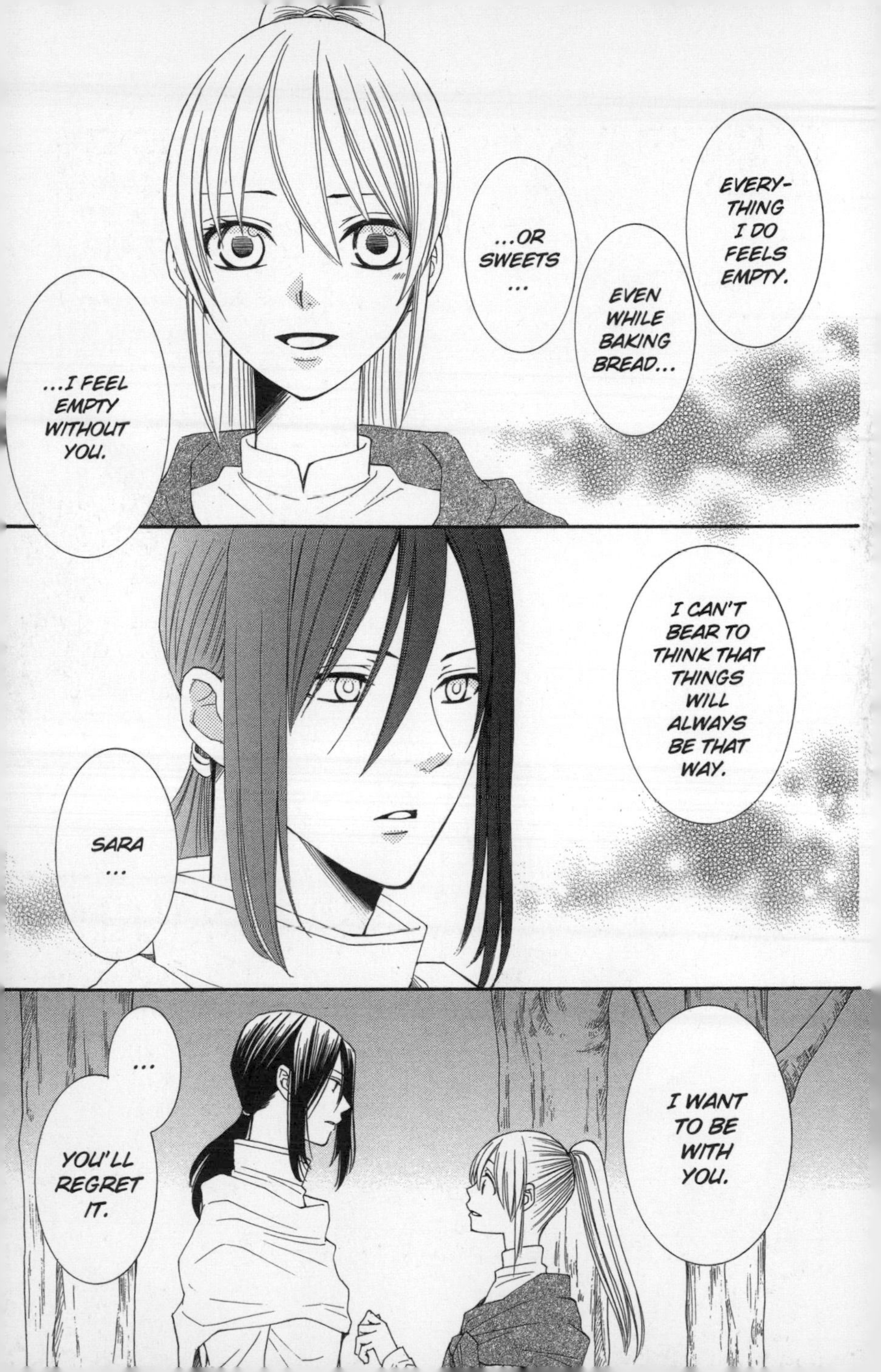
EVERY-THING I DO FEELS EMPTY.
EVEN WHILE BAKING BREAD...
...OR SWEETS...
...I FEEL EMPTY WITHOUT YOU.
I CAN'T BEAR TO THINK THAT THINGS WILL ALWAYS BE THAT WAY.
SARA...
I WANT TO BE WITH YOU.
... YOU'LL REGRET IT.

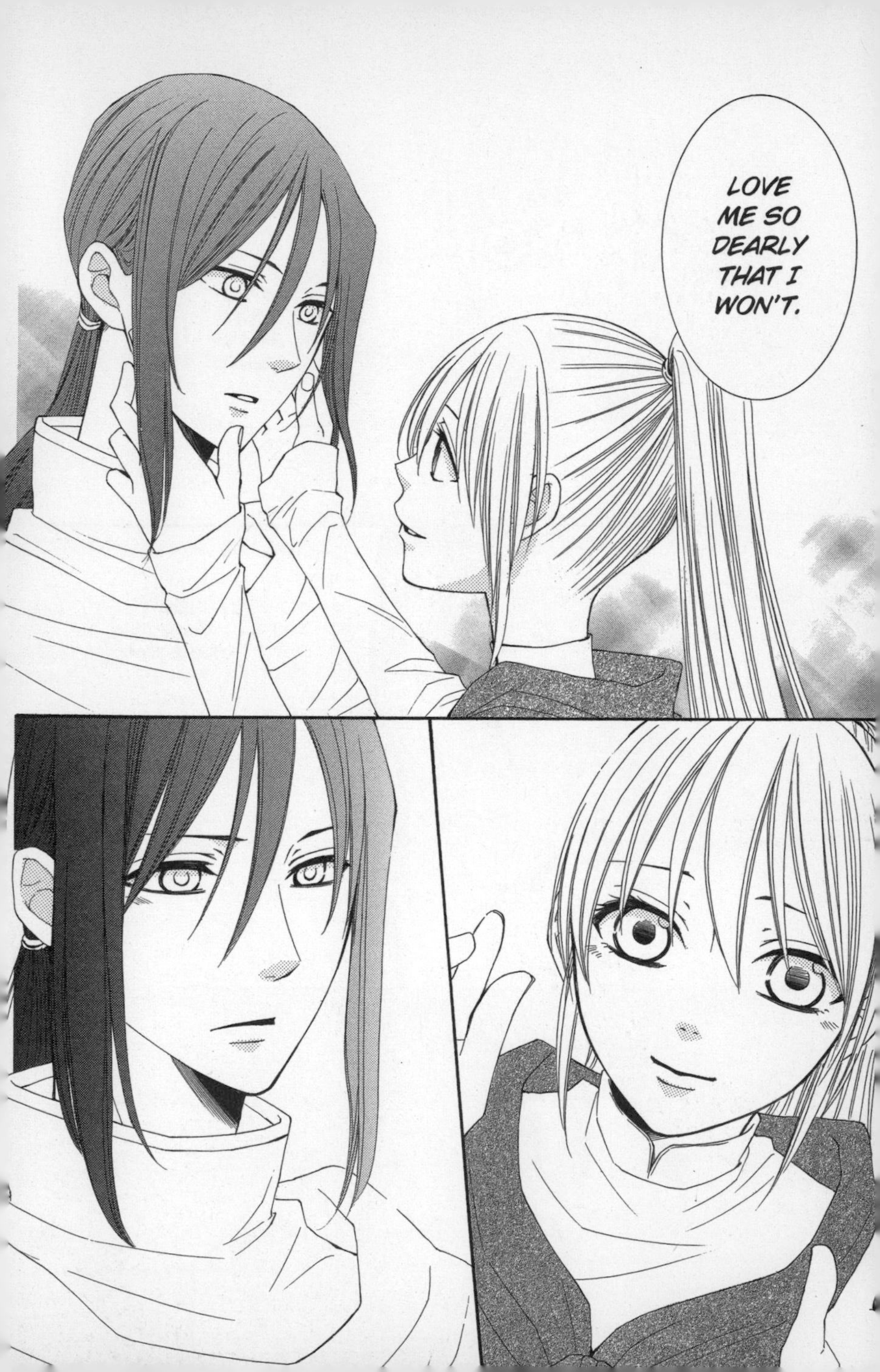
LOVE ME SO DEARLY THAT I WON'T.

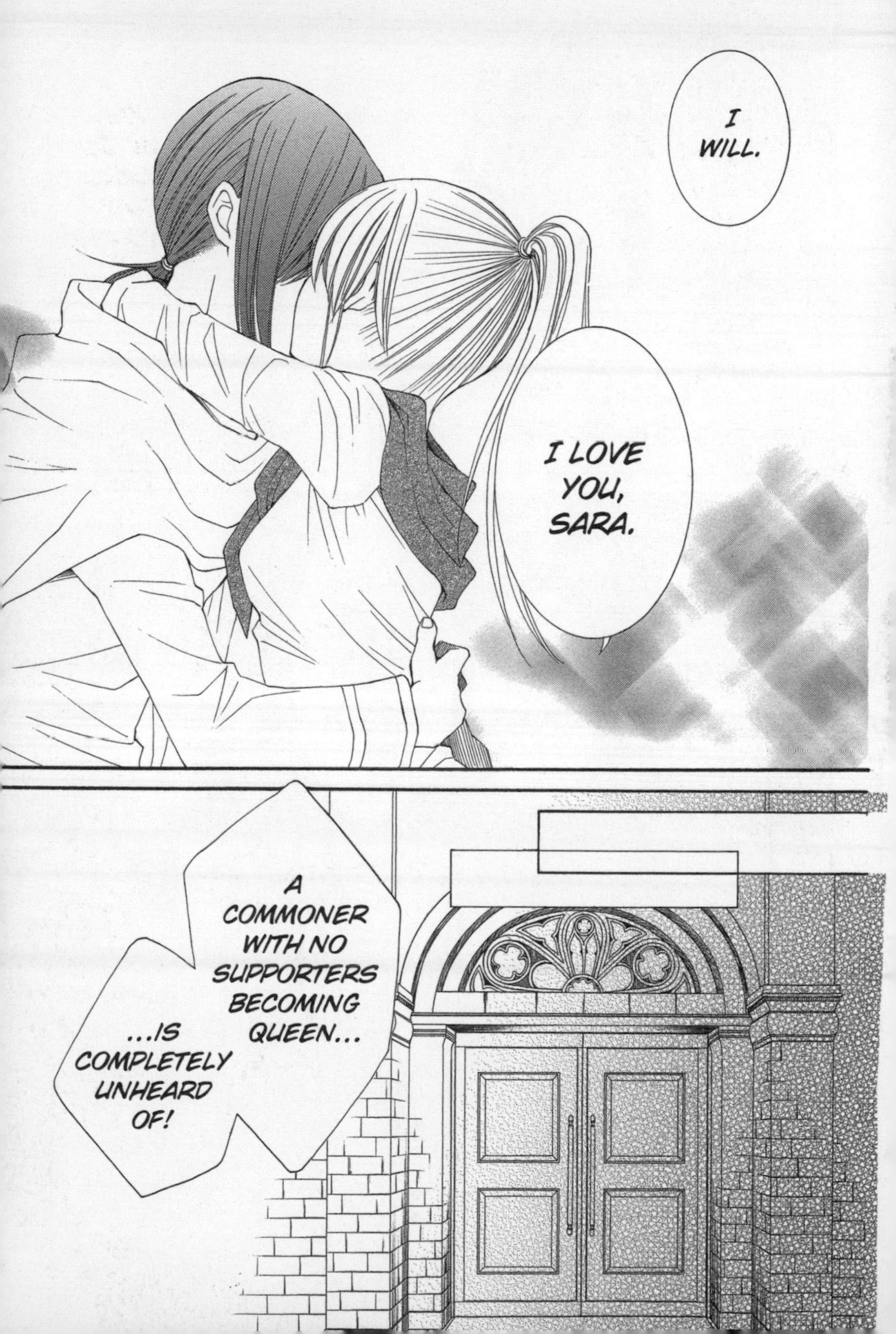
I WILL.
I LOVE YOU, SARA.
A COMMONER WITH NO SUPPORTERS BECOMING QUEEN...
...IS COMPLETELY UNHEARD OF!

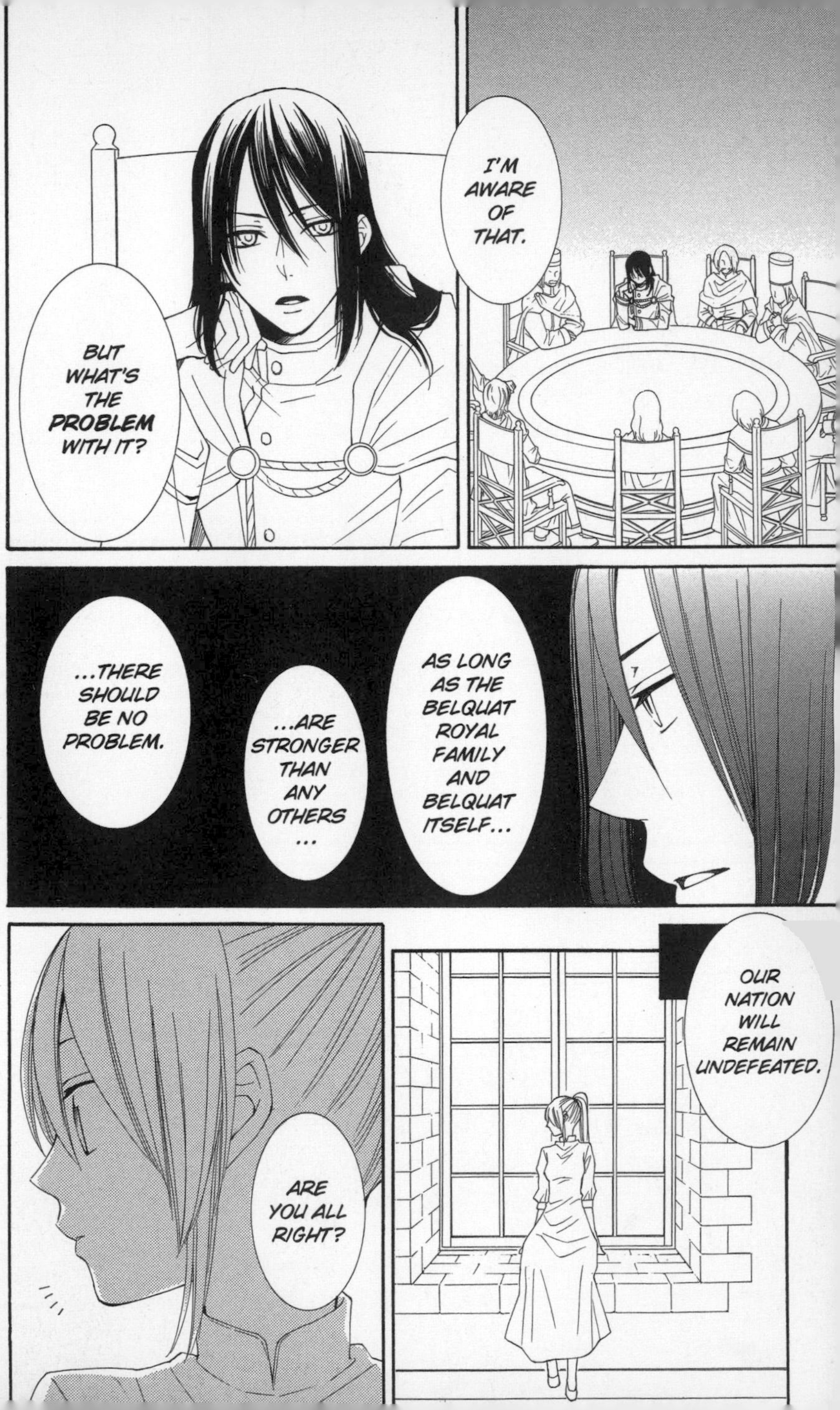
I'M AWARE OF THAT.
BUT WHAT'S THE **PROBLEM** WITH IT?
AS LONG AS THE BELQUAT ROYAL FAMILY AND BELQUAT ITSELF...
...ARE STRONGER THAN ANY OTHERS...
...THERE SHOULD BE NO PROBLEM.
OUR NATION WILL REMAIN UNDEFEATED.
ARE YOU ALL RIGHT?

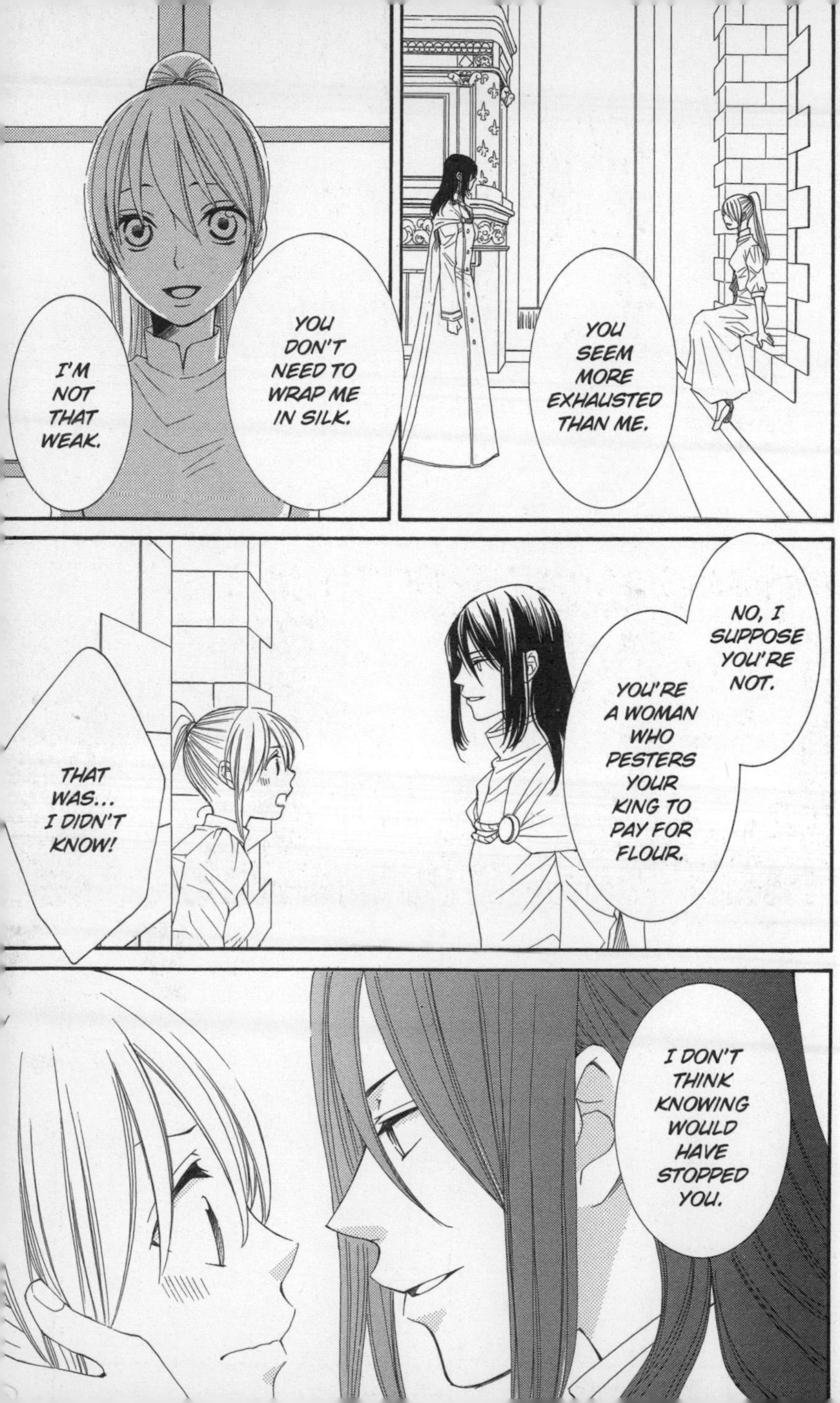
YOU SEEM MORE EXHAUSTED THAN ME.
YOU DON'T NEED TO WRAP ME IN SILK.
I'M NOT THAT WEAK.
NO, I SUPPOSE YOU'RE NOT.
YOU'RE A WOMAN WHO PESTERS YOUR KING TO PAY FOR FLOUR.
THAT WAS... I DIDN'T KNOW!
I DON'T THINK KNOWING WOULD HAVE STOPPED YOU.

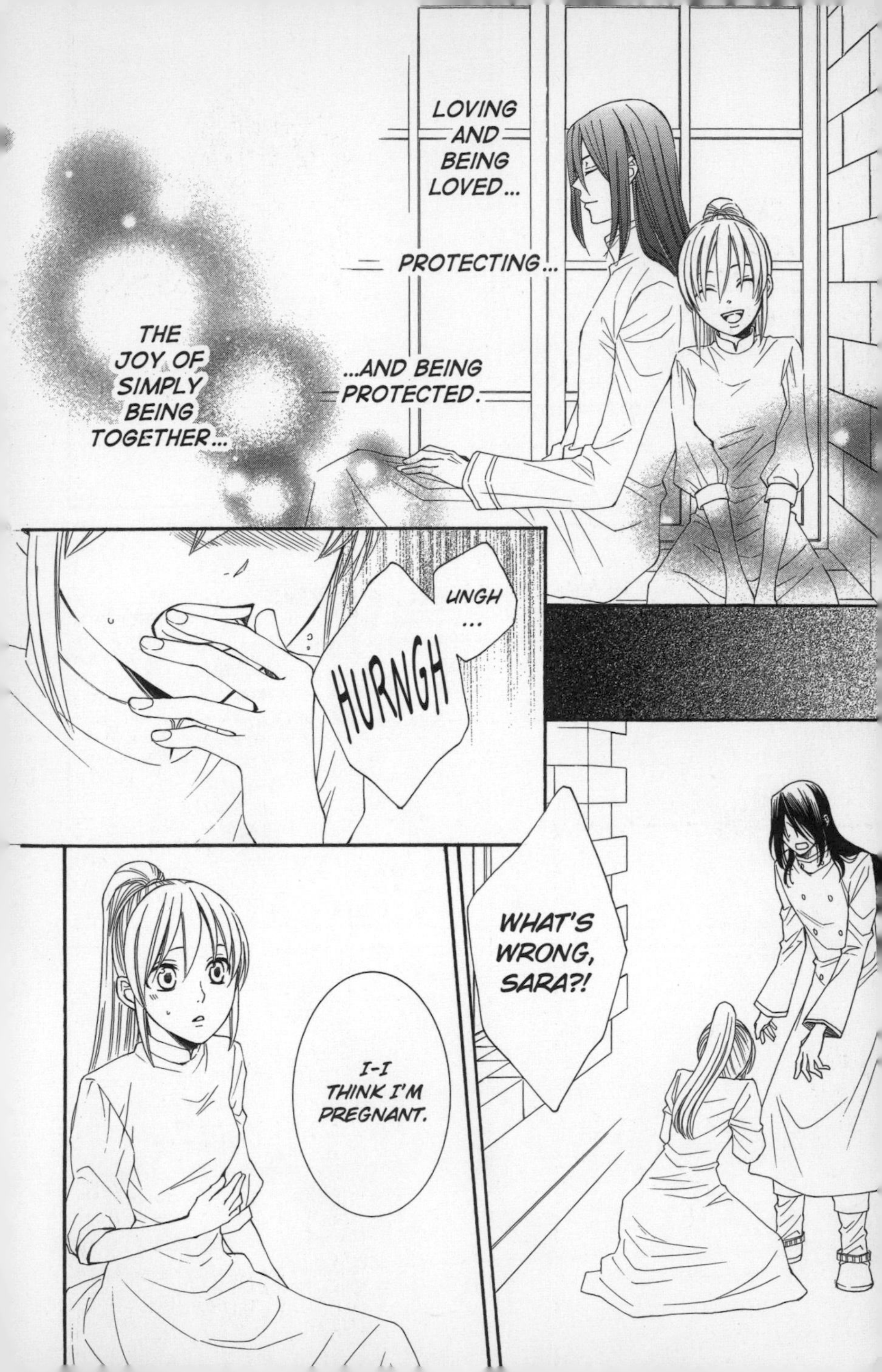
LOVING AND BEING LOVED...
PROTECTING...
...AND BEING PROTECTED.
THE JOY OF SIMPLY BEING TOGETHER...
UNGH ...
HURNGH
WHAT'S WRONG, SARA?!
I-I THINK I'M PREGNANT.

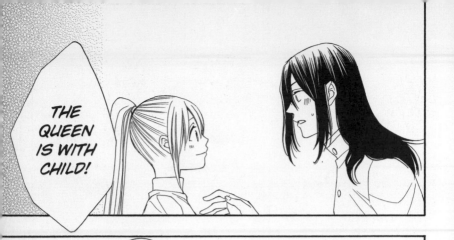

THE QUEEN IS WITH CHILD!

WELL, NOW.

I WAS WORRIED ABOUT A COMMONER BECOMING QUEEN.

ESPECIALLY WHEN THE FAMILY OF HIS MAJESTY'S CONCUBINE, ROSENTA, GIVES HIM SUCH SUPPORT.

BUT IF ANYTHING...

Da...

Aa...

...HIS MAJESTY HAS MELLOWED.

HA HA! THAT'S TRUE.

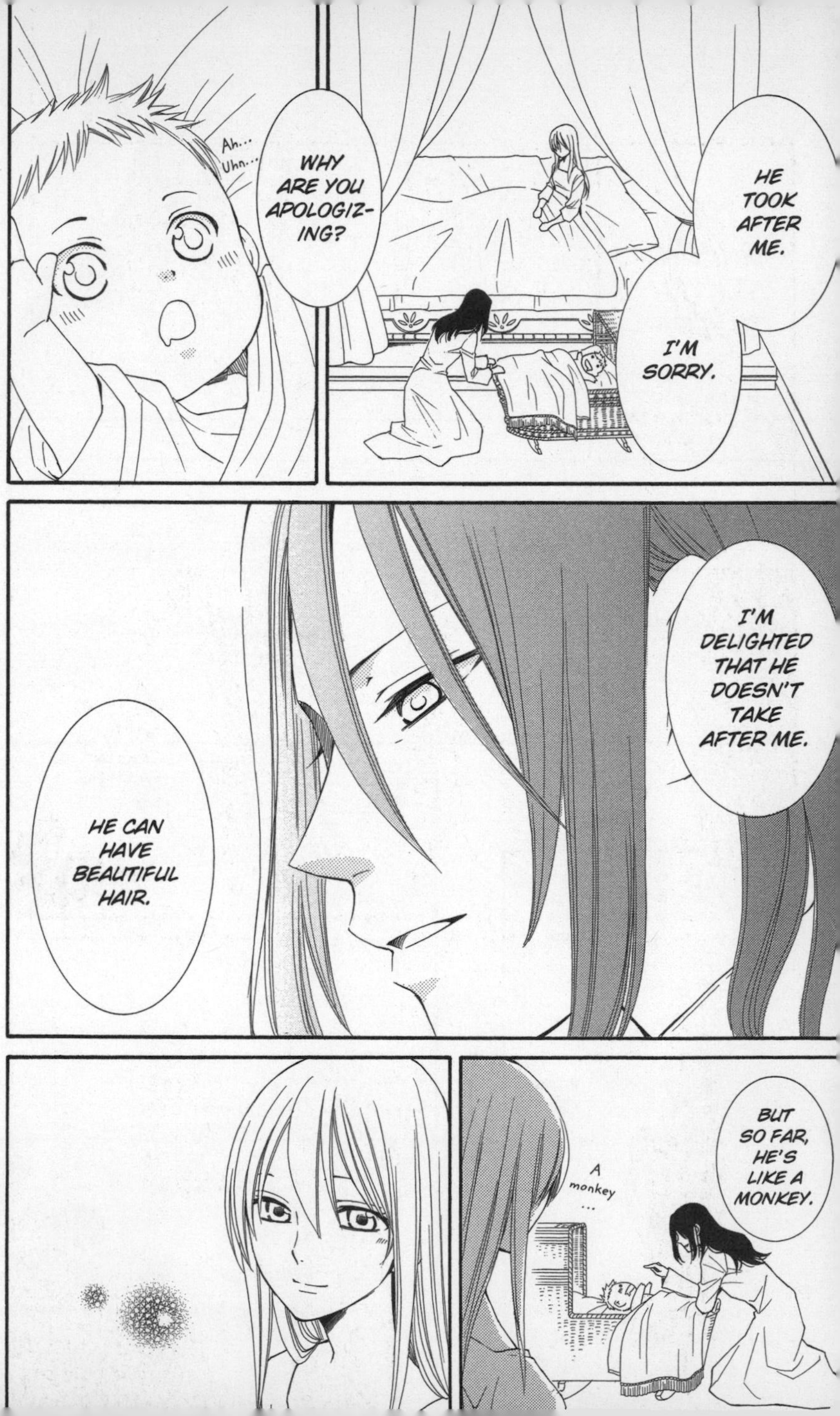
HE TOOK AFTER ME.
I'M SORRY.
WHY ARE YOU APOLOGIZ-ING?
Ah... Uhn...
I'M DELIGHTED THAT HE DOESN'T TAKE AFTER ME.
HE CAN HAVE BEAUTIFUL HAIR.
BUT SO FAR, HE'S LIKE A MONKEY.
A monkey...

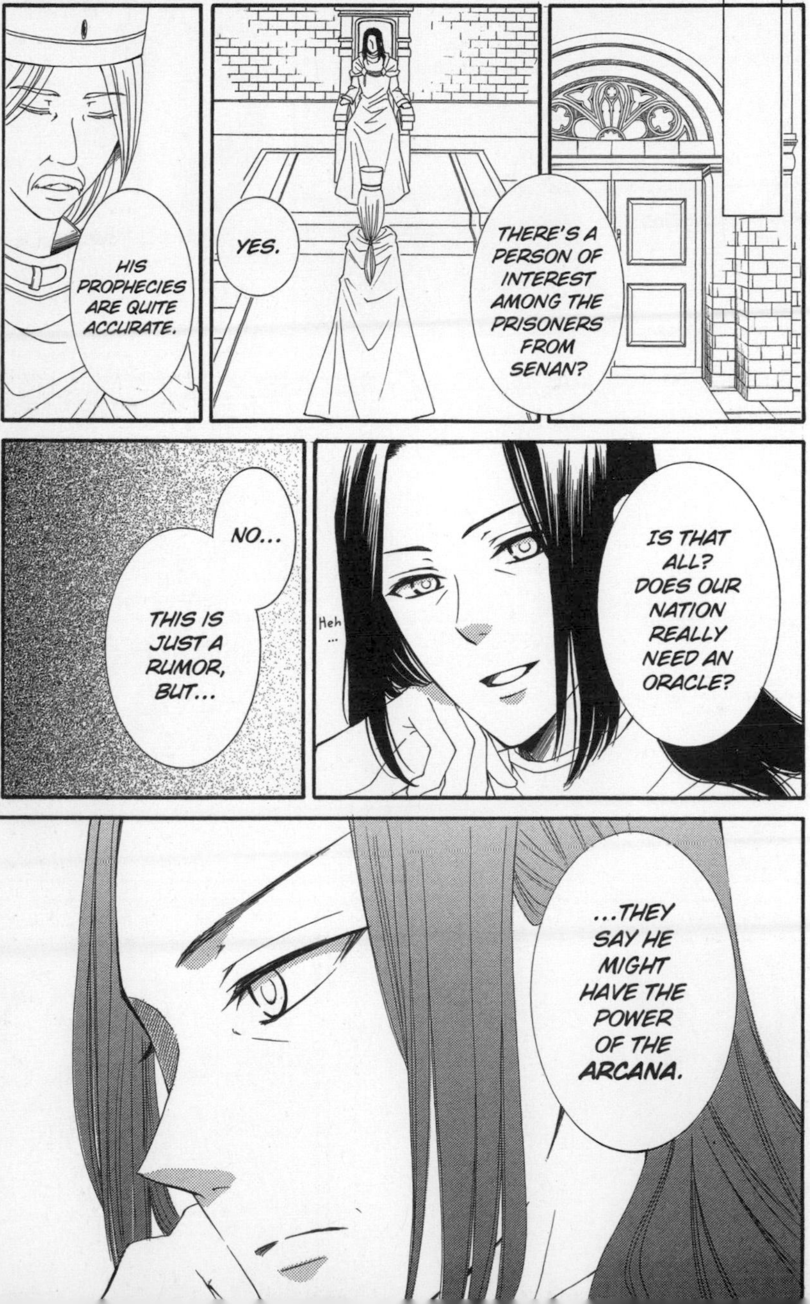
THERE'S A PERSON OF INTEREST AMONG THE PRISONERS FROM SENAN?
YES.
HIS PROPHECIES ARE QUITE ACCURATE.
IS THAT ALL? DOES OUR NATION REALLY NEED AN ORACLE?
Heh...
NO...
THIS IS JUST A RUMOR, BUT...
...THEY SAY HE MIGHT HAVE THE POWER OF THE ARCANA.

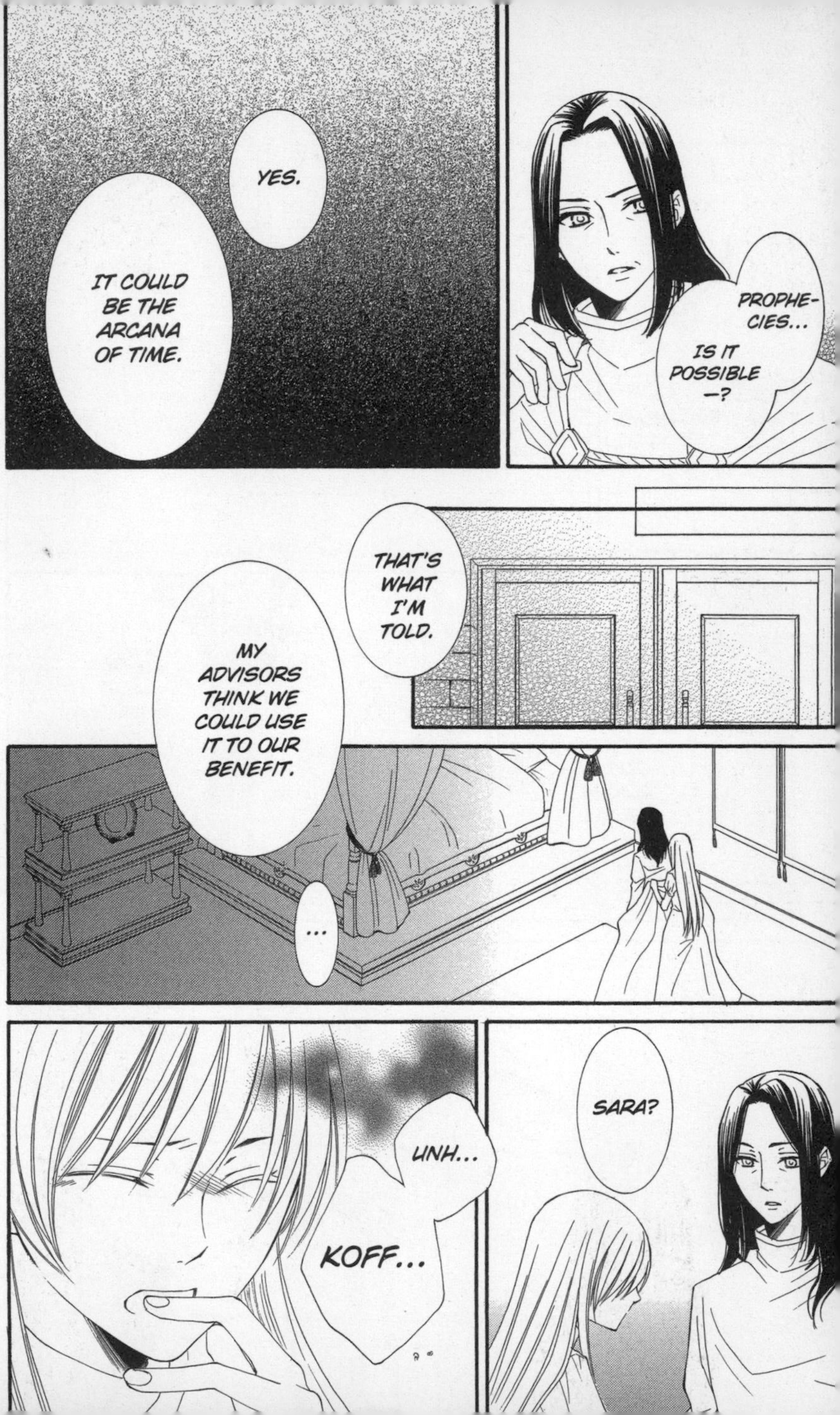
PROPHE-CIES...
IS IT POSSIBLE —?
YES.
IT COULD BE THE ARCANA OF TIME.
THAT'S WHAT I'M TOLD.
MY ADVISORS THINK WE COULD USE IT TO OUR BENEFIT.
...
SARA?
UNH...
KOFF...

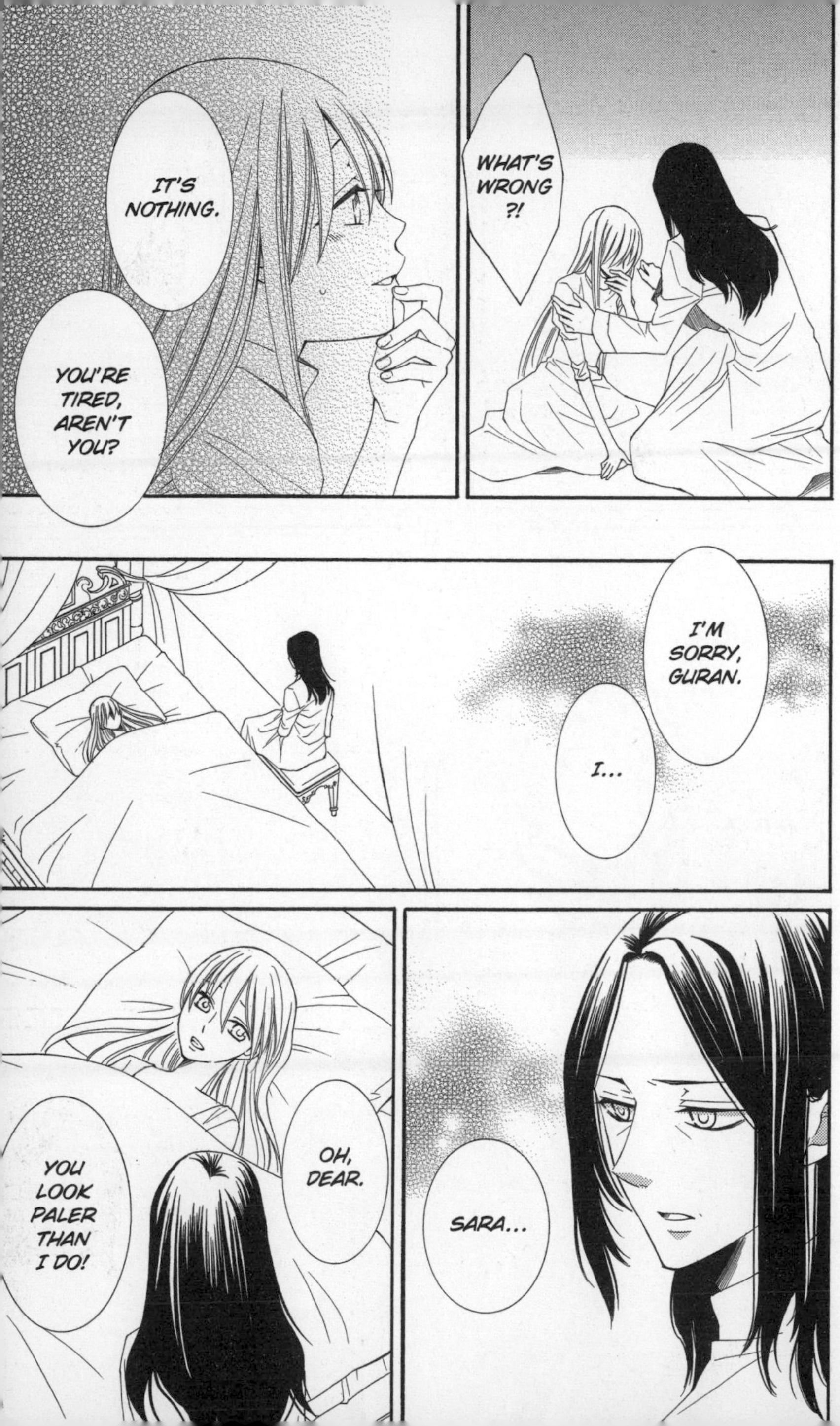
WHAT'S WRONG?!
IT'S NOTHING.
YOU'RE TIRED, AREN'T YOU?
I'M SORRY, GURAN.
I...
SARA...
OH, DEAR.
YOU LOOK PALER THAN I DO!

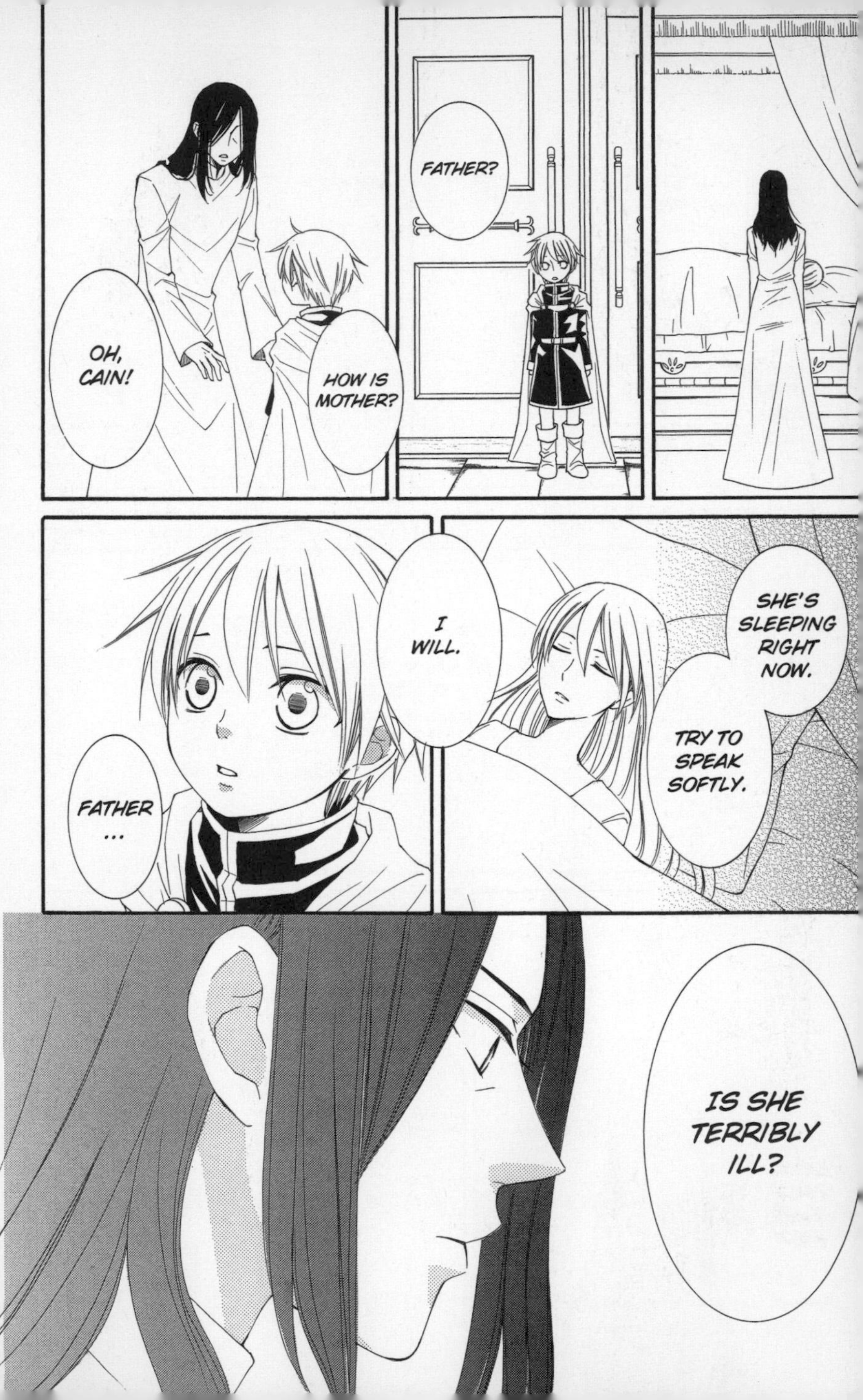
FATHER?
OH, CAIN!
HOW IS MOTHER?
SHE'S SLEEPING RIGHT NOW.
TRY TO SPEAK SOFTLY.
I WILL.
FATHER ...
IS SHE TERRIBLY ILL?

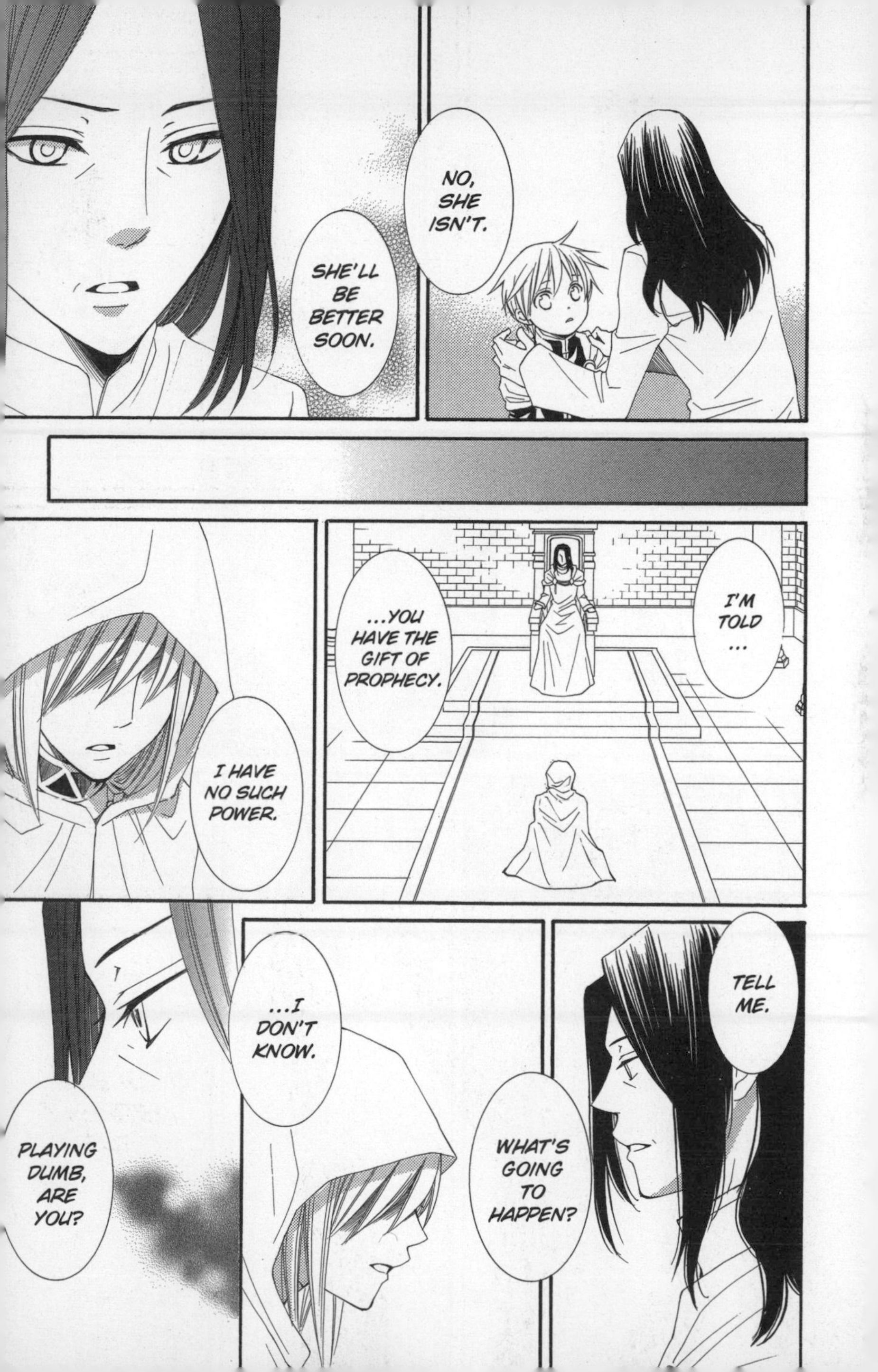
NO, SHE ISN'T.
SHE'LL BE BETTER SOON.
I'M TOLD ...
...YOU HAVE THE GIFT OF PROPHECY.
I HAVE NO SUCH POWER.
TELL ME.
WHAT'S GOING TO HAPPEN?
...I DON'T KNOW.
PLAYING DUMB, ARE YOU?

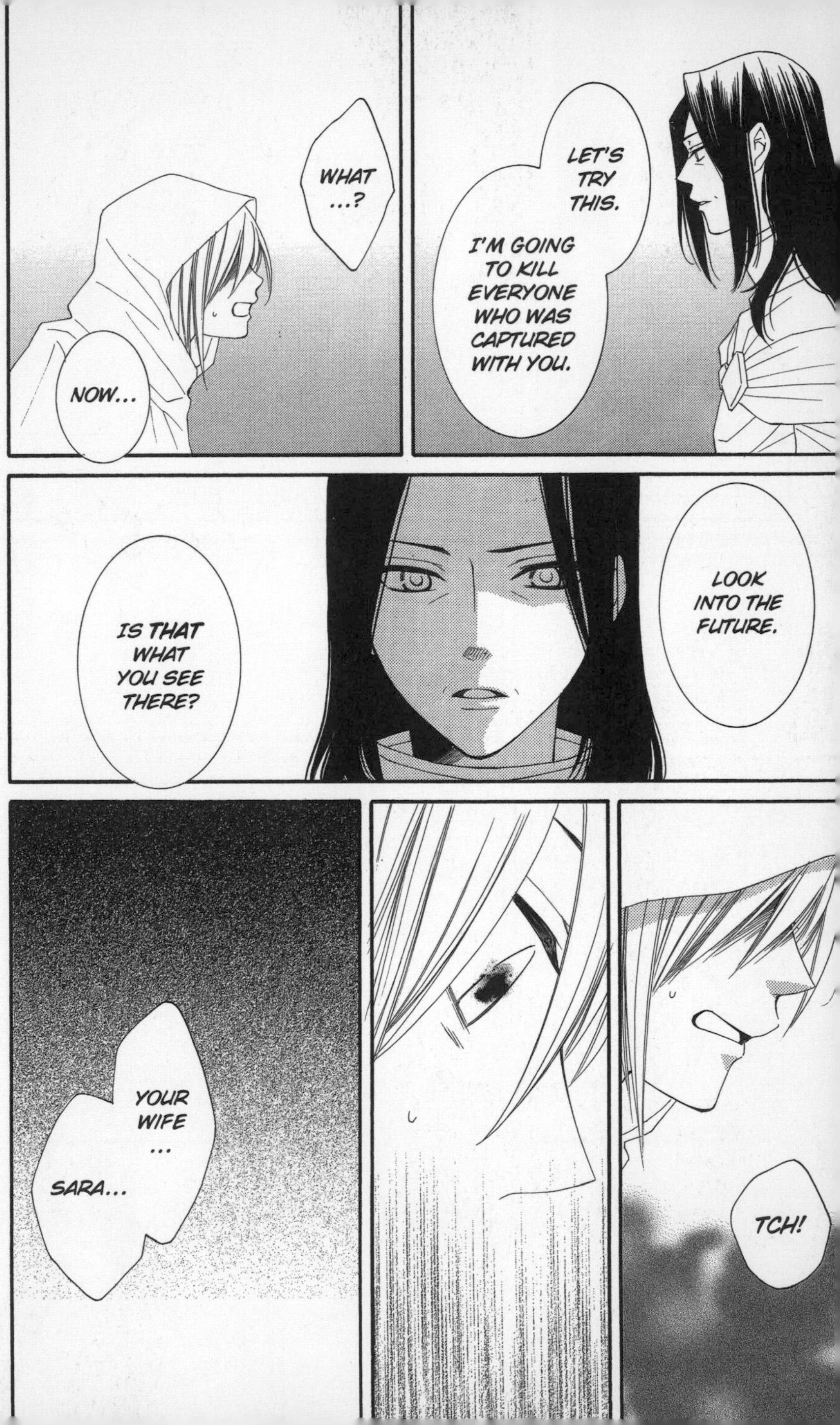
LET'S TRY THIS.
I'M GOING TO KILL EVERYONE WHO WAS CAPTURED WITH YOU.
WHAT ...?
NOW...
LOOK INTO THE FUTURE.
IS THAT WHAT YOU SEE THERE?
TCH!
YOUR WIFE ...
SARA...

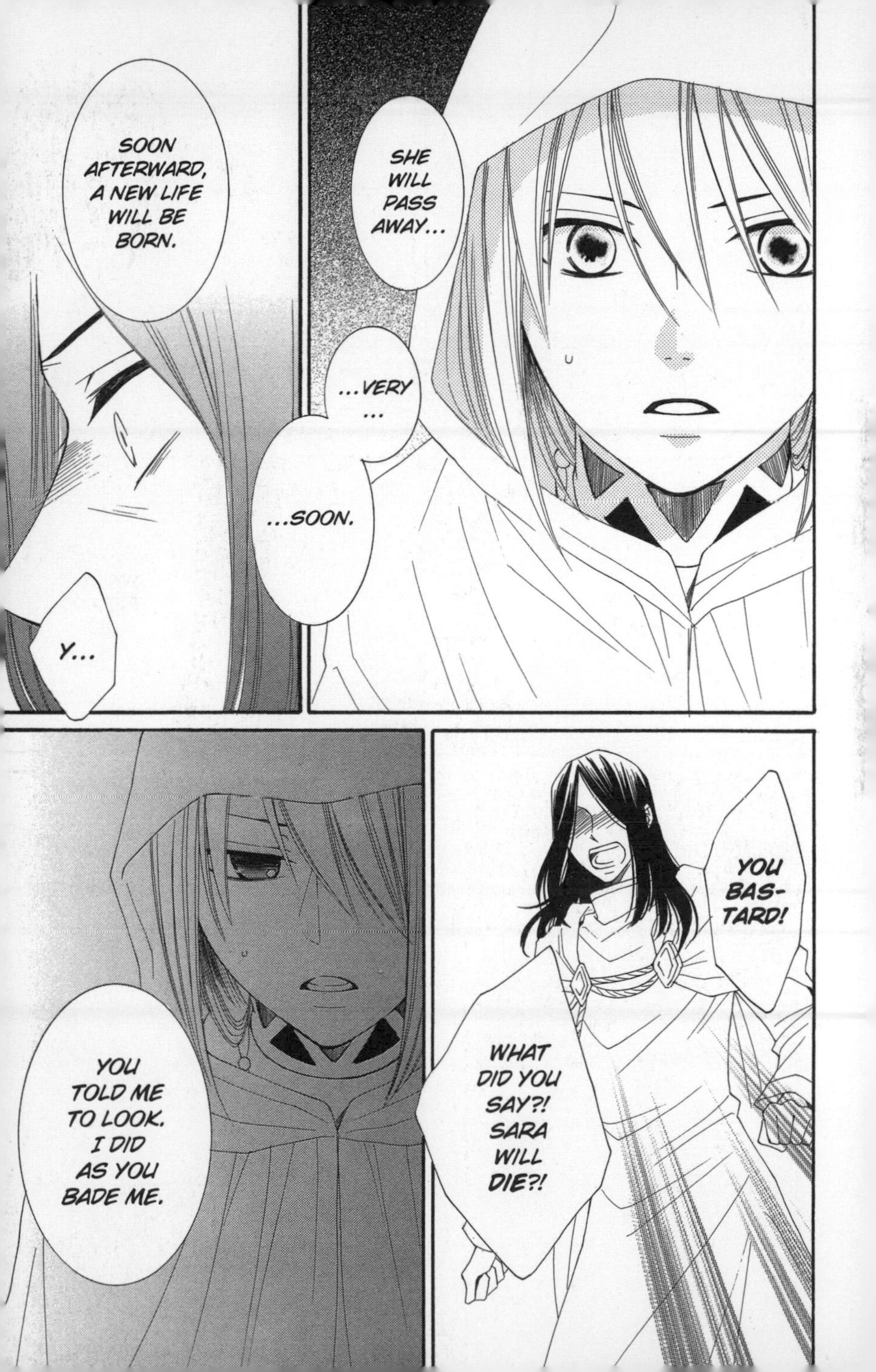
SHE WILL PASS AWAY...
...VERY ...
...SOON.
SOON AFTERWARD, A NEW LIFE WILL BE BORN.
Y...
YOU BAS-TARD!
WHAT DID YOU SAY?! SARA WILL DIE?!
YOU TOLD ME TO LOOK. I DID AS YOU BADE ME.

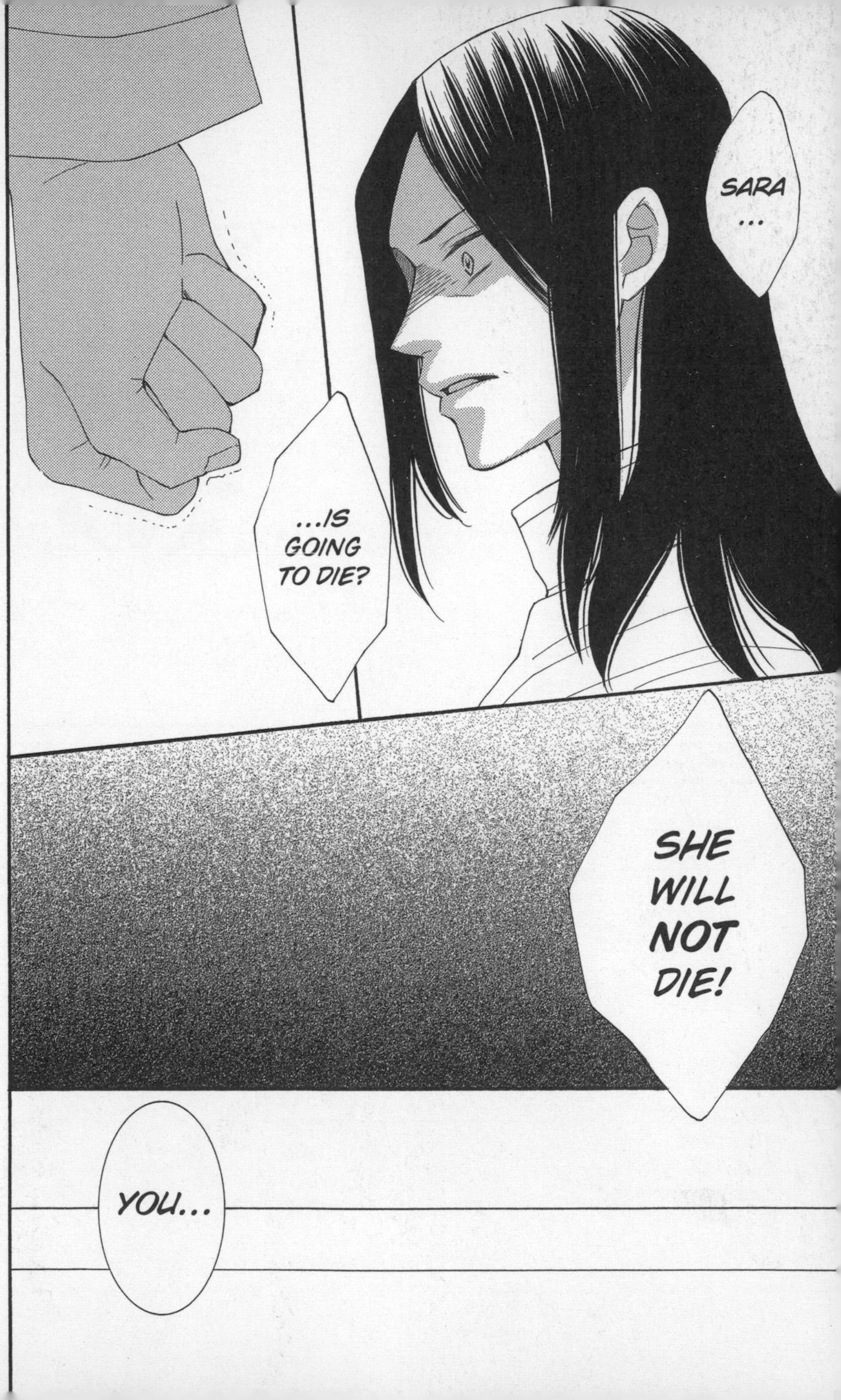
SARA...
...IS GOING TO DIE?
SHE WILL NOT DIE!
YOU...

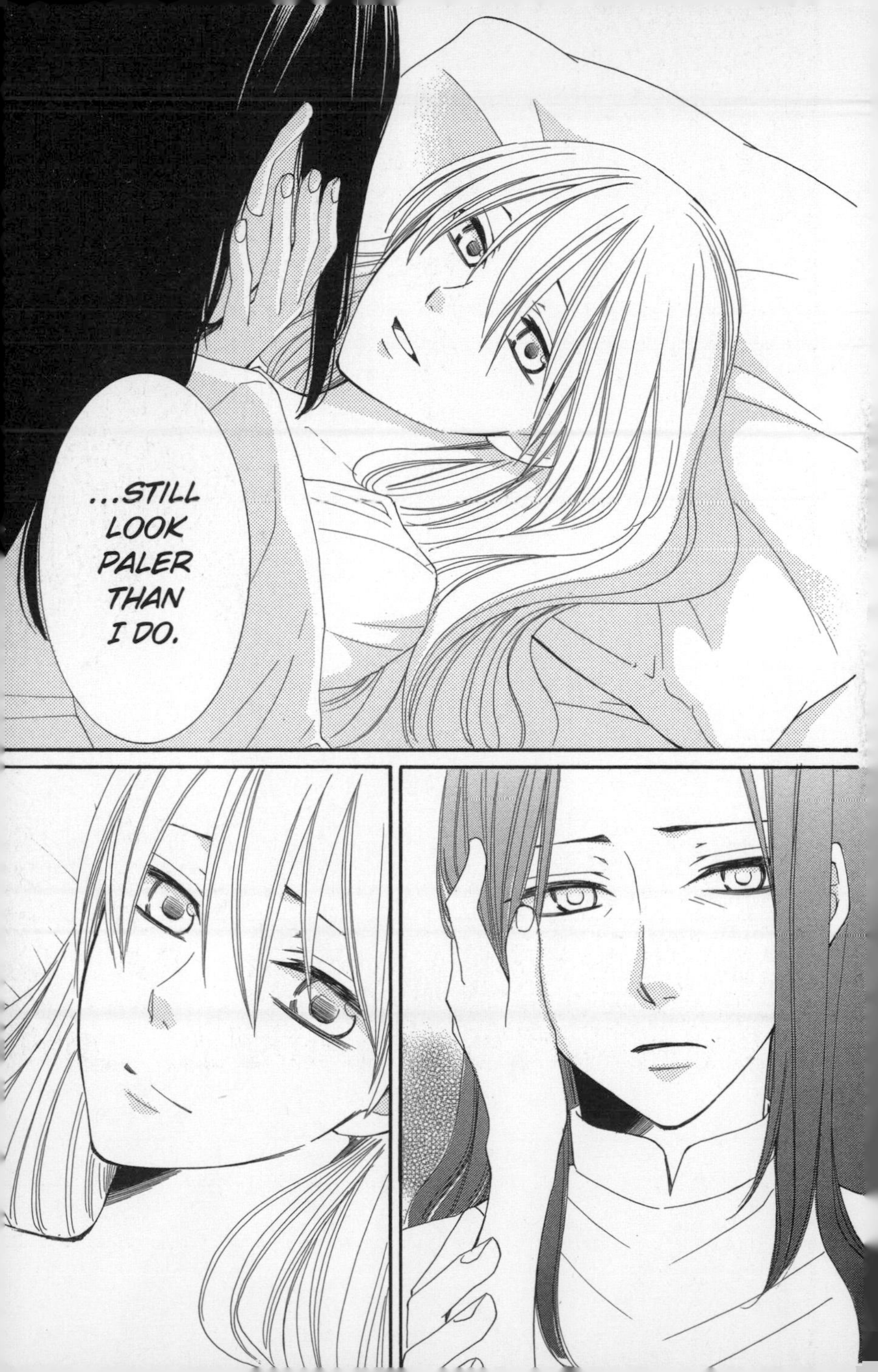
...STILL LOOK PALER THAN I DO.

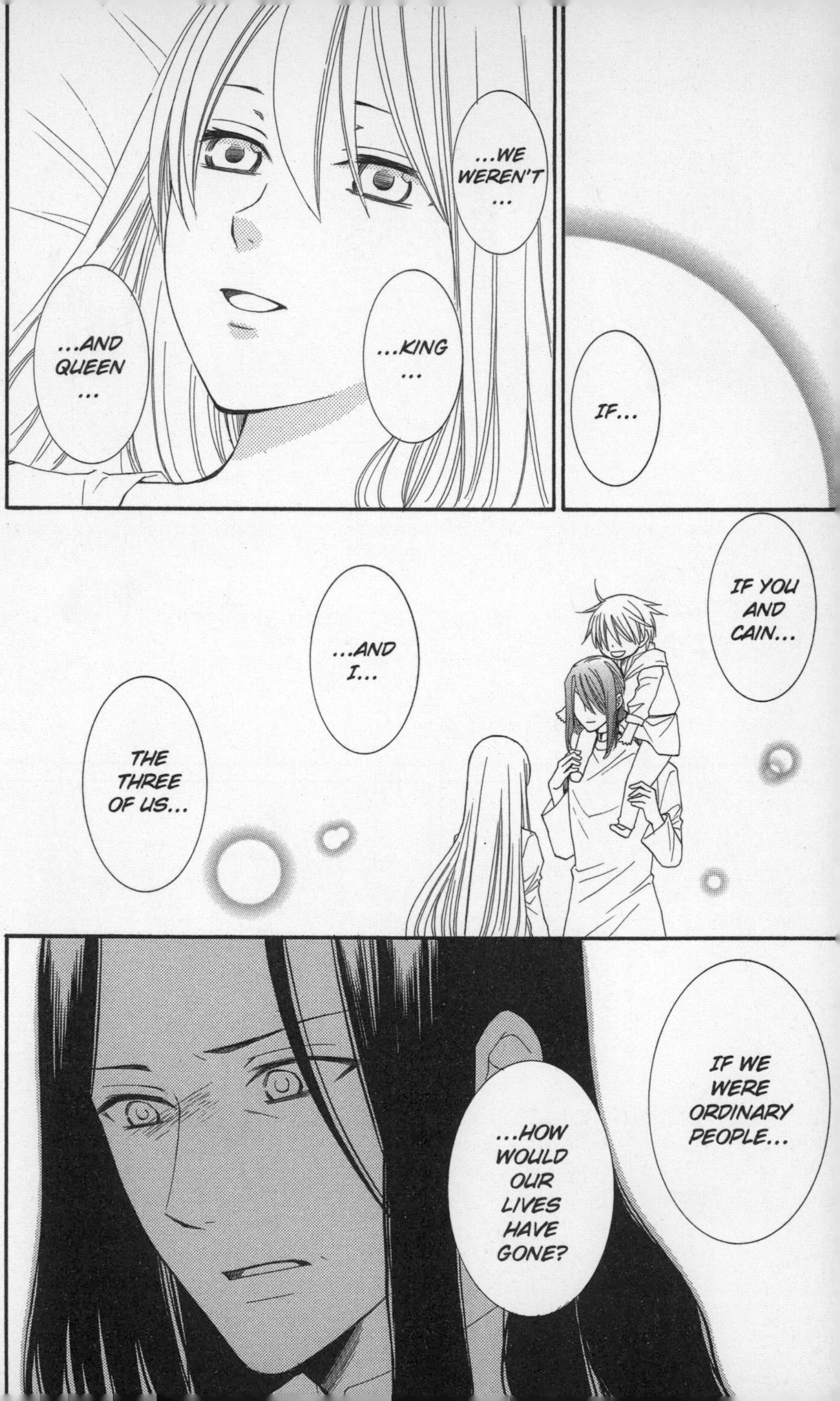
IF...
...WE WEREN'T ...
...KING ...
...AND QUEEN ...
IF YOU AND CAIN...
...AND I...
THE THREE OF US...
IF WE WERE ORDINARY PEOPLE...
...HOW WOULD OUR LIVES HAVE GONE?

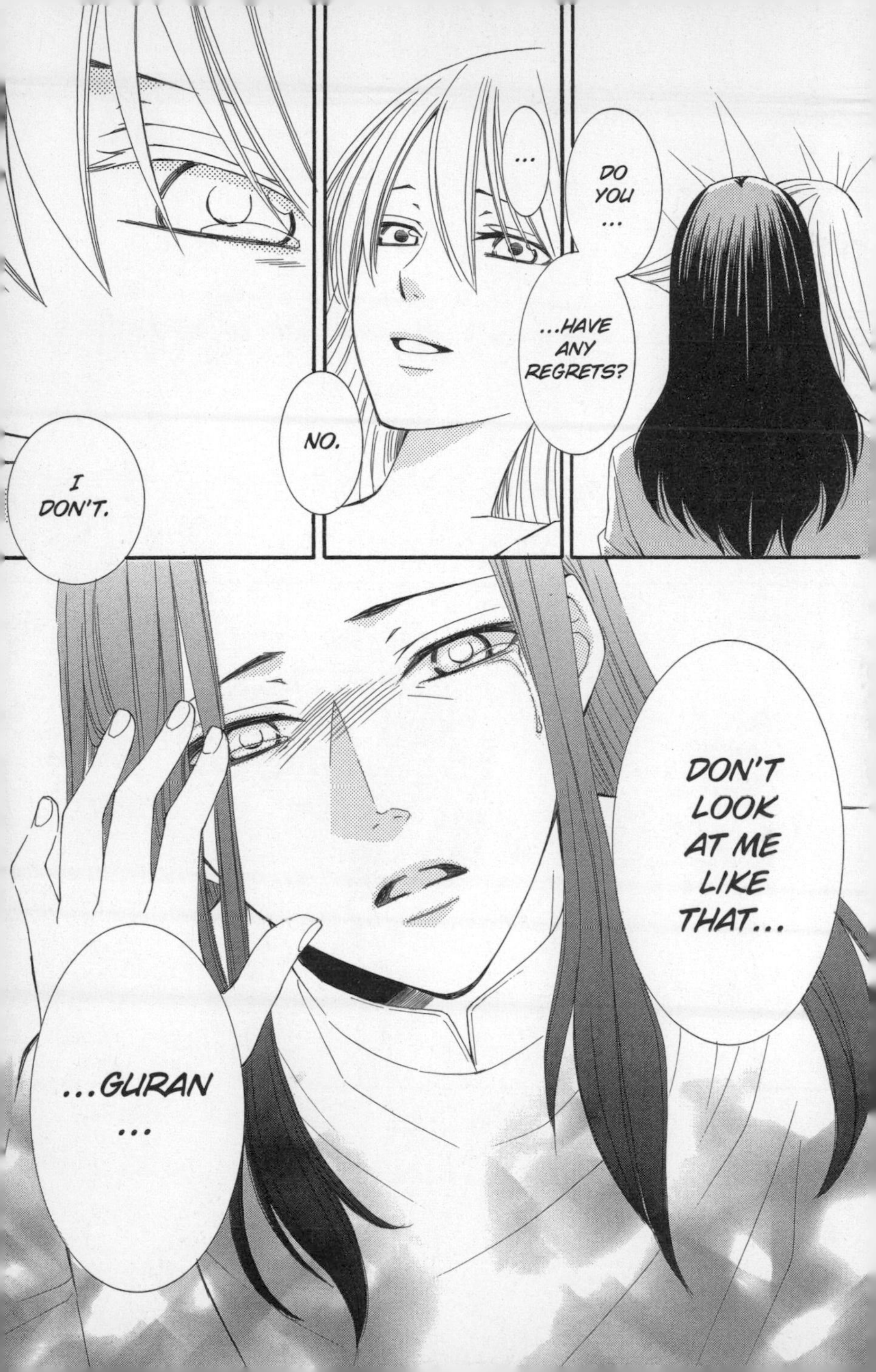
DO YOU ...
...HAVE ANY REGRETS?
...
NO.
I DON'T.
DON'T LOOK AT ME LIKE THAT...
...GURAN ...

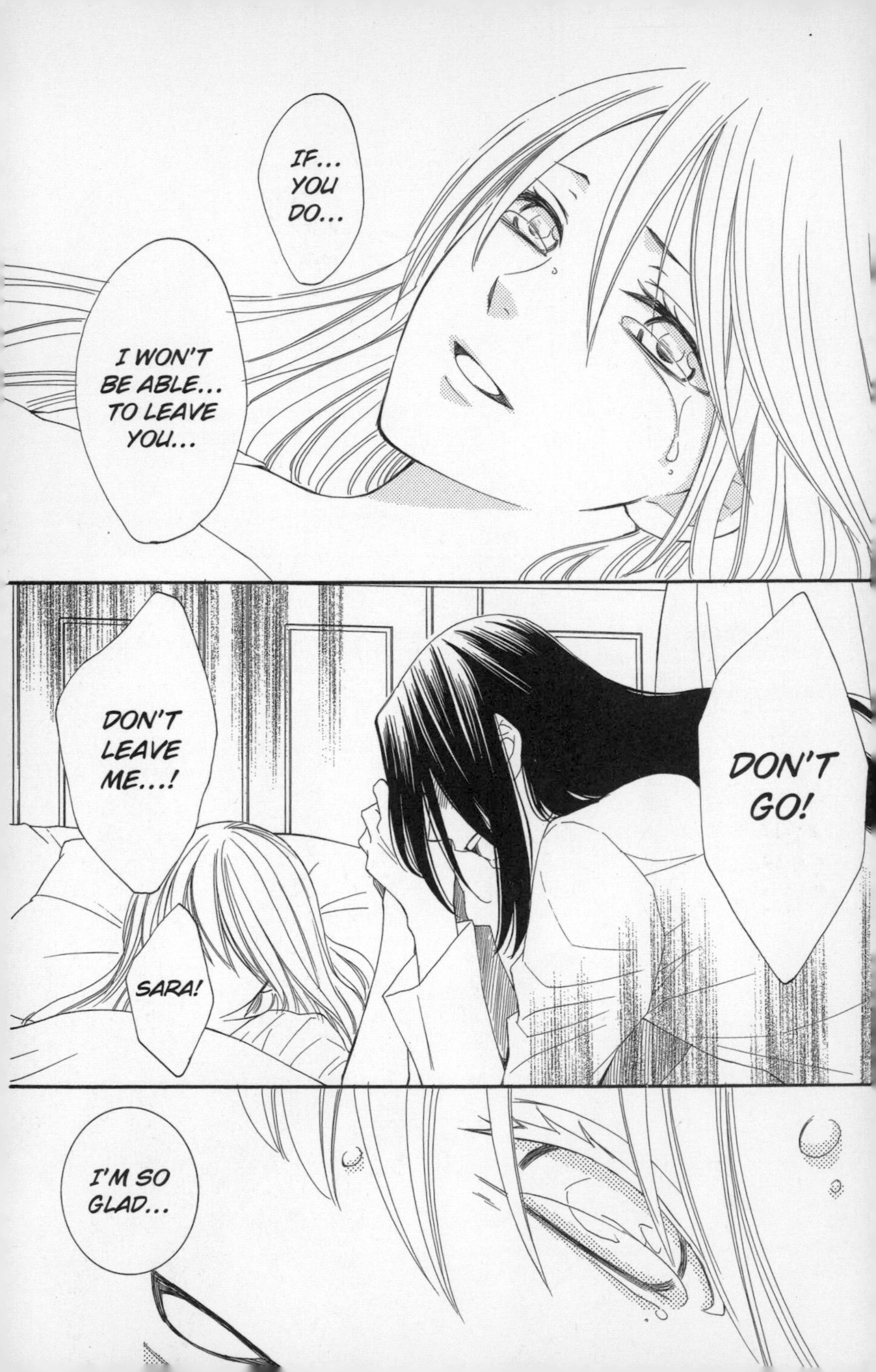
IF... YOU DO...
I WON'T BE ABLE... TO LEAVE YOU...
DON'T GO!
DON'T LEAVE ME...!
SARA!
I'M SO GLAD...

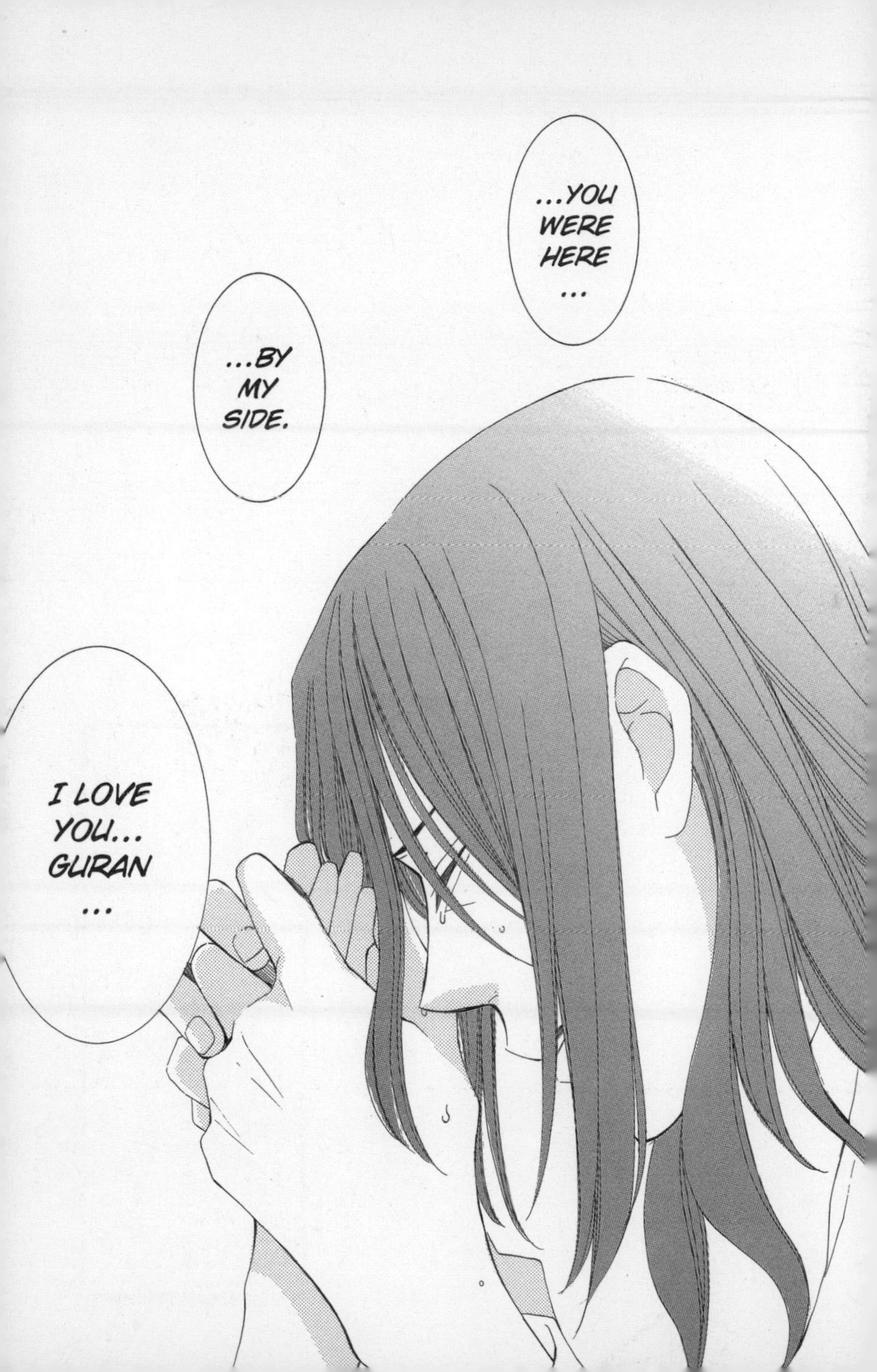
...YOU WERE HERE...
...BY MY SIDE.
I LOVE YOU... GURAN...

Chapter 48

HAPPY
NEW
YEAR

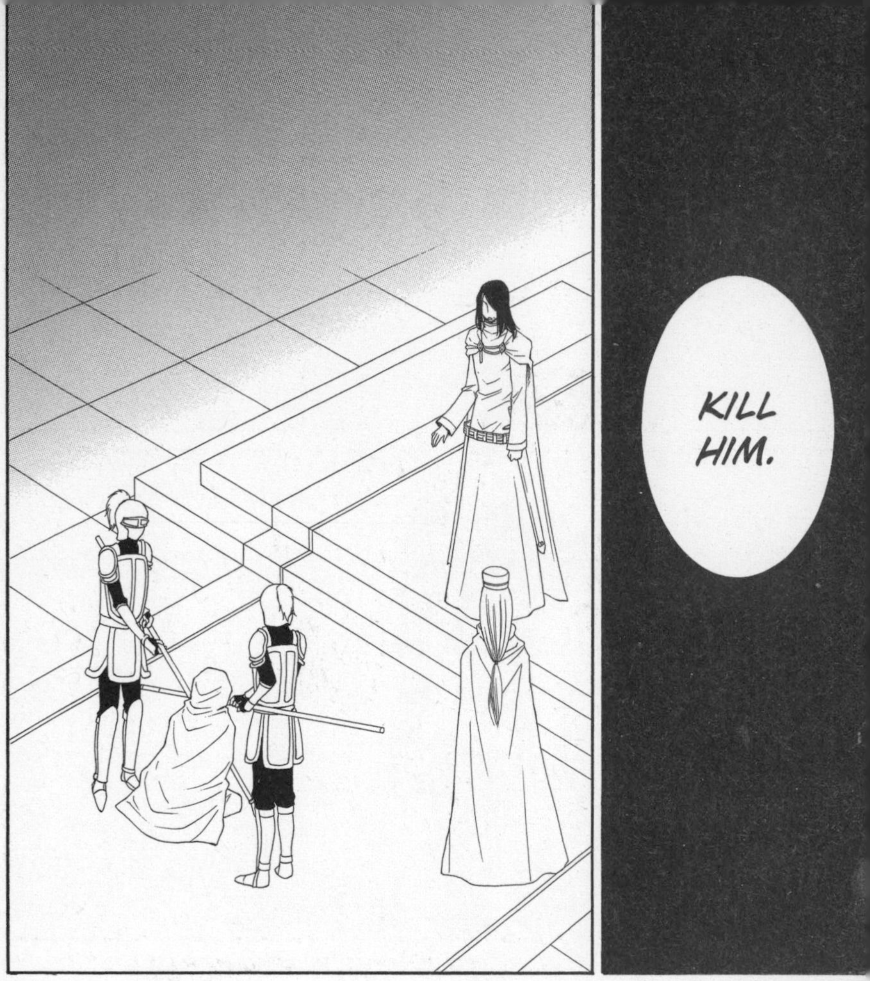
KILL HIM.

Dawn of the Arcana

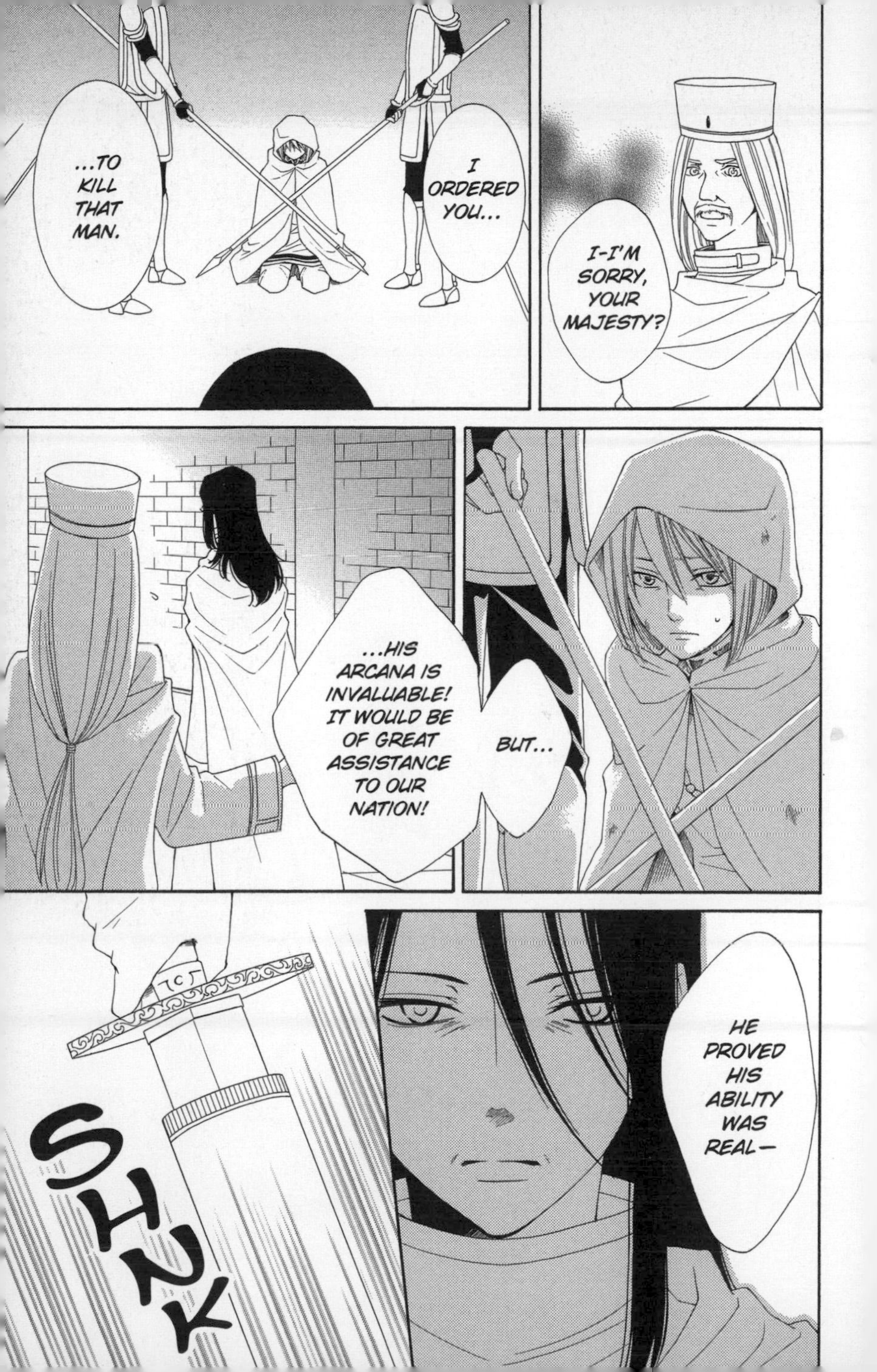
I-I'M SORRY, YOUR MAJESTY?
I ORDERED YOU...
...TO KILL THAT MAN.
BUT...
...HIS ARCANA IS INVALUABLE! IT WOULD BE OF GREAT ASSISTANCE TO OUR NATION!
HE PROVED HIS ABILITY WAS REAL—
SHNK

Y...

YOUR... MAJESTY ...

SHLIK

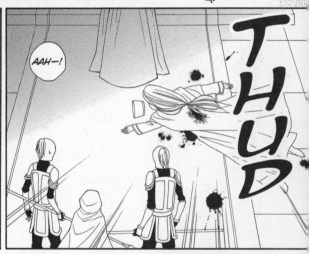

AAH—!

REAL?

THUD

YES, IT CERTAINLY WAS THAT.

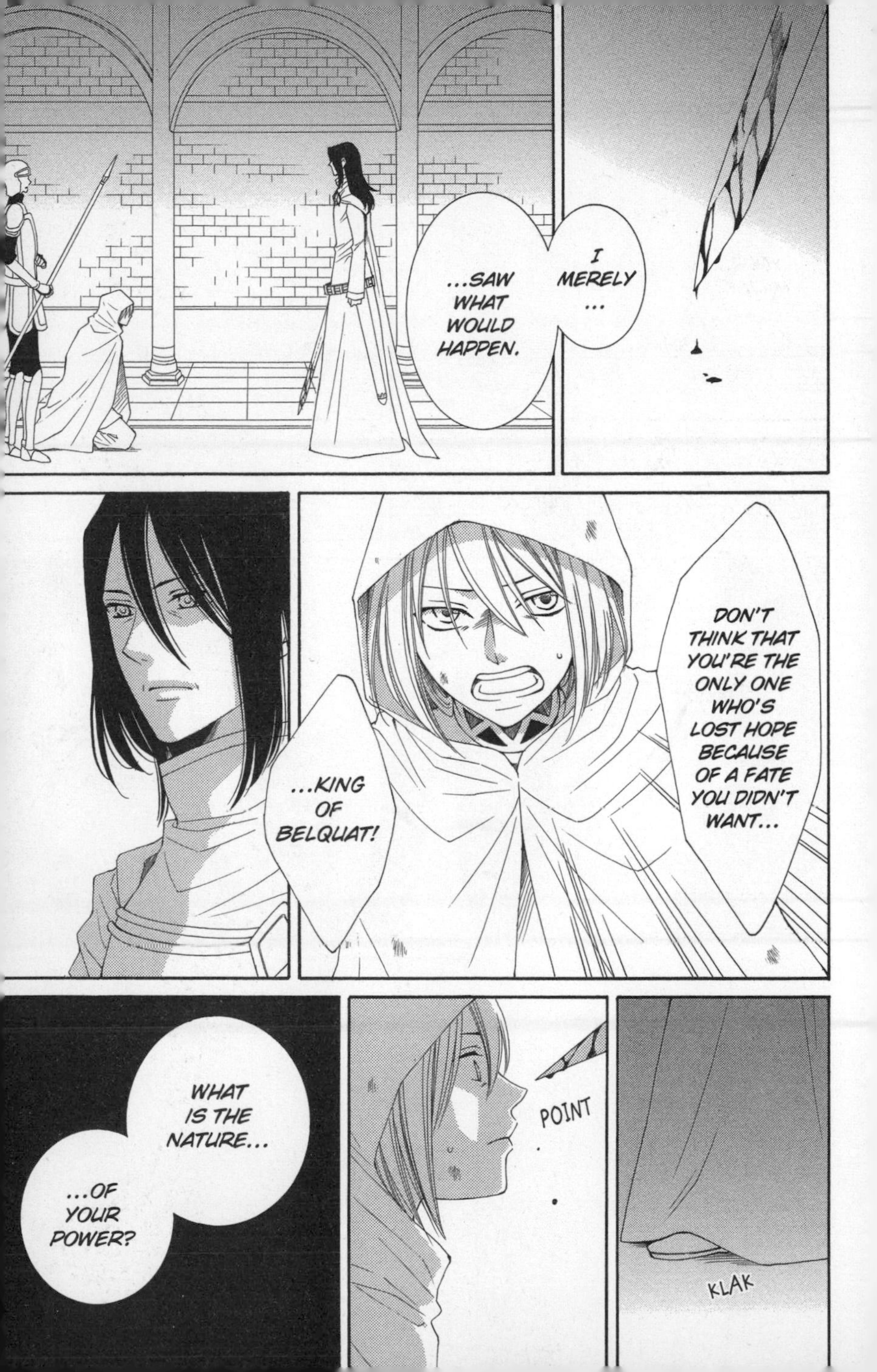
I MERELY...
...SAW WHAT WOULD HAPPEN.
DON'T THINK THAT YOU'RE THE ONLY ONE WHO'S LOST HOPE BECAUSE OF A FATE YOU DIDN'T WANT...
...KING OF BELQUAT!
KLAK
POINT
WHAT IS THE NATURE...
...OF YOUR POWER?

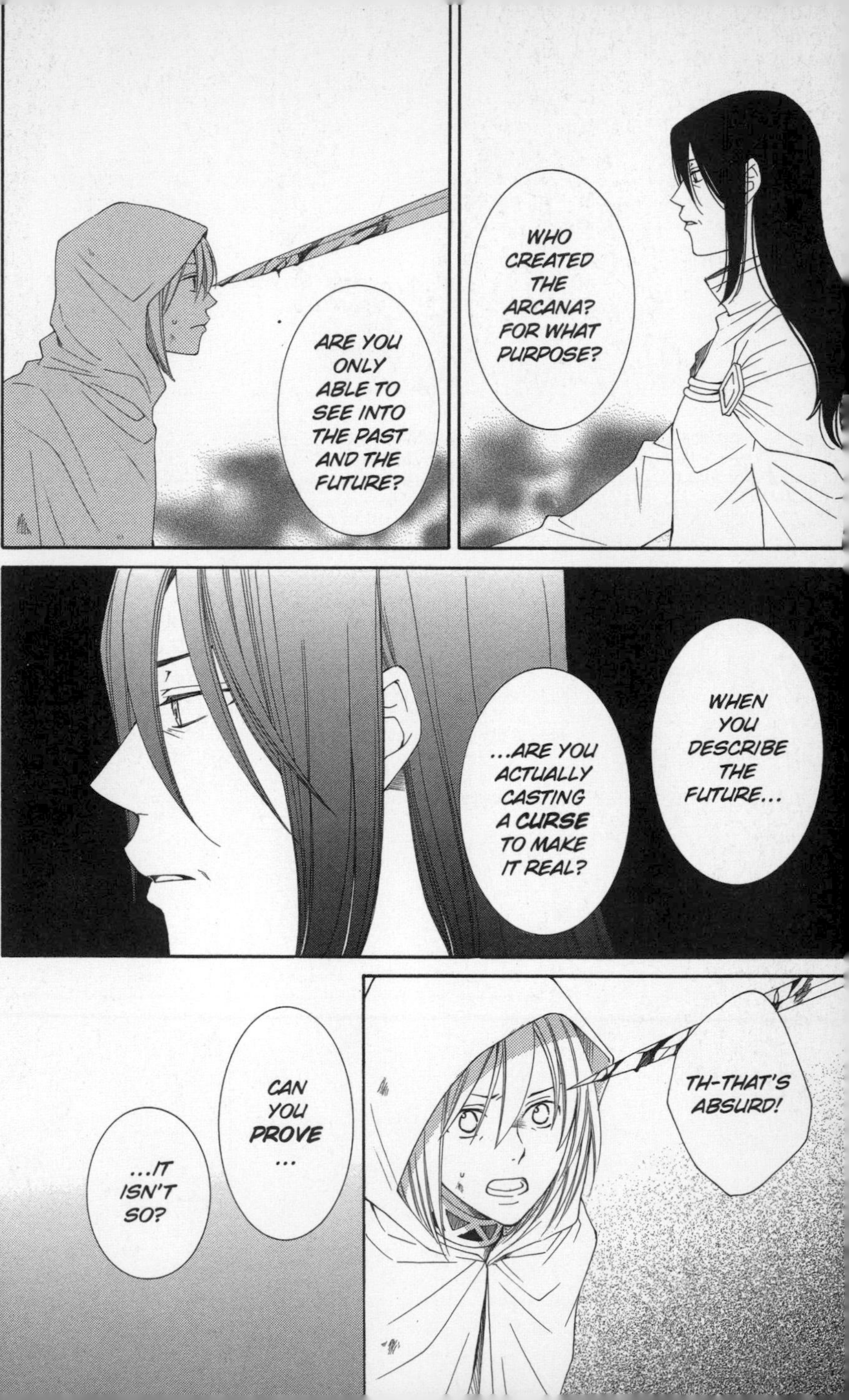
WHO CREATED THE ARCANA? FOR WHAT PURPOSE?
ARE YOU ONLY ABLE TO SEE INTO THE PAST AND THE FUTURE?
WHEN YOU DESCRIBE THE FUTURE...
...ARE YOU ACTUALLY CASTING A CURSE TO MAKE IT REAL?
TH-THAT'S ABSURD!
CAN YOU PROVE...
...IT ISN'T SO?

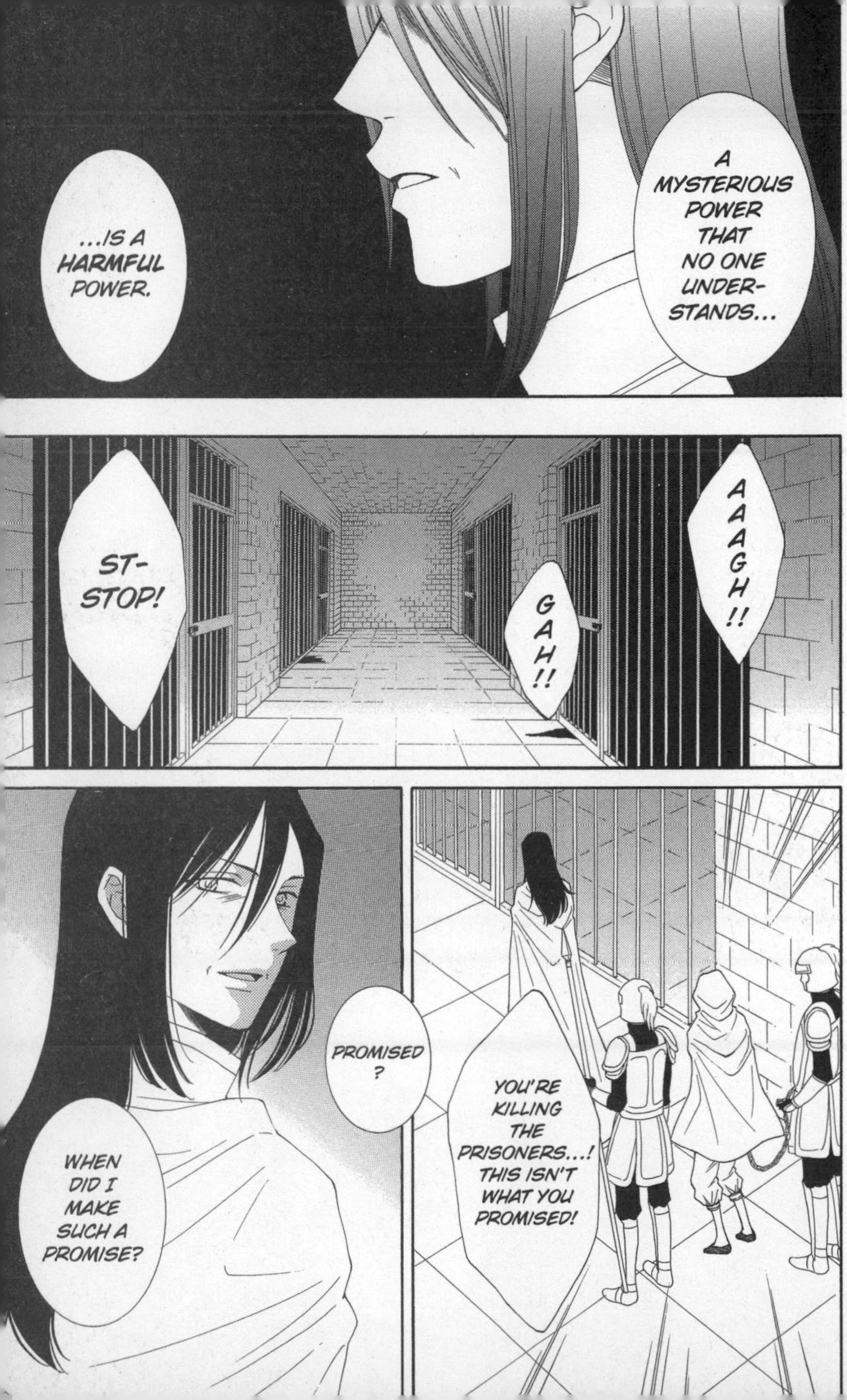
A MYSTERIOUS POWER THAT NO ONE UNDER-STANDS...
...IS A HARMFUL POWER.
AAAAGH!!
GAH!!
ST-STOP!
YOU'RE KILLING THE PRISONERS...! THIS ISN'T WHAT YOU PROMISED!
PROMISED?
WHEN DID I MAKE SUCH A PROMISE?

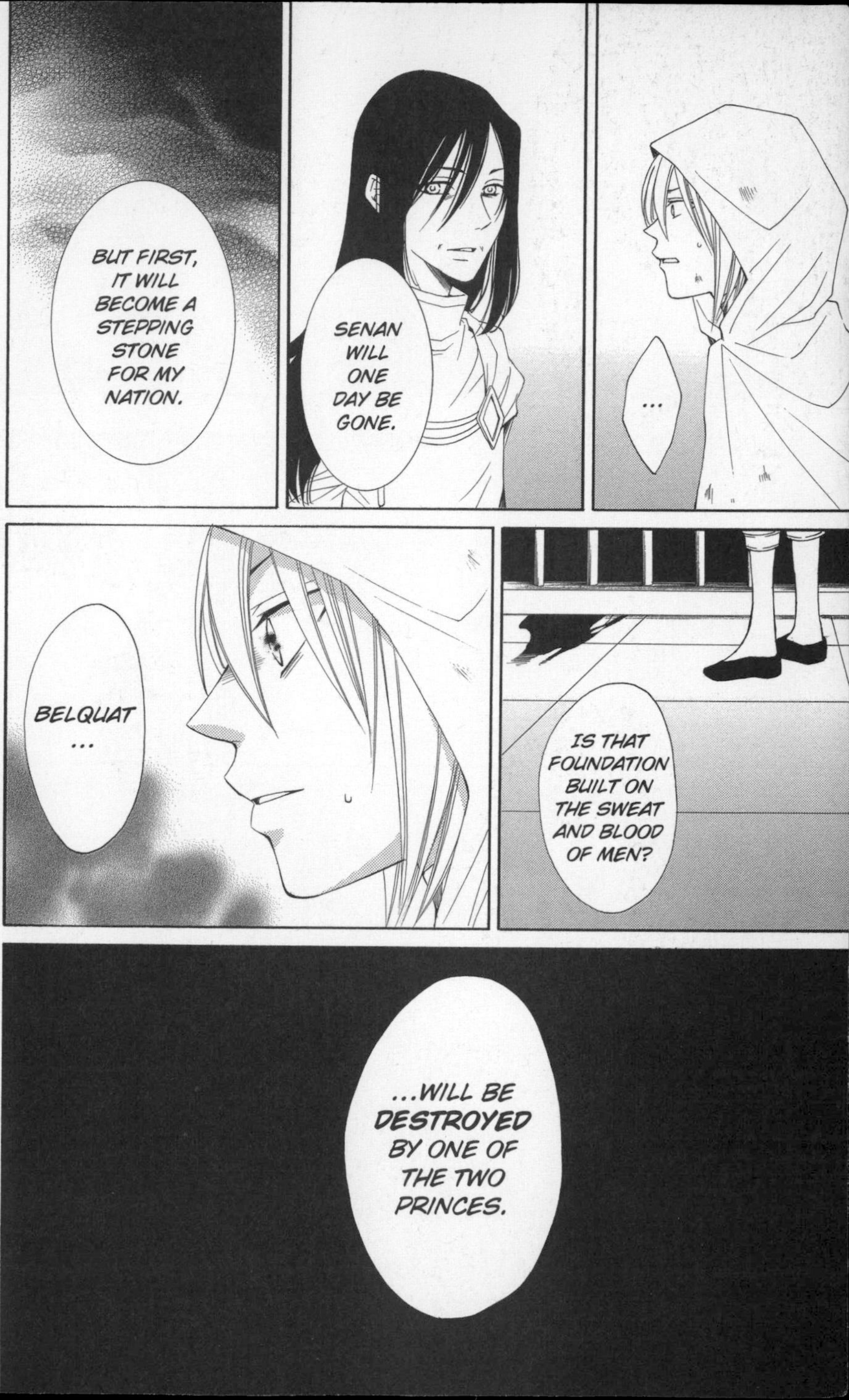
...
SENAN WILL ONE DAY BE GONE.
BUT FIRST, IT WILL BECOME A STEPPING STONE FOR MY NATION.
IS THAT FOUNDATION BUILT ON THE SWEAT AND BLOOD OF MEN?
BELQUAT ...
...WILL BE DESTROYED BY ONE OF THE TWO PRINCES.

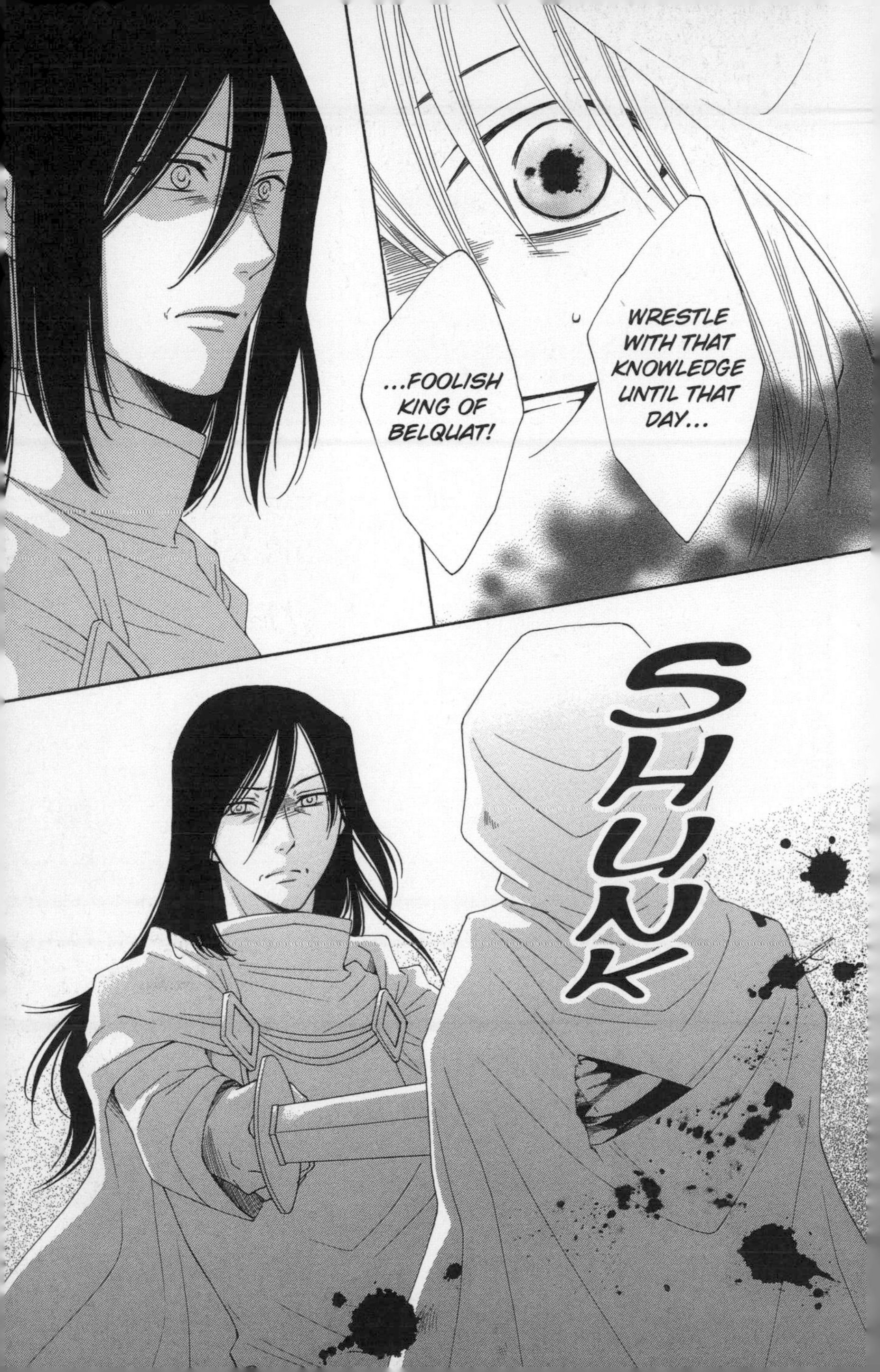
WRESTLE WITH THAT KNOWLEDGE UNTIL THAT DAY...
...FOOLISH KING OF BELQUAT!
SHUNK

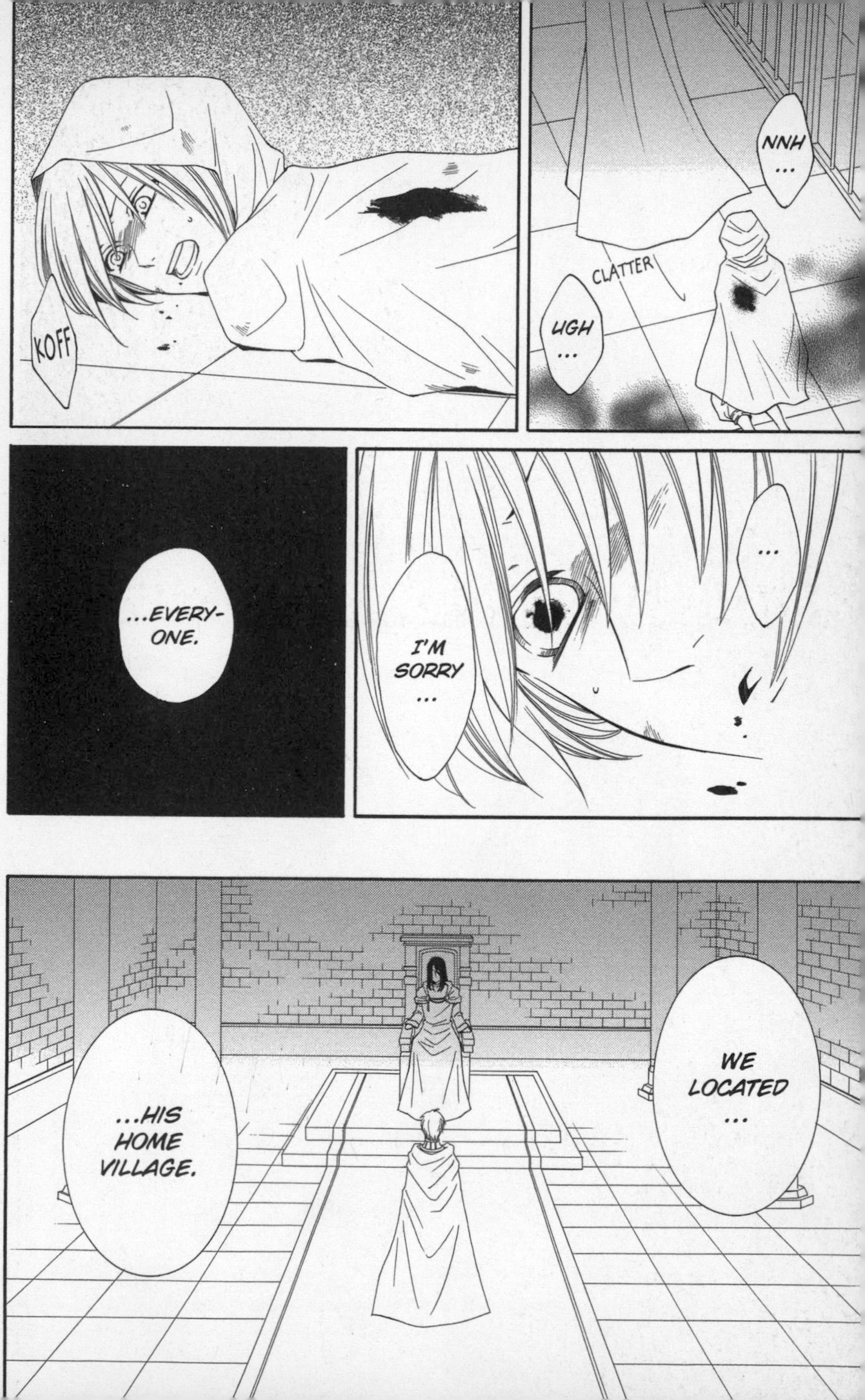
NNH...
CLATTER
UGH...
KOFF
...
I'M SORRY...
...EVERY-ONE.
WE LOCATED...
...HIS HOME VILLAGE.

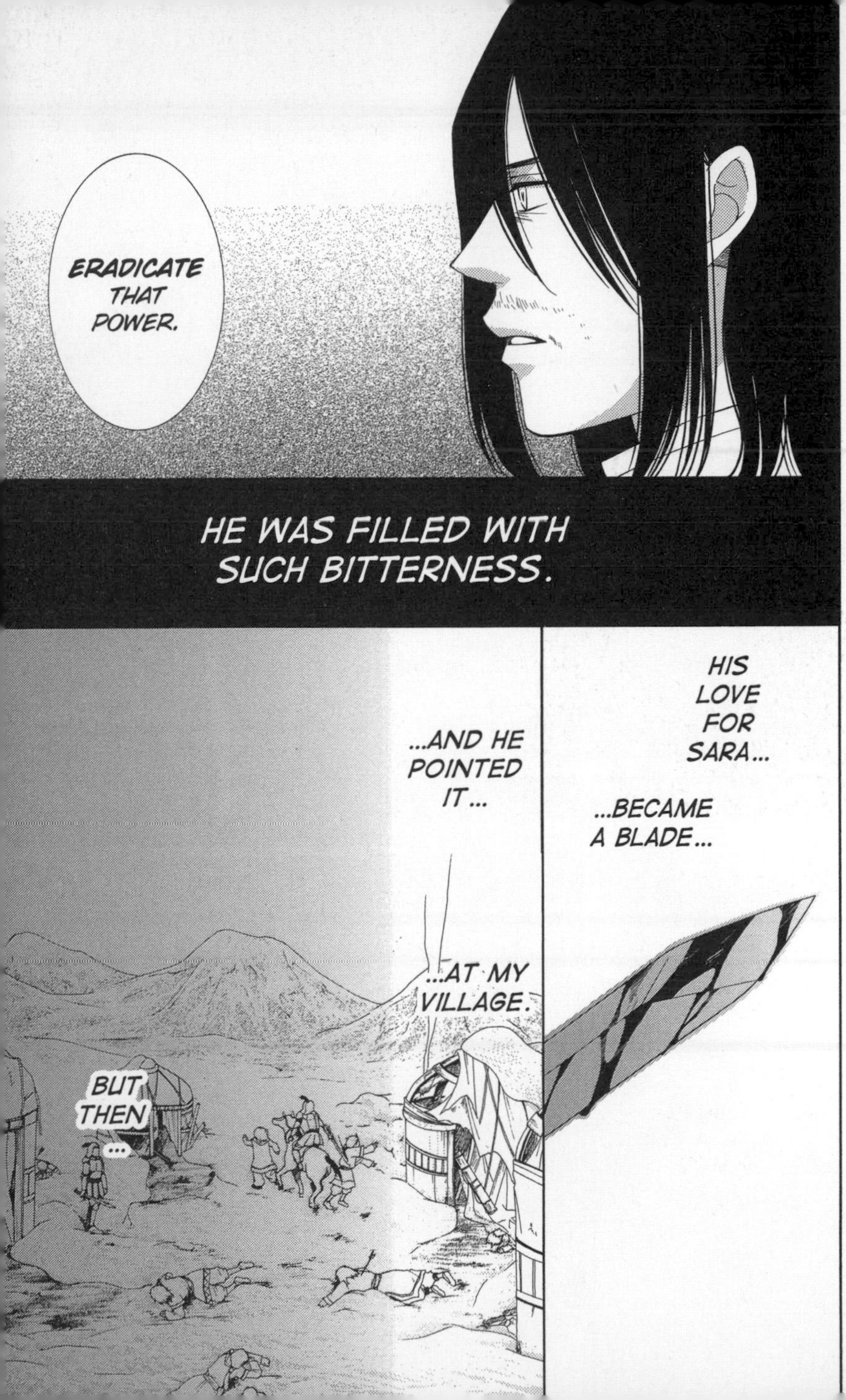
ERADICATE THAT POWER.
HE WAS FILLED WITH SUCH BITTERNESS.
HIS LOVE FOR SARA...
...BECAME A BLADE...
...AND HE POINTED IT...
...AT MY VILLAGE.
BUT THEN ...

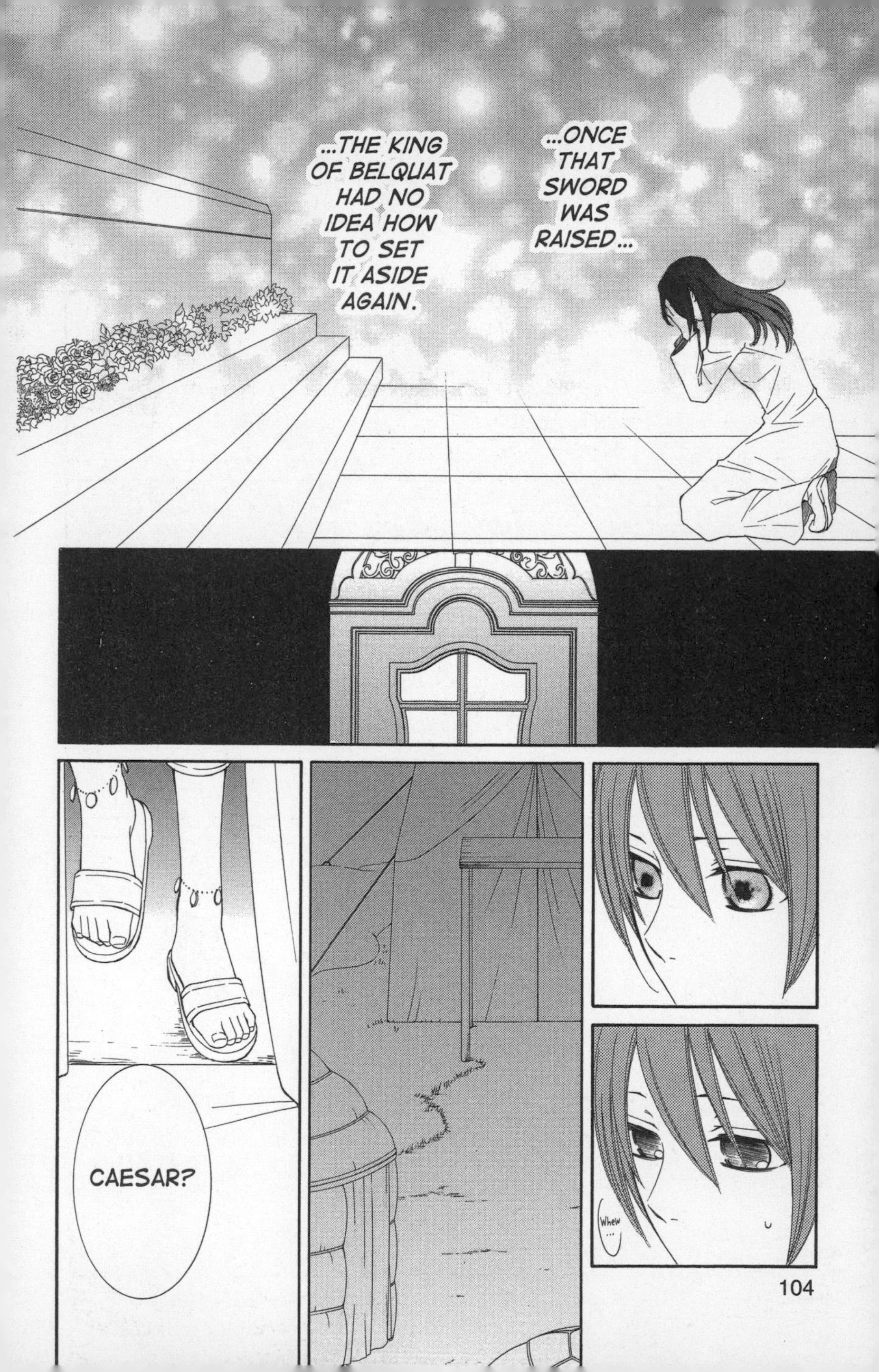
...ONCE THAT SWORD WAS RAISED...
...THE KING OF BELQUAT HAD NO IDEA HOW TO SET IT ASIDE AGAIN.
Whew...
CAESAR?

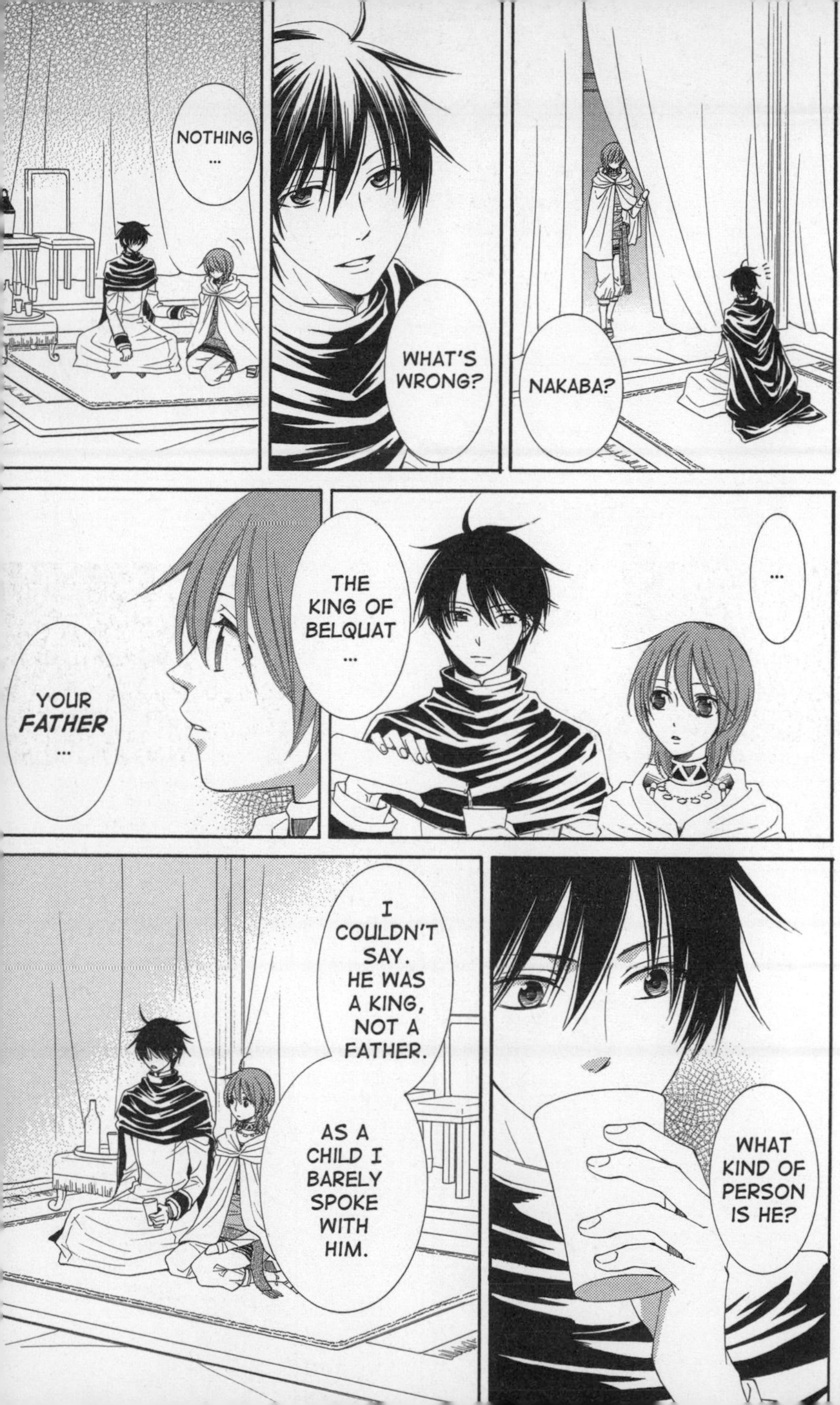
NAKABA?
WHAT'S WRONG?
NOTHING ...
...
THE KING OF BELQUAT ...
YOUR *FATHER* ...
WHAT KIND OF PERSON IS HE?
I COULDN'T SAY. HE WAS A KING, NOT A FATHER.
AS A CHILD I BARELY SPOKE WITH HIM.

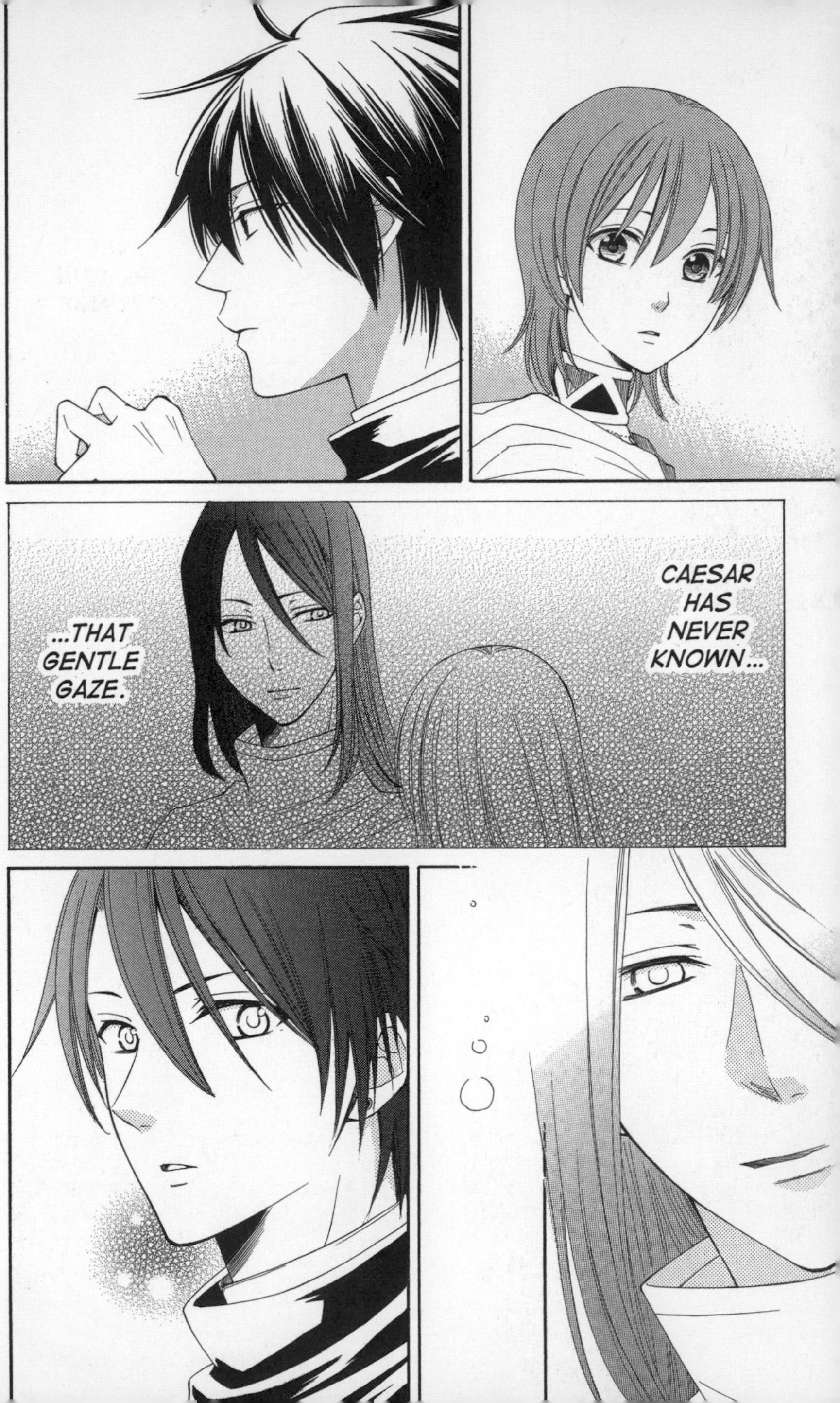
CAESAR HAS NEVER KNOWN...
...THAT GENTLE GAZE.

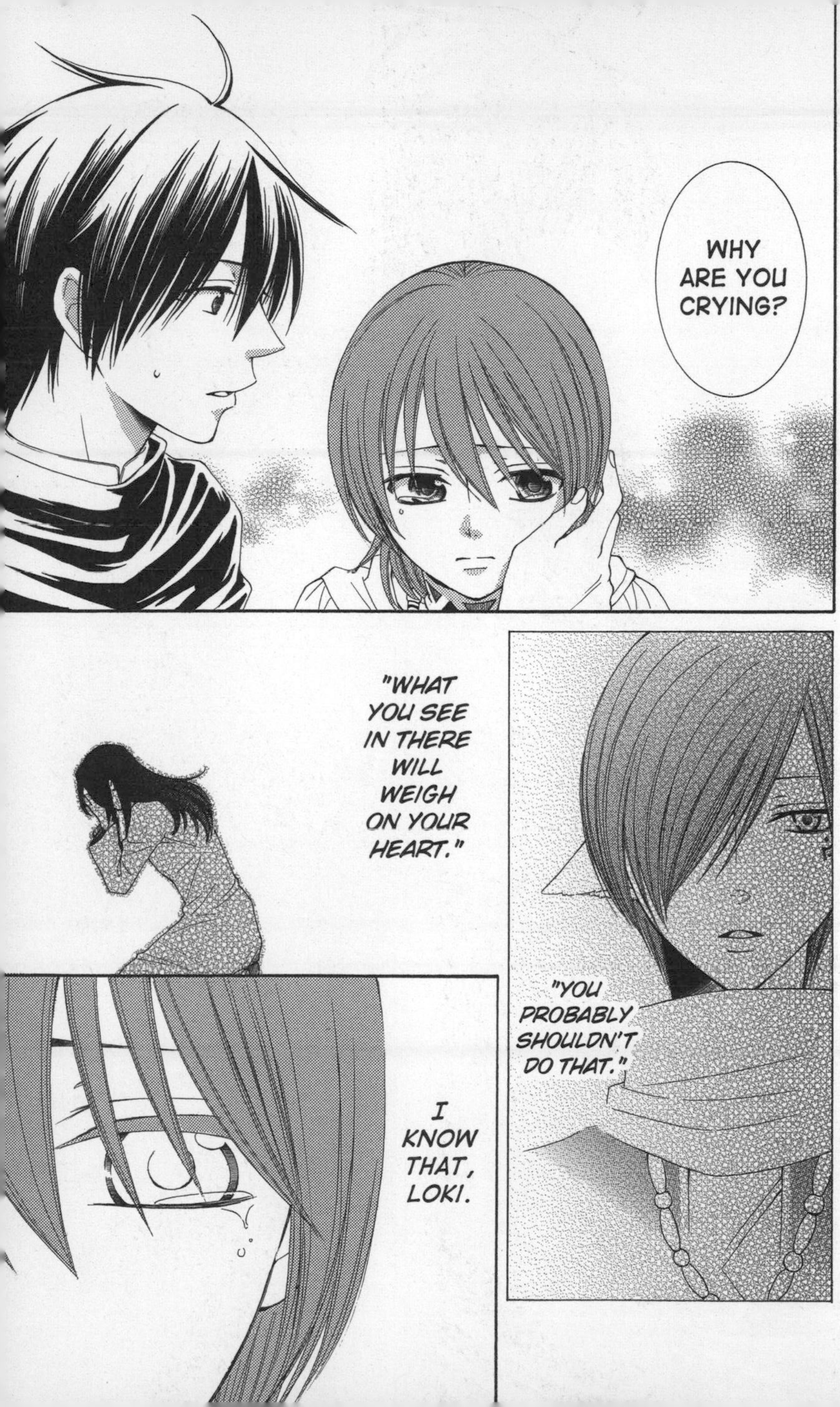
WHY ARE YOU CRYING?
"YOU PROBABLY SHOULDN'T DO THAT."
"WHAT YOU SEE IN THERE WILL WEIGH ON YOUR HEART."
I KNOW THAT, LOKI.

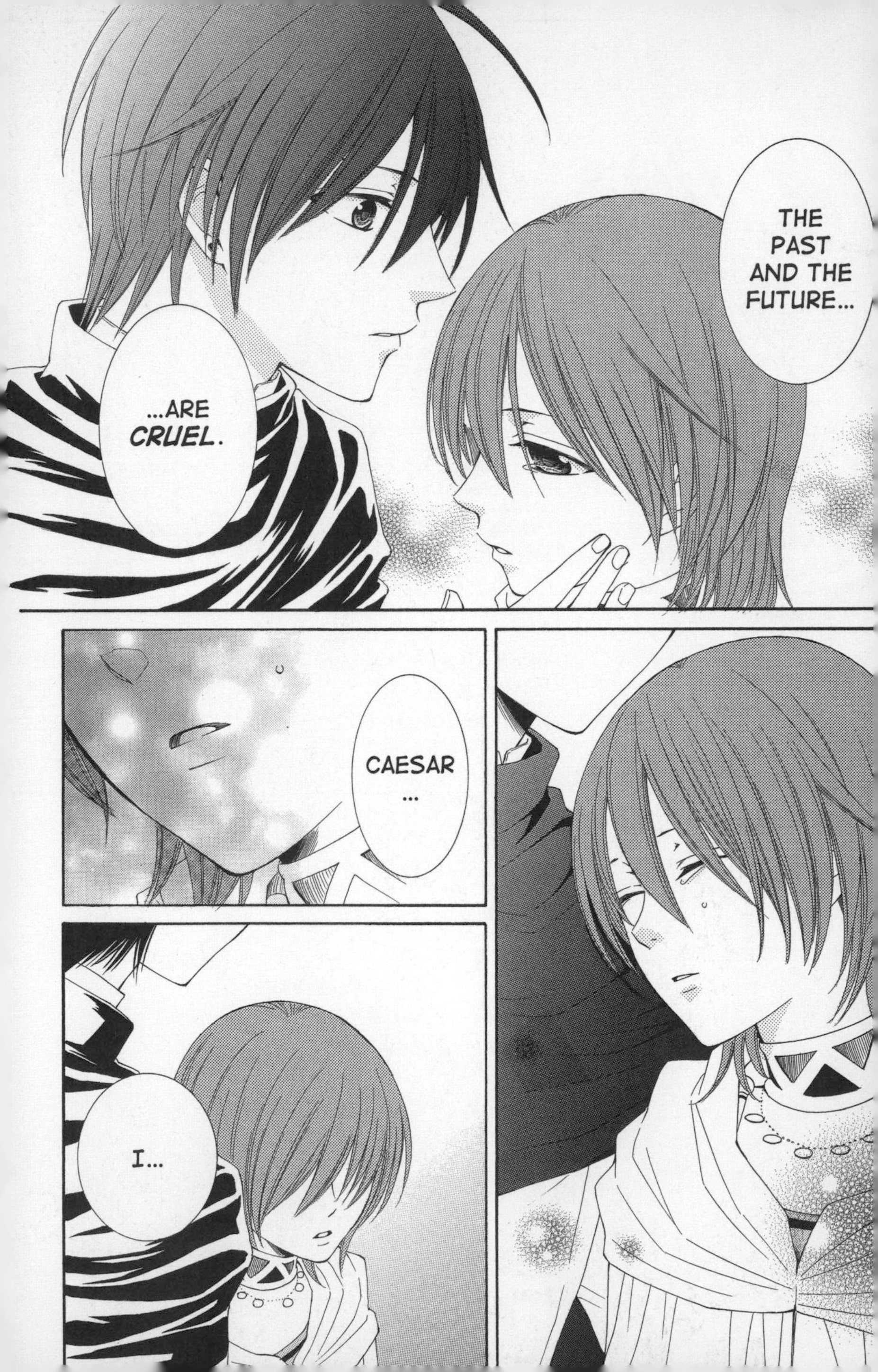
THE PAST AND THE FUTURE...
...ARE CRUEL.
CAESAR ...
I...

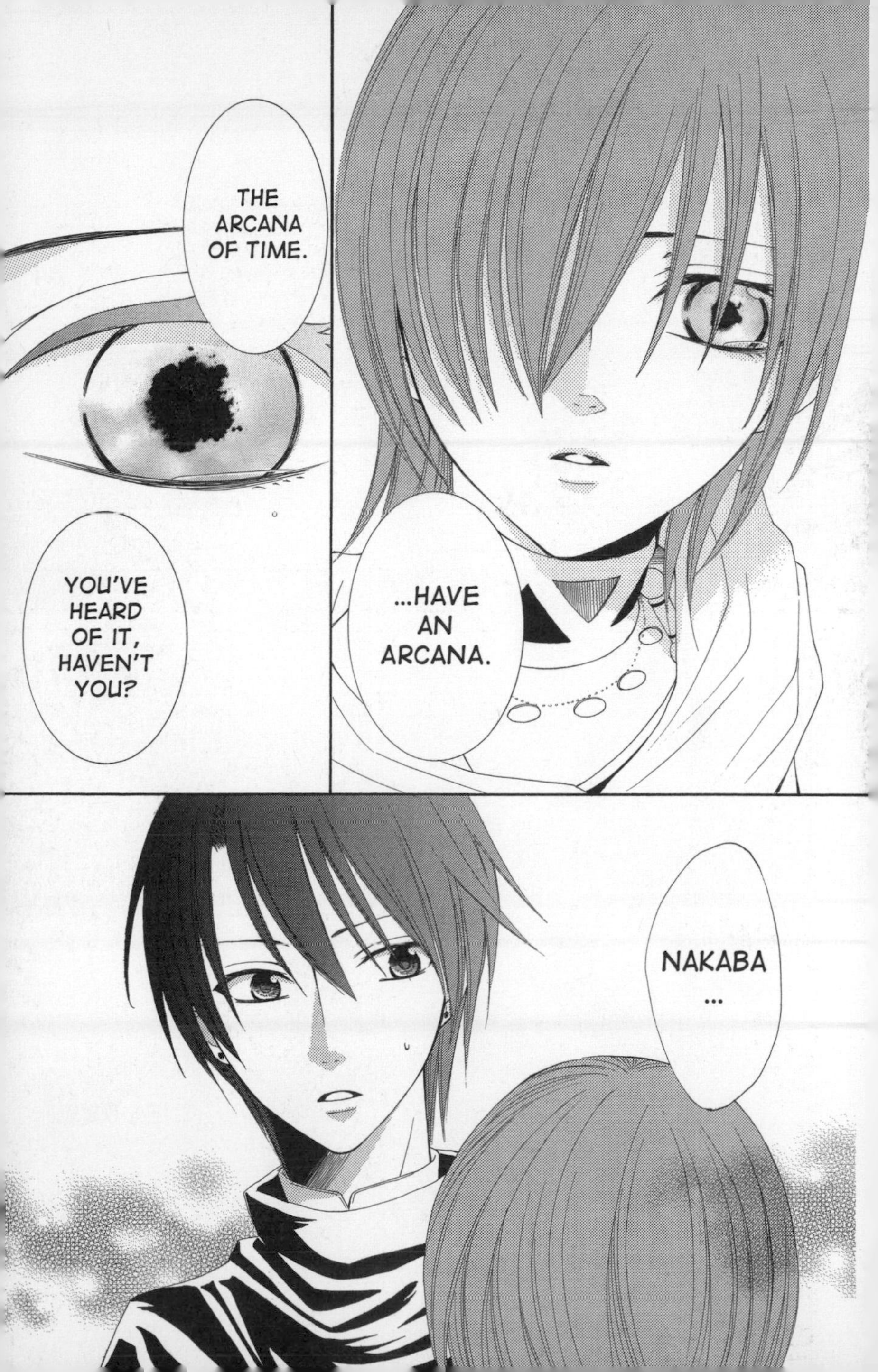
...HAVE AN ARCANA.
THE ARCANA OF TIME.
YOU'VE HEARD OF IT, HAVEN'T YOU?
NAKABA ...

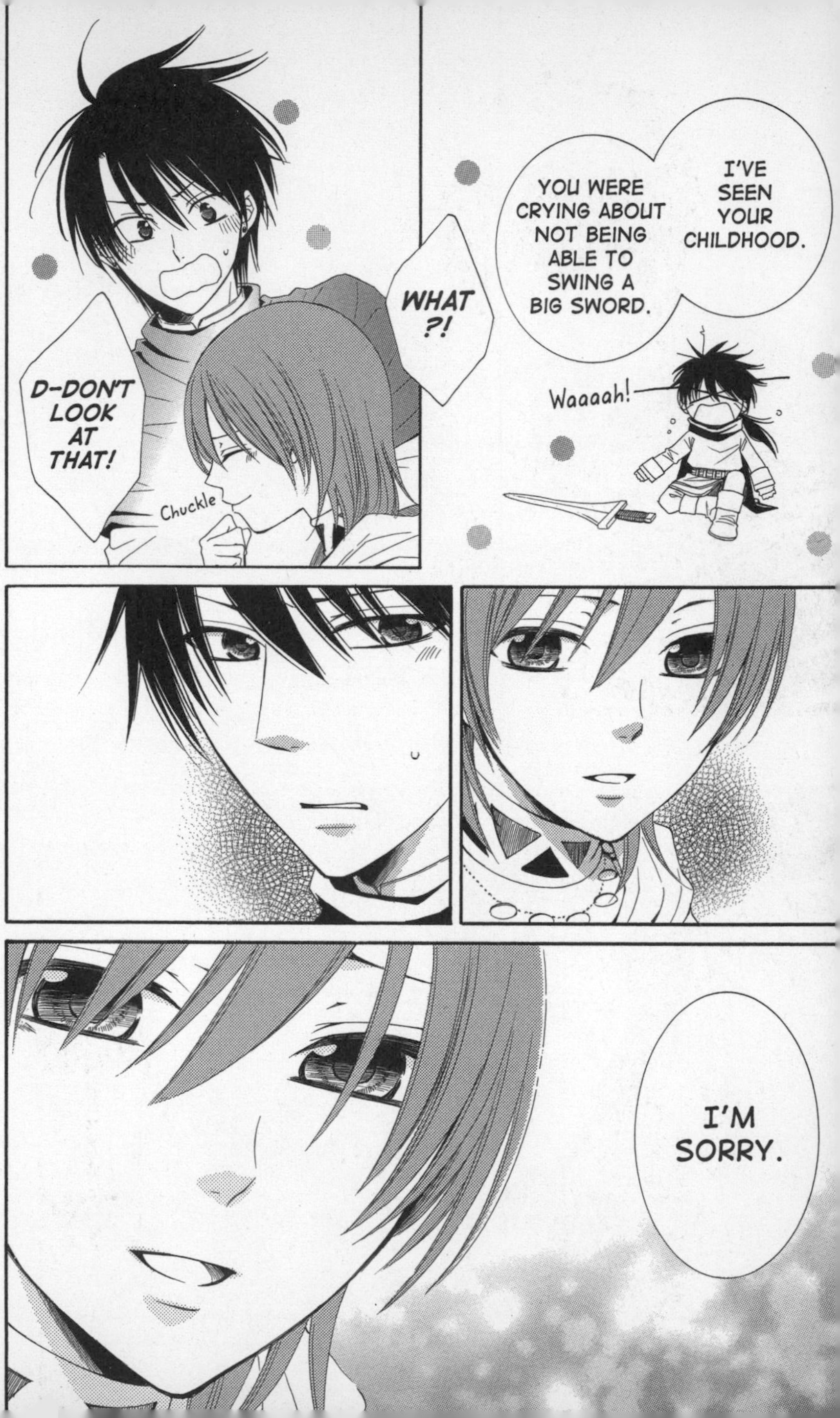
I'VE SEEN YOUR CHILDHOOD.
YOU WERE CRYING ABOUT NOT BEING ABLE TO SWING A BIG SWORD.
Waaaah!
WHAT?!
D-DON'T LOOK AT THAT!
Chuckle
I'M SORRY.

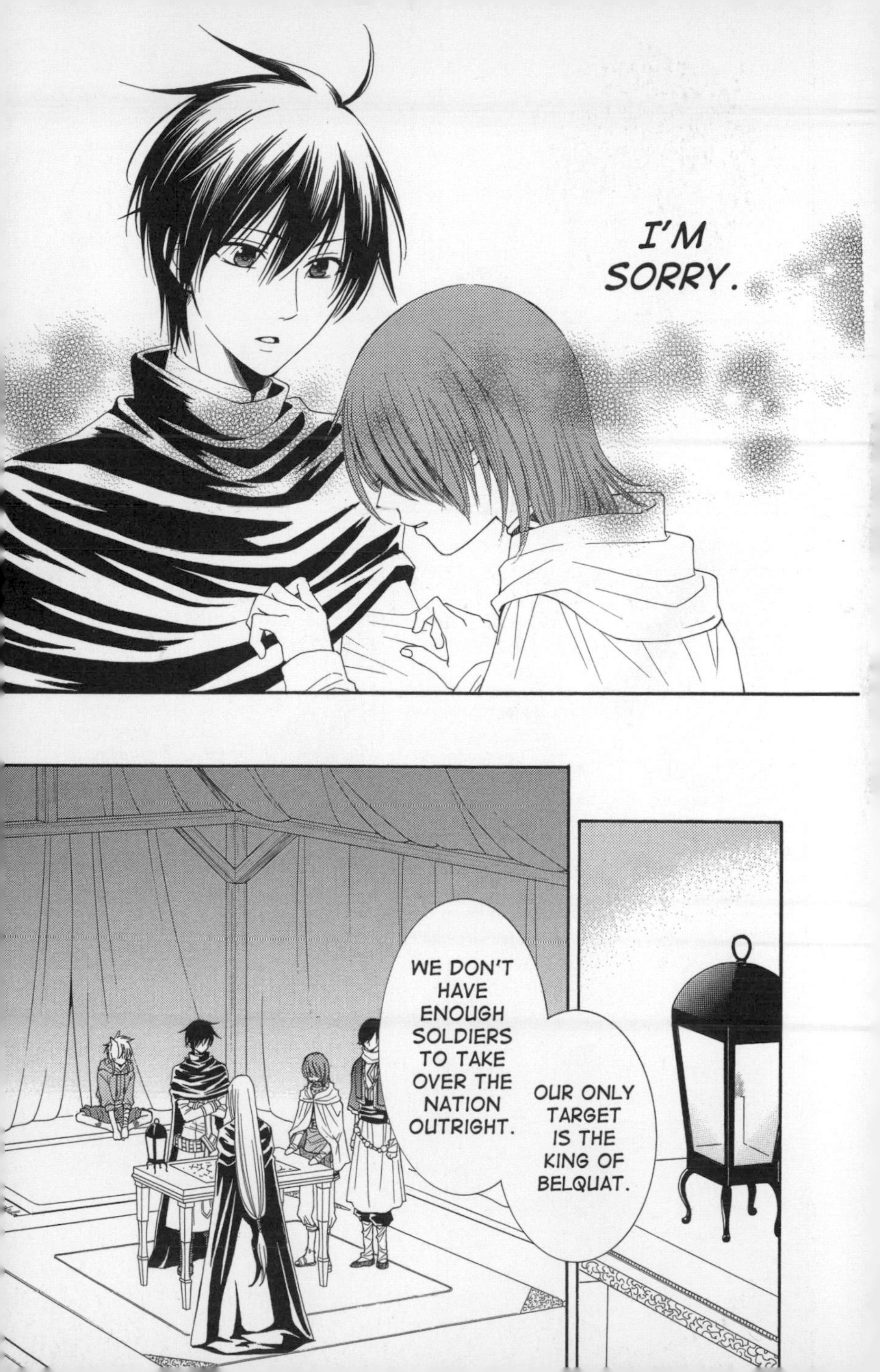
I'M SORRY.
WE DON'T HAVE ENOUGH SOLDIERS TO TAKE OVER THE NATION OUTRIGHT.
OUR ONLY TARGET IS THE KING OF BELQUAT.

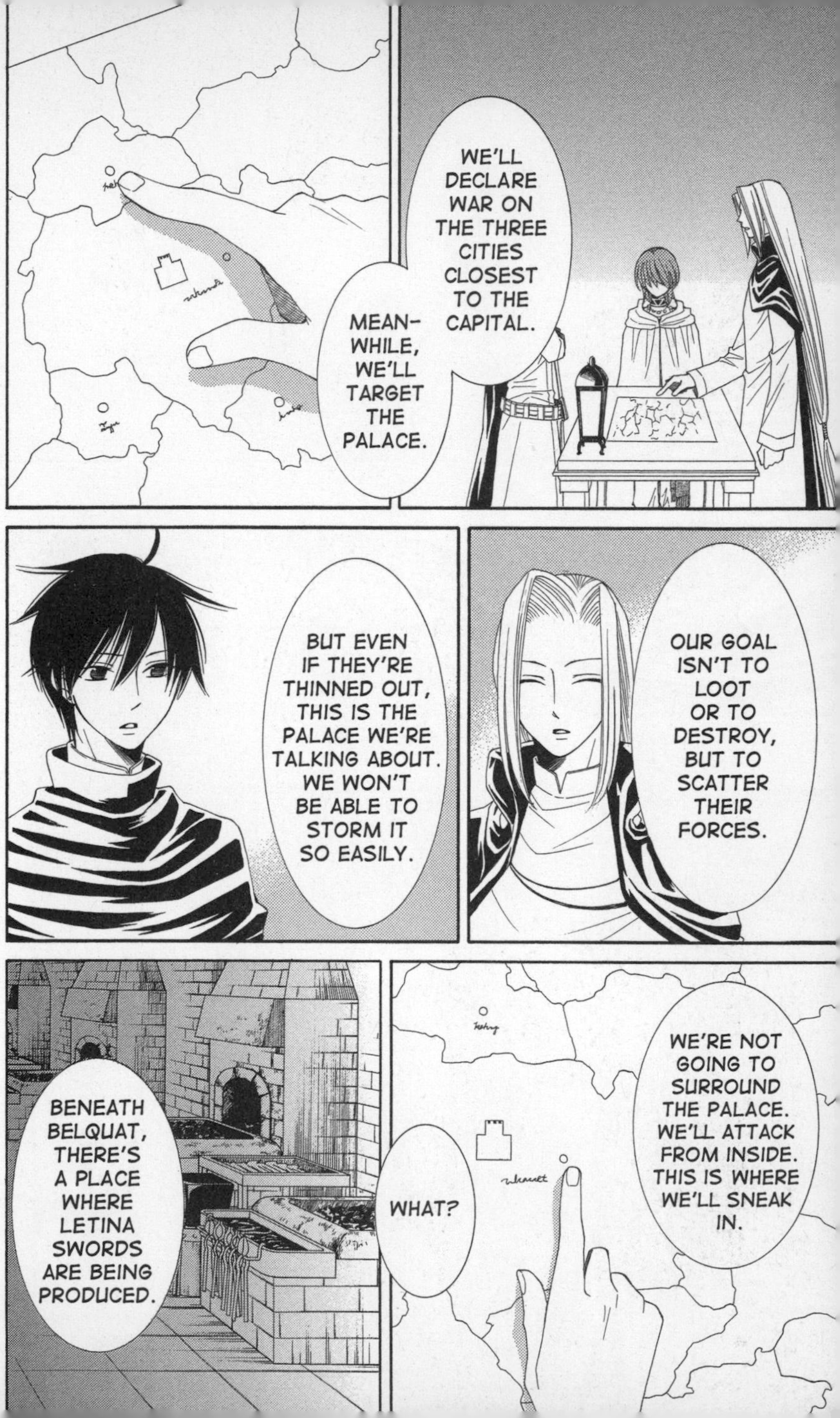
WE'LL DECLARE WAR ON THE THREE CITIES CLOSEST TO THE CAPITAL.
MEAN-WHILE, WE'LL TARGET THE PALACE.
OUR GOAL ISN'T TO LOOT OR TO DESTROY, BUT TO SCATTER THEIR FORCES.
BUT EVEN IF THEY'RE THINNED OUT, THIS IS THE PALACE WE'RE TALKING ABOUT. WE WON'T BE ABLE TO STORM IT SO EASILY.
WE'RE NOT GOING TO SURROUND THE PALACE. WE'LL ATTACK FROM INSIDE. THIS IS WHERE WE'LL SNEAK IN.
WHAT?
BENEATH BELQUAT, THERE'S A PLACE WHERE LETINA SWORDS ARE BEING PRODUCED.

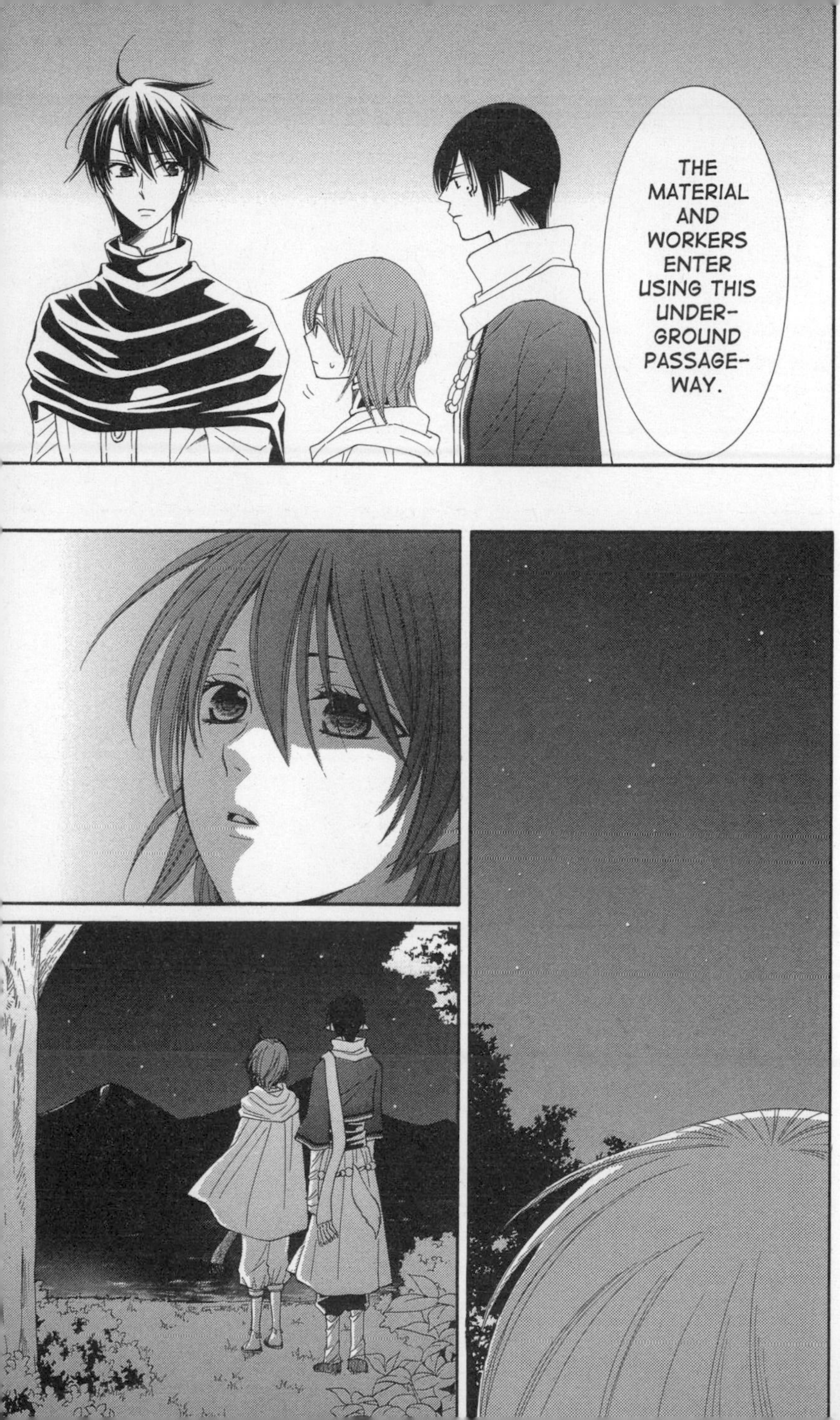
THE MATERIAL AND WORKERS ENTER USING THIS UNDER-GROUND PASSAGE-WAY.

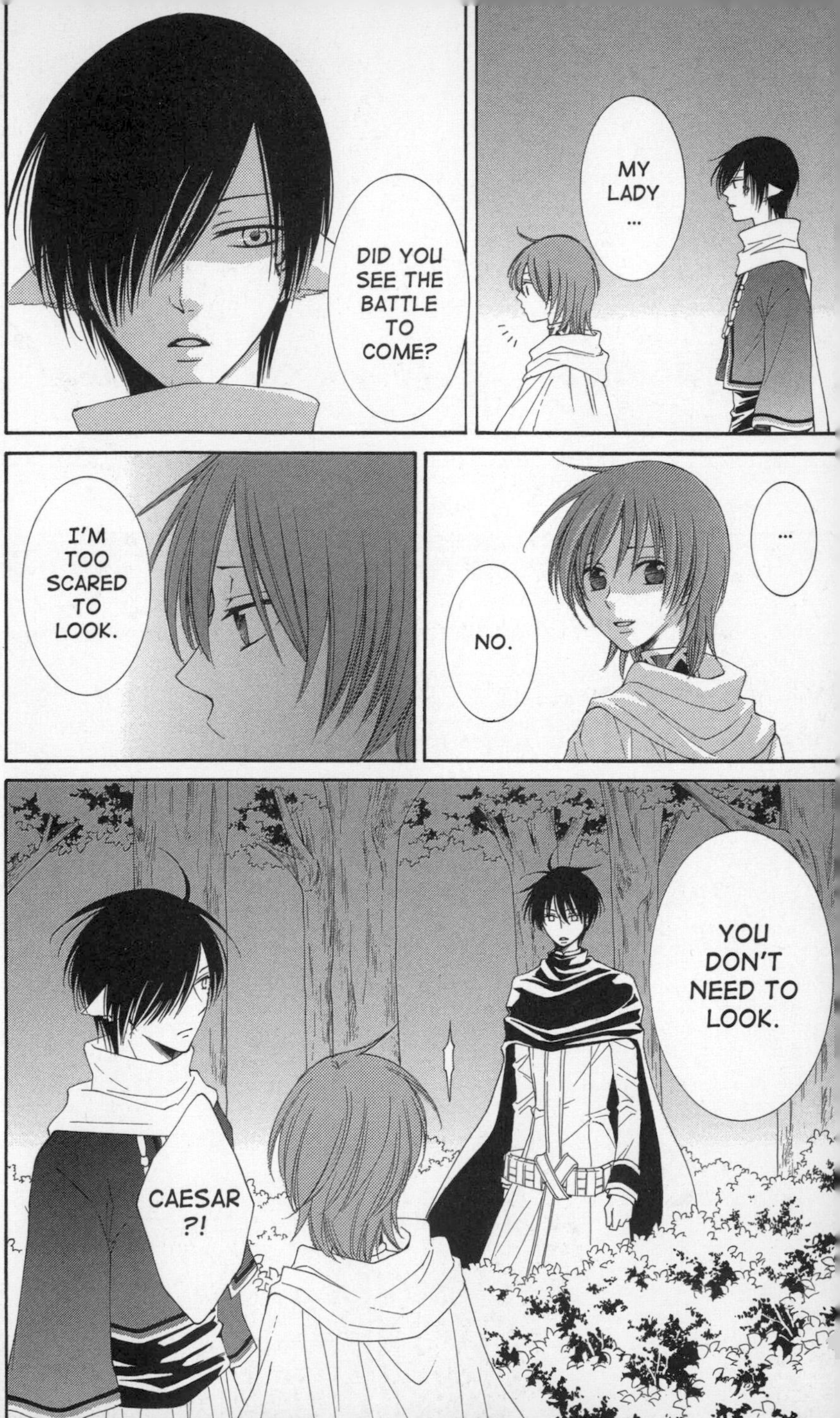
MY LADY ...
DID YOU SEE THE BATTLE TO COME?
...
NO.
I'M TOO SCARED TO LOOK.
YOU DON'T NEED TO LOOK.
CAESAR?!

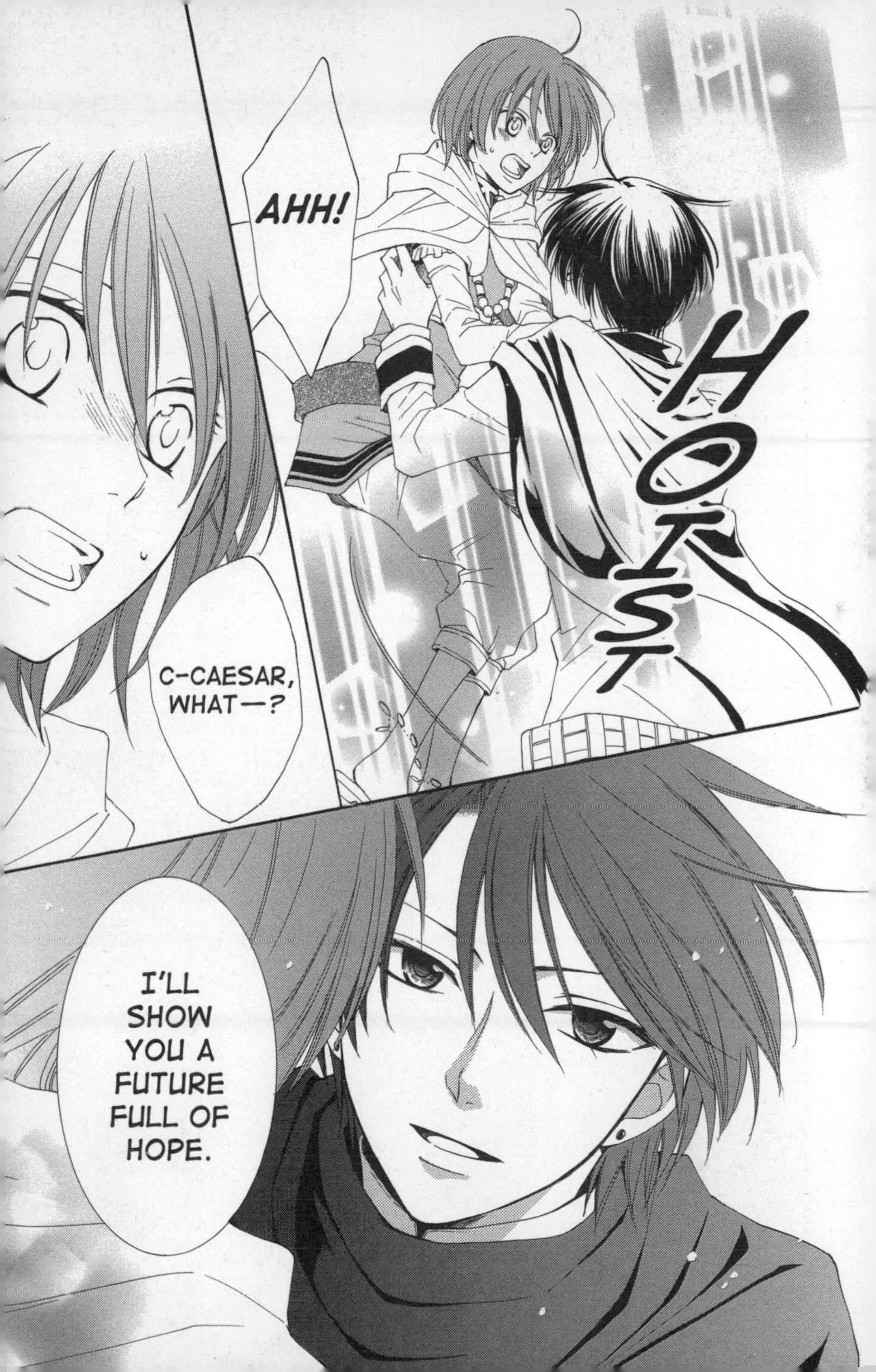
AHH!
HOIST
C-CAESAR, WHAT—?
I'LL SHOW YOU A FUTURE FULL OF HOPE.

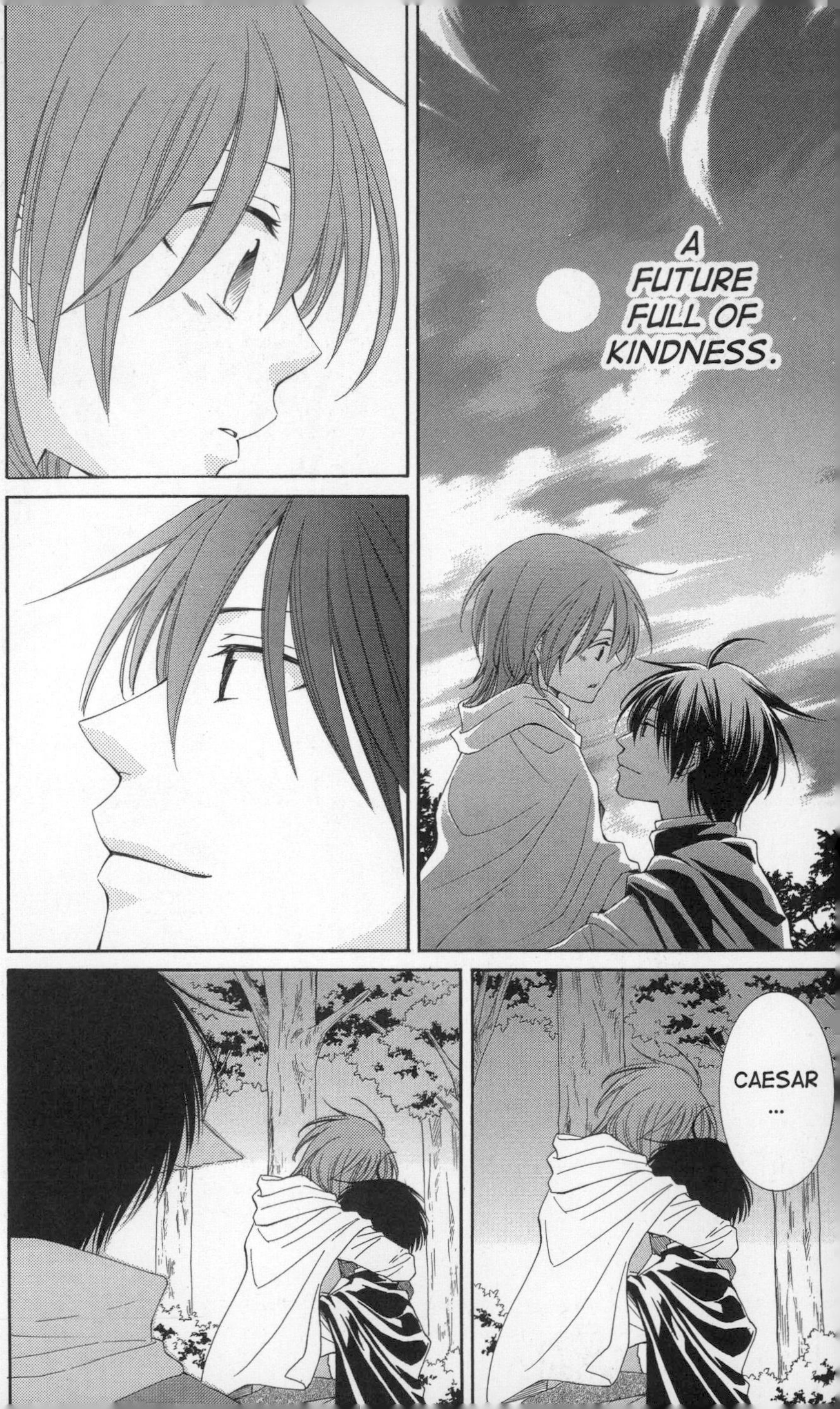
A FUTURE FULL OF KINDNESS.
CAESAR ...

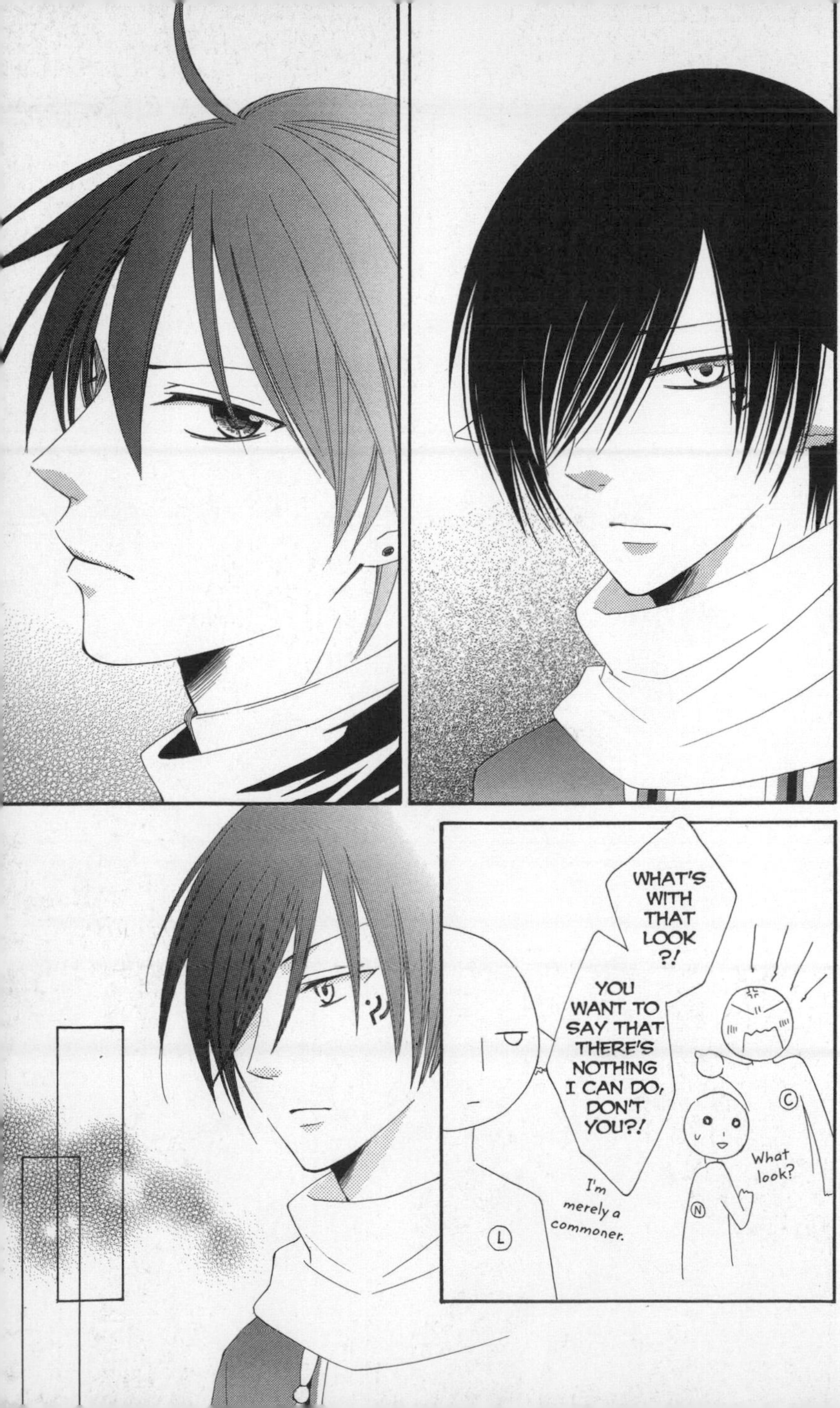
WHAT'S WITH THAT LOOK?!
YOU WANT TO SAY THAT THERE'S NOTHING I CAN DO, DON'T YOU?!
C
What look?
N
I'm merely a commoner.
L

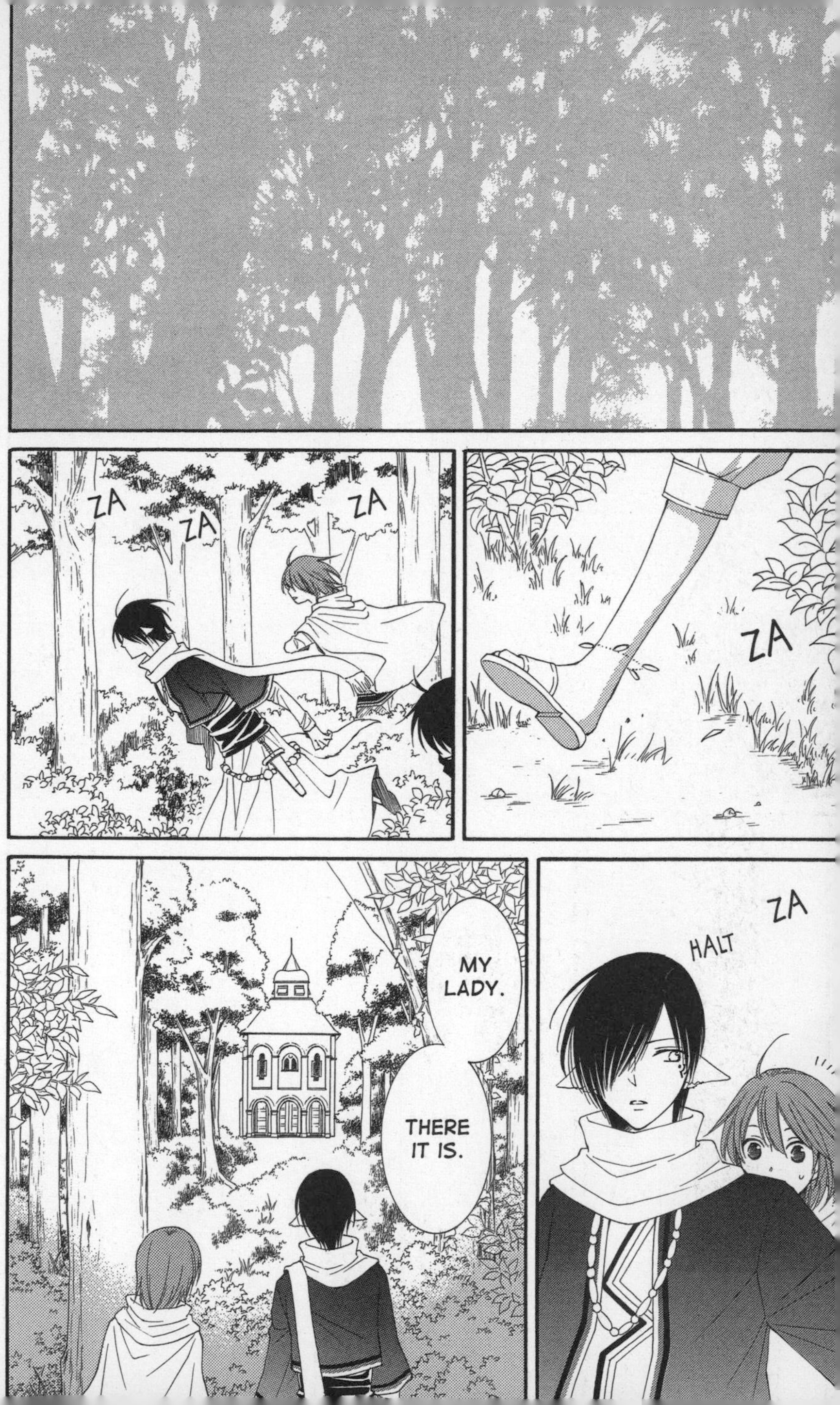
ZA
ZA
ZA
ZA
ZA
HALT
MY LADY.
THERE IT IS.

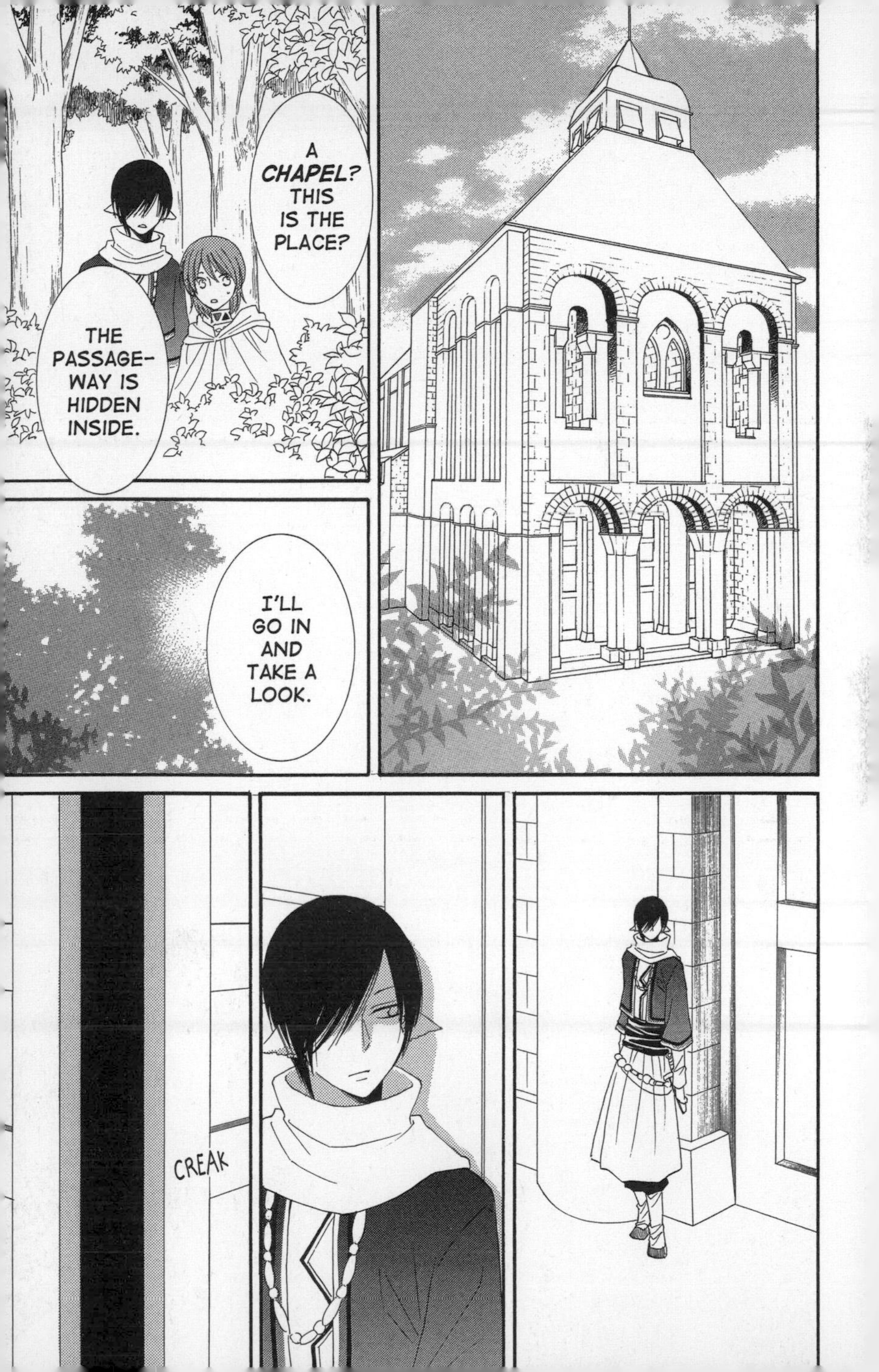
A CHAPEL? THIS IS THE PLACE?
THE PASSAGE-WAY IS HIDDEN INSIDE.
I'LL GO IN AND TAKE A LOOK.
CREAK

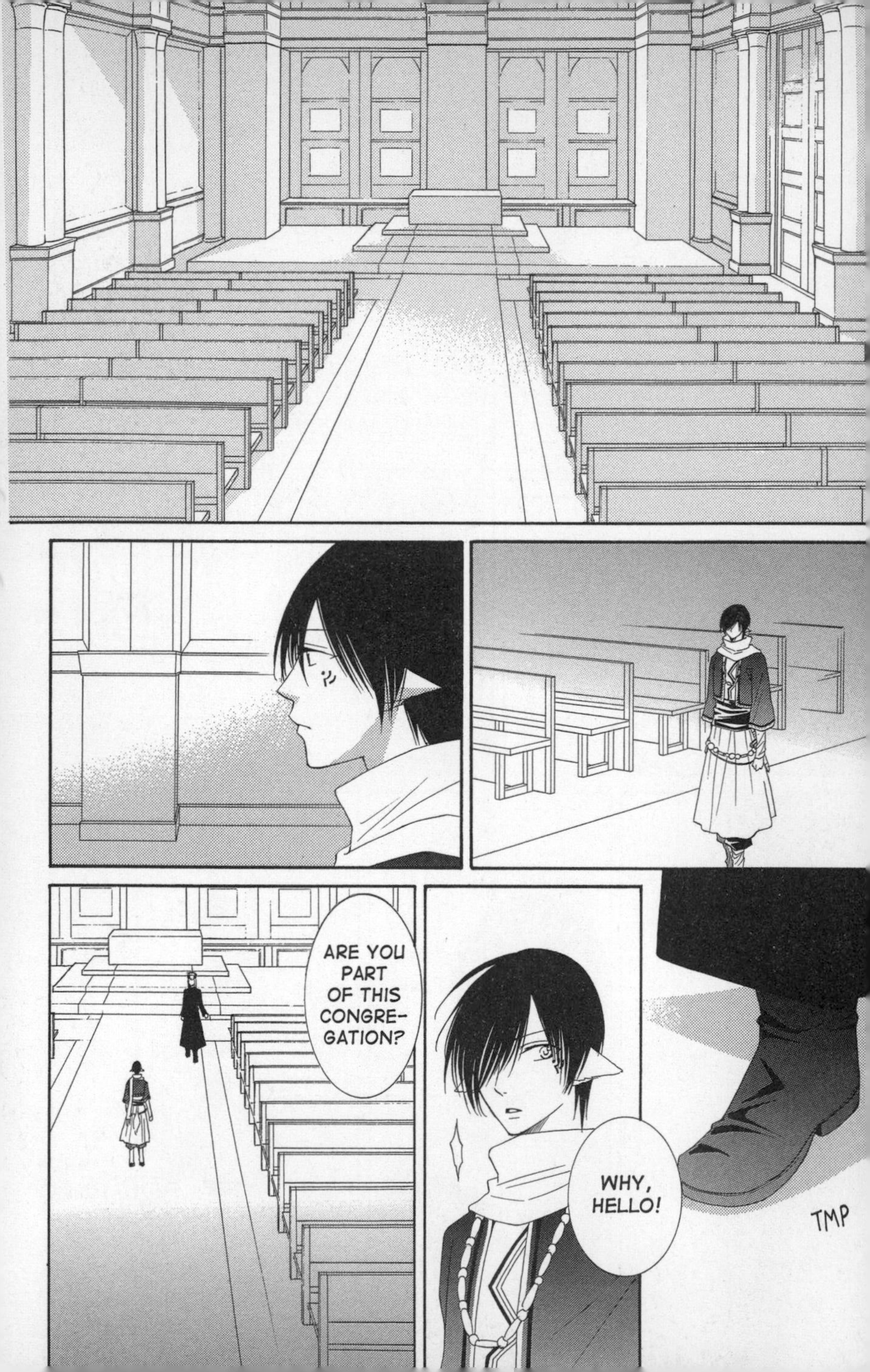
TMP
WHY, HELLO!
ARE YOU PART OF THIS CONGREGATION?

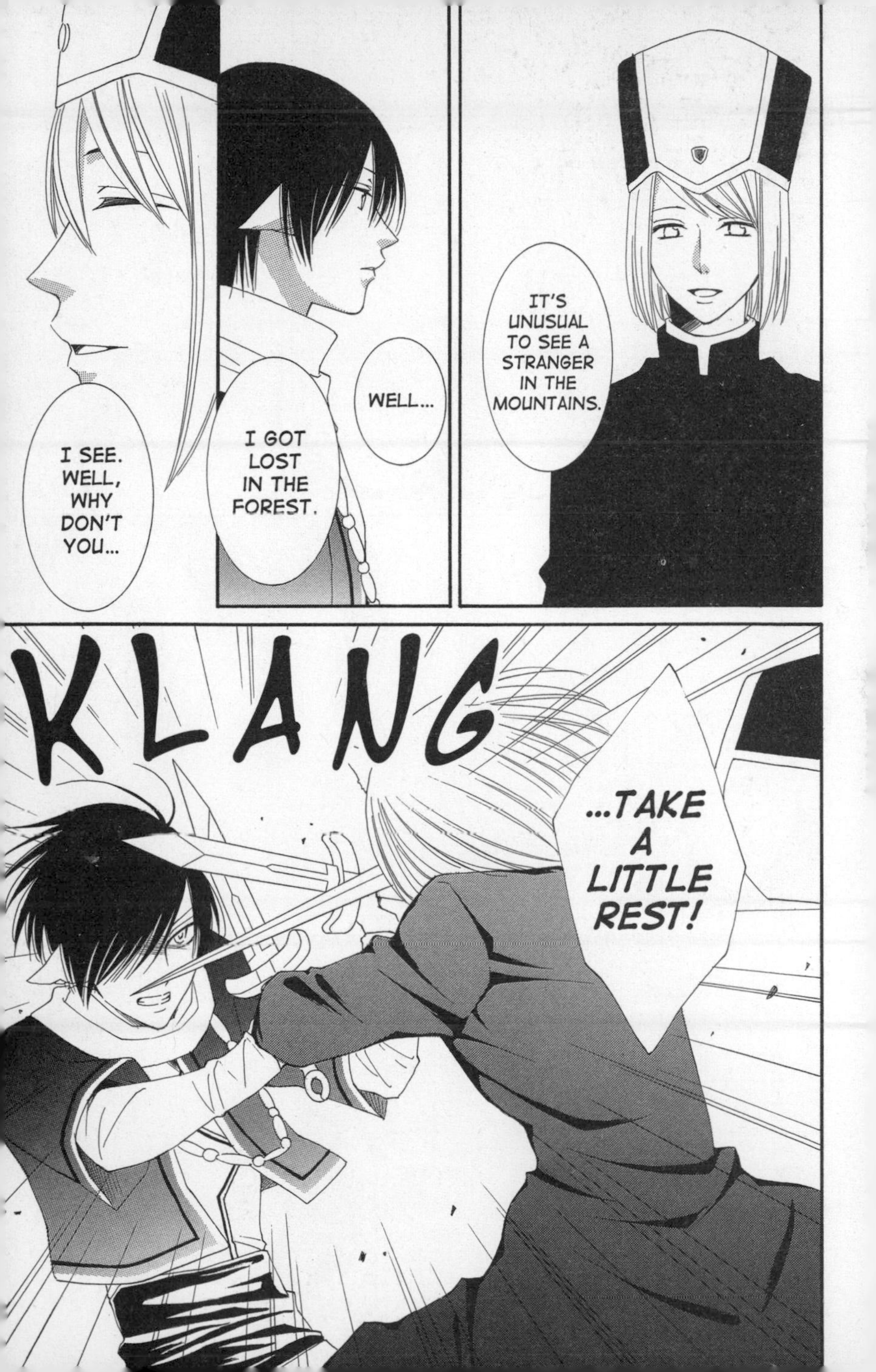
IT'S UNUSUAL TO SEE A STRANGER IN THE MOUNTAINS.
WELL...
I GOT LOST IN THE FOREST.
I SEE. WELL, WHY DON'T YOU...
...TAKE A LITTLE REST!
KLANG

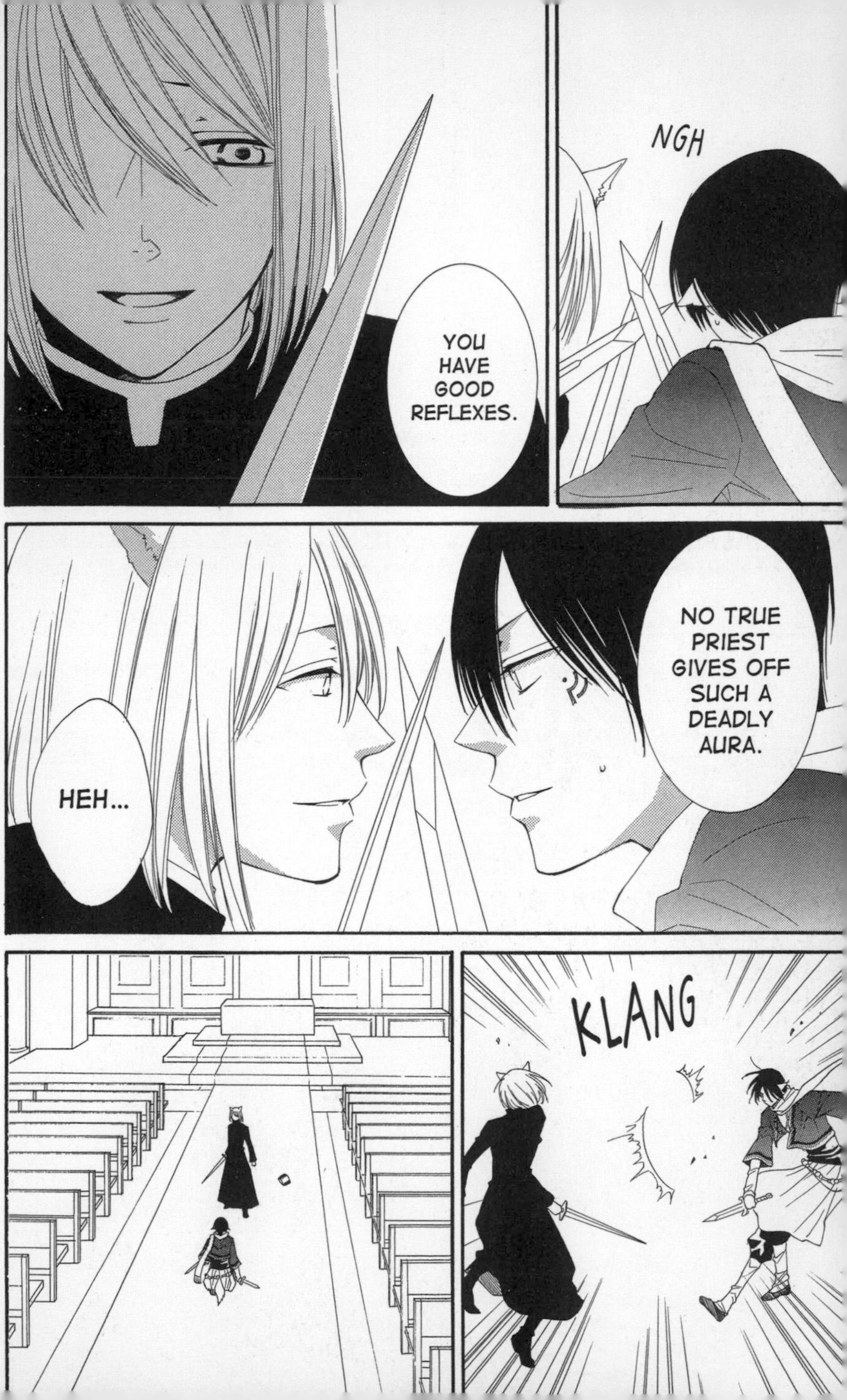
NGH
YOU HAVE GOOD REFLEXES.
NO TRUE PRIEST GIVES OFF SUCH A DEADLY AURA.
HEH...
KLANG

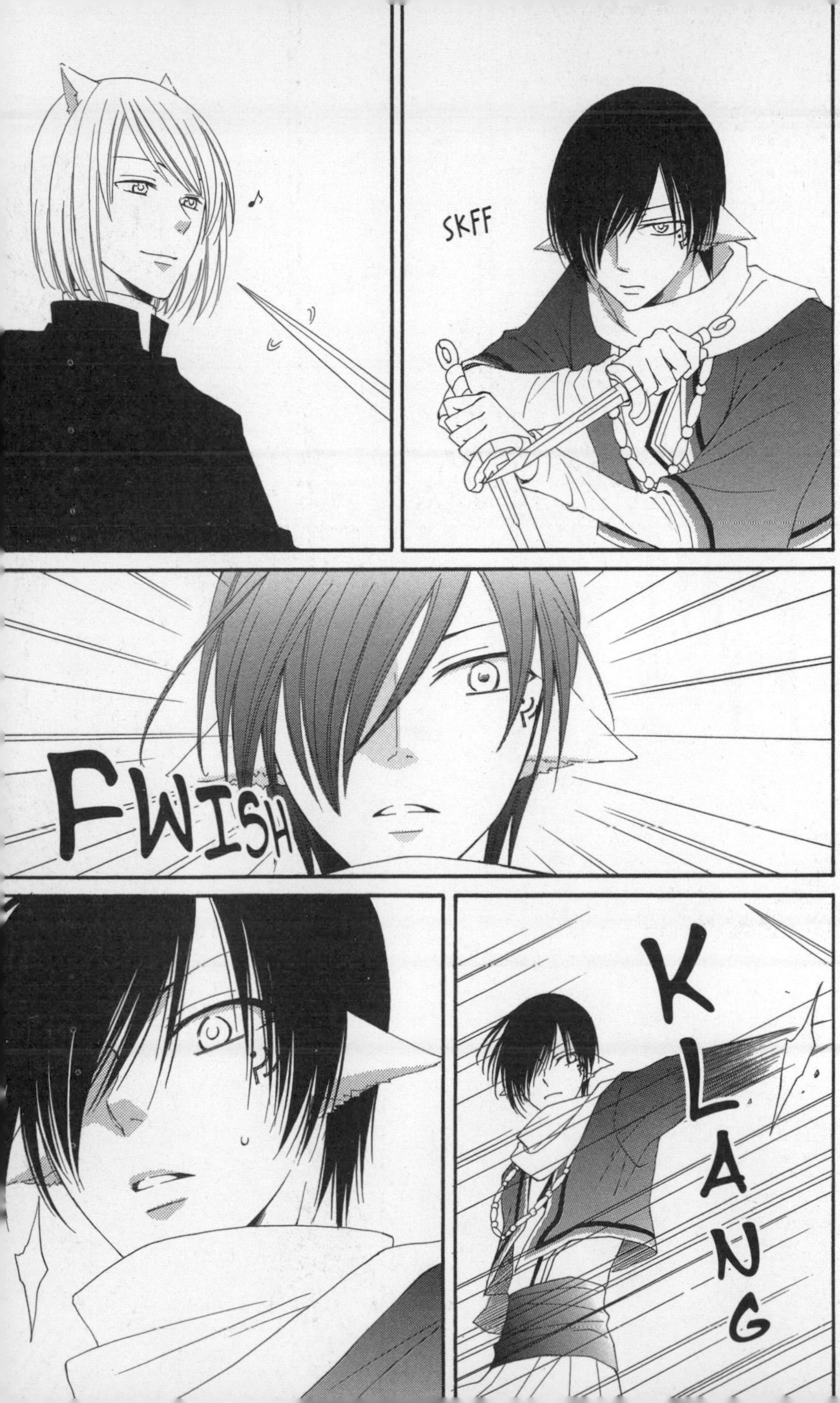
SKFF
FWISH
KLANG

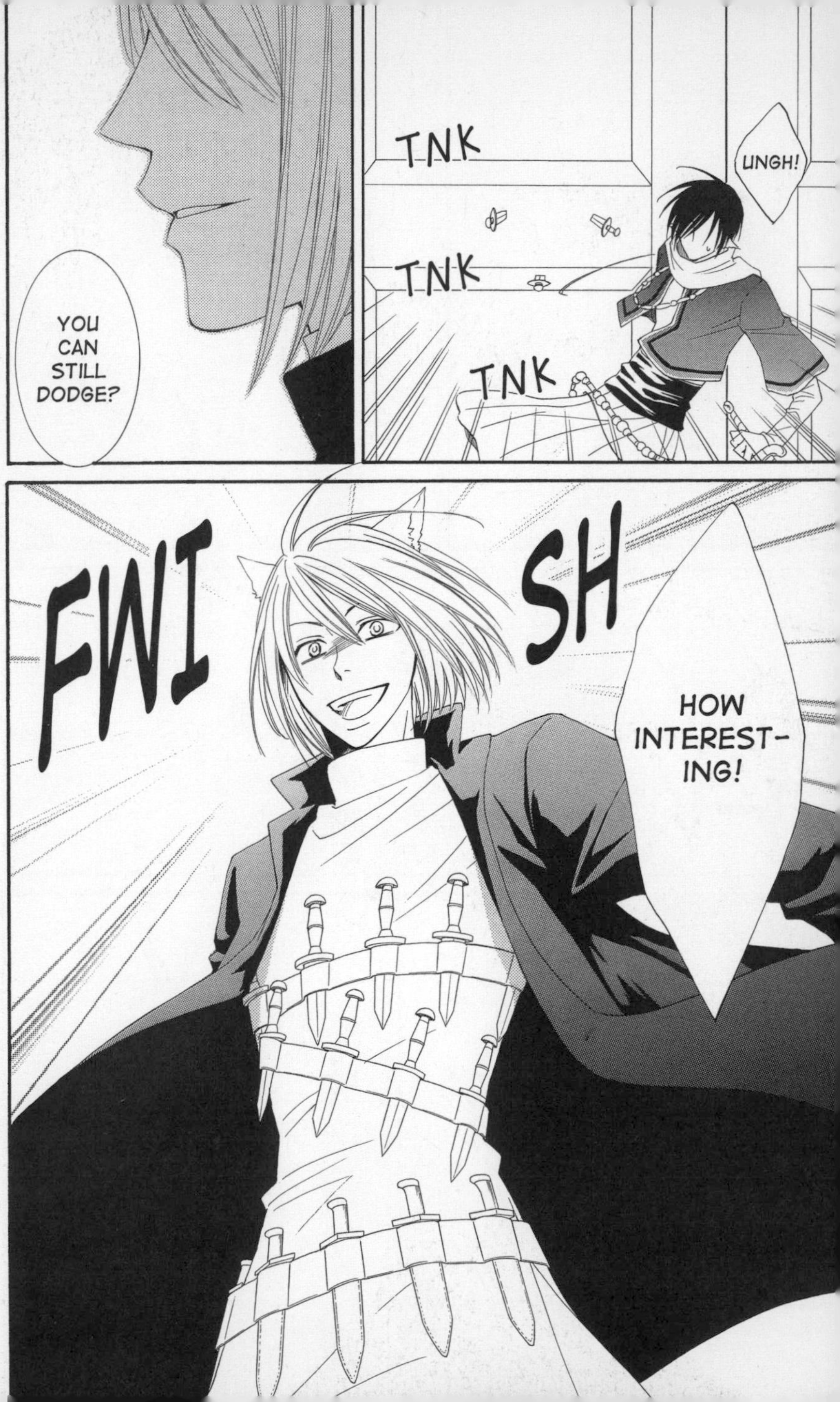
UNGH!
TNK
TNK
TNK
YOU CAN STILL DODGE?
HOW INTEREST-ING!
FWISH

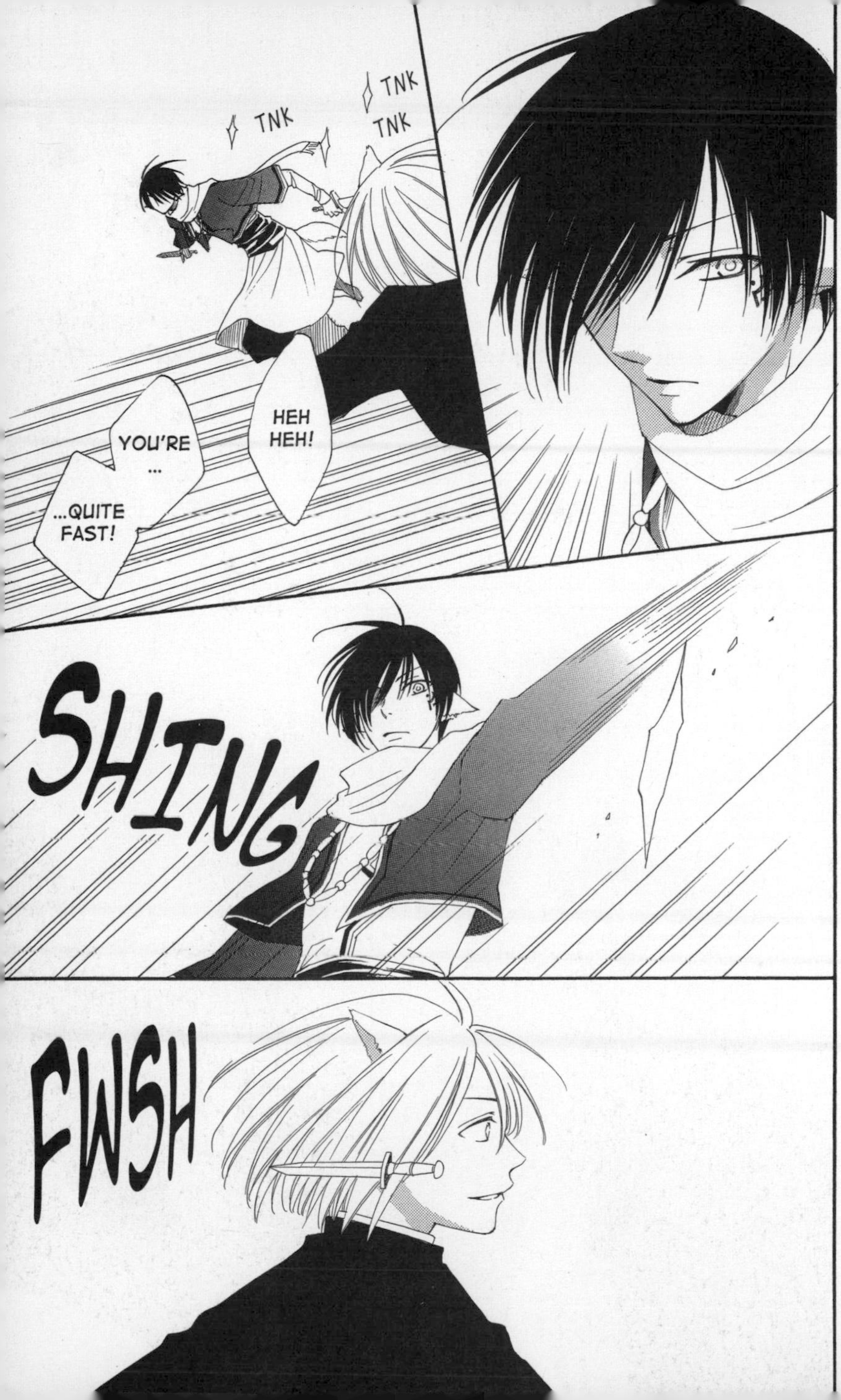
TNK
TNK
TNK
HEH HEH!
YOU'RE ...
...QUITE FAST!
SHING
FWSH

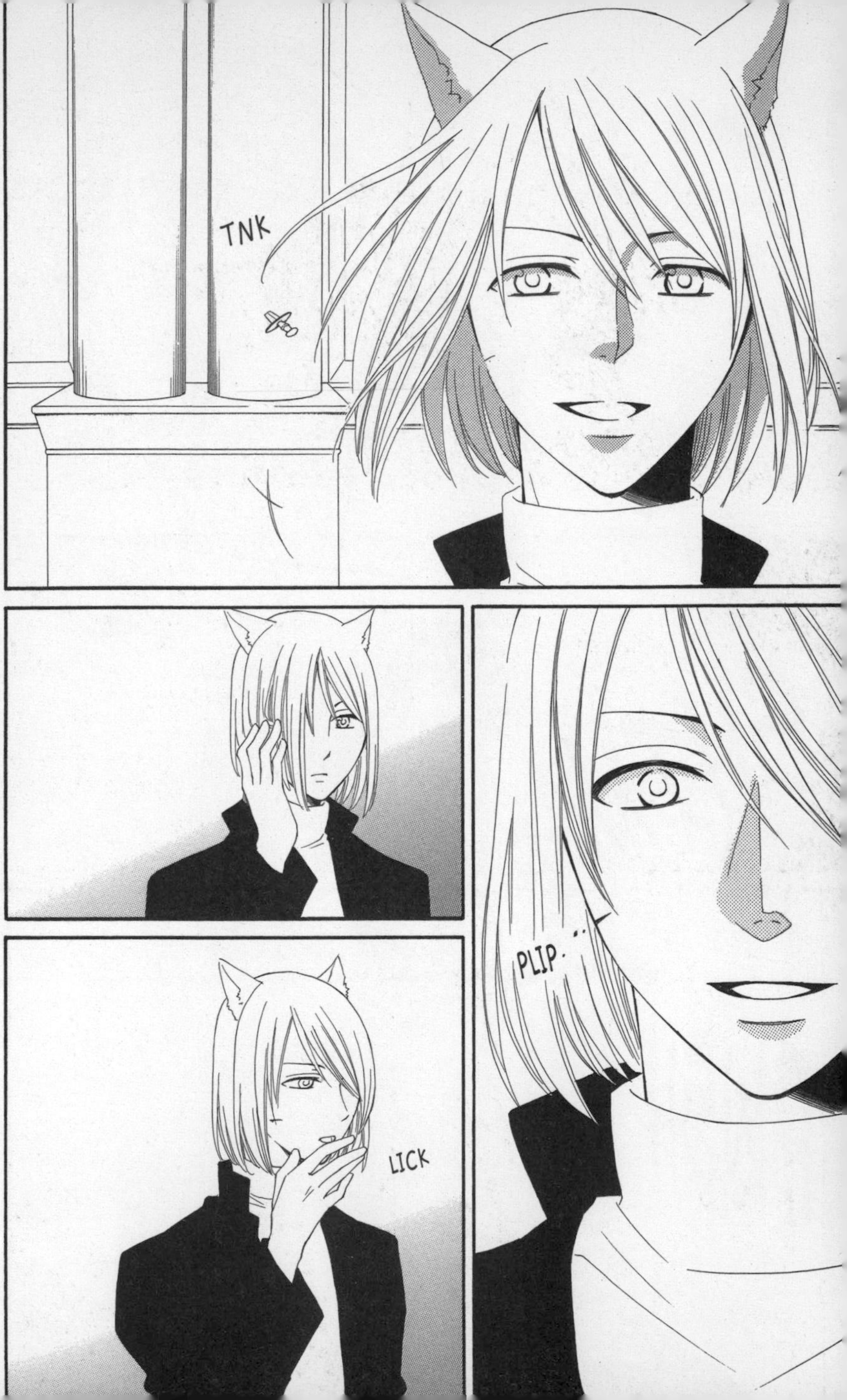
TNK
PLIP...
LICK

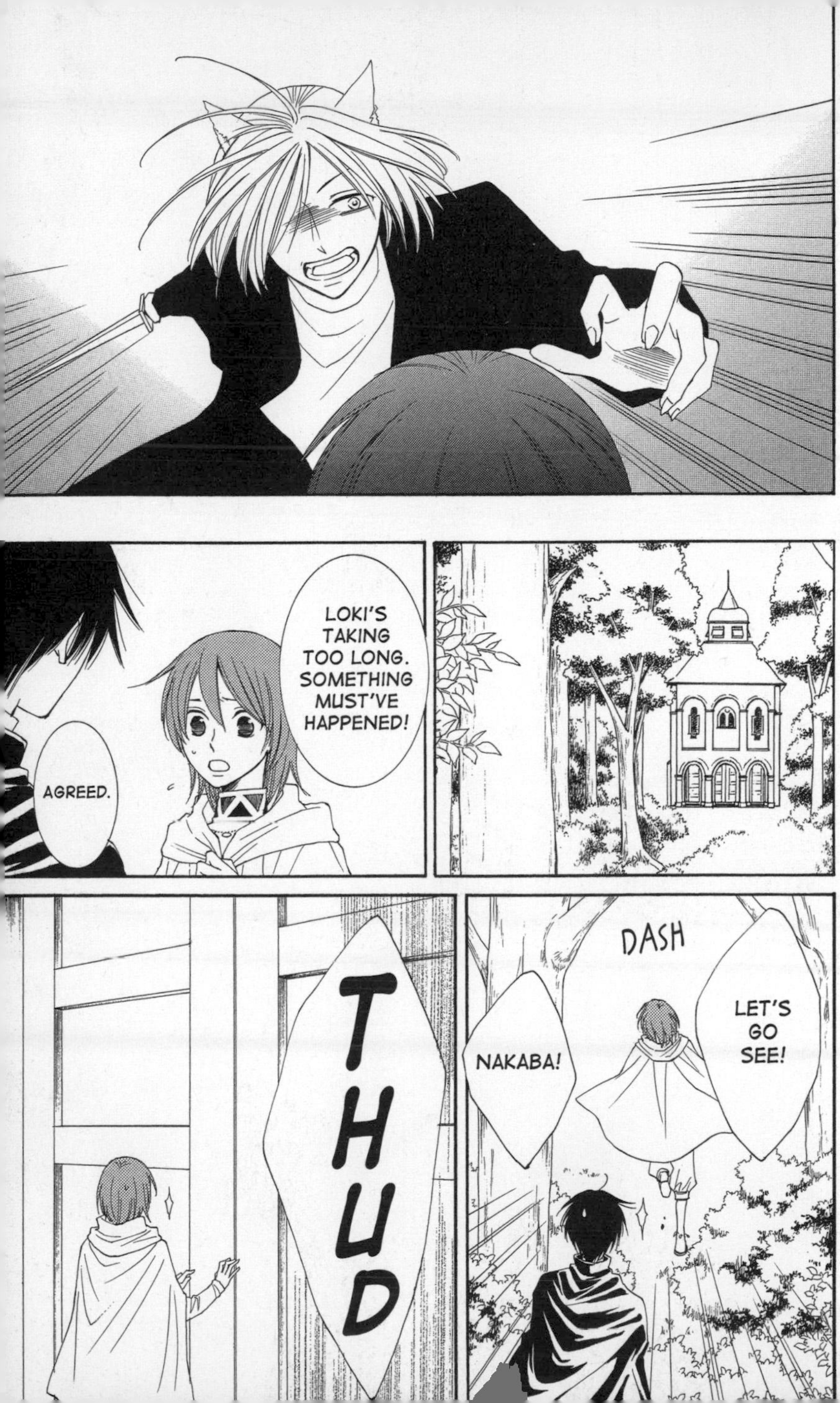
LOKI'S TAKING TOO LONG. SOMETHING MUST'VE HAPPENED!
AGREED.
DASH
LET'S GO SEE!
NAKABA!
THUD

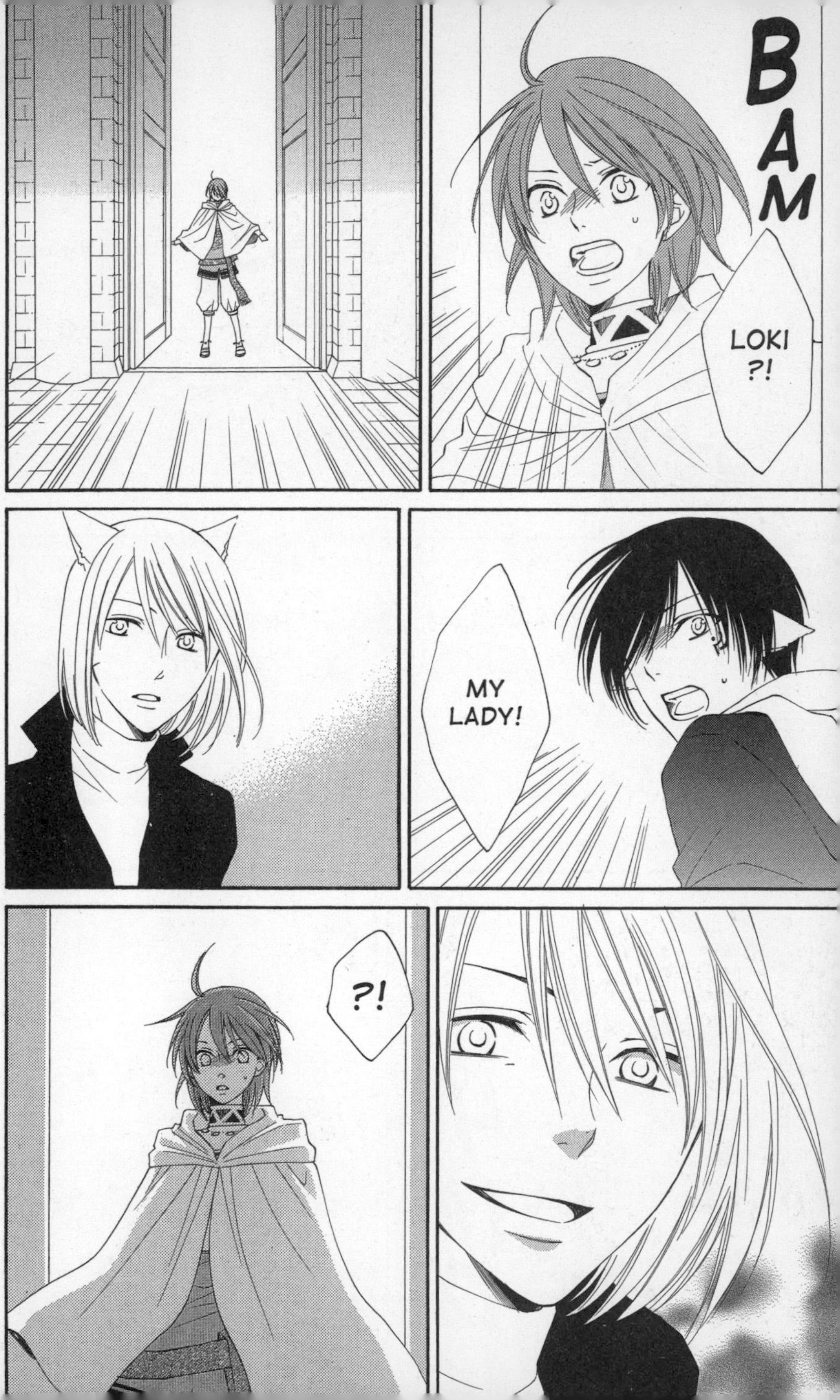
BAM
LOKI ?!
MY LADY!
?!

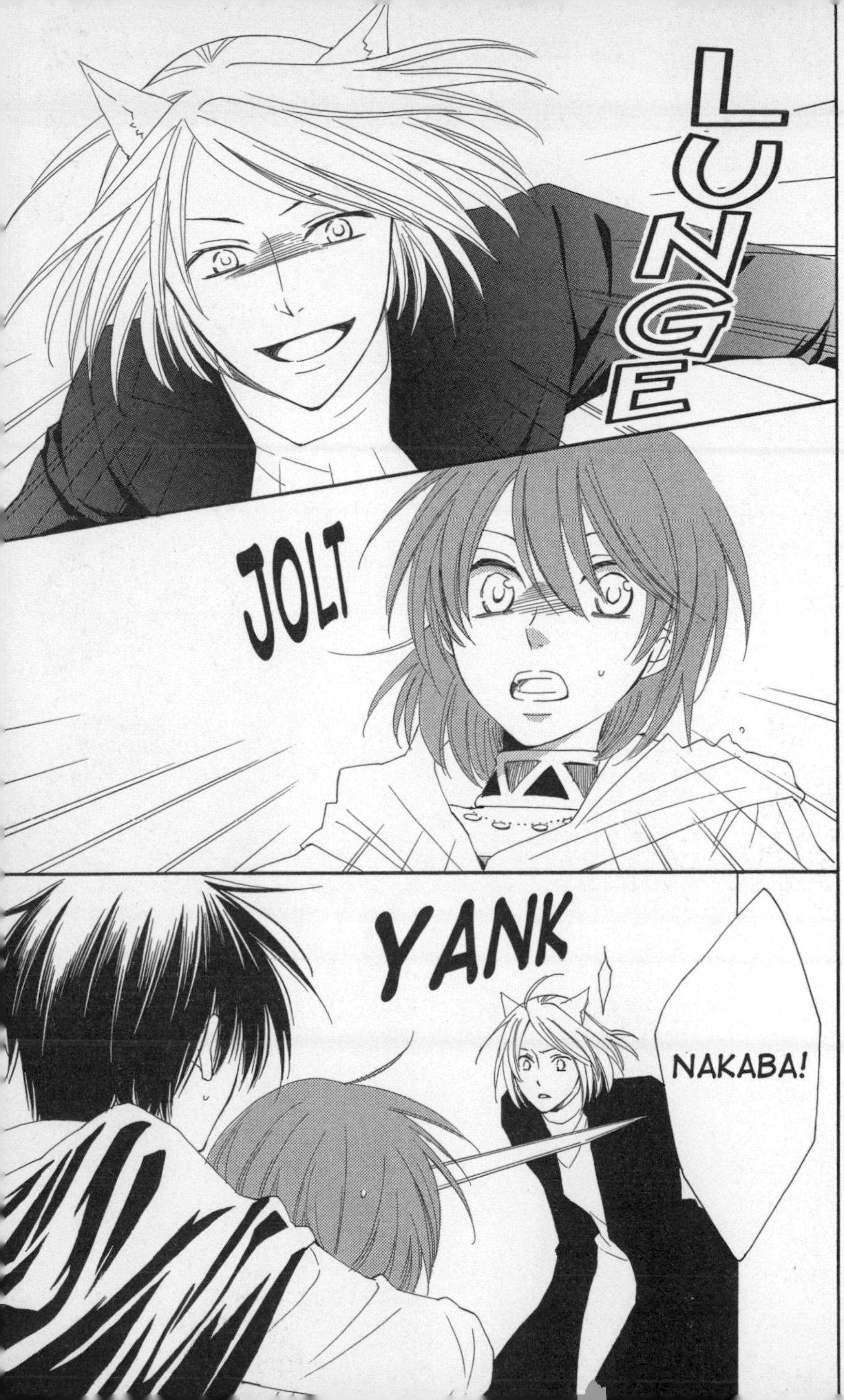
LUNGE
JOLT
YANK
NAKABA!

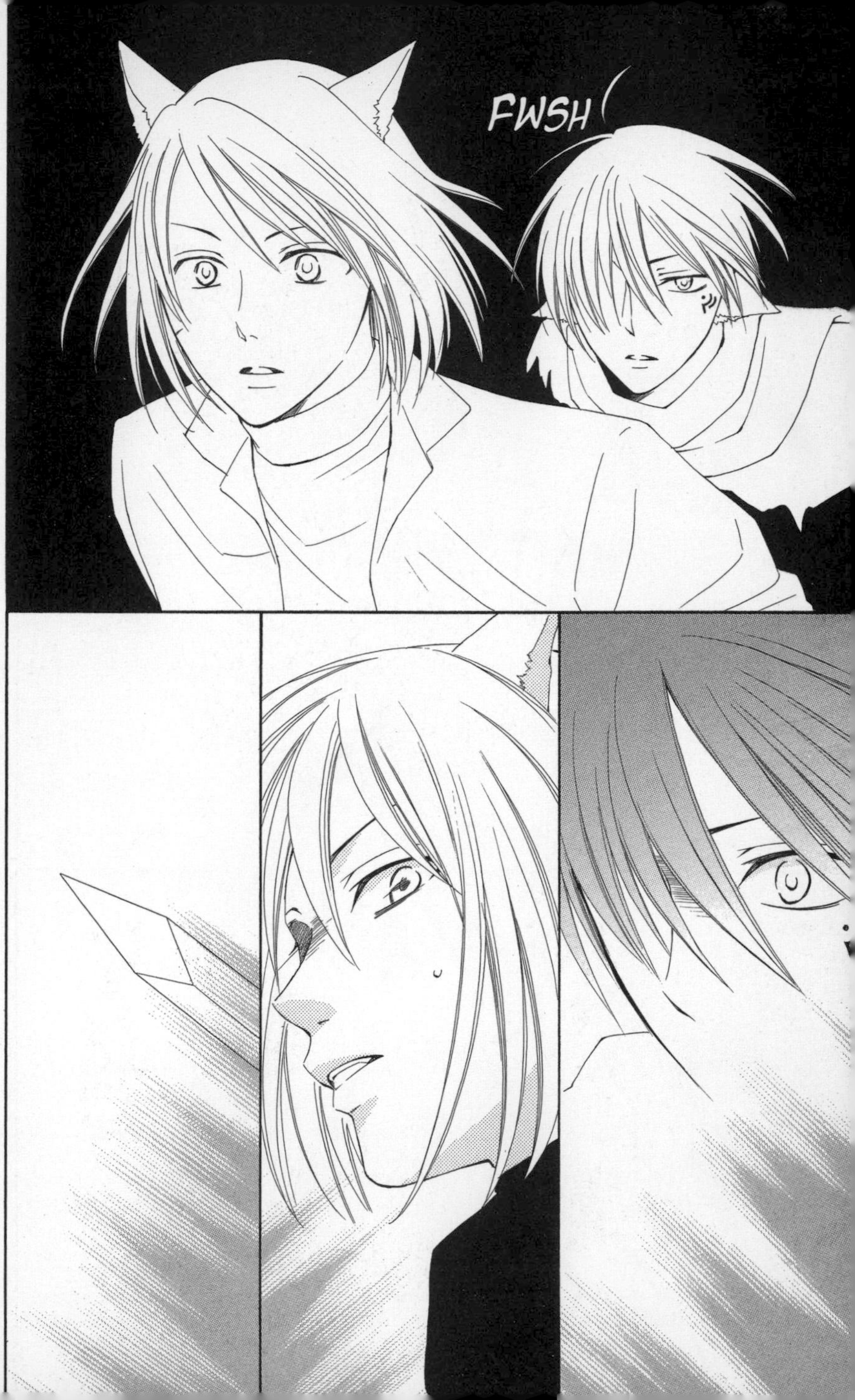
FWSH

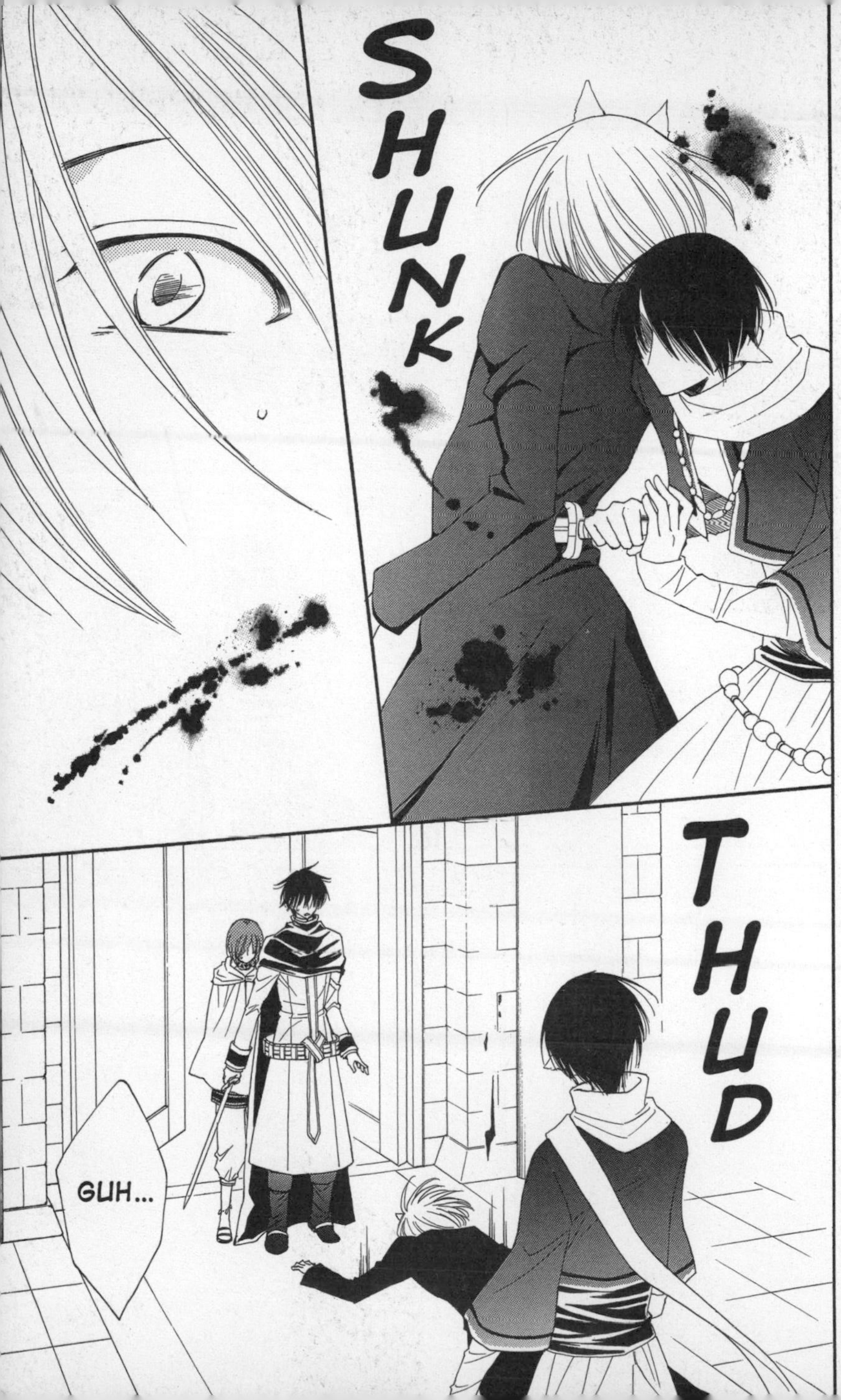
SHUNK
THUD
GUH...

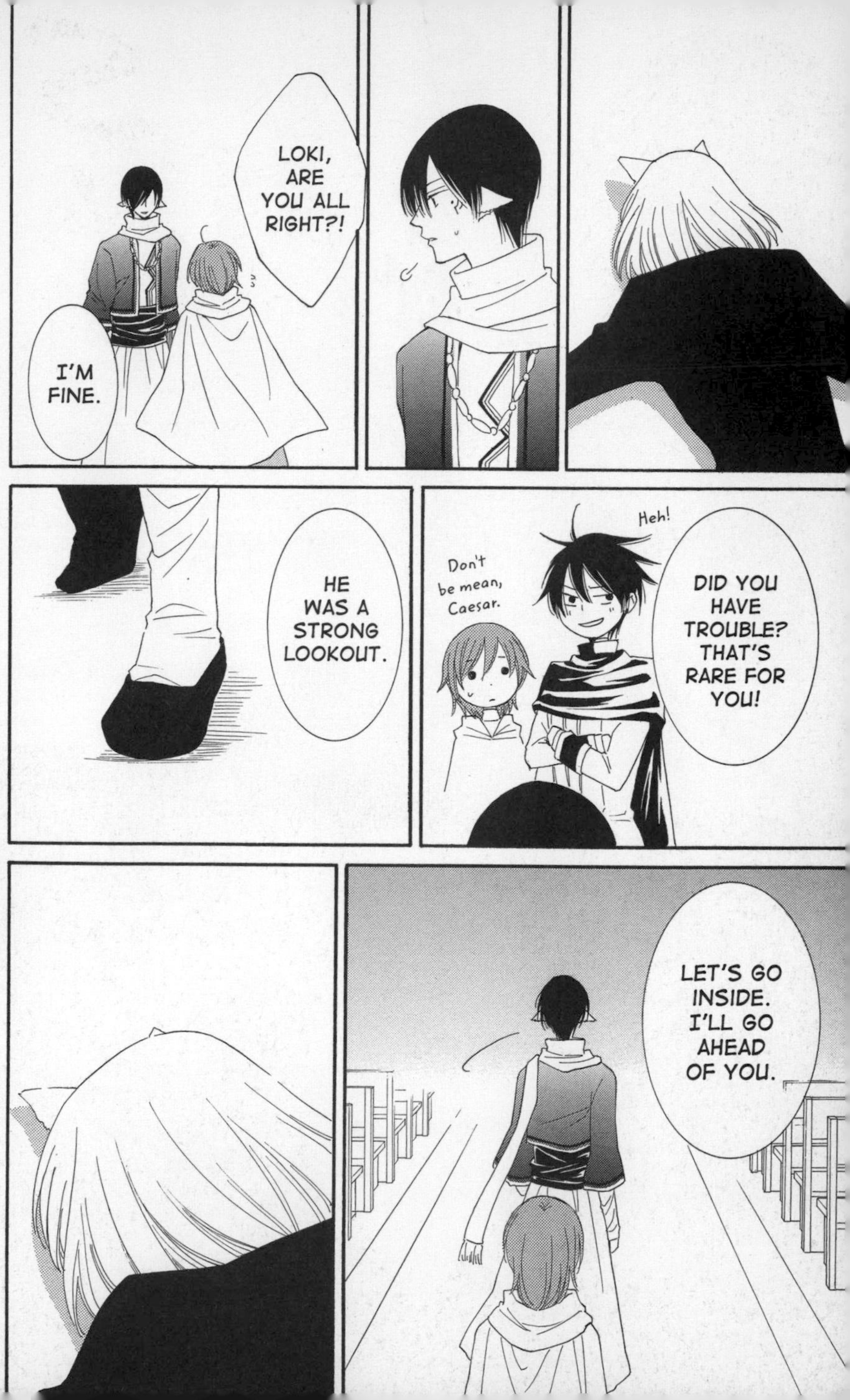
LOKI, ARE YOU ALL RIGHT?!
I'M FINE.
Heh!
DID YOU HAVE TROUBLE? THAT'S RARE FOR YOU!
Don't be mean, Caesar.
HE WAS A STRONG LOOKOUT.
LET'S GO INSIDE. I'LL GO AHEAD OF YOU.

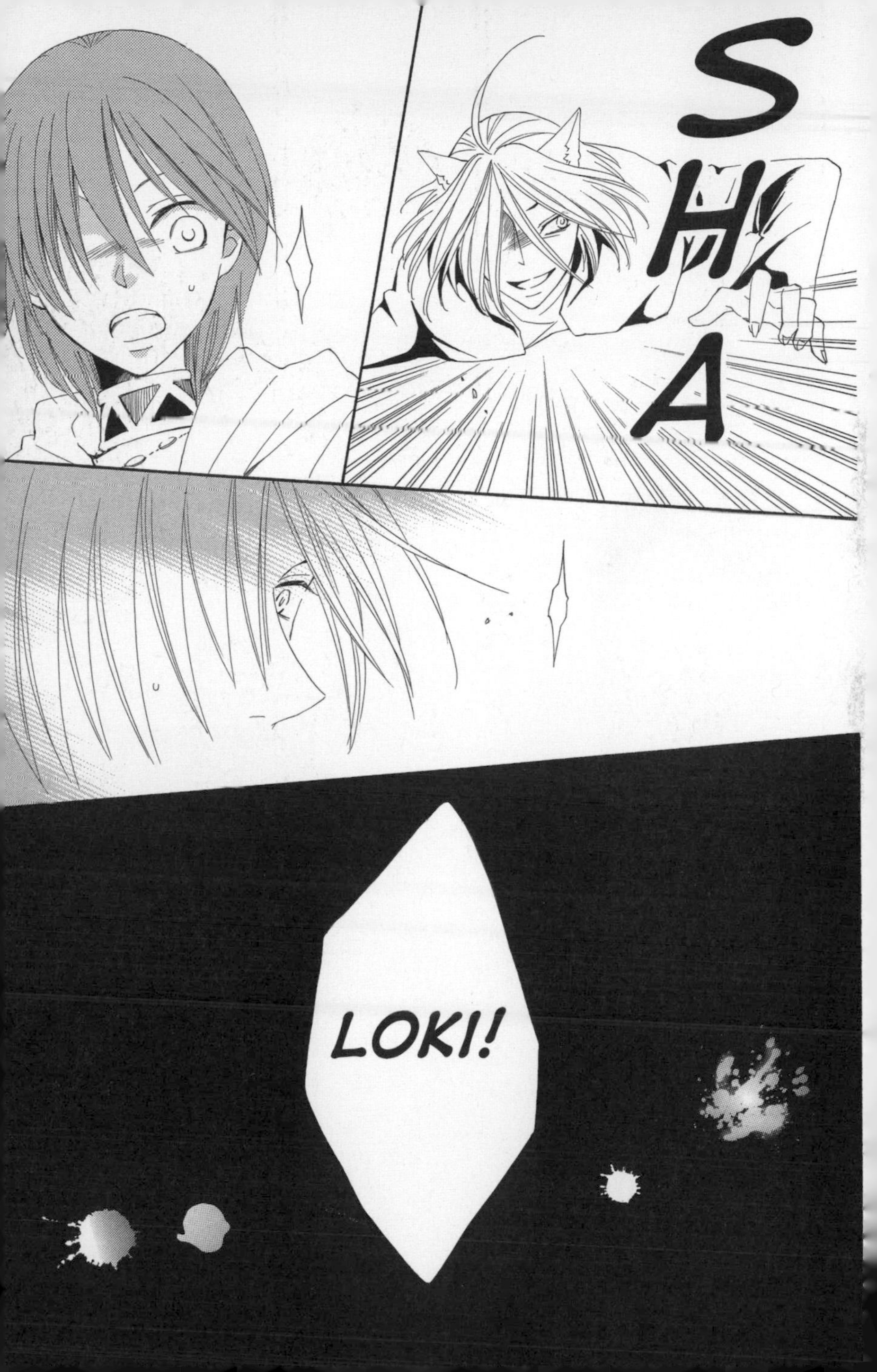
SHA
LOKI!

Chapter 49

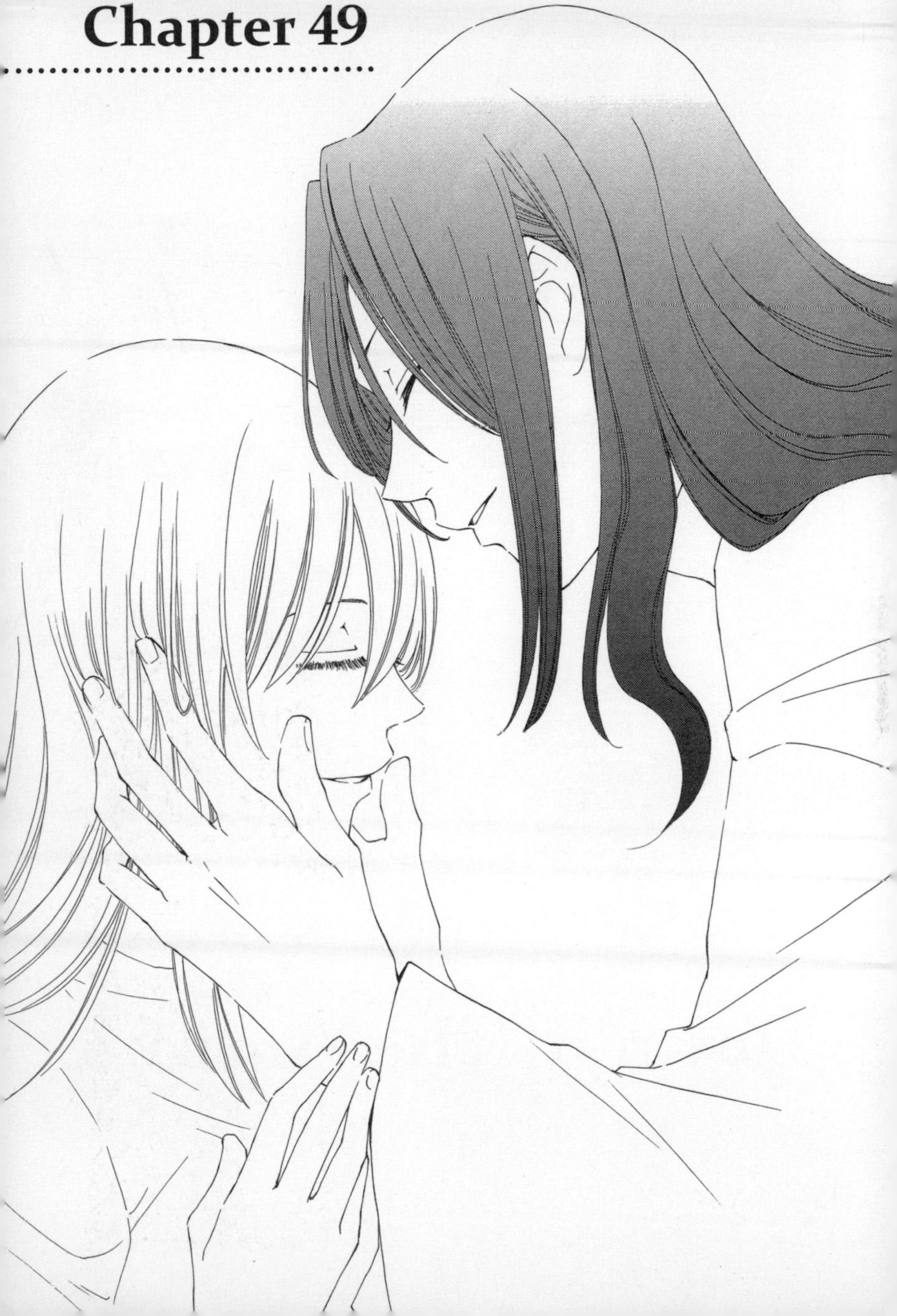

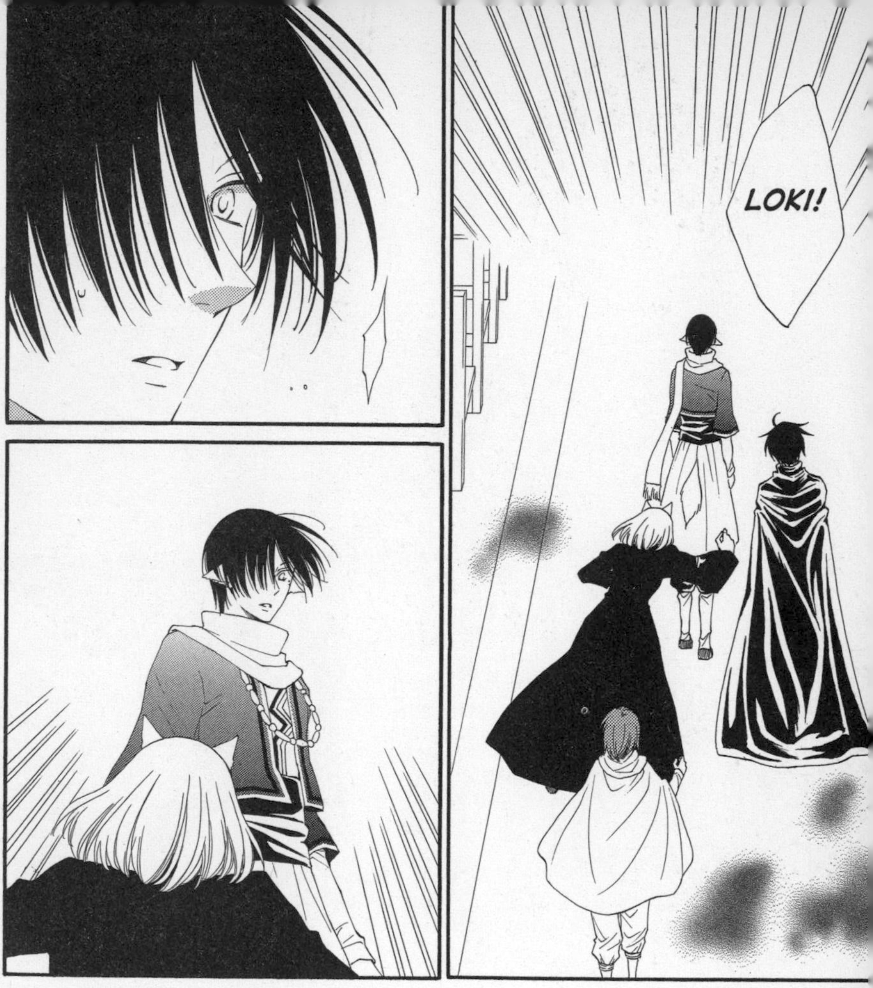
LOKI!

Dawn of the Arcana

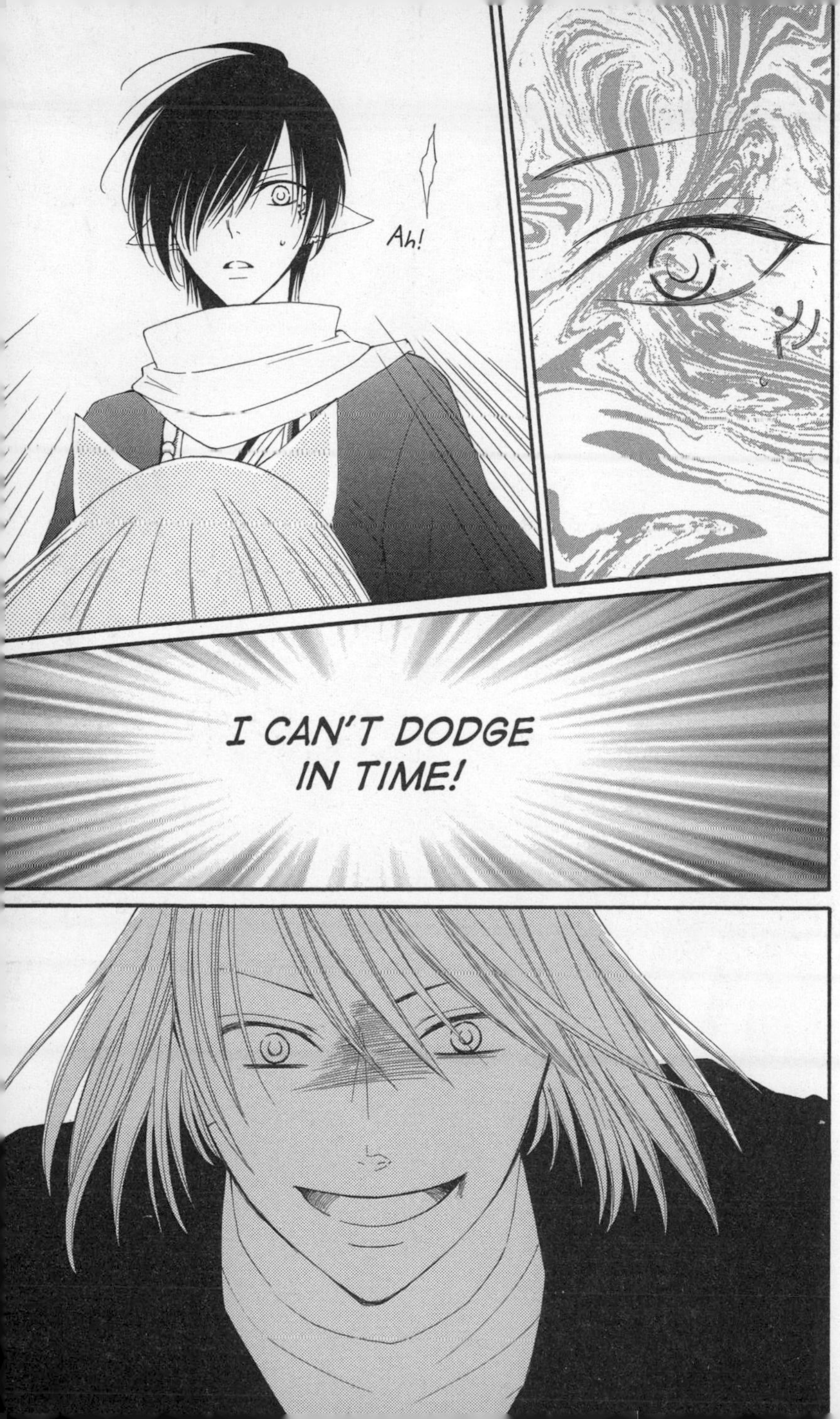
Ah!
I CAN'T DODGE IN TIME!

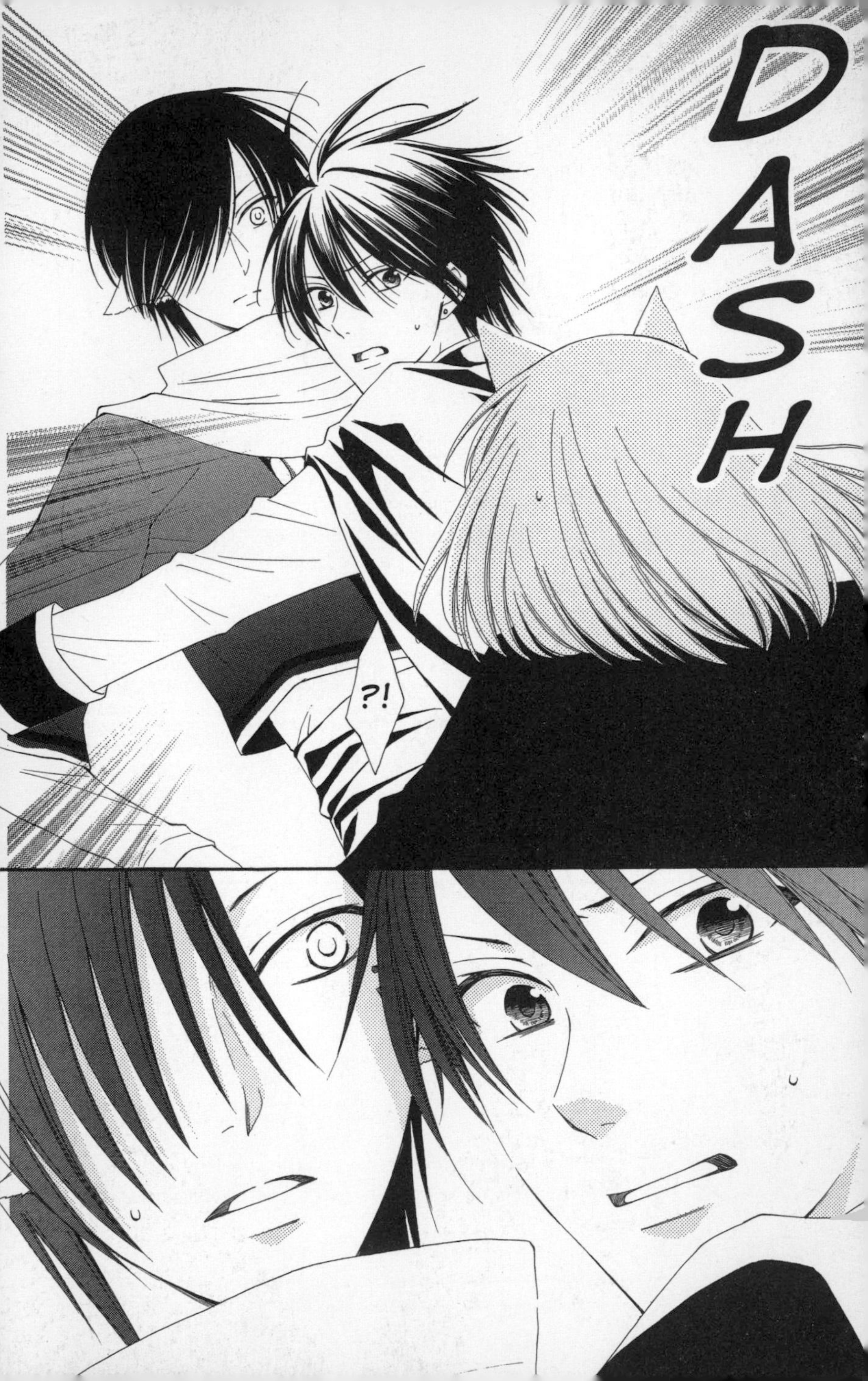
DASH
?!

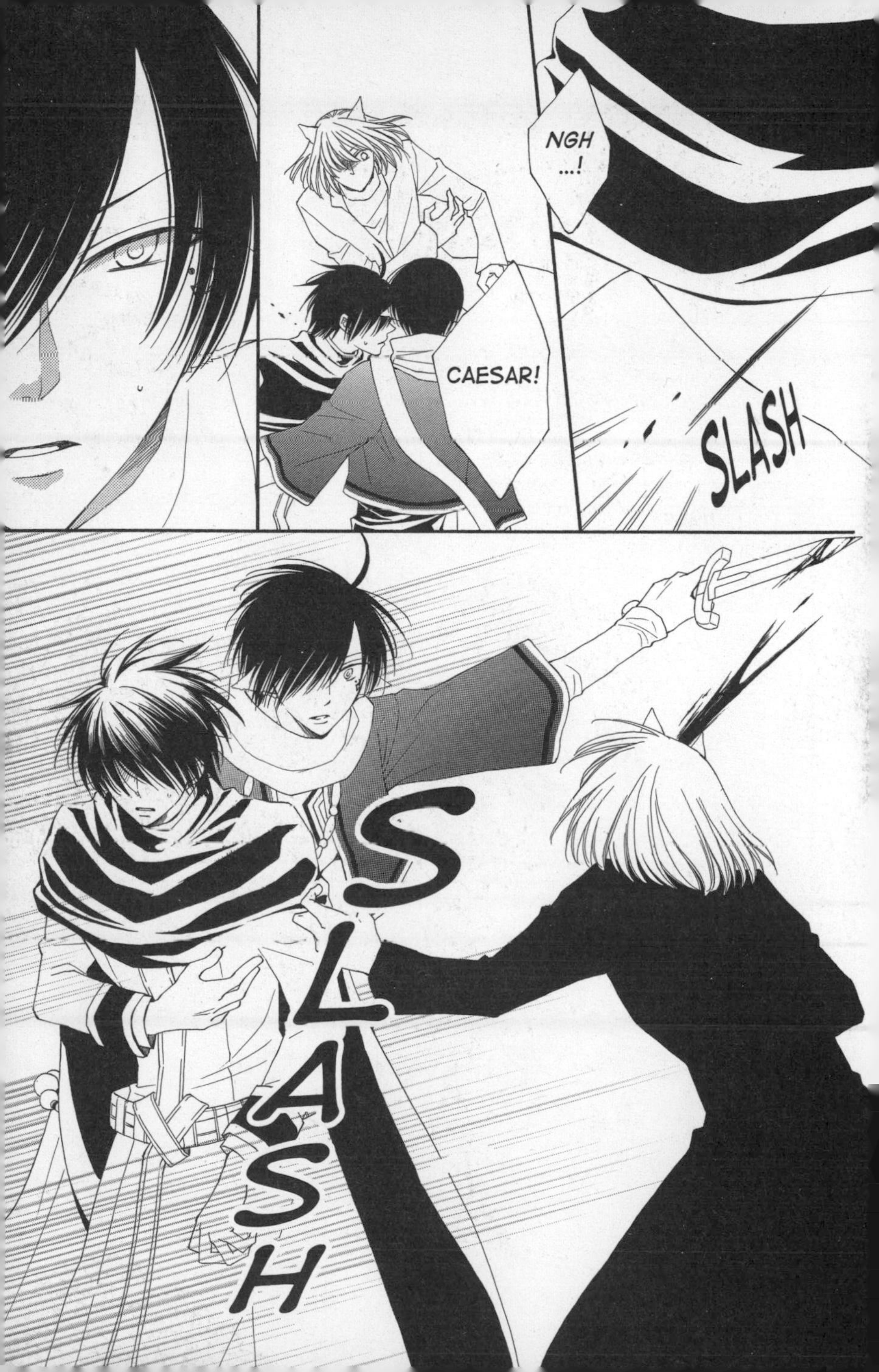
NGH ...!
SLASH
CAESAR!
SLASH

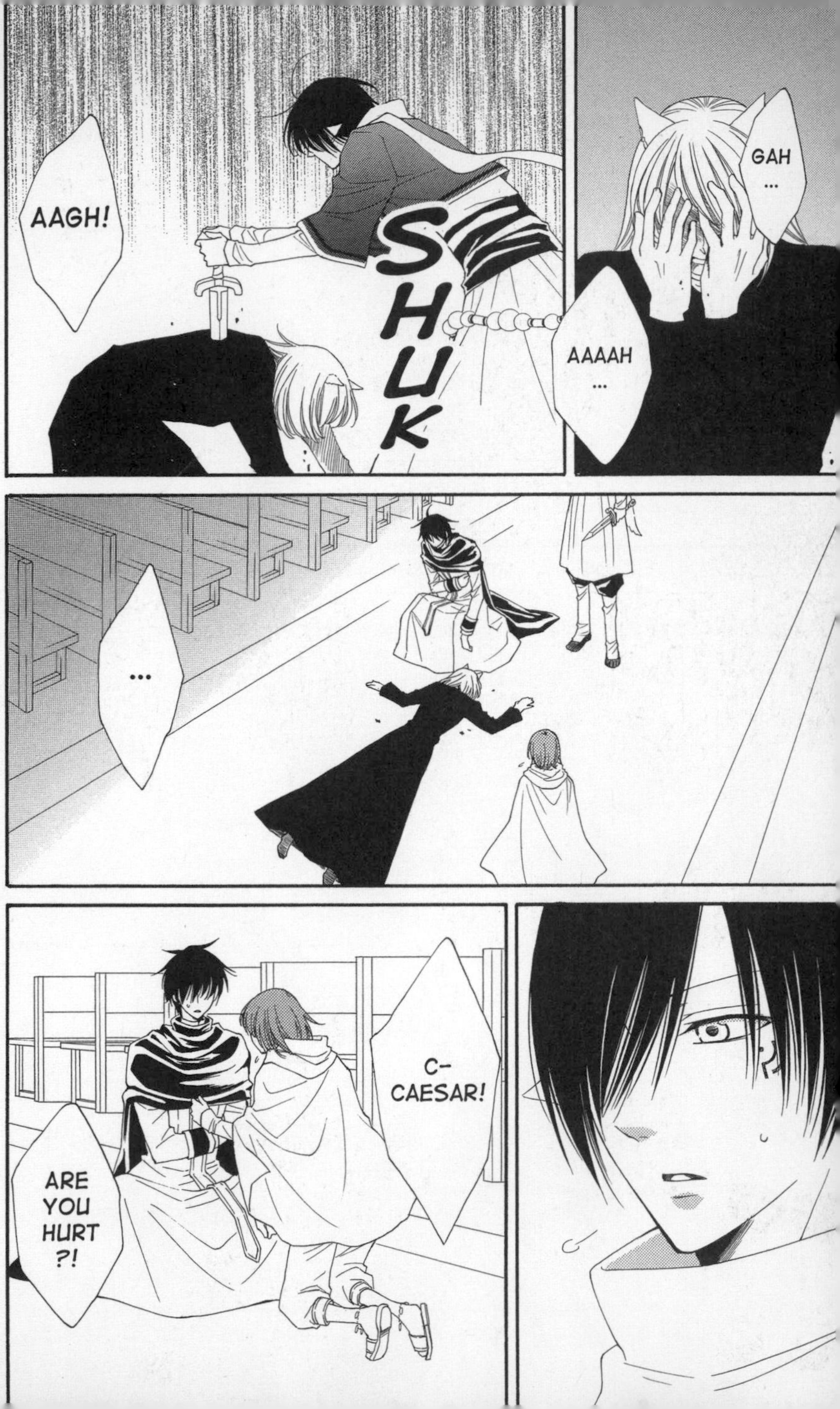
GAH ...
AAAAH ...
AAGH!
SHUK
...
C-CAESAR!
ARE YOU HURT ?!

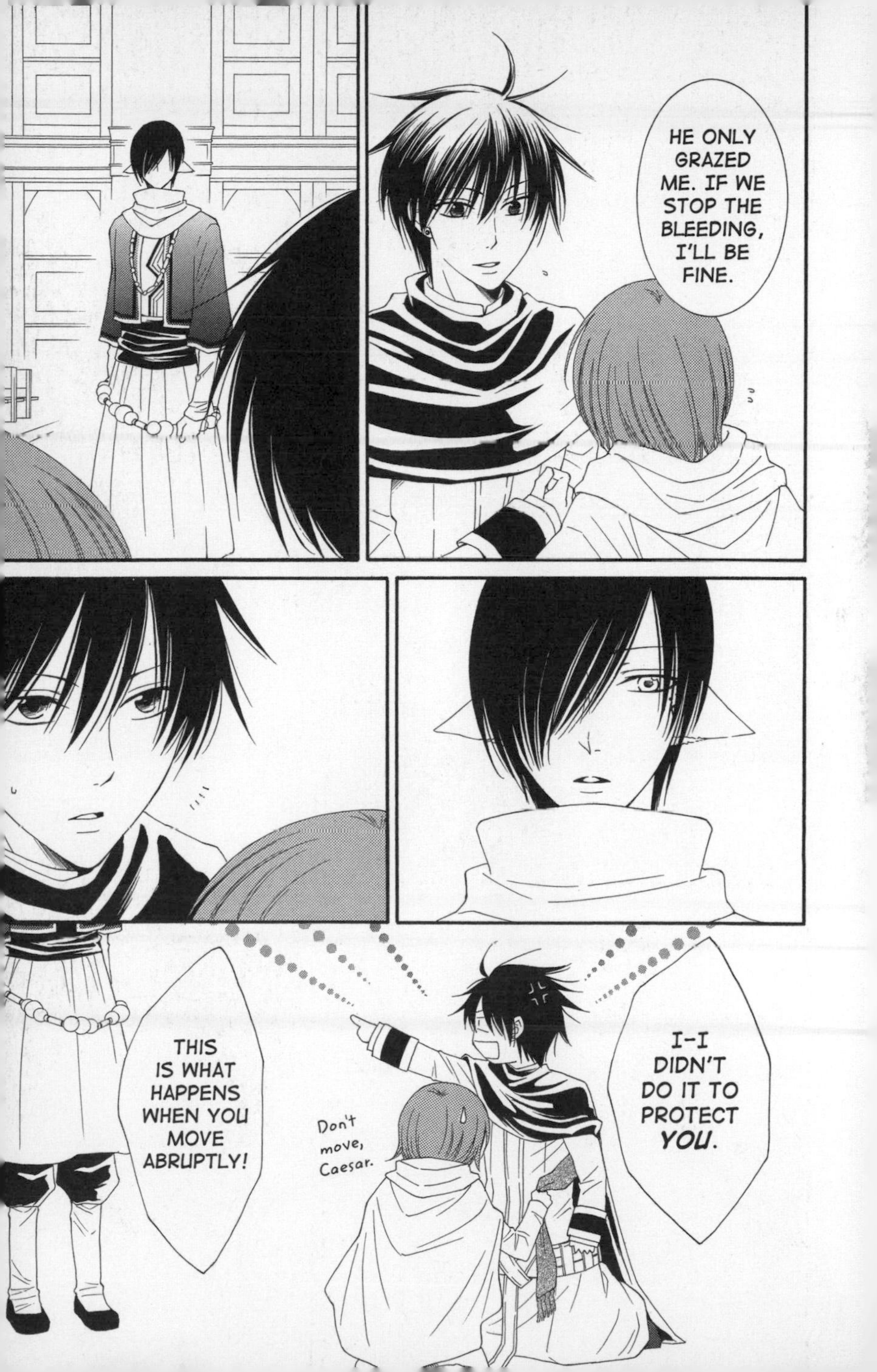
HE ONLY GRAZED ME. IF WE STOP THE BLEEDING, I'LL BE FINE.
I-I DIDN'T DO IT TO PROTECT YOU.
Don't move, Caesar.
THIS IS WHAT HAPPENS WHEN YOU MOVE ABRUPTLY!

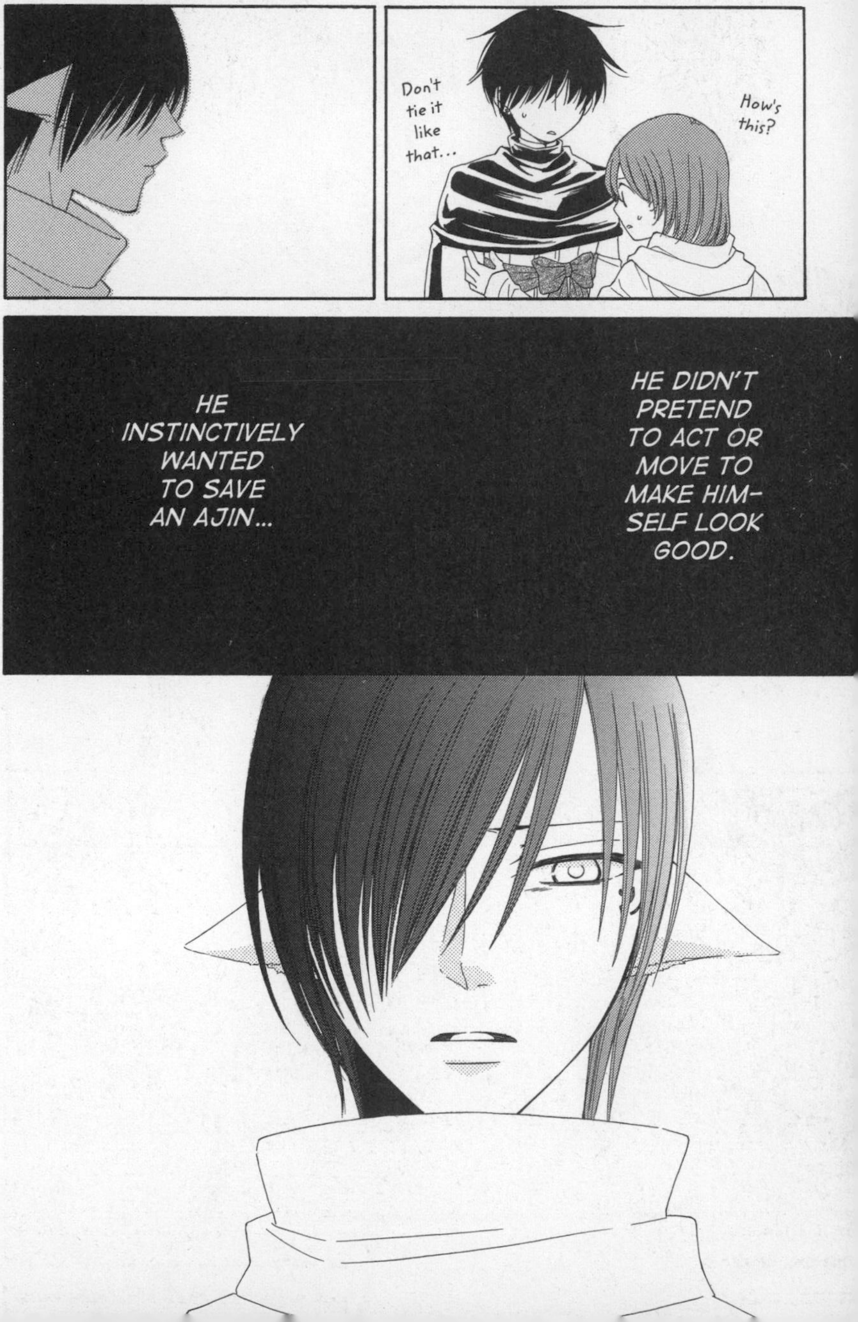
How's this?
Don't tie it like that...
HE DIDN'T PRETEND TO ACT OR MOVE TO MAKE HIM-SELF LOOK GOOD.
HE INSTINCTIVELY WANTED TO SAVE AN AJIN...

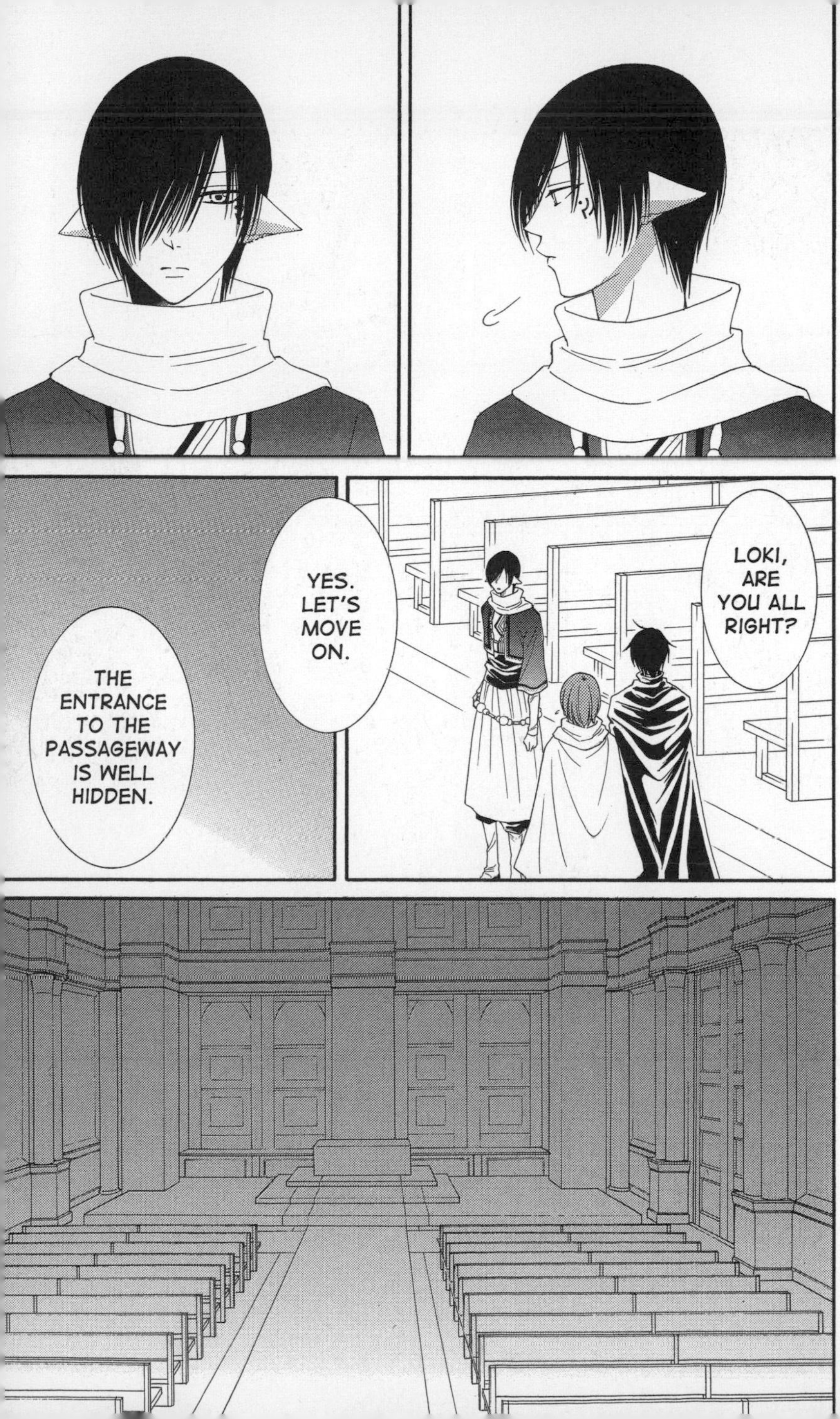
LOKI, ARE YOU ALL RIGHT?
YES. LET'S MOVE ON.
THE ENTRANCE TO THE PASSAGEWAY IS WELL HIDDEN.

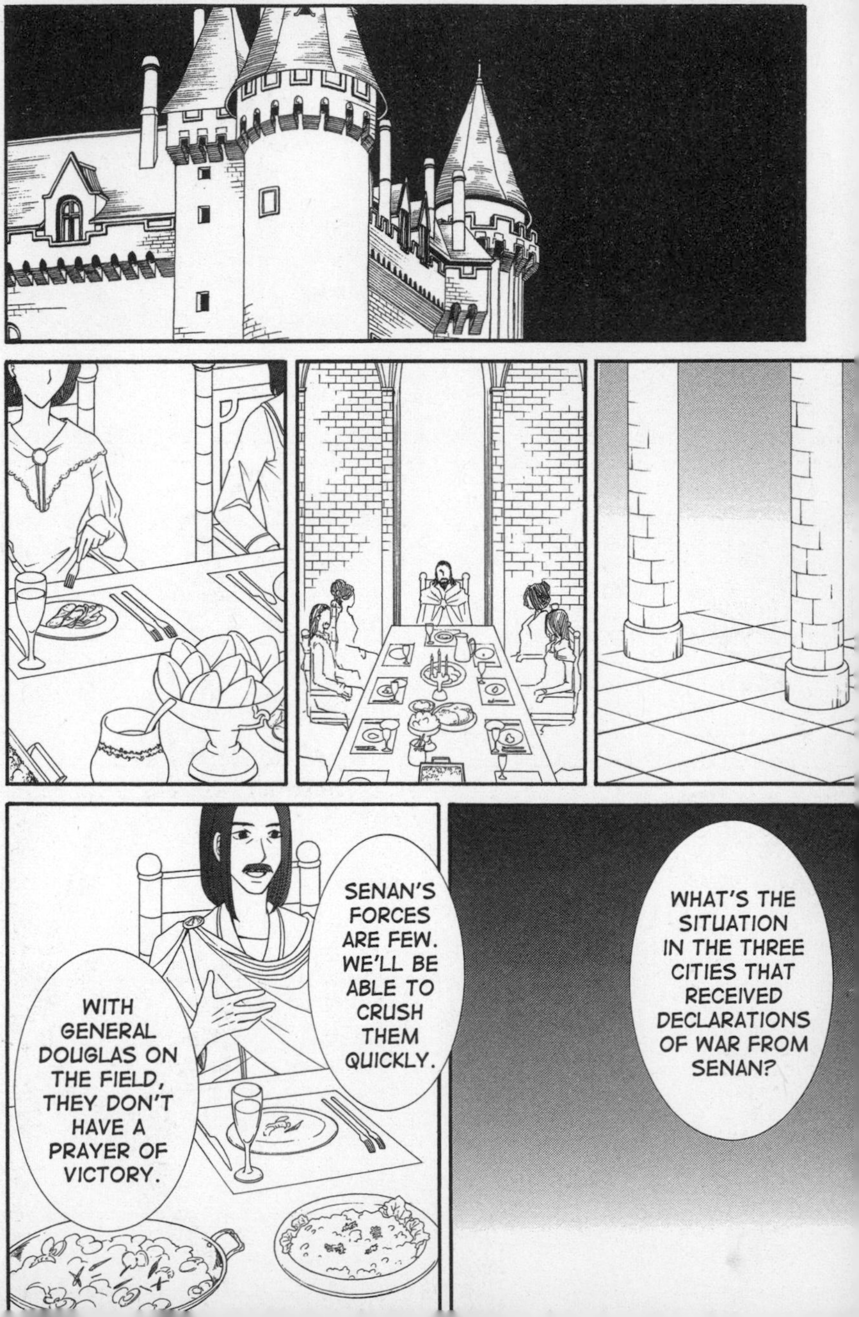
WHAT'S THE SITUATION IN THE THREE CITIES THAT RECEIVED DECLARATIONS OF WAR FROM SENAN?
SENAN'S FORCES ARE FEW. WE'LL BE ABLE TO CRUSH THEM QUICKLY.
WITH GENERAL DOUGLAS ON THE FIELD, THEY DON'T HAVE A PRAYER OF VICTORY.

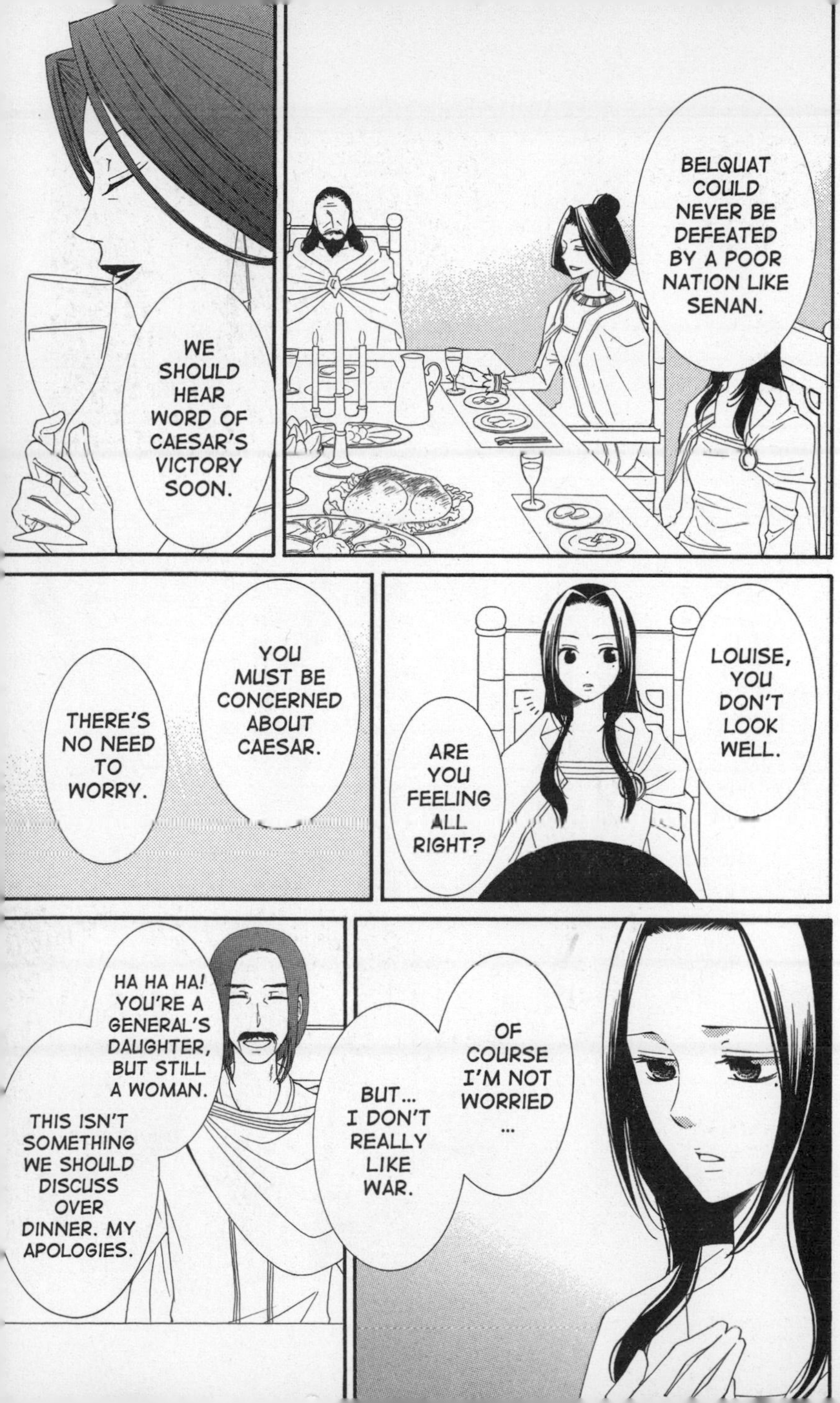
BELQUAT COULD NEVER BE DEFEATED BY A POOR NATION LIKE SENAN.
WE SHOULD HEAR WORD OF CAESAR'S VICTORY SOON.
LOUISE, YOU DON'T LOOK WELL.
ARE YOU FEELING ALL RIGHT?
YOU MUST BE CONCERNED ABOUT CAESAR.
THERE'S NO NEED TO WORRY.
OF COURSE I'M NOT WORRIED...
BUT... I DON'T REALLY LIKE WAR.
HA HA HA! YOU'RE A GENERAL'S DAUGHTER, BUT STILL A WOMAN.
THIS ISN'T SOMETHING WE SHOULD DISCUSS OVER DINNER. MY APOLOGIES.

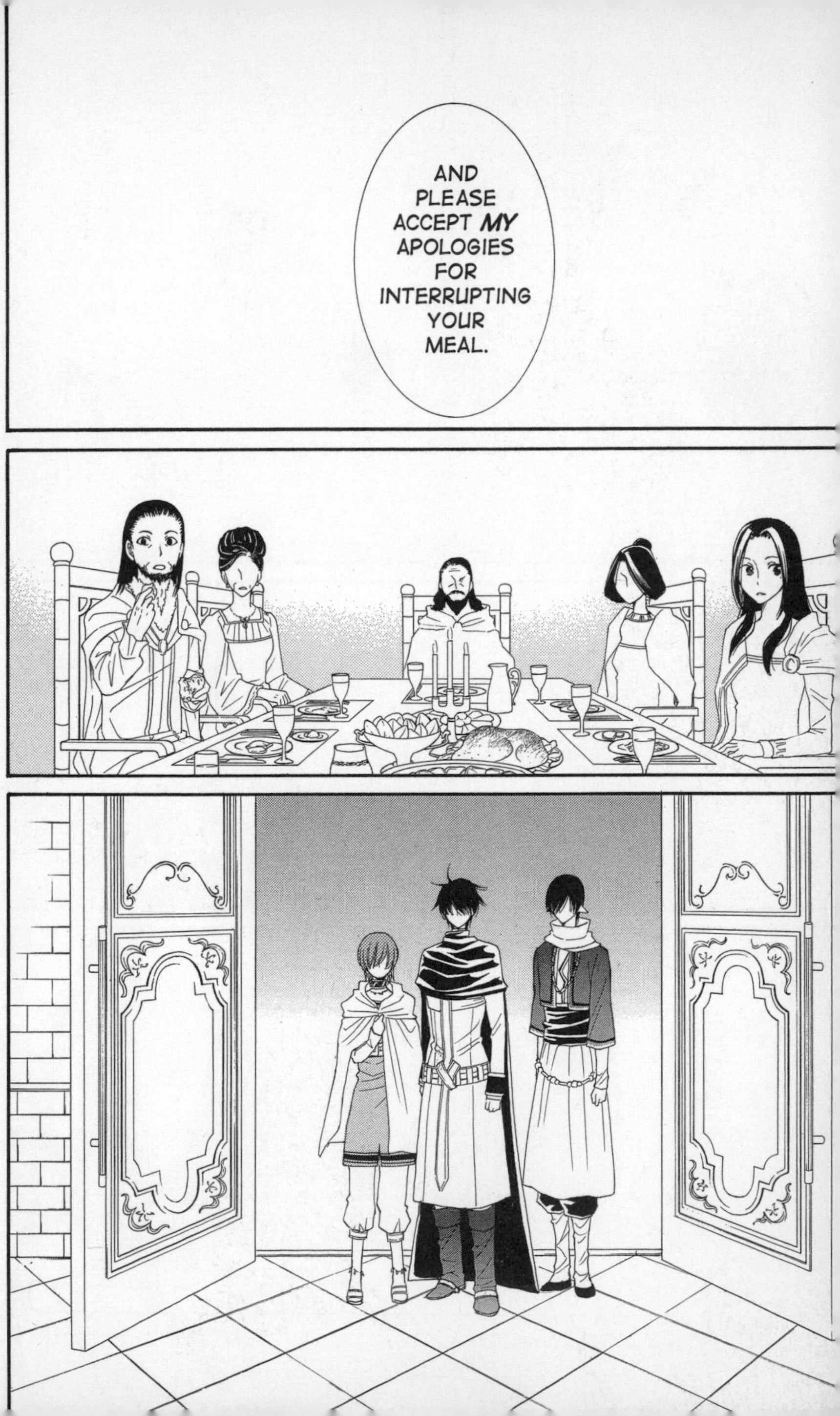
AND PLEASE ACCEPT *MY* APOLOGIES FOR INTERRUPTING YOUR MEAL.

PRINCE CAESAR?!

WH-WHO ARE *THEY*?

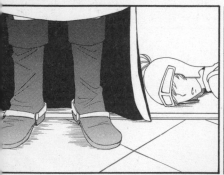

YOU...!

RATTLE

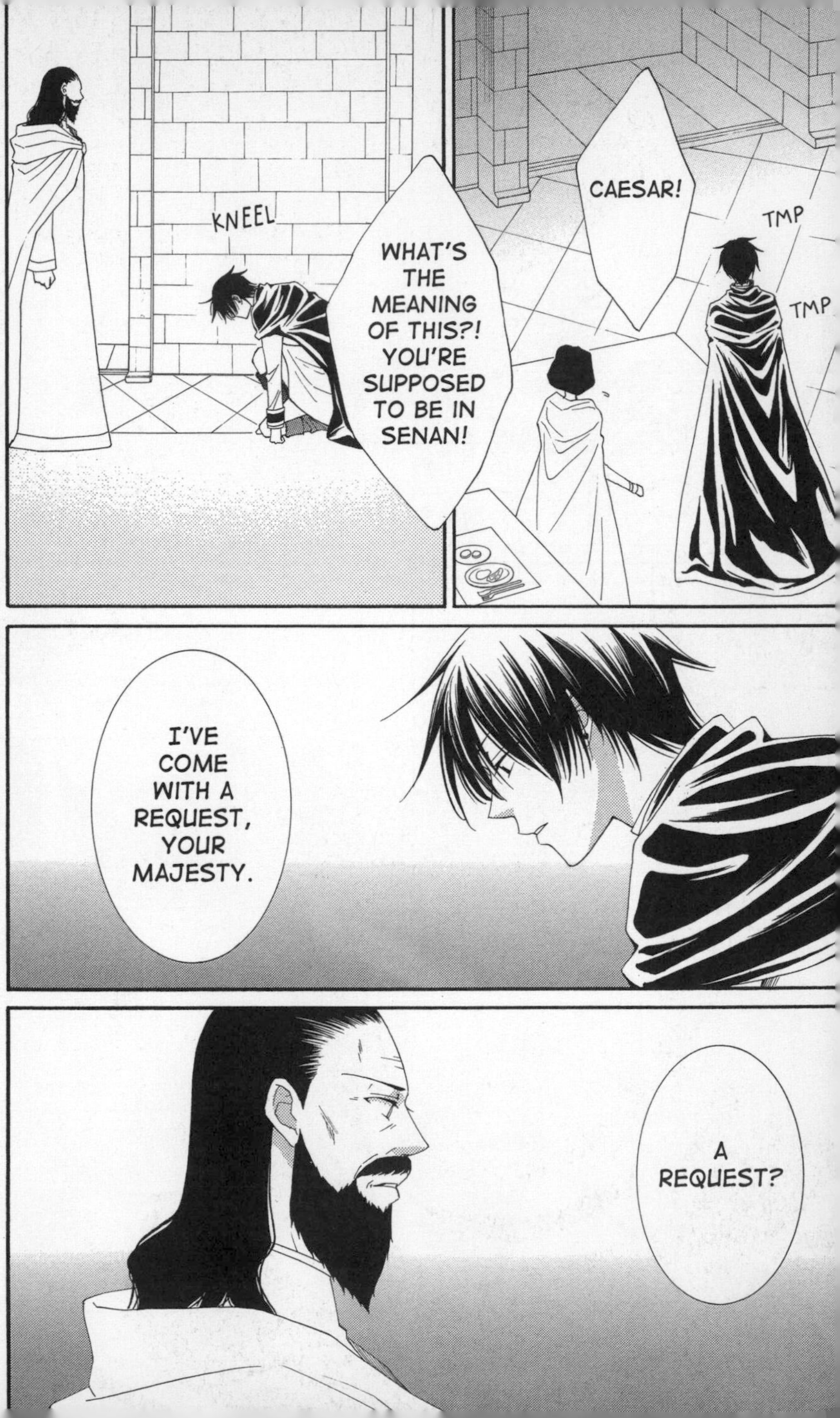
TMP
TMP
CAESAR!
WHAT'S THE MEANING OF THIS?! YOU'RE SUPPOSED TO BE IN SENAN!
KNEEL
I'VE COME WITH A REQUEST, YOUR MAJESTY.
A REQUEST?

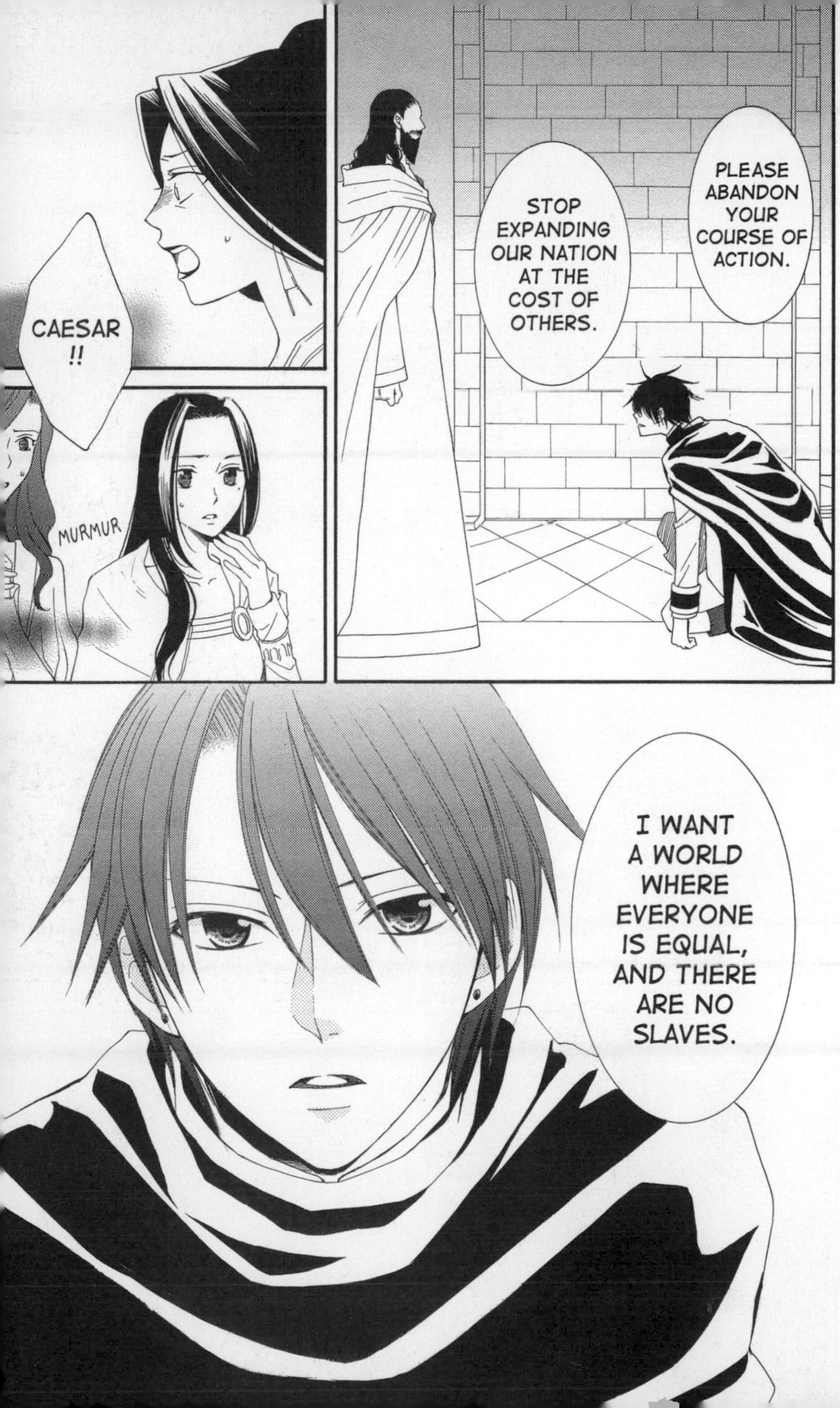
PLEASE ABANDON YOUR COURSE OF ACTION.
STOP EXPANDING OUR NATION AT THE COST OF OTHERS.
CAESAR !!
MURMUR
I WANT A WORLD WHERE EVERYONE IS EQUAL, AND THERE ARE NO SLAVES.

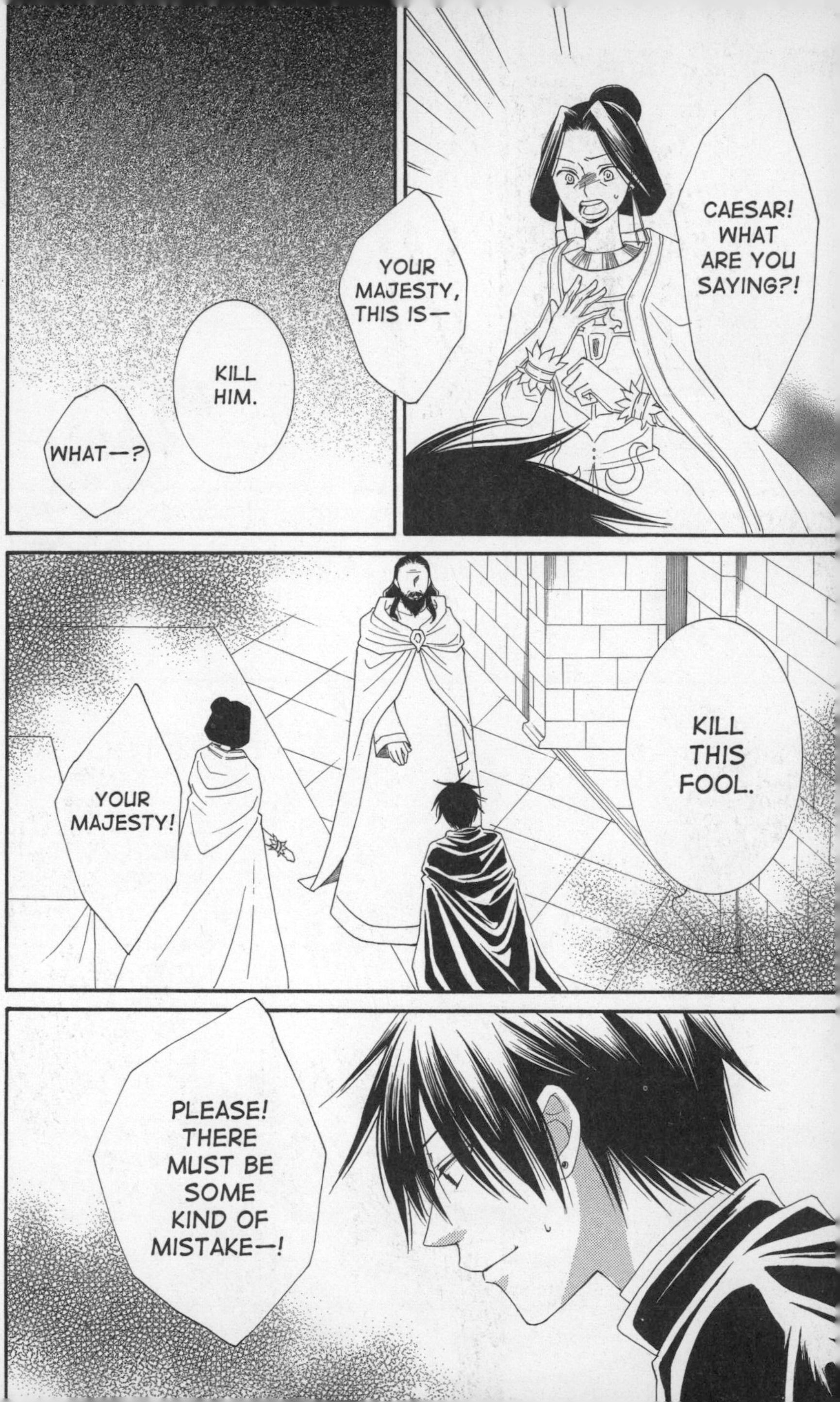
CAESAR! WHAT ARE YOU SAYING?!
YOUR MAJESTY, THIS IS—
KILL HIM.
WHAT—?
KILL THIS FOOL.
YOUR MAJESTY!
PLEASE! THERE MUST BE SOME KIND OF MISTAKE—!

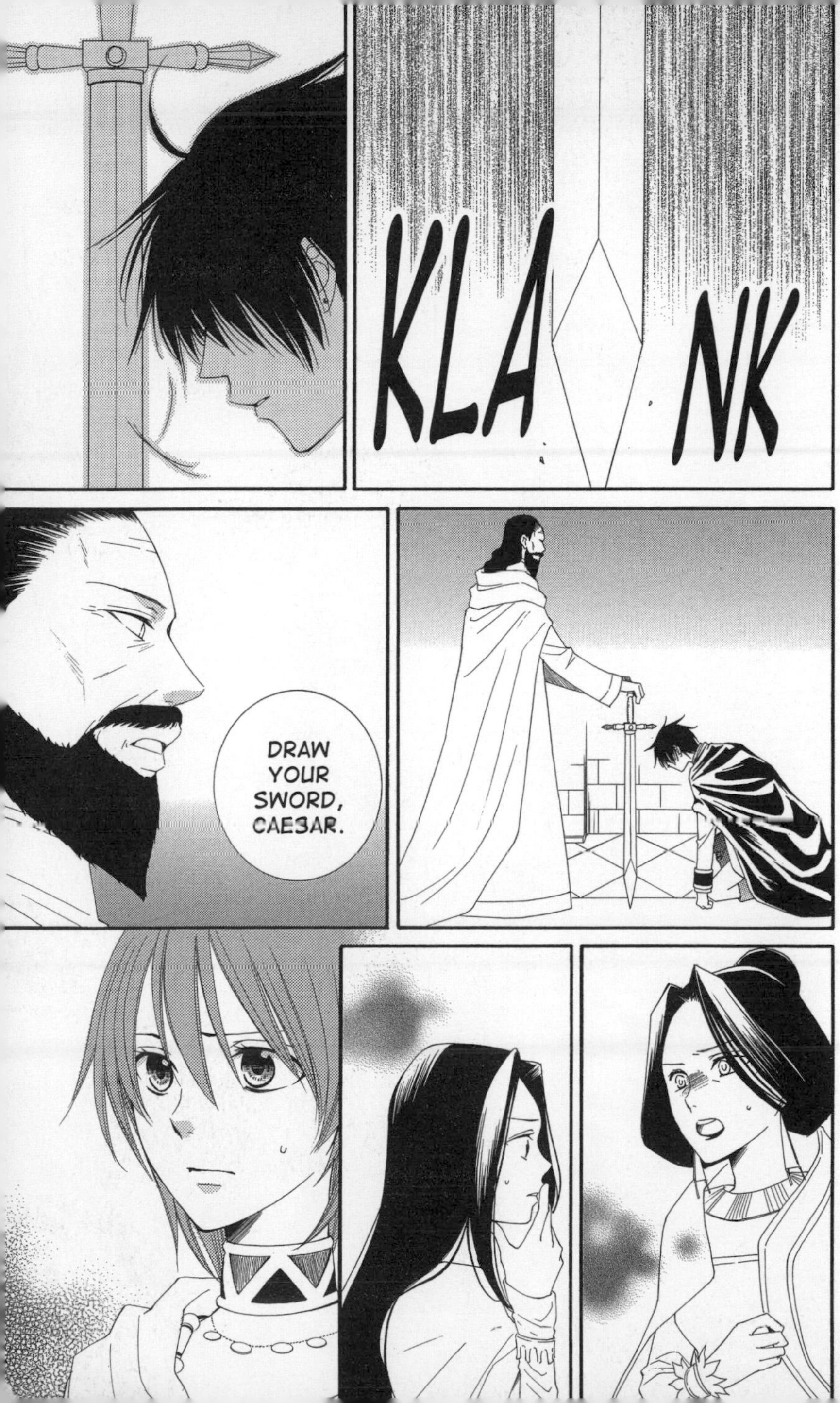
KLA NK
DRAW YOUR SWORD, CAESAR.

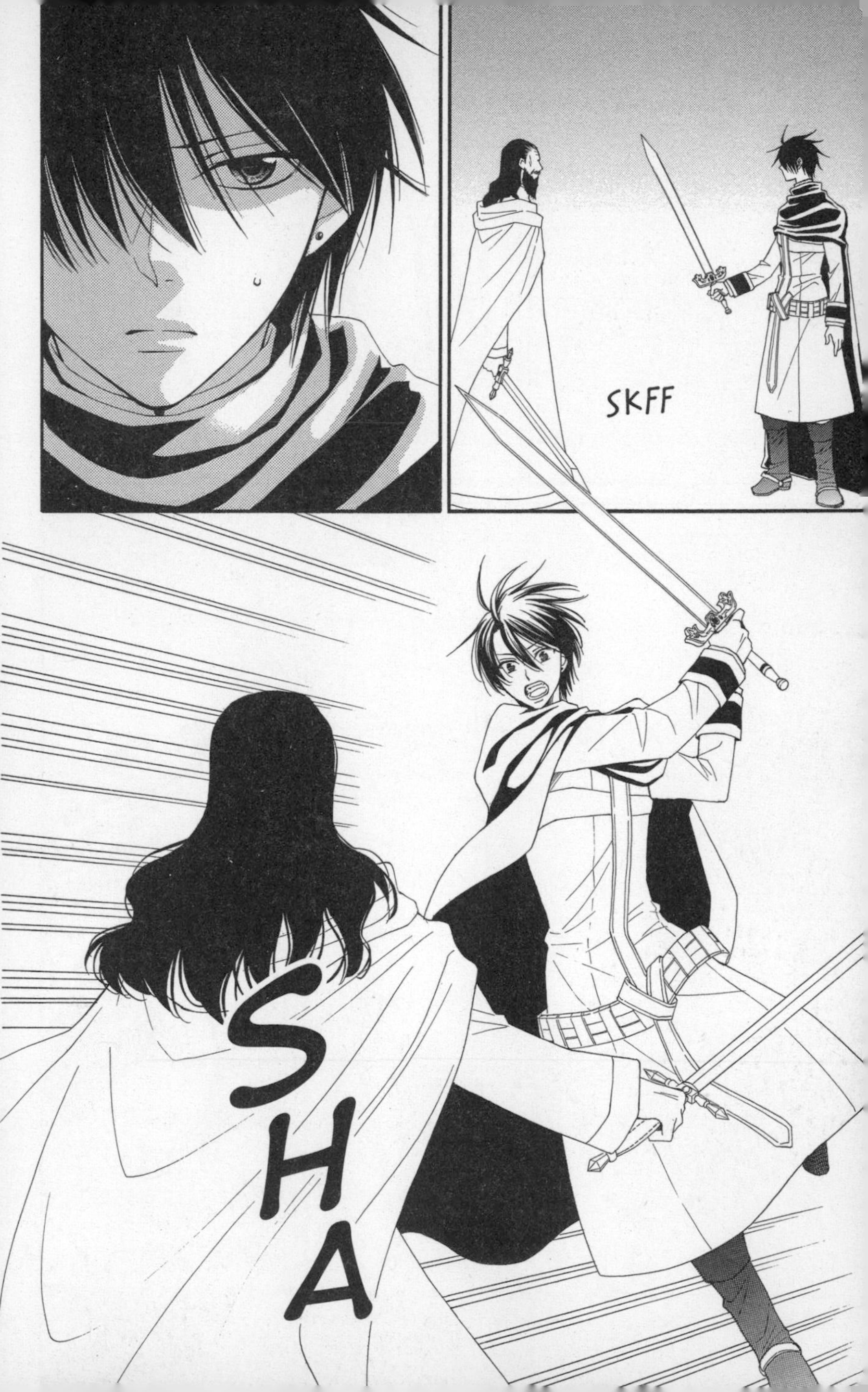
SKFF
SHA

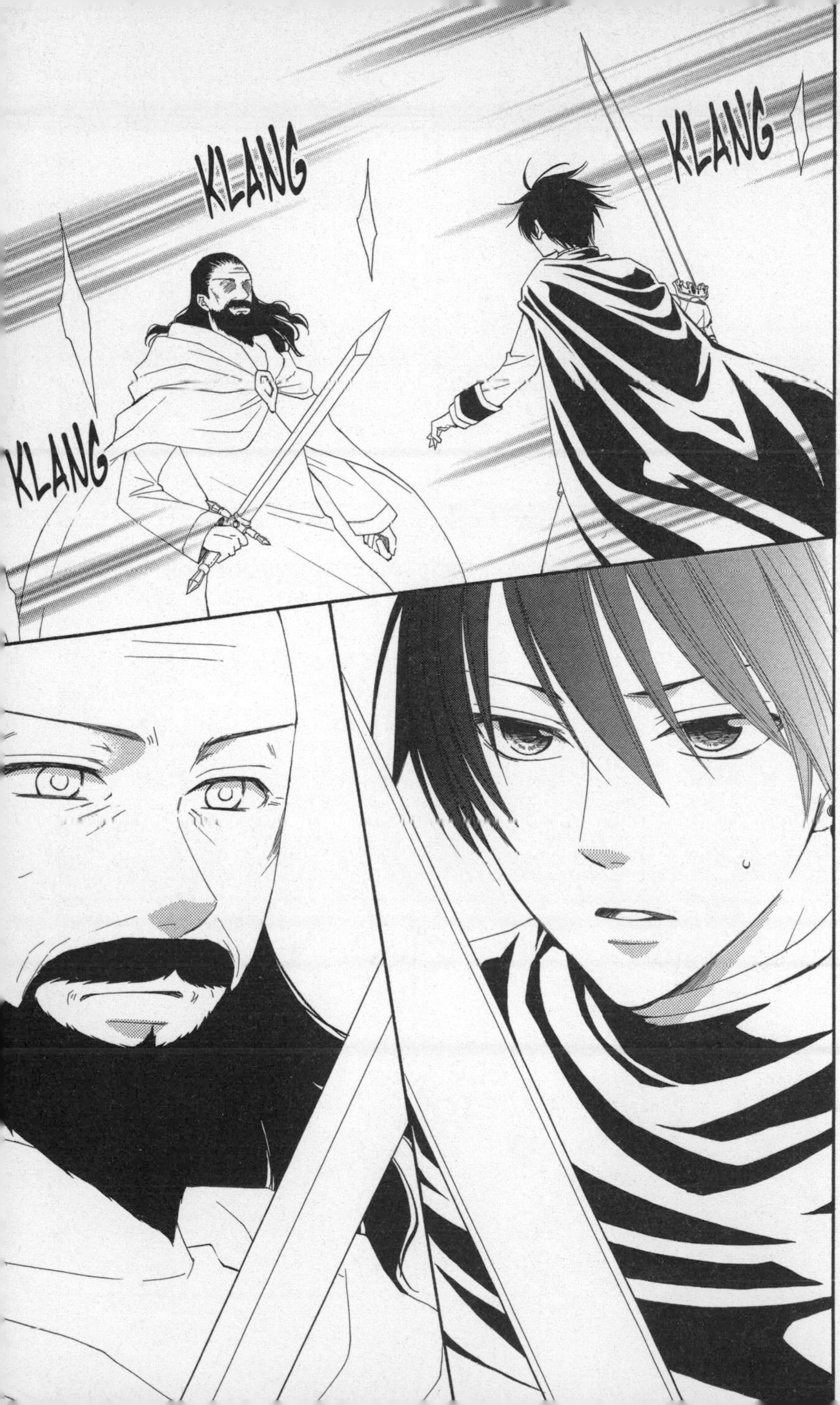
KLANG
KLANG
KLANG

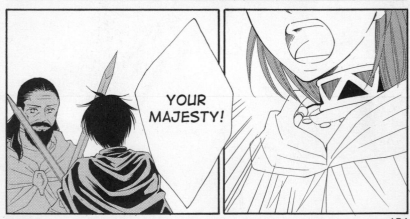

YOUR
MAJESTY!

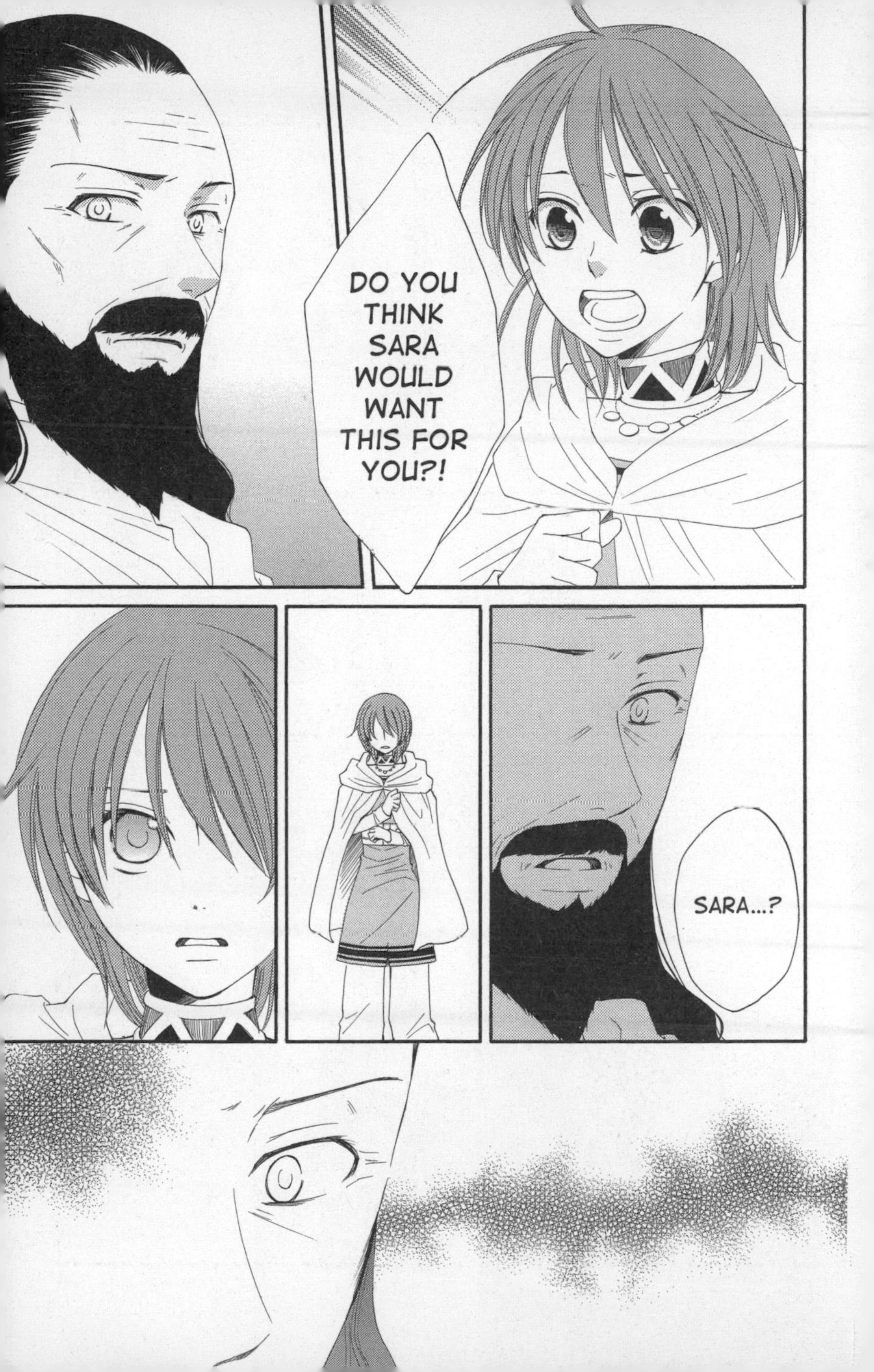
DO YOU THINK SARA WOULD WANT THIS FOR YOU?!
SARA...?

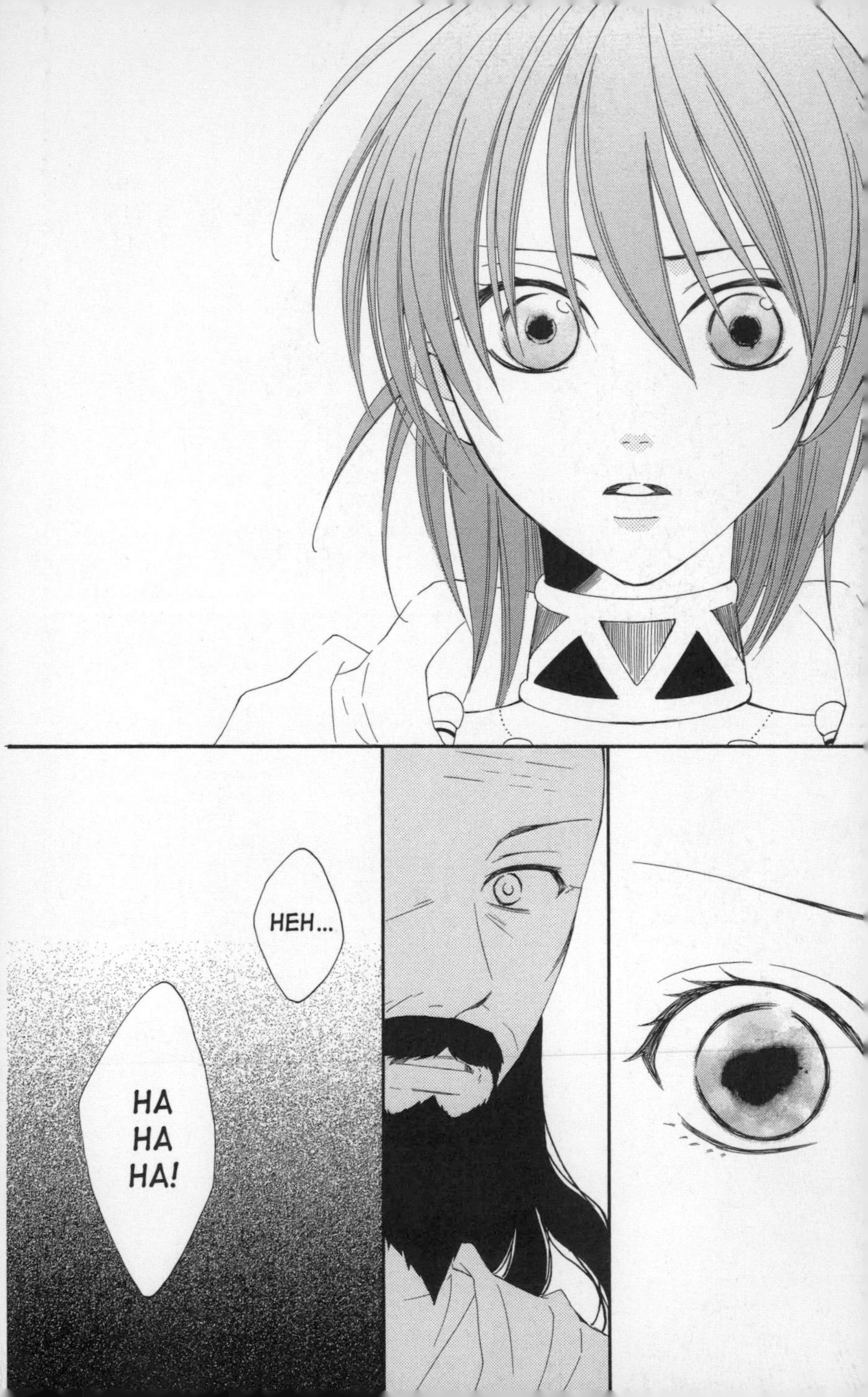
HEH...
HA HA HA!

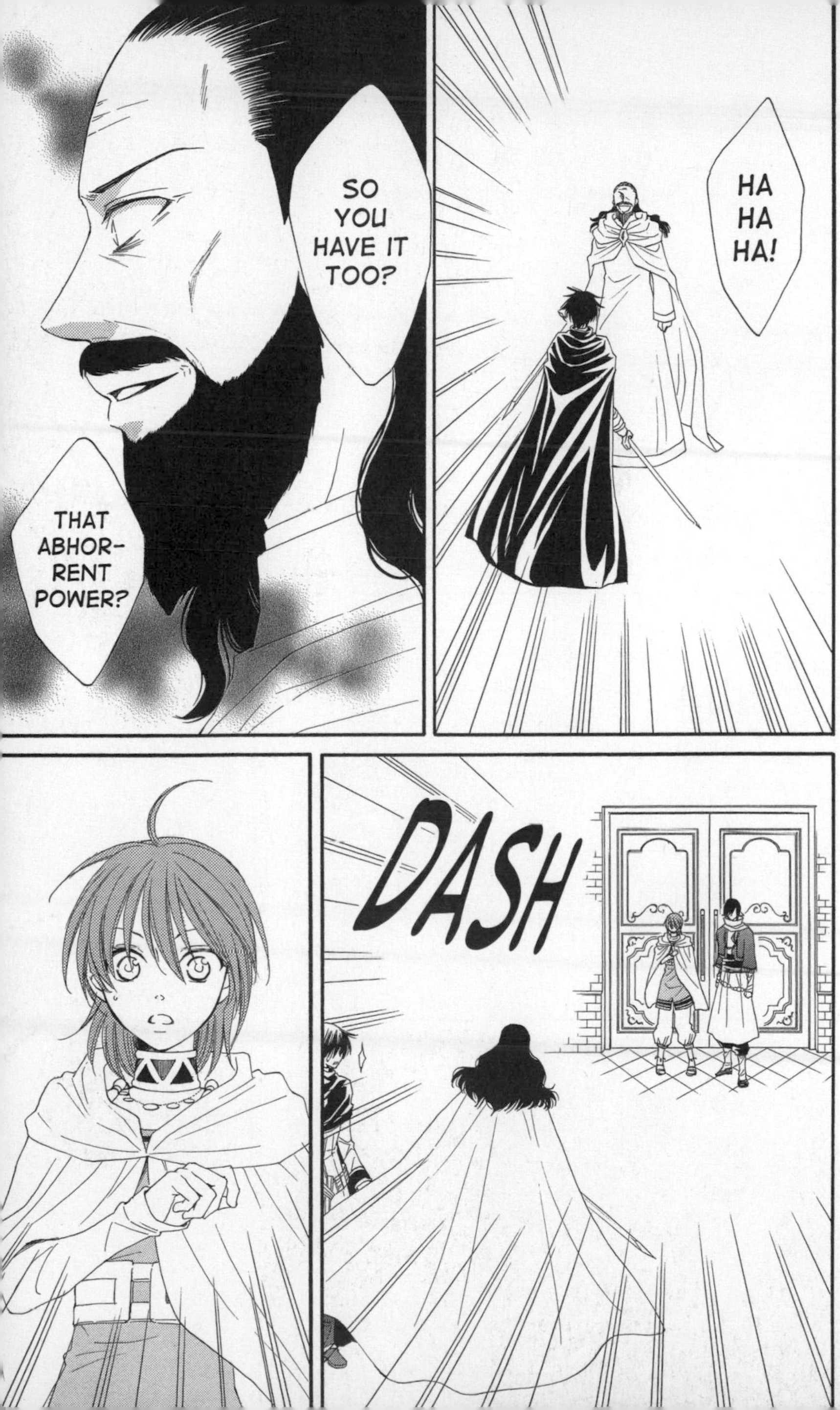
HA HA HA!
SO YOU HAVE IT TOO?
THAT ABHOR-RENT POWER?
DASH

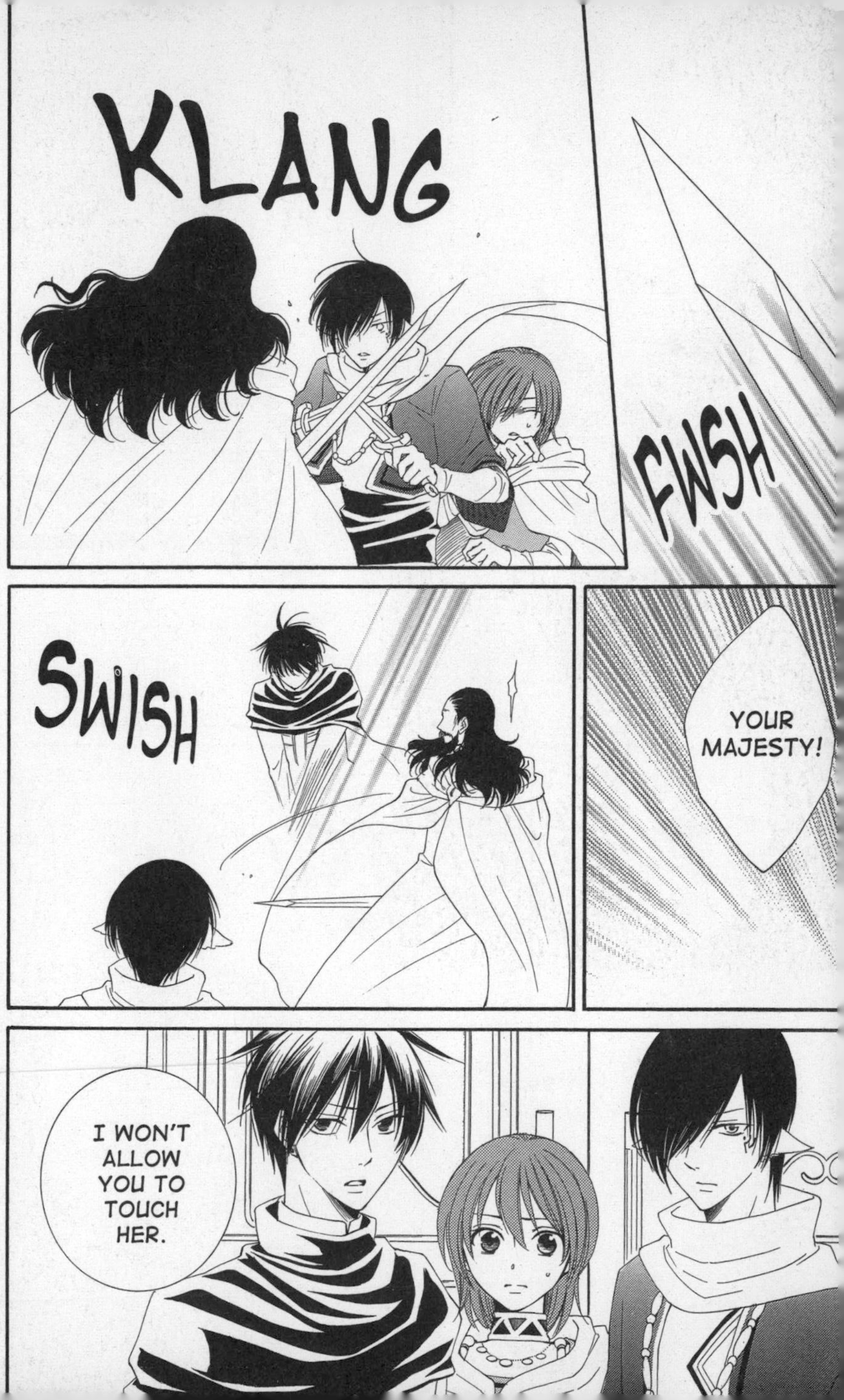
FWSH
KLANG
YOUR MAJESTY!
SWISH
I WON'T ALLOW YOU TO TOUCH HER.

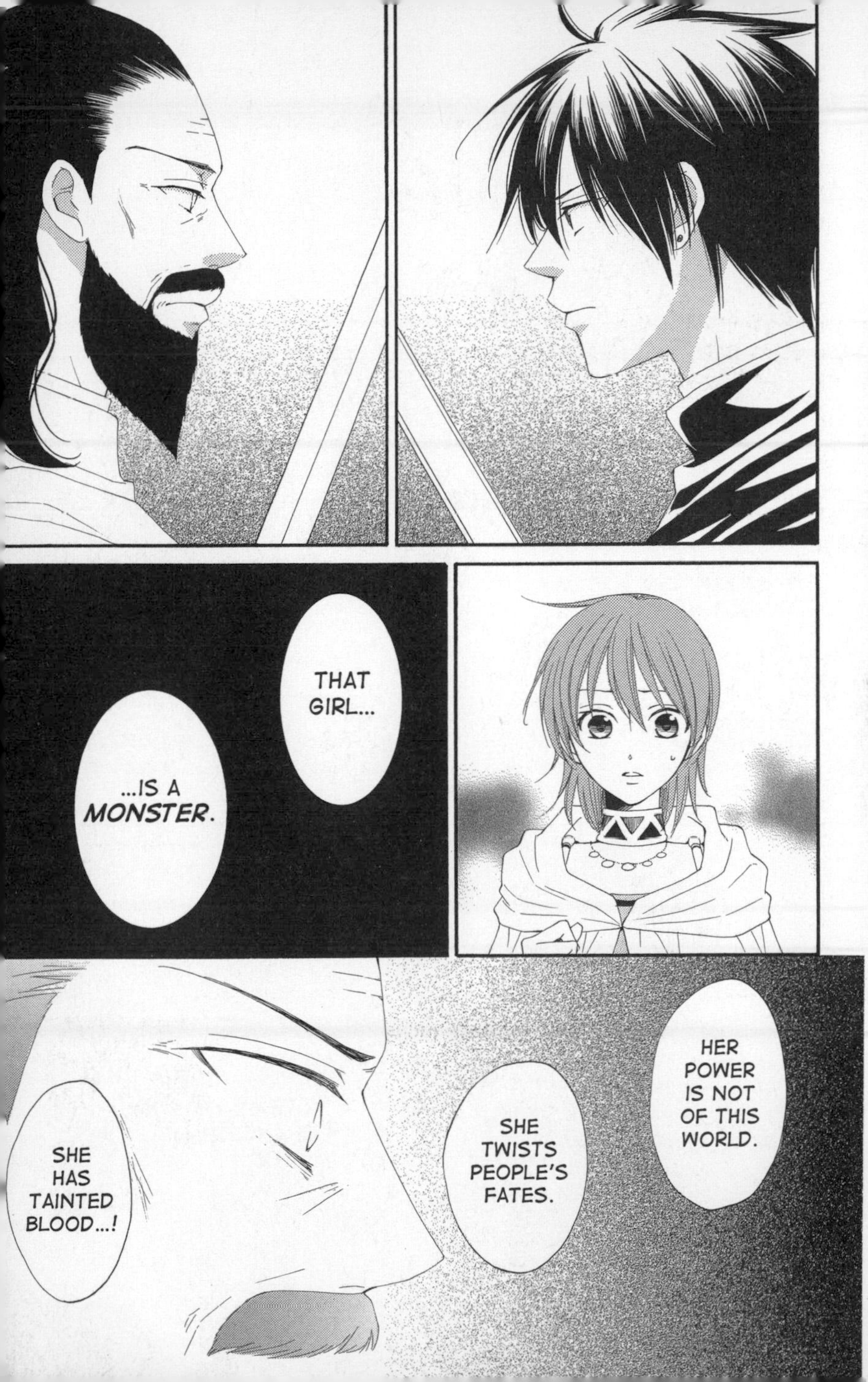
THAT GIRL...
...IS A *MONSTER*.
HER POWER IS NOT OF THIS WORLD.
SHE TWISTS PEOPLE'S FATES.
SHE HAS TAINTED BLOOD...!

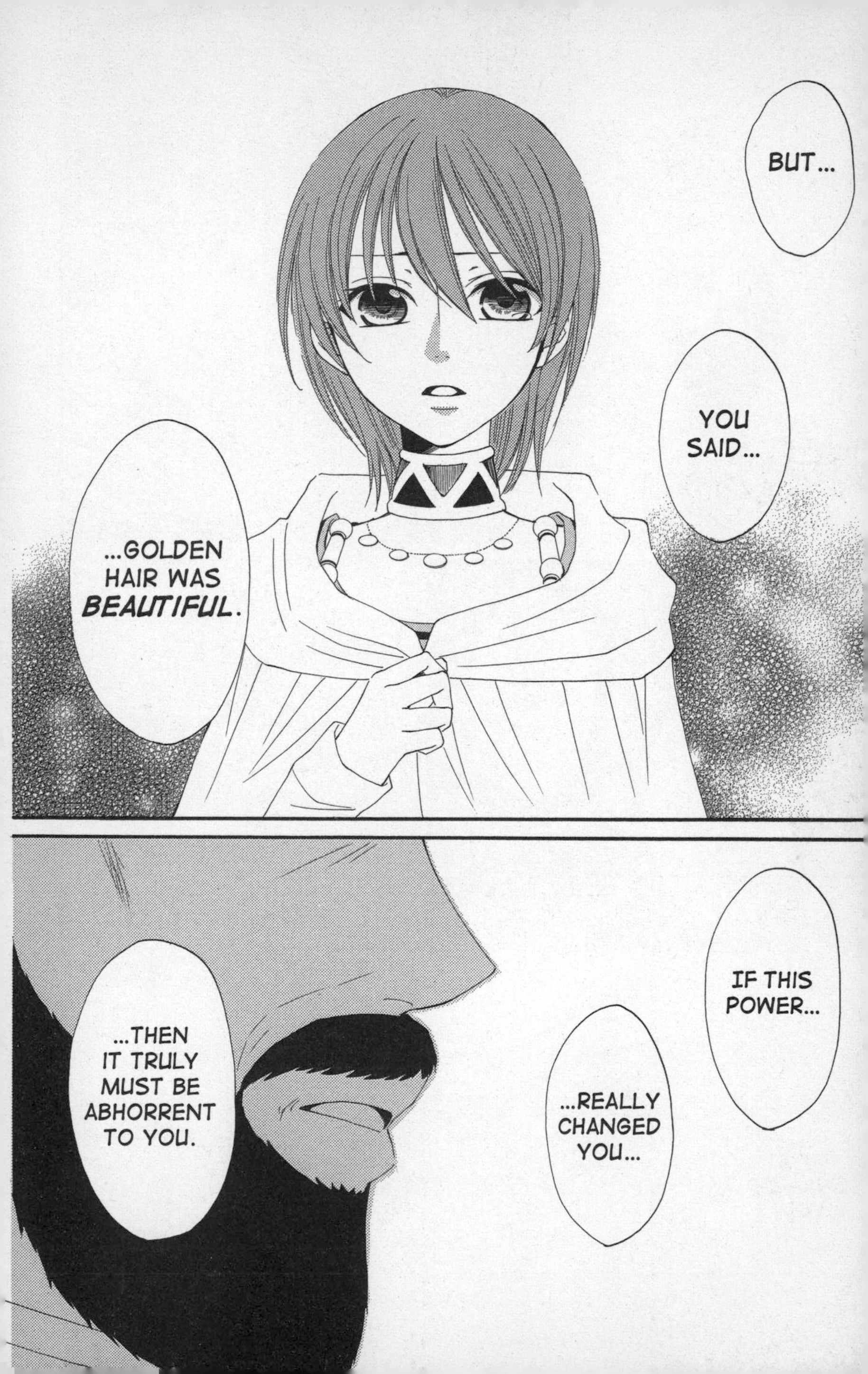
BUT...
YOU SAID...
...GOLDEN HAIR WAS BEAUTIFUL.
IF THIS POWER...
...REALLY CHANGED YOU...
...THEN IT TRULY MUST BE ABHORRENT TO YOU.

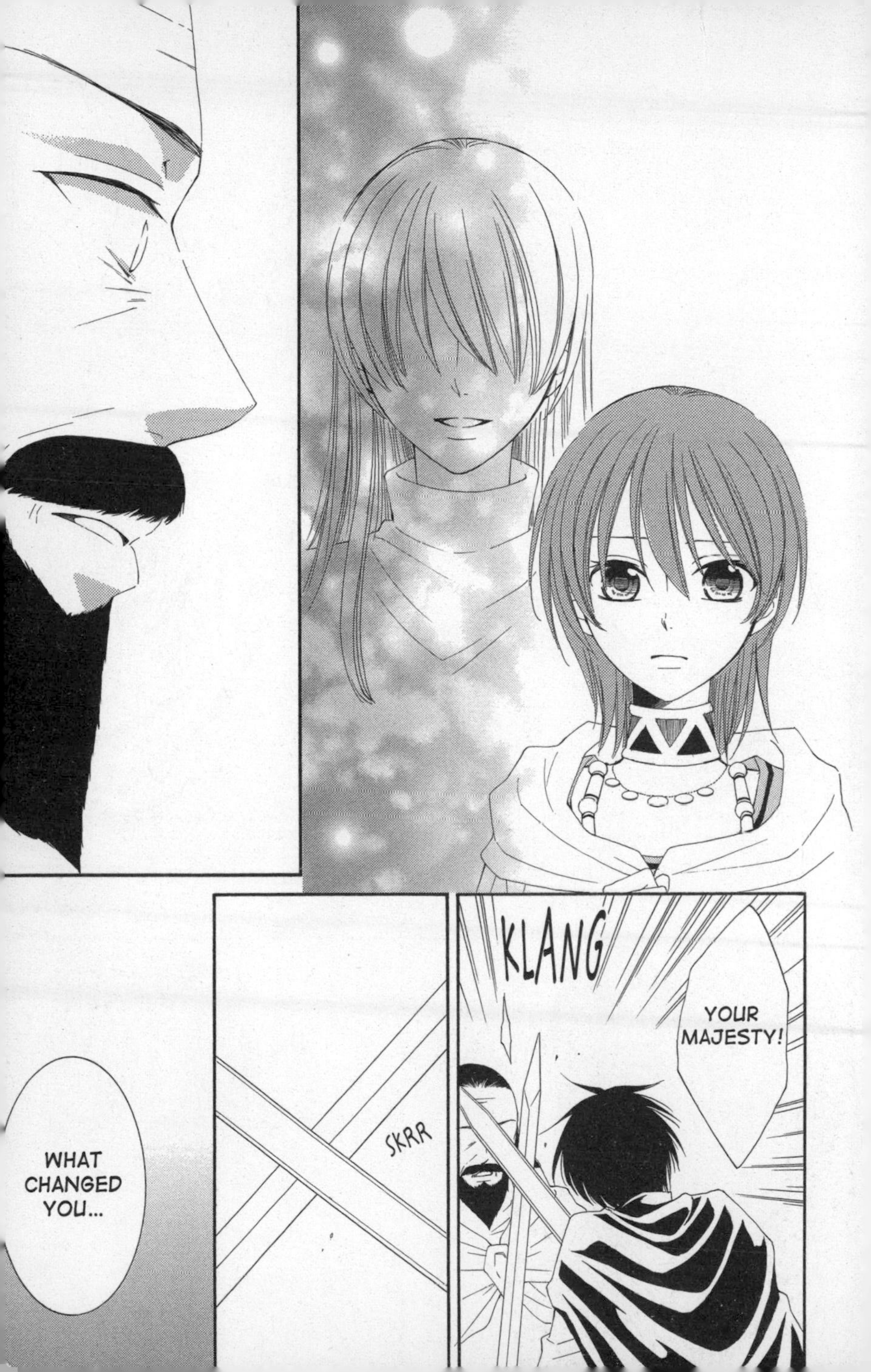
KLANG
YOUR MAJESTY!
SKRR
WHAT CHANGED YOU...

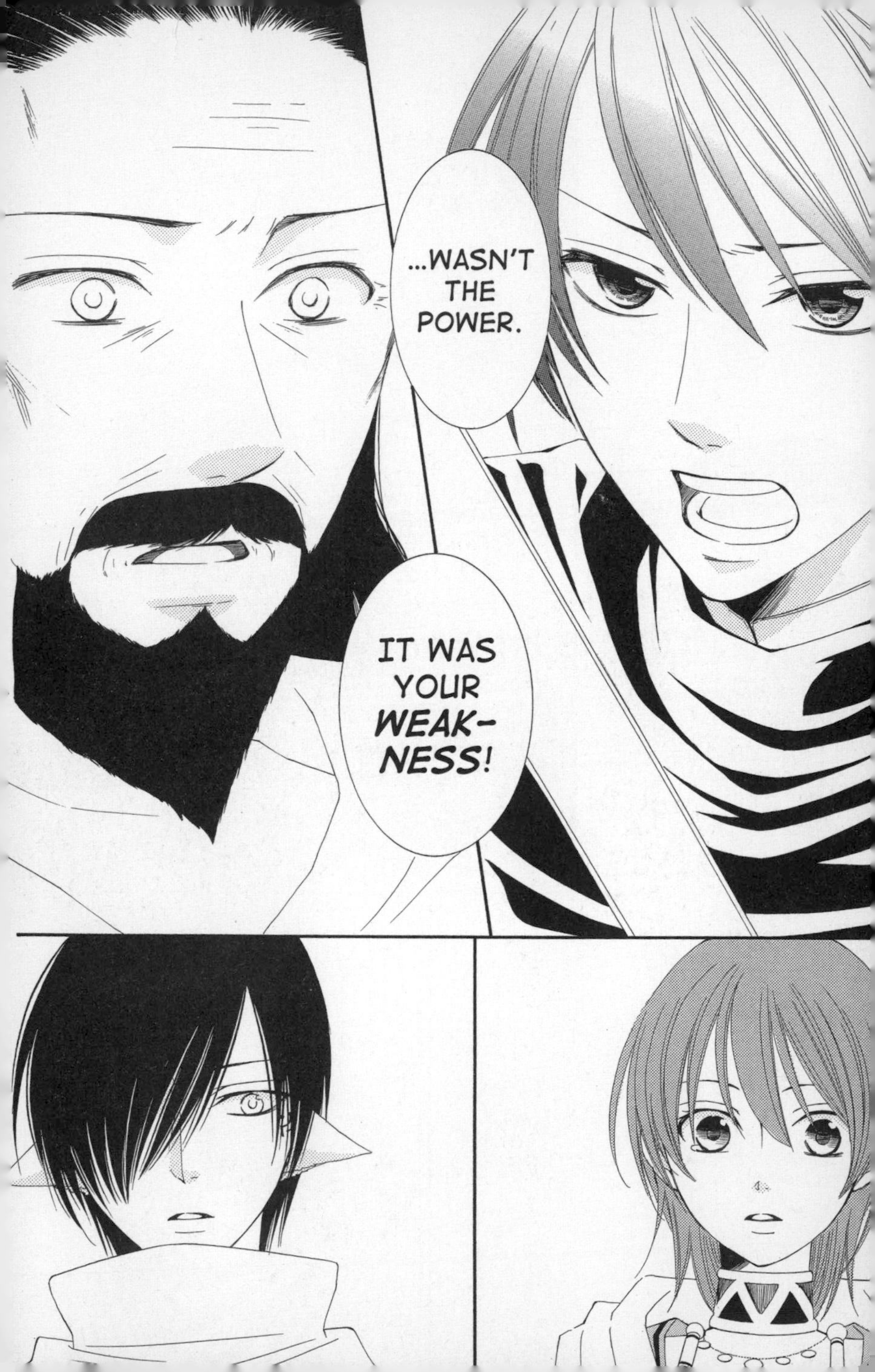
...WASN'T THE POWER.
IT WAS YOUR WEAK-NESS!

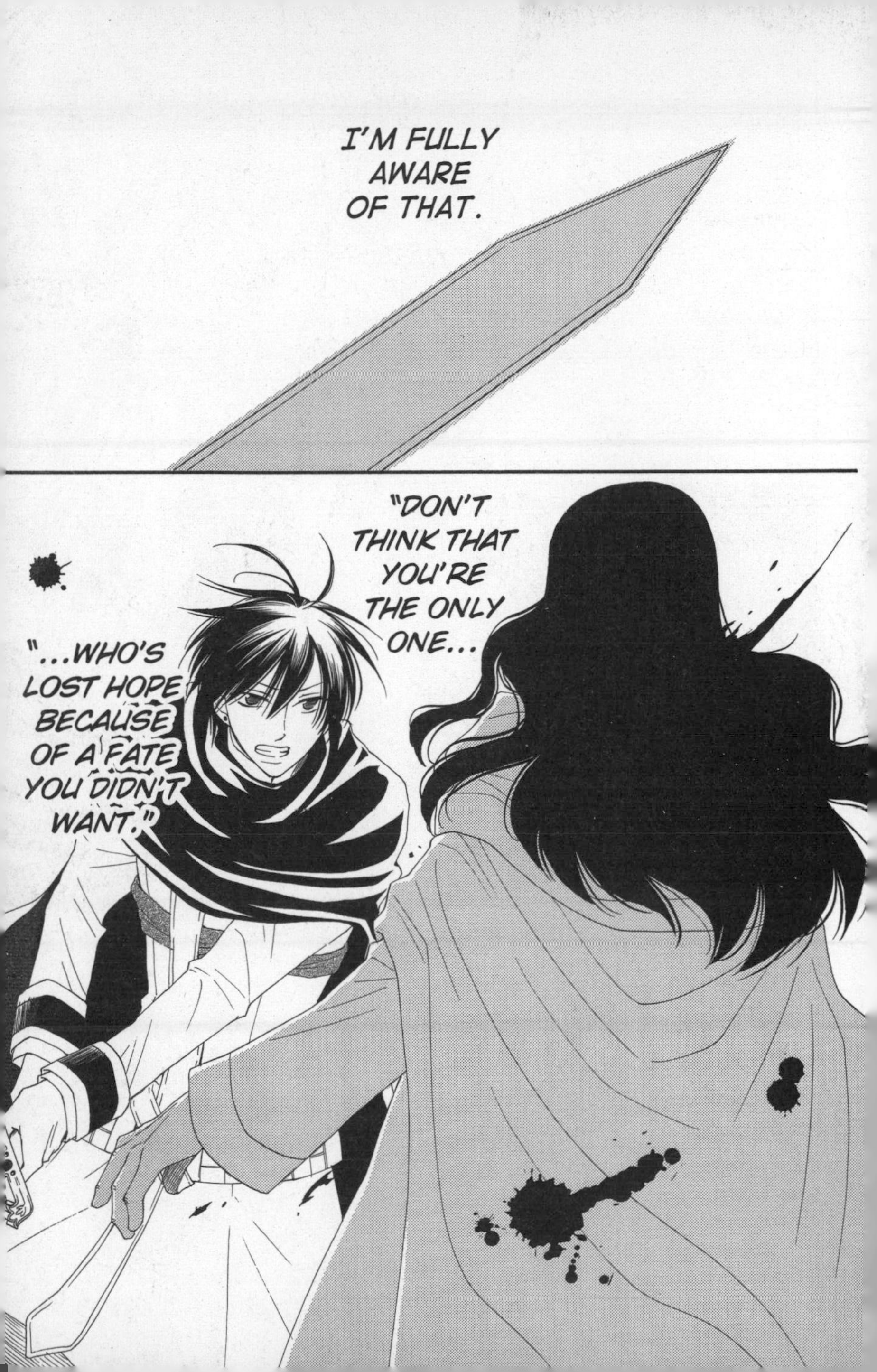
I'M FULLY AWARE OF THAT.
"DON'T THINK THAT YOU'RE THE ONLY ONE...
"...WHO'S LOST HOPE BECAUSE OF A FATE YOU DIDN'T WANT."

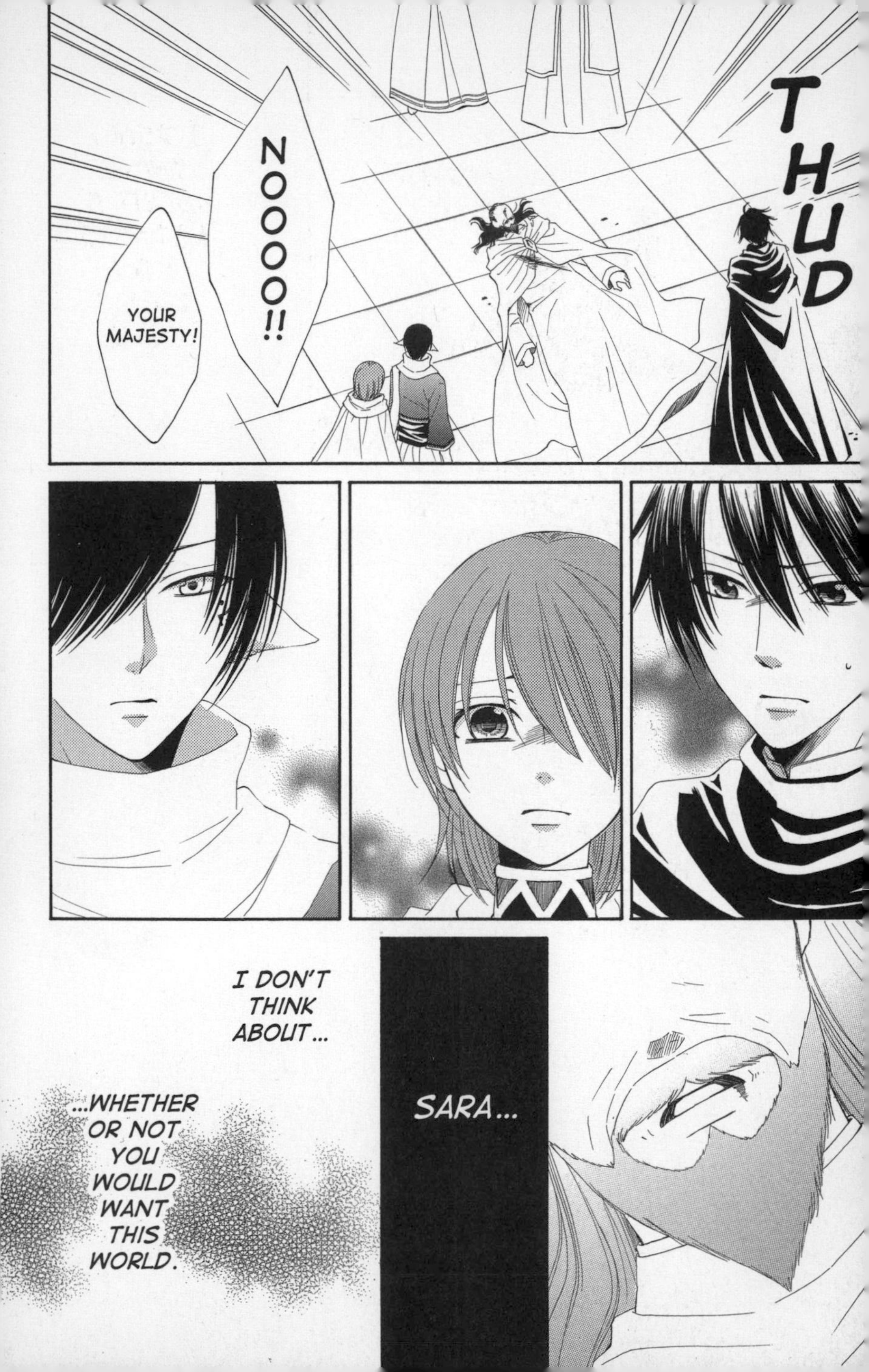
THUD
NOOOO!!
YOUR MAJESTY!
SARA...
I DON'T THINK ABOUT...
...WHETHER OR NOT YOU WOULD WANT THIS WORLD.

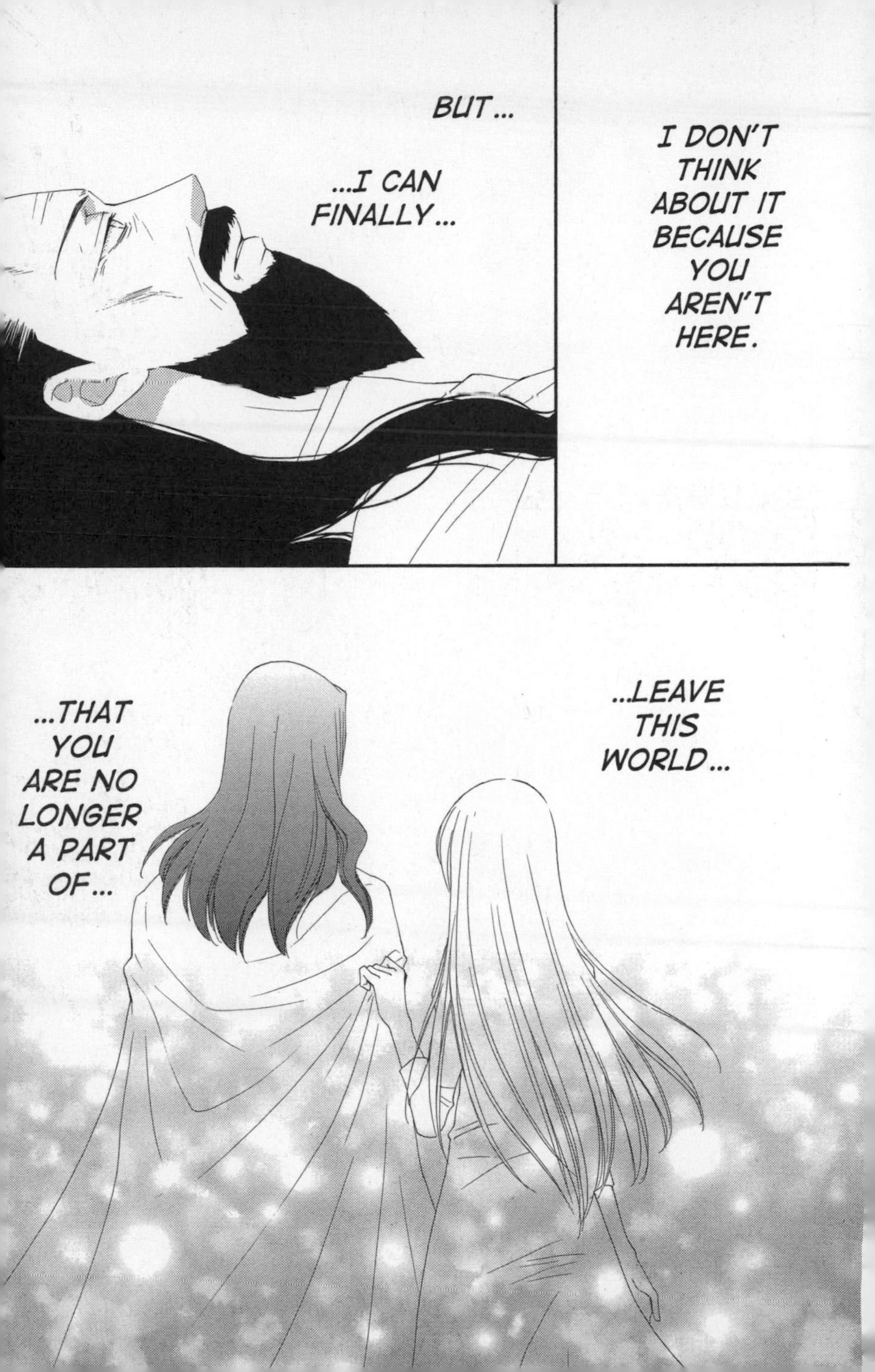
I DON'T THINK ABOUT IT BECAUSE YOU AREN'T HERE.
BUT...
...I CAN FINALLY...
...LEAVE THIS WORLD...
...THAT YOU ARE NO LONGER A PART OF...

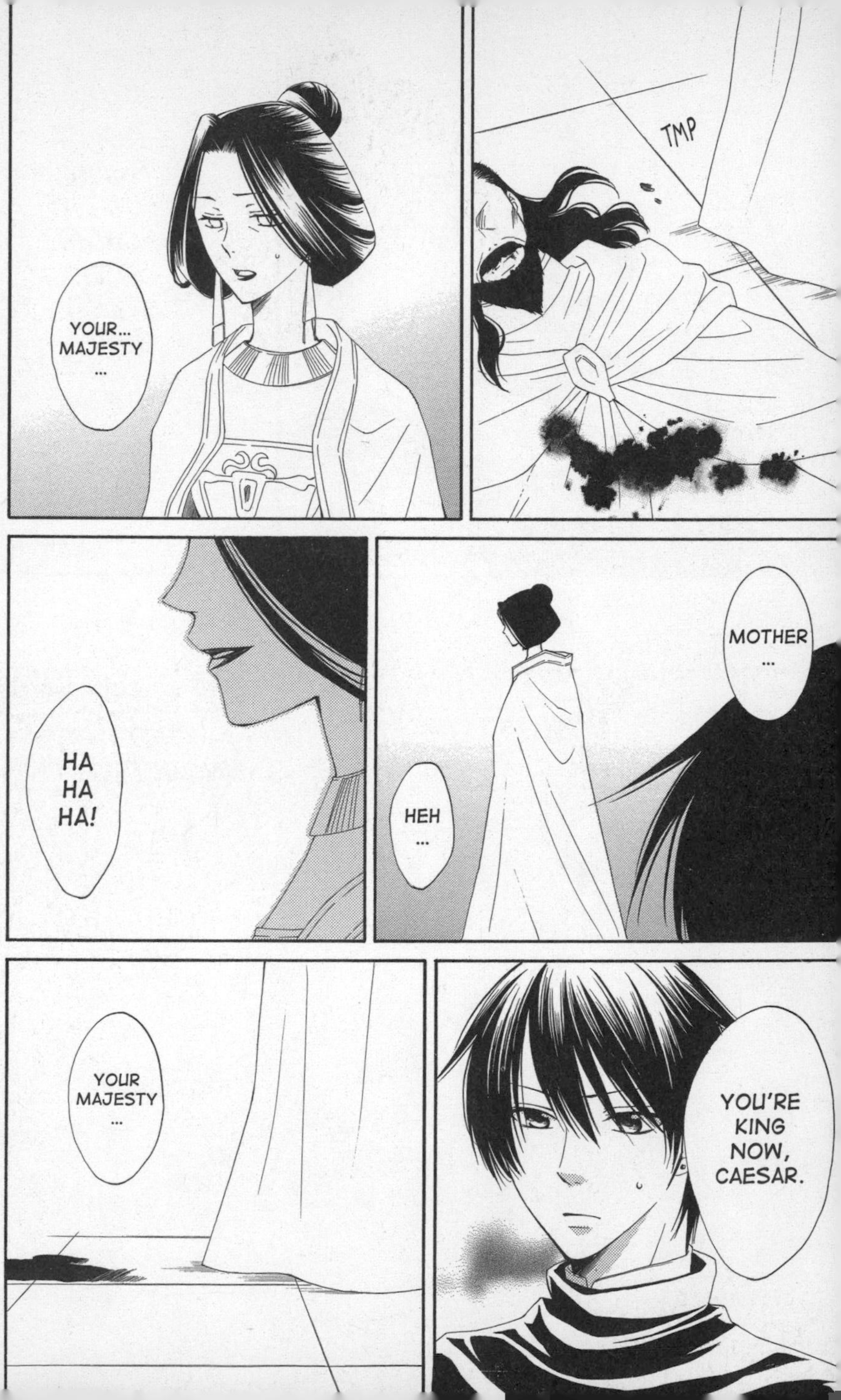
TMP
YOUR... MAJESTY ...
MOTHER ...
HEH ...
HA HA HA!
YOU'RE KING NOW, CAESAR.
YOUR MAJESTY ...

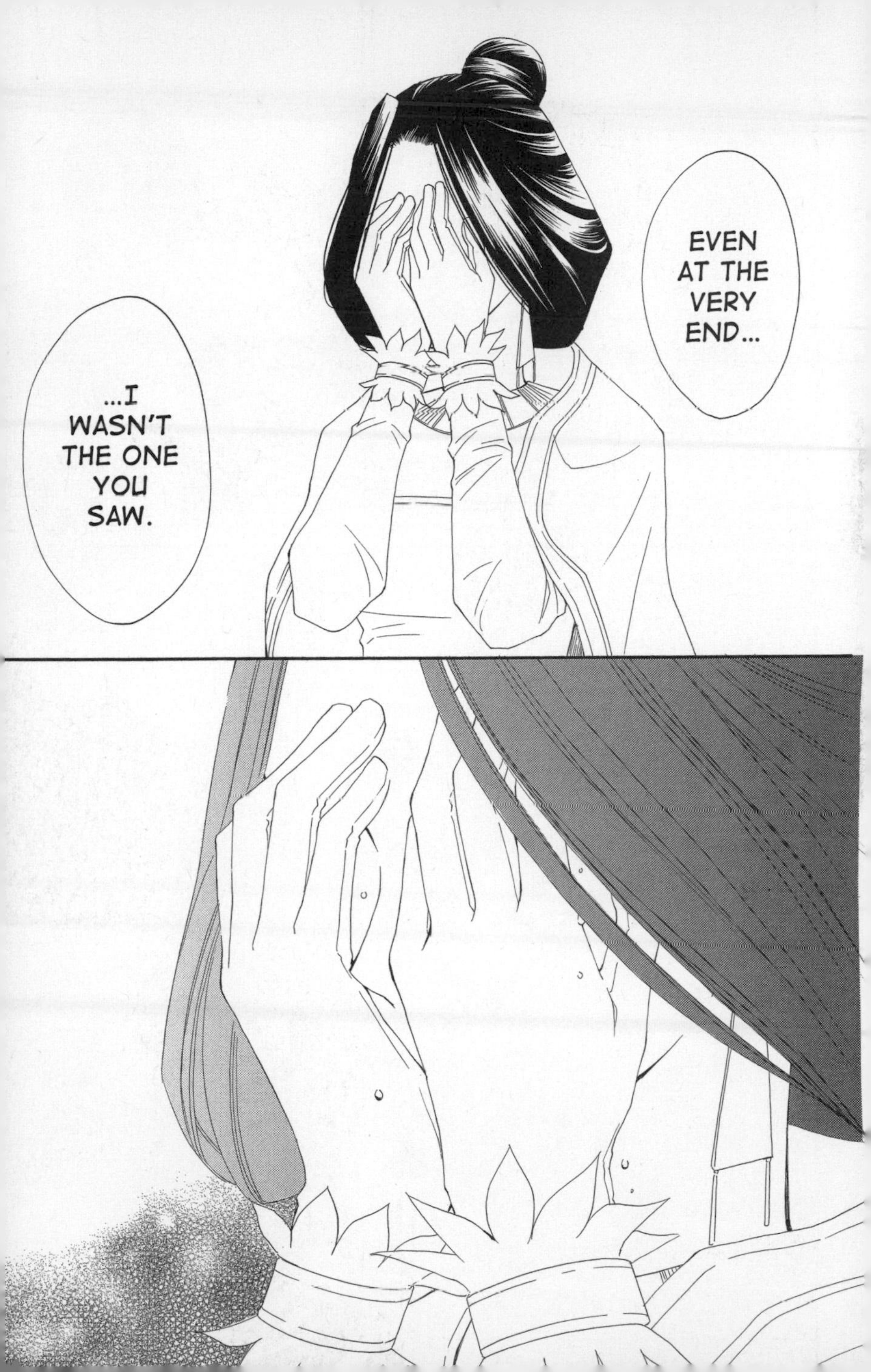
EVEN AT THE VERY END...
...I WASN'T THE ONE YOU SAW.

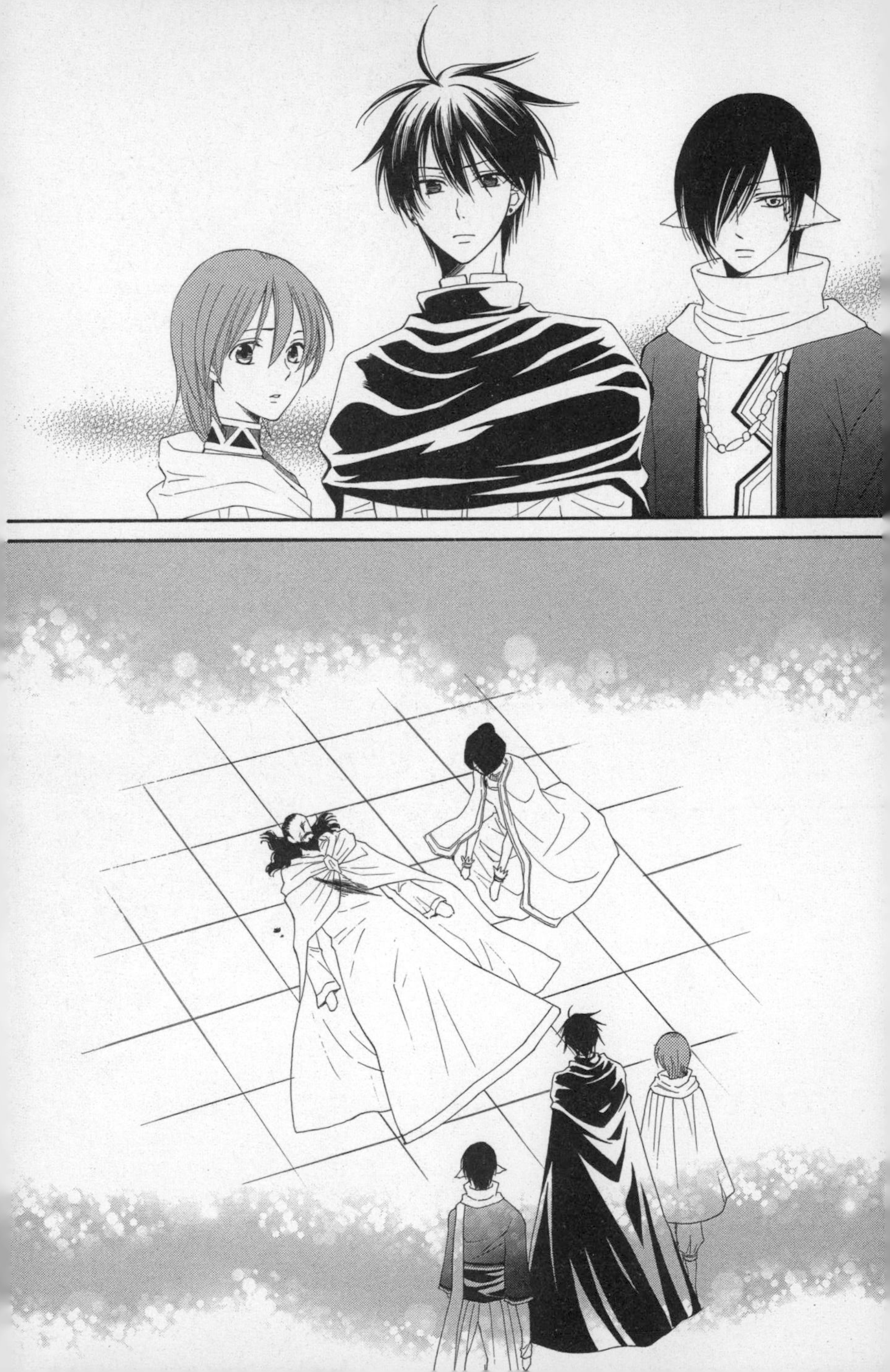

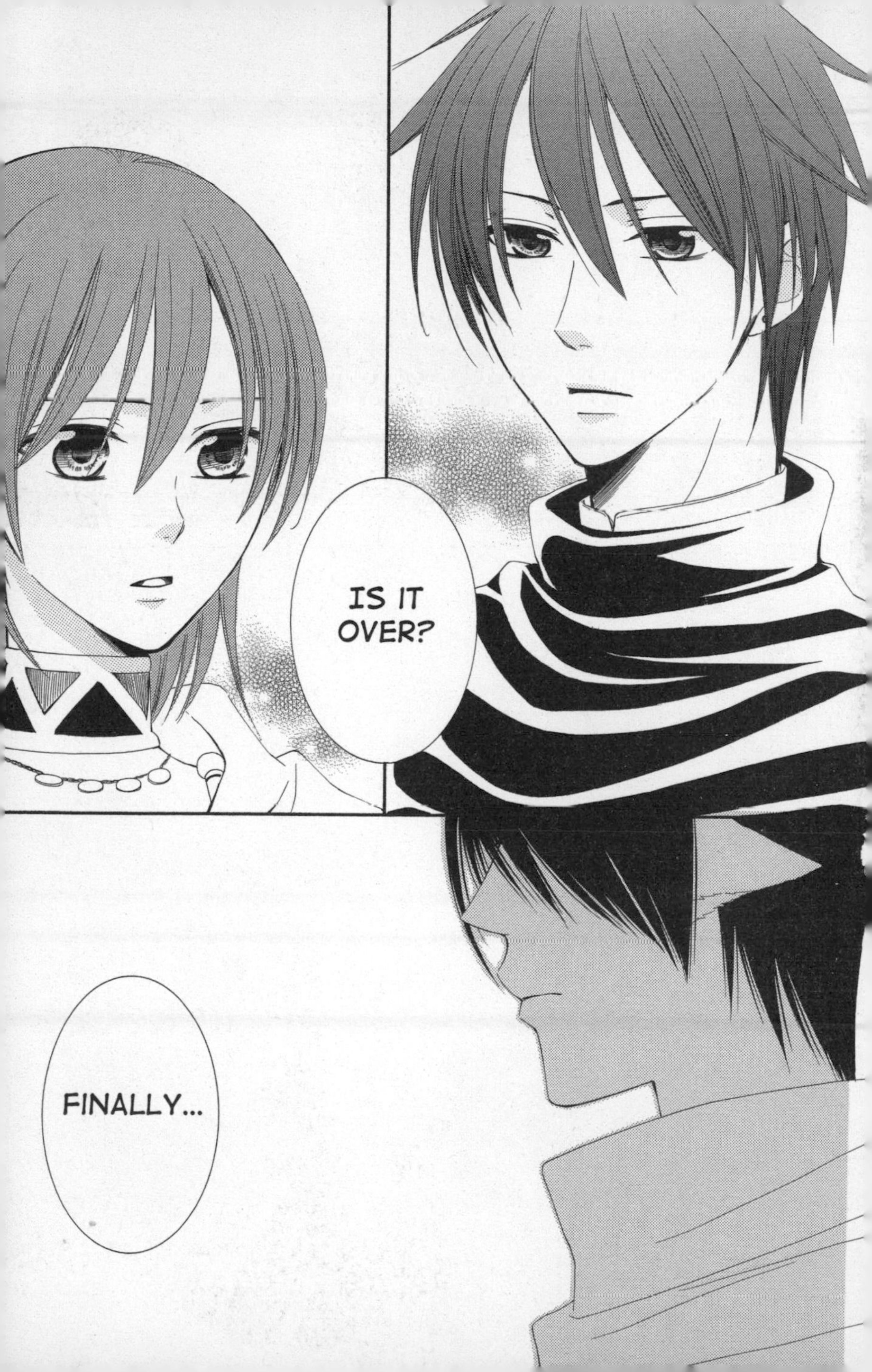
IS IT OVER?
FINALLY...

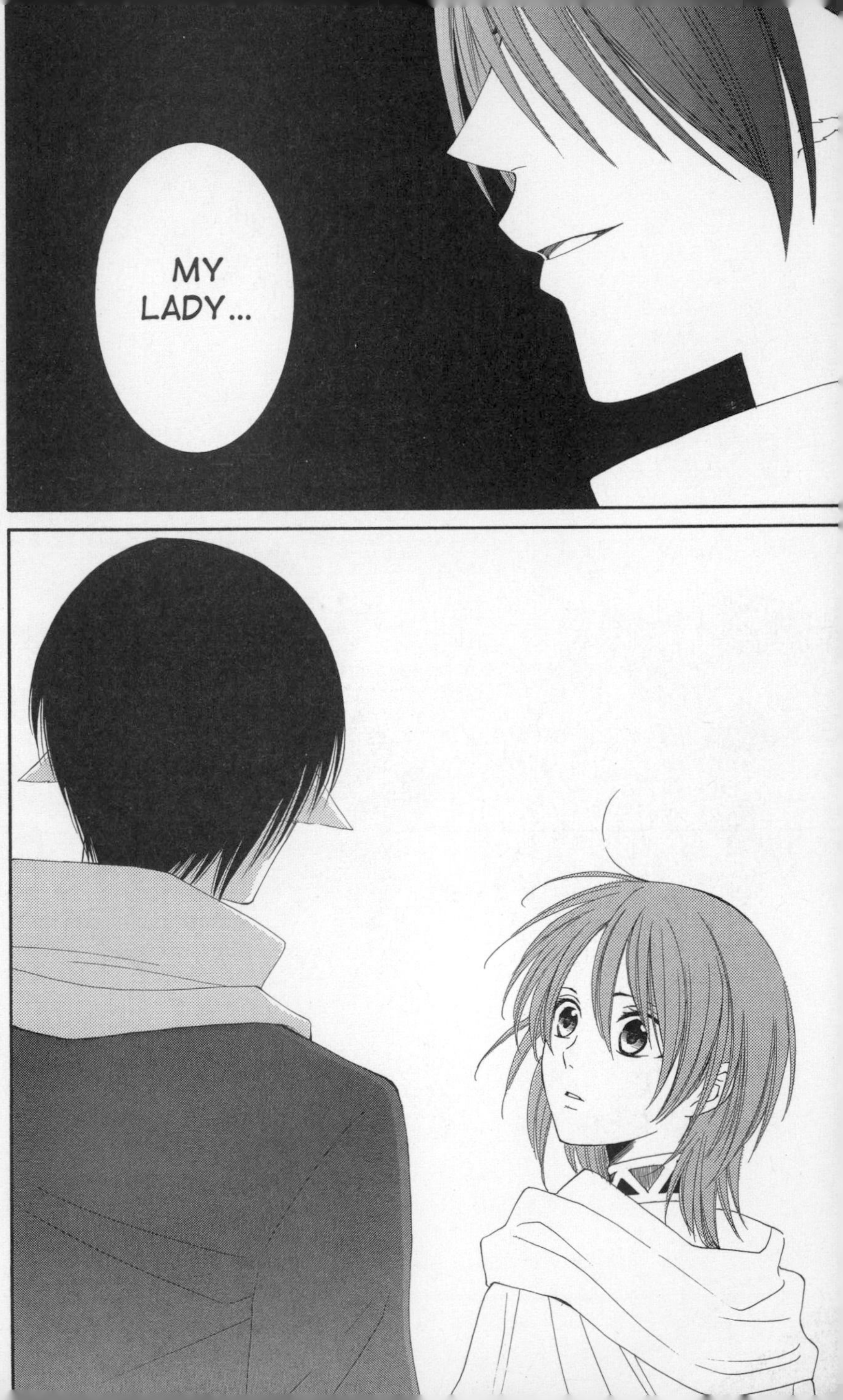
MY LADY...

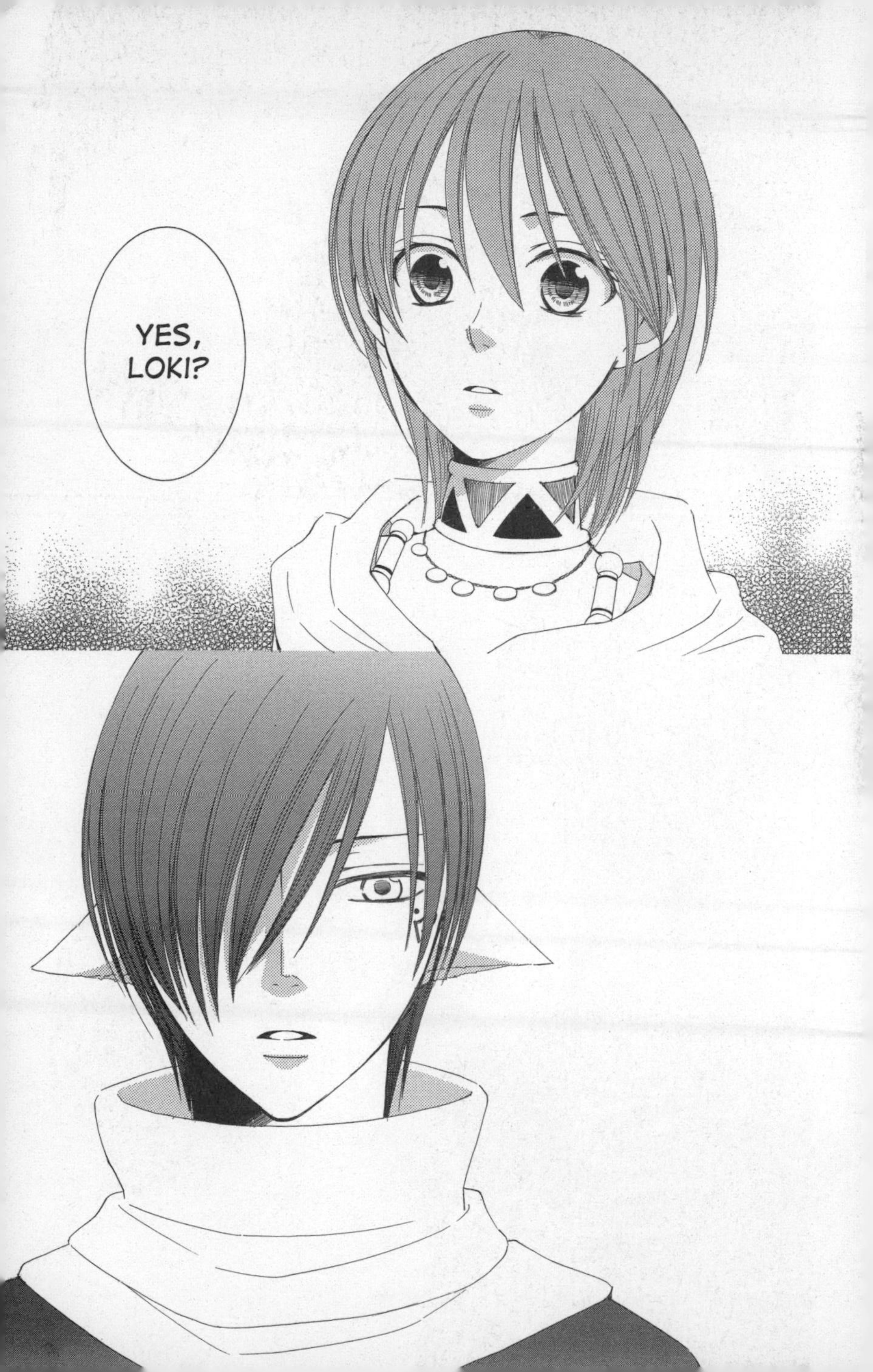
YES, LOKI?

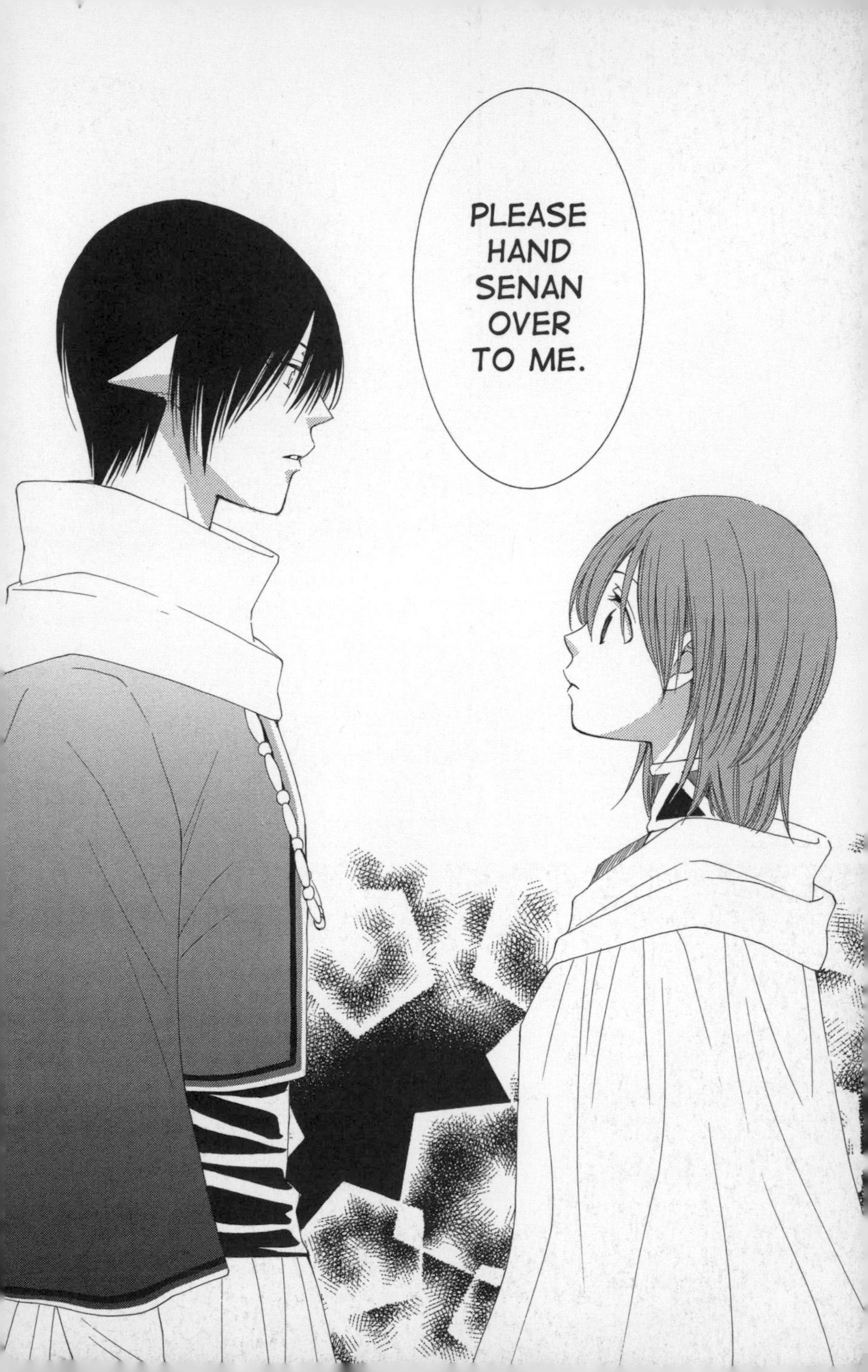
PLEASE HAND SENAN OVER TO ME.

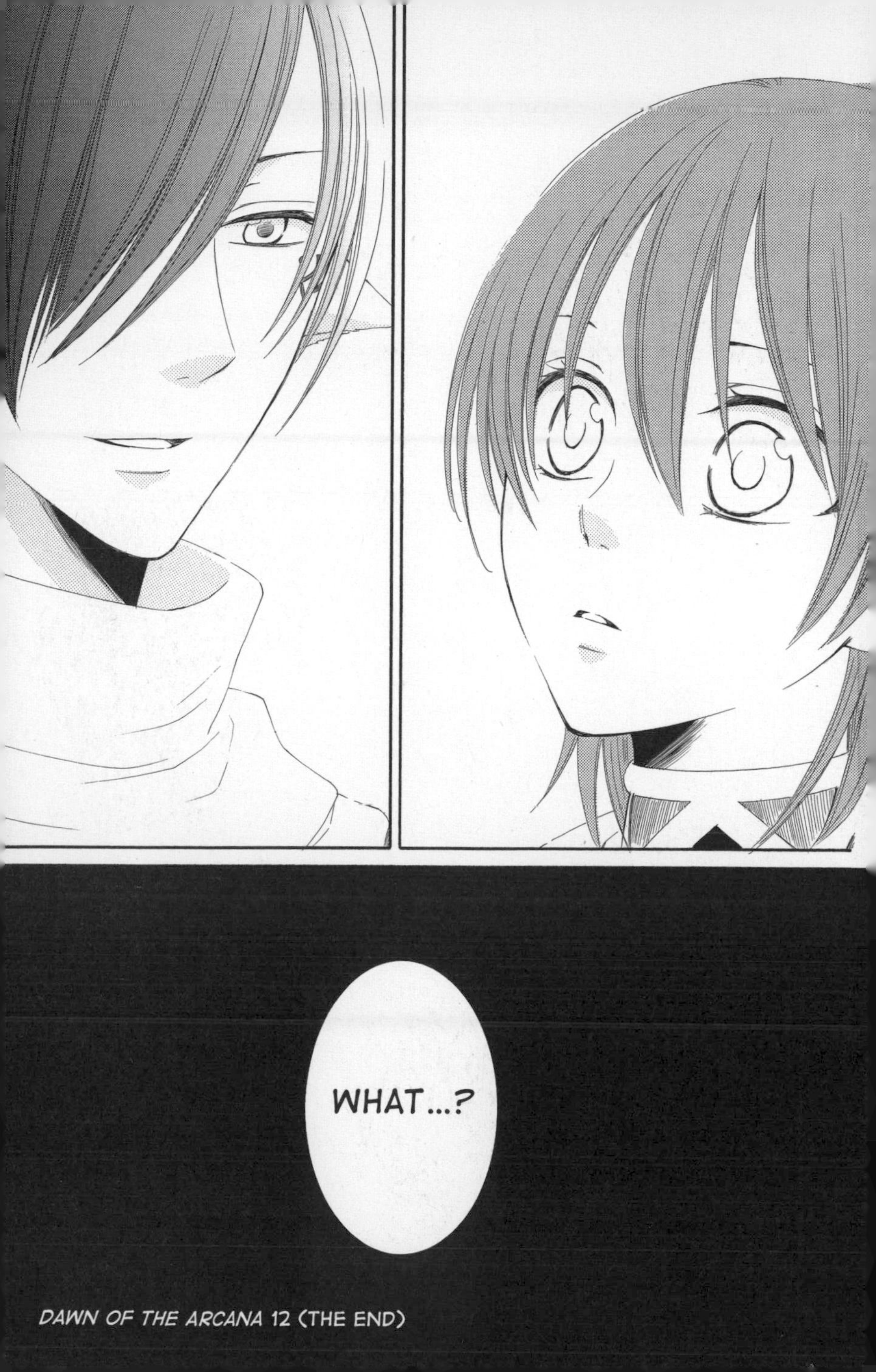
WHAT...?
DAWN OF THE ARCANA 12 (THE END)

THE COMIC ON THE
FOLLOWING PAGES WAS
WRITTEN FOR A PLANNER
THAT WAS INCLUDED WITH
CHEESE! PLAY AROUND WITH
IT BY PUTTING MESSAGES IN
THE BUBBLES AND SPACES,
OR ADD WHATEVER
DIALOGUE YOU LIKE! ♪

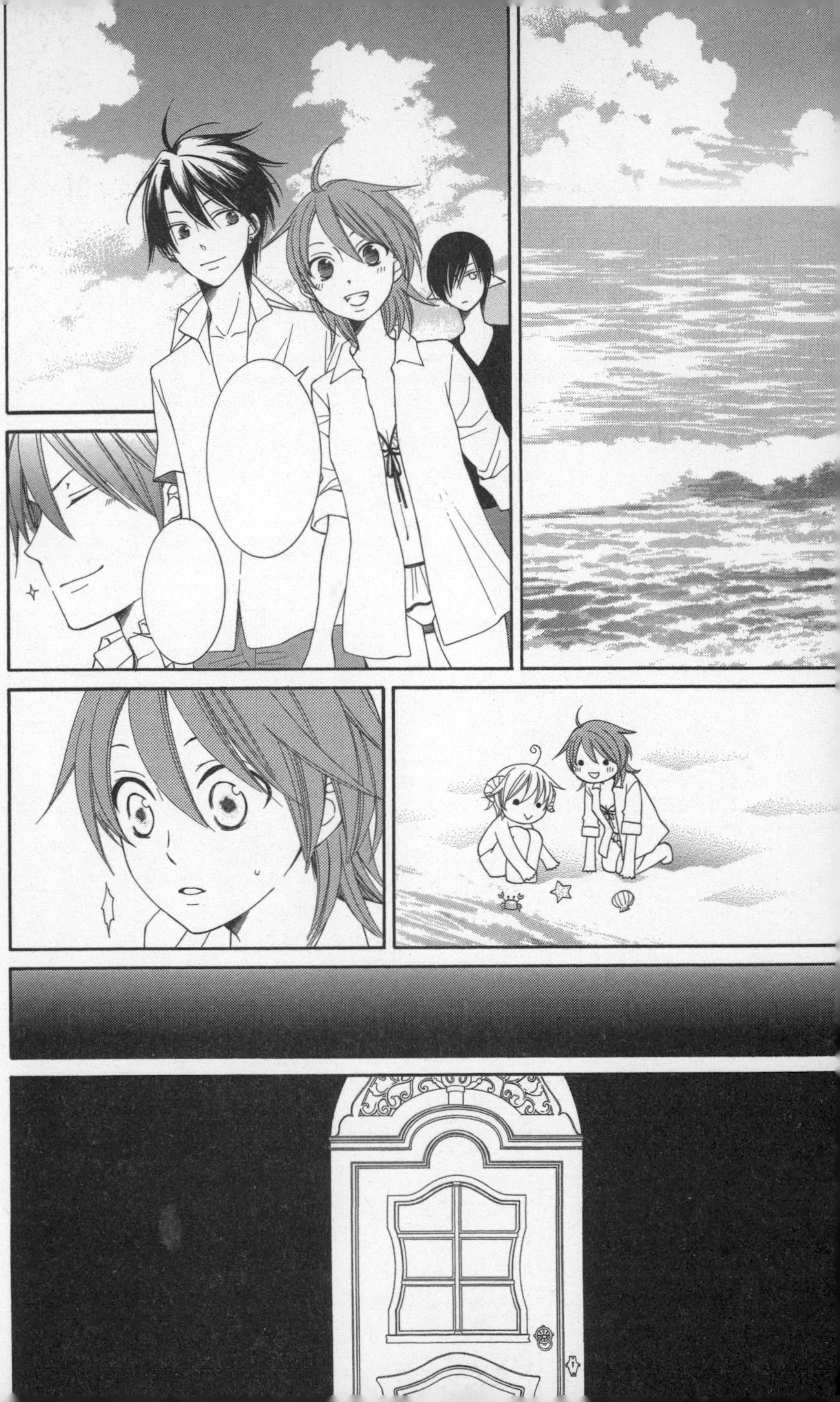

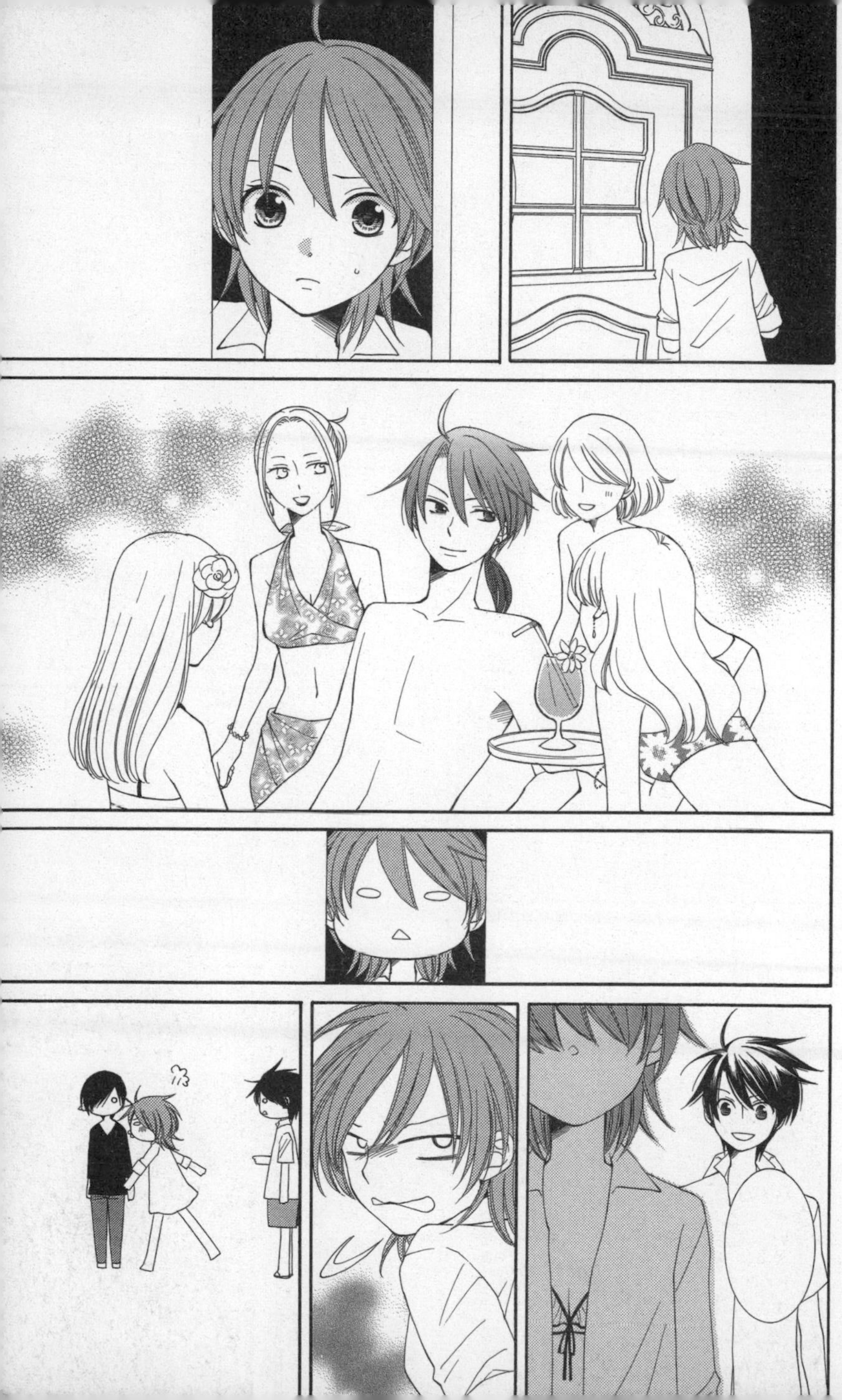

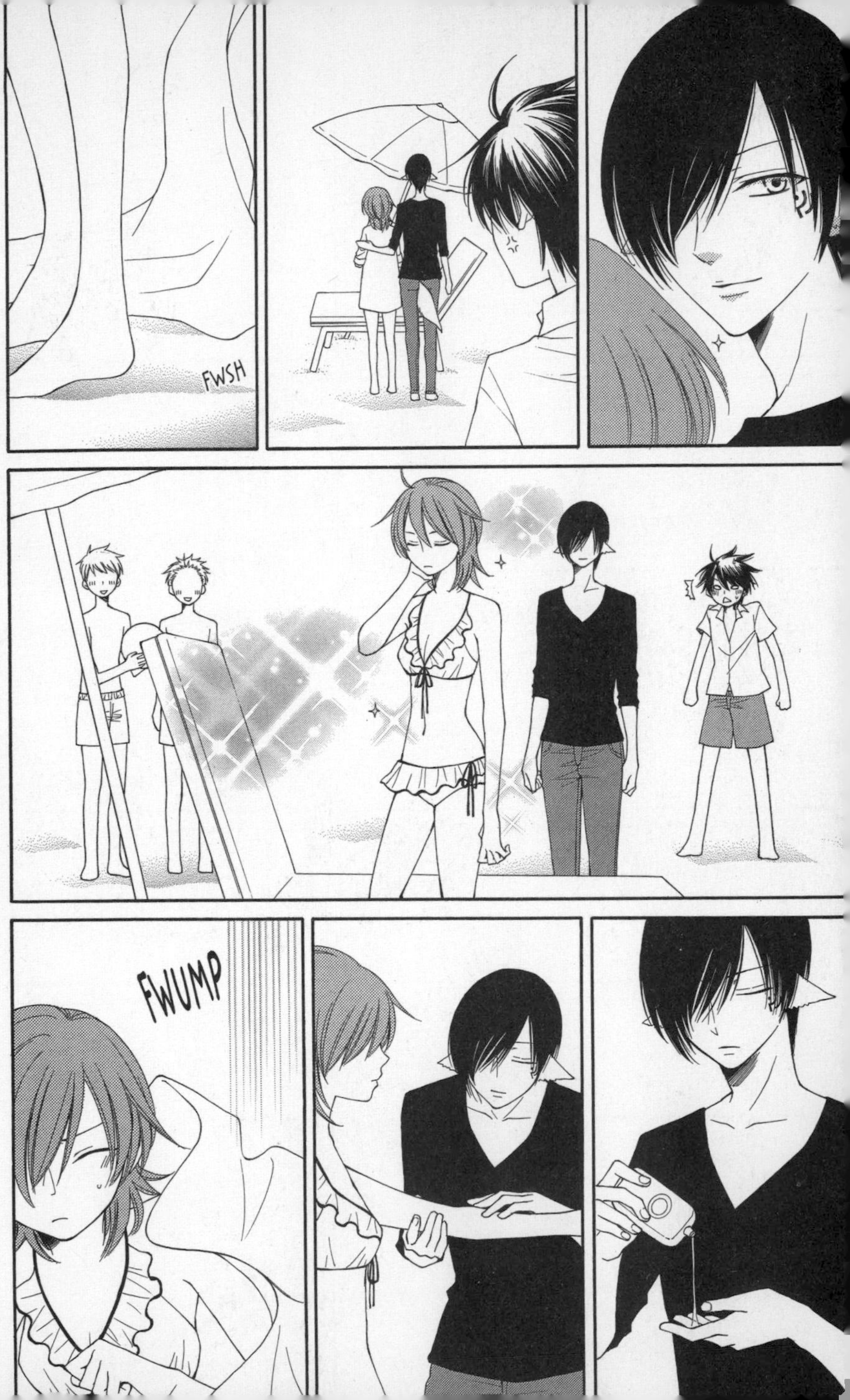
FWSH
FWUMP

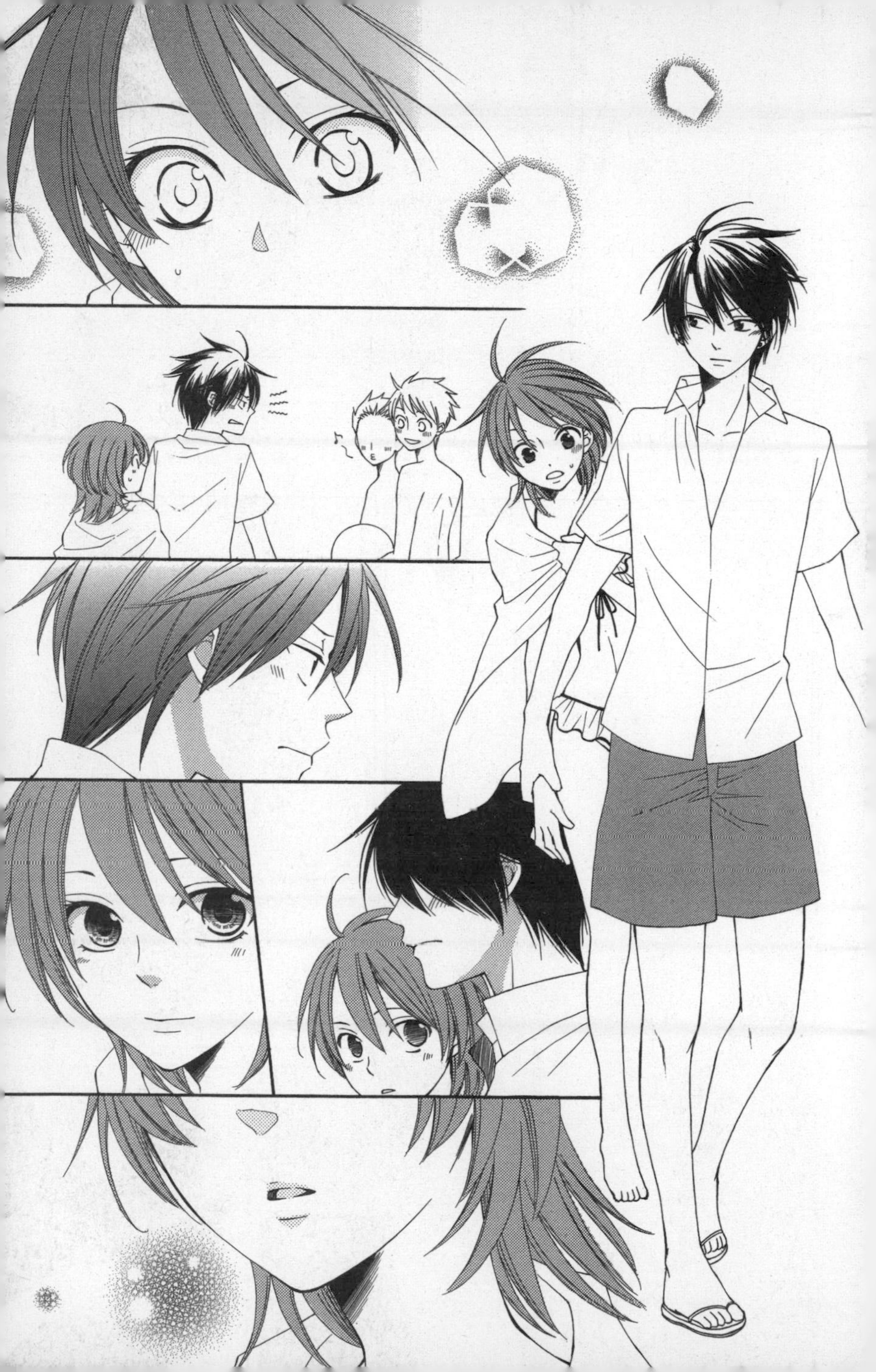

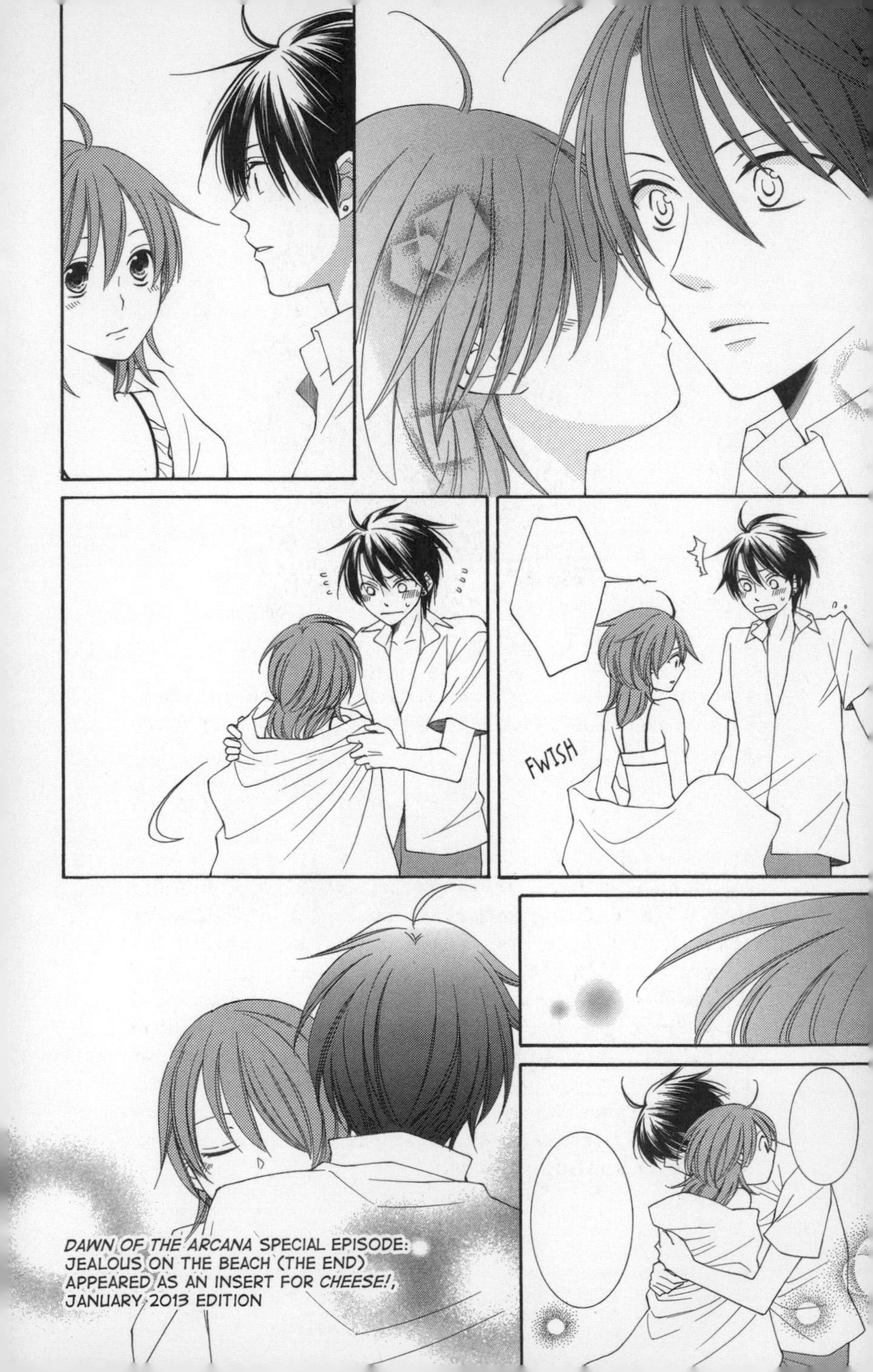
FWISH

DAWN OF THE ARCANA SPECIAL EPISODE:
JEALOUS ON THE BEACH (THE END)
APPEARED AS AN INSERT FOR *CHEESE!*,
JANUARY 2013 EDITION

The young king and Sarah are on the cover this time. The young king is (probably) pretty popular with some people.

—Rei Toma

Rei Toma has been drawing since childhood, but she only began drawing manga because of her graduation project in design school. When she drew a short-story manga, *Help Me, Dentist,* for the first time, it attracted a publisher's attention and she made her debut right away. Her magnificent art style became popular, and after she debuted as a manga artist, she became known as an illustrator for novels and video game character designs. Her current manga series, *Dawn of the Arcana,* is her first long-running manga series, and it has been a hit in Japan, selling over a million copies.

DAWN OF THE ARCANA
VOLUME 12
Shojo Beat Edition

STORY AND ART BY
REI TOMA

REIMEI NO ARCANA Vol. 12
by Rei TOMA
© 2009 Rei TOMA
All rights reserved.
Original Japanese edition published by SHOGAKUKAN.
English translation rights in the United States of America and
Canada arranged with SHOGAKUKAN.

English Adaptation/Ysabet MacFarlane
Translation/JN Productions
Touch-up Art & Lettering/Freeman Wong
Design/Yukiko Whitley
Editor/Amy Yu

Printed in Canada

Published by VIZ Media, LLC
P.O. Box 77010
San Francisco, CA 94107

10 9 8 7 6 5 4 3 2 1
First printing, April 2014

www.viz.com   www.shojobeat.com

This is the last page.

In keeping with the original Japanese comic format, this book reads from right to left—so action, sound effects, and word balloons are completely reversed. This preserves the orientation of the original artwork—plus, it's fun! Check out the diagram shown here to get the hang of things, and then turn to the other side of the book to get started!

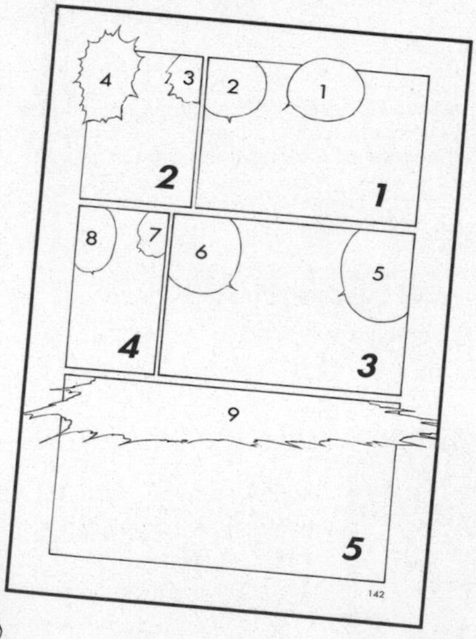

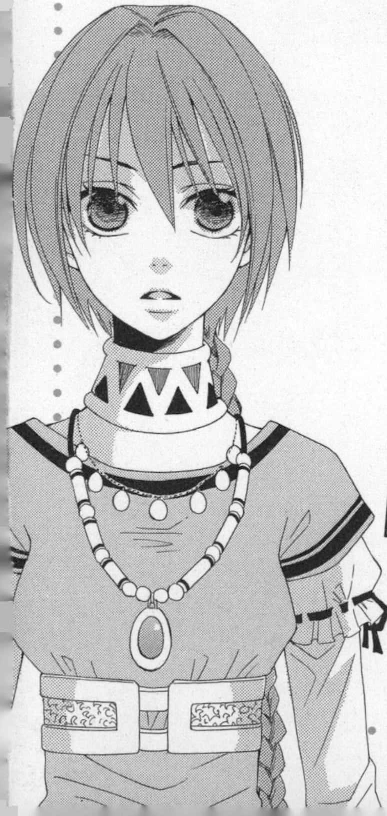